Theorising NATO

Scholarship on NATO is often preoccupied with key episodes in the development of the organisation and so, for the most part, has remained inattentive to theory.

This book addresses that gap in the literature. It provides a comprehensive analysis of NATO through a range of theoretical perspectives that includes realism, liberalism and constructivism, and lesser-known approaches centred on learning, public goods, securitisation and risk. Focusing on NATO's post–Cold War development, it considers the conceptualisation, purpose and future of the Alliance.

This book will be of interest to students and scholars of international organisation, international relations, security and European politics.

Mark Webber is Professor of International Politics and Head of the School of Government and Society at the University of Birmingham, UK.

Adrian Hyde-Price is Professor of Political Science at Gothenburg University, Sweden.

For the late Dave Allen

Contents

Illustrations

Figures

Tables

Contributors

Trine Flockhart is Professor of International Relations at the University of Kent. She was previously Senior Researcher at the Danish Institute for International Studies and Senior Fellow at the Transatlantic Academy in Washington, D.C. Her research focuses on liberal international order, transatlantic relations, European security (especially the EU and NATO) and explaining processes of change from a constructivist perspective. Her articles have appeared in journals such as *International Relations, Journal of Common Market Studies, European Security* and *European Journal of International Relations*. Her most recent publications are (co-edited with Tim Dunne) *Liberal World Orders* (Oxford University Press, 2013) and the Transatlantic Academy Report *Liberal Order in a Post-Western World*.

Adrian Hyde-Price is Professor of Political Science at Gothenburg University, Sweden, and the European editor of *European Journal of International Security*. He has previously held chairs of international politics at the universities of Bath and Leicester, and academic posts at the universities of Birmingham, Southampton and Manchester. Among his many publications are *European Security in the Twenty-First Century: The Challenge of Multipolarity* (Routledge, 2007), *Germany and European Order: Enlarging NATO and the EU* (Manchester University Press, 2000), *The International Politics of East Central Europe* (Manchester University Press, 1996) and *European Security Beyond the Cold War: Four Scenarios for the Year 2010* (Sage, 1991). He is the co-editor of *British Foreign Policy and the Anglican Church: Christian Engagement with the Contemporary World* (Ashgate, 2008) and has had articles published in a wide variety of journals, including *European Security, Globalisations, International Affairs, Journal of Common Market Studies, Journal of European Public Policy* and *Studia Diplomatica*.

Jörg Noll studied political science at the Vrije Universiteit in Amsterdam (1991–1998). He holds a doctorate from Leiden University for his thesis on Dutch and Swedish political and military leadership in post–Cold War defence reforms (2005). Since 2007 he has been Associate Professor of International Conflict Studies at the Netherlands Defence Academy. He is editor of *Political* *and Military Exit Strategies* (Asser, 2015). Jörg Noll is also lieutenant colonel of the German army reserve and is currently assigned to the German Ministry of Defence as analyst (referent) at the section Strategy and Operations.

Benjamin Pohl is Senior Project Manager at Adelphi in Berlin. He obtained his PhD from Leiden University in the Netherlands and was a postdoctoral research fellow at the University of Aberdeen in the UK. Prior to his PhD, he was a desk officer in the German Foreign Office. He is the author of *EU Foreign Policy and Crisis Management Operations: Power, Purpose and Domestic Politics* (Routledge, 2014) and has published in *European Security, Contemporary Security Policy, Cooperation and Conflict* and *Global Society*.

Sebastiaan Rietjens, PhD, an engineer by training, is Associate Professor at the Netherlands Defence Academy and a reserve major in the Dutch army. He is a member of the editorial boards of *Armed Forces and Society* and the *Journal of Humanitarian Logistics and Supply Chain Management*, as well as the editor of two volumes on civil–military interaction (Ashgate, 2008; Springer, forthcoming 2015), a special issue on defence logistics (*International Journal of Physical Distribution and Logistics Management*, 2013) and the *Routledge Handbook of Research Methods in Military Studies* (Routledge, 2014).

Jens Ringsmose is Associate Professor at the Centre for War Studies, and Head of the Department of Political Science and Public Management, University of Southern Denmark. He has published widely, including articles in *International Politics, Contemporary Security Policy, European Security, Journal of Transatlantic Studies* and *Cooperation and Conflict*; on NATO burden sharing; transatlantic cooperation and Danish security and defence policy. He has recently published two books: *Frontlinjer. Med medierne og militæret i krig* (2014) with Charlotte Aagaard and H.-C. Mathiesen and *Strategic Narratives, Public Opinion and War: Winning Support for Foreign Military Missions* (2015, eds.) with Beatrice A. de Graaf and George Dimitriu.

Frank Schimmelfennig is Professor of European Politics and a member of the Centre for Comparative and International Studies at ETH Zurich, Switzerland. He has published, *inter alia*, in *Comparative Political Studies, European Journal of International Relations, European Union Politics, International Organization, Journal of Common Market Studies, Journal of European Integration* and *Journal of European Public Policy*. He is the author of *The EU, NATO and the Integration of Europe: Rules and Rhetoric* (Cambridge University Press, 2003). His most recent book is *Differentiated Integration: Explaining Variation in the European Union* (Palgrave, 2015), with Dirk Leuffen and Berthold Rittberger.

Gabi Schlag is Teaching Associate and Research Fellow at the Otto-von-Guericke-University of Magdeburg (Germany). Her research and teaching interests include international political theory, securitisation theory and visual culture in IR. Her most recent publications are 'The West: A Securitizing Community?', in *Journal of International Relations and Development*, 17(3), 2014 (co-authored with Gunther Hellmann, Benjamin Herborth, Christian Weber) and 'Securitizing Images: The Female Body and the War in Afghanistan', *European Journal of International Relations*, 19(4), 2013 (co-authored by Axel Heck). She has also contributed a chapter to Monica Juneja and Gerrit Jasper Schenk (eds), *Disaster as Image: Iconographies and Media Strategies across Europe and Asia* (Regensburg: Schnell and Steiner, 2014).

James Sperling is Professor of Political Science University of Akron. He was Fernand Braudel Senior Fellow, the European University Institute, and Senior Fellow at the Institute for Advanced Studies, the University of Bologna, in 2015. His research and publications have focused on various aspects of transatlantic relations, German foreign policy, security governance, EU foreign and defence policy and NATO. He is editor of the *Handbook on Governance and Security* (Edward Elgar, 2014) and co-author (with Mark Webber and Martin Smith) of *NATO's Post-Cold-War Trajectory: Decline or Regeneration?* (Palgrave, 2012). He is currently co-authoring a book with Mark Webber entitled *What's Wrong with NATO and How to Fix It*. (Polity Press).

Mark Webber is Professor of International Politics and Head of the School of Government and Society at the University of Birmingham. His work on NATO has been published in the journals *International Affairs, British Journal of Politics and International Relations, Journal of European Integration, Civil Wars* and *Great Decisions*. He is the co-author (with James Sperling and Martin Smith) of *NATO's Post-Cold-War Trajectory: Decline or Regeneration?* (Palgrave, 2012). He is currently co-authoring a book with James Sperling entitled *What's Wrong with NATO and How to Fix It* (Polity Press).

Michael John Williams is Clinical Professor of International Relations and director of the Graduate Programme in International Relations at New York University. His most recent publications include *Science, Law and Liberalism in the American Way of War: The Quest for Humanity in Conflict* (Cambridge University Press, 2015), 'The Afghan War, 2001–2012' in the *Oxford Encyclopedia of American Military and Diplomatic History* (Oxford, 2012) and *The Good War: NATO and the Liberal Conscience in Afghanistan* (Palgrave, 2011). Dr Williams is Senior Associate Scholar at the Centre for European Policy Analysis in Washington, D.C. and editor-in-chief of the journal *International Politics Reviews*.

Acknowledgements

This volume is the end product of a collaboration initiated at the Joint Sessions of Workshops held under the auspices of the European Consortium for Political Research (ECPR) in Lisbon in April 2009. The editors would like to thank all the original participants in the workshop on 'Theorising NATO' as well as those who took part in a subsequent panel on NATO at the ECPR General Conference in Reykjavik the following year. Papers developed on those two occasions were, in turn, refined and revised at a workshop hosted by the Netherlands Defence Academy, Breda, also in 2010, and our thanks are extended to Jörg Noll for facilitating that event.

Delivery of the manuscript was delayed on more than one occasion, and the editors would like to extend their particular thanks to the editorial team at Routledge for its patience and forbearance.

The project benefitted from work carried out by Mark Webber while principal investigator on the seminar series, 'NATO after Afghanistan', funded by the Economic and Social Research Council (ES/J022063/1). He would like to acknowledge the work of his co-investigators on that project, Ellen Hallams and Martin Smith, who have helped shape some of the thinking behind the Introduction.

Adrian Hyde-Price (Gothenberg)
Mark Webber (Birmingham)

Abbreviations

ARRC	Allied Rapid Reaction Corps
AWAC	Airborne Warning and Control System
BRIC	Brazil, Russia, India and China
CDU	Christian Democratic Union
CEE	Central and East Europe
CEEC	Central and East European country
CENTCOM	United States Central Command
CIMIC	civil–military cooperation
CSCE	Conference on Security and Cooperation in Europe
CSDP	Common Security and Defence Policy
ESDI	European Security and Defence Identity
EU	European Union
FDI	foreign direct investment
FDP	Free Democratic Party
GDP	gross domestic product
IFOR	Implementation Force
IR	International Relations
ISAF	International Security Assistance Force
ISIS	Islamic State
KFOR	Kosovo Force
KLA	Kosovo Liberation Army
MAP	Membership Action Plan
MBFR	Mutual and Balanced Force Reductions
MD	Mouvement Démocrate
NACC	North Atlantic Cooperation Council
NATO	North Atlantic Treaty Organisation
NCR	neo-classical realism
NRF	NATO Response Force
OEF	Operation Enduring Freedom
OL	organisational learning
OOD	Operation Odyssey Dawn
OSCE	Organisation for Security and Cooperation in Europe
OUP	Operation Unified Protector

PfP	Partnership for Peace
PGT	public goods theory
PRT	Provincial Reconstruction Team
PSO	peace support operation
RAP	Readiness Action Plan
SACEUR	Supreme Allied Commander Europe
SFOR	Stabilisation Force
SHAPE	Supreme Headquarters Allied Powers Europe
SRA	strategic relational approach
ST	securitisation theory
UMP	Union pour un Mouvement Populaire
UN	United Nations
UNMIK	United Nations Mission in Kosovo
UNSCR	United Nations Security Council Resolution
US	United States
WEU	Western European Union

1   Introduction

Is NATO a theory-free zone?

Mark Webber

In September 2014, the twenty-eight members of the North Atlantic Treaty Organisation (NATO) gathered in Newport, Wales, for a summit meeting of heads of state and government. The timing of the event was portentous. Held six months after Russia's annexation of the Ukrainian territory of Crimea and amidst dire warnings of a Russian manoeuvre against NATO's Baltic members, many saw the Alliance as at a turning point, facing its gravest crisis since the end of the Cold War (Bergeron 2014; Burns 2014; Rumer 2014). The Wales summit was thus championed as the most important coming together of NATO leaders in years, if not decades (Rasmussen 2014). If NATO did not respond to Russian assertiveness, then, so it was argued, its credibility and purpose would be severely compromised (Niblett 2014; Wolfson 2014). But Russia was not the only challenge. Equally worrying was the catastrophic situation in Syria and Iraq; having already baulked at intervening in the civil conflicts in these two countries, NATO faced fresh calls for action in response to the rise of the violent Islamist movement, ISIS (Kamp 2014). And if this were not enough, Afghanistan, too, was a continuing source of concern. There, NATO's largest-ever operation stood on a knife edge; the International Security Assistance Force (ISAF) was due to wind up operations in December 2014, but the follow-on force (Operation Resolute Support) still lacked a proper mandate from the Afghan government as the Wales summit approached, thus calling into question the chances of long-term stability in the country (Gordon 2014).

The gravity of these converging crises is not to be doubted; indeed, the Wales summit declaration itself was informed by an appreciation that the Alliance stood at an important watershed. The longest in NATO's history, the declaration ranged widely: from the relationship with the European Union (EU) to support for African peace and security; from energy security to climate change; and from political dialogue with the United Nations (UN) to support for a 'comprehensive approach' to conflict management and cooperative security (NATO 2014). The headline commitments, however, were a series of practical measures, including rises in defence spending, the creation of a new Very High-Readiness Joint Task Force and a NATO Readiness Action Plan, none of which would have found itself on the summit agenda if not for the Ukraine crisis.

But whatever the air of impending disaster, NATO had found itself in a similar position many times before. Certainly since the end of the Cold War, pitching the business of a summit as a make-or-break event has become part of the normal life cycle of the Alliance. Recourse to the rhetoric of danger and resolve reflects, in part, the politics and purpose of high-level summitry. But it is also indicative of NATO's unsettled character. The Alliance since the end of the 1980s has been a body in a constant state of flux, unable to enjoy the luxury of managing routine. It has experienced a near doubling of its membership (from sixteen states to twenty-eight), undertaken some forty separate operations (the largest of which, in Afghanistan, has seen NATO forces engaged in combat for a period twice as long as World War II) and absorbed into its terms of reference (as authoritatively expressed in three separate Strategic Concepts in 1991, 1999 and 2010) a set of security concerns extending from terrorism to piracy to cyber attacks. Such far-ranging changes have tested not just NATO's operational character but also its political unity. Over the Balkans, Afghanistan and, most damagingly, Iraq in 2003, NATO has experienced an exhausting internal struggle aimed at preserving a common front. The visibility and difficulty of that effort has given rise to a view of the Alliance as ineffectual, divided and perched constantly on the verge of collapse (for discussion see Cottey 2004 and Menon 2007: 53–99).

This 'NATO in crisis' narrative is one that has, however, come in for some telling criticism – as being exaggerated, imprecise and neglectful of the Alliance's staying power (Thies 2009). Yet the broader point – of a NATO somehow disoriented by its environment, engaged in a constant search for purpose and thus the object of ongoing anxiety for policy makers – is not far off the mark. It is this turbulence which renders NATO a source of fascination for observers and the subject of questions which sometimes brook no obvious answer. If NATO has changed so much, then how do we pinpoint its essential character? Further, if NATO's operational and strategic vision has shifted beyond the narrow horizons of the Cold War, how do we explain the organisation's ranking of priorities and the occasions on which it has decided to act? And when NATO has acted, in whose interest has this been done: all allies, some allies or some overarching NATO aggregate? And looming over all of these questions is perhaps the most important – why does NATO persist at all?

Analysing NATO

It is questions such as these which frame the current volume (more on this later), but addressing them gives rise to another: Why yet another book on NATO? Isn't the interested reader already well served by an extensive and healthily expanding literature on the subject? That question could well be answered in the affirmative, but a deficiency in NATO scholarship remains nonetheless – namely, its inattention to theory; it is this gap we wish to address. That such a gap exists can be illustrated by a brief survey. Considering works published in the period since the end of the Cold War, much of the NATO-relevant literature can be placed under one of four headings.[1]

The first focuses on key episodes of NATO's recent history – a history that has undoubtedly been dramatic. The Alliance was a key actor at the Cold War's end and has been central to the reshaping of European (and, to some degree, international) order thereafter. A good deal of attention has thus been paid to moments of crisis and historical turning points. Take, for instance, treatments of NATO's predicament in the wake of the Cold War. The uncertainty that confronted the Allies at this juncture was unique – not since its creation in 1949 had existential questions of NATO's purpose and likelihood of survival been presented in such stark form. Much of the consequent analysis was practical in its concerns, focussing on how the Alliance ought to repurpose itself: by reaching out to the former communist East, reorganising its conventional and nuclear force posture, embracing out-of-area missions and facilitating a greater European role in defence (Corterier 1990; Lunn 1992; Sloan 1989). In parallel, a rich vein of work focused on debates within NATO, how distinct national positions emerged over the Alliance's future and, as an important corollary to this, how the position of the US as NATO's leading power was viewed (de Wijk 1997; Goldstein 1994; Levine 1992). Given the significance of the issues at hand, much of this work had a reflective quality. NATO, for some, was doomed to wither away, given the disappearance of its long-time Soviet adversary (De Santis 1991). Others, by contrast, saw it as the best guarantee against possible future dangers (a resurgent Russia or war in Eastern Europe), the most reliable expression of transatlantic interests and a body superior to others (for instance, the Western European Union [WEU] and the Conference on Security and Cooperation in Europe [CSCE]) in its ability to adapt to multiple and new security tasks (Duffield 1994–1995; Glaser 1993; McInnes 1995).

Debates on NATO's future were sustained by the re-emergence of conflict in Europe. Throughout much of the 1990s, the crucible of change for NATO was in the Balkans. In both Bosnia and Kosovo, decisive NATO interventions (Operation Deliberate Force in 1995 and Operation Allied Force in 1999, respectively)[2] were preceded by intimations of crisis in the Alliance as well as charges of ineptitude and indecisiveness (Webber 2012). The outcome in each case – a NATO aerial intervention paving the way for local political settlements and long-term NATO peacekeeping missions – had consequences for both Balkan stability and NATO's own evolution. On the latter, scholarly analysis has focused on a number of themes: NATO capabilities (Lambeth 2001; Schulte 1997), the combination of force and diplomacy in achieving mission outcomes (Daalder and O'Hanlon 2000; Henriksen 2007; Kaufman 2002: 91–136), intra-Alliance debates on the strategy of force (Allin 2002; Martin and Brawley 2000) and how mission outcomes went on to shape NATO's operational, doctrinal and political development (Allin 2002: 92–100; Kaufman 2002: 209–232; Latawski and Smith 2003: 39–65; Sperling and Webber, 2009: 498–500).

NATO's forays in the Balkans were premised on an assumption that the organisation's core purposes were related to the provision of European security (Kay 1998: 59–87). That assumption was overturned by the al Qaeda attacks of 9/11 on the US mainland. In response, for the first (and still only) time in its history, the Alliance invoked the collective defence provisions of Article Five of the North

Atlantic Treaty and so NATO followed the US into the long campaign against the Taliban in Afghanistan. That campaign was bookmarked by two notable and related episodes elsewhere, both of which were illustrative of debates on NATO's extra-European role. The first occurred in 2003 over the merits of the US-led intervention in Iraq – a mission firmly opposed by France and Germany and one which became the subject of NATO's most bitter dispute of the entire post–Cold War period (Gordon and Shapiro 2004; Pond 2004).The second, Operation Unified Protector against the Qaddafi regime in Libya in 2011, was seen to mark something of a departure, given the willingness of NATO's European allies to undertake a significant proportion of flight missions (Hallams and Schreer 2012). Although regarded by many as operational successfully (albeit within narrow parameters), NATO's intervention in Libya was not viewed as indicative of a new focus on North Africa and the Middle East (Barry 2011; Englelbert, Mohlin and Wagnsson 2014). The circumstances which had given rise to the operation were largely fortuitous, and as NATO's reluctance to become involved in Syria in subsequent years would demonstrate, the Alliance lacked the political will to involve itself in any mission to which the United States was not prepared to commit.

As for Afghanistan itself, this has seen NATO's largest, longest and costliest mission to date[3] and so the occasion for a good deal of commentary on how the Alliance has fared. In this regard, much attention has been placed on problems of alliance management (a consequence, in large part, of inequitable burden and risk sharing), capability shortfalls, military transformation and the challenges of mounting a prolonged expeditionary operation against a determined enemy (Chaudhuri and Farrell 2011; Farrell and Rynning 2010; Siegel 2009; Sperling and Webber 2012). The downbeat tone of these writings has been mirrored in more general assessments. That the ISAF mission went on for so many years with no certainty of success and no defined end point (at least until 2012 when decisions were made to transition away from kinetic operations to an advisory role in support of local Afghan forces) means it has come to be viewed as a failure on NATO's part, one that has undermined Alliance credibility, political will and ability to act (Noetzel and Schreer 2009). Alongside this negative assessment, however, a much more positive view has also emerged. A decade of war would have cracked most alliances, but NATO, so some have argued, managed to demonstrate a resilience and a collective resolve unparalleled in modern warfare (Mattelaer 2011–2012; Rynning 2012: 213). Yet even sympathetic assessments have come to regard the Afghan episode as unrepeatable, indicative of the geographic and practical limits of allied efforts and a mission whose costs have largely outweighed the strategic and political benefits (Williams 2011: 142–143).

The end of NATO's ISAF mission closed a chapter in NATO's history. Although a smaller follow-on force remained in the country, it was clear that NATO's extra-European role had become increasingly unsustainable. Such missions have been seen as intrinsically very difficult but also very costly (something given added emphasis by the pressures of defence austerity following the 2008 global financial crash). Talk of a 'global NATO' – something that had been very much part of the analysis of NATO in the decade after 9/11 (Medcalf 2008; Moore 2007) –

consequently faded away. By the time of the Ukraine crisis of 2014, NATO was, therefore, already primed to give closer attention to its European heartland (Webber, Hallams and Smith 2014).

The focus of a good deal of NATO literature on key episodes adds up to a seemingly compelling picture of how the Alliance has developed. It scotches the notion of a NATO about to suffer some irreparable crisis (NATO may have had an episodic history in the post–Cold War period, but none of the episodes noted earlier has proven fatal), yet also makes clear that NATO has not always fared well when put under intense (and prolonged) pressure. The limited objectives of NATO action in the Balkans and Libya, for instance, were more readily achievable (but even then not without difficulty) than the open-ended mandate in Afghanistan (Hodge 2013). Key episodes also allow us to consider NATO's wider significance. Taken together, they are indicative of the expanding (and post-ISAF) then contracting terms of reference of the Alliance. They also connect to wider currents of international politics (the notion of 'liberal' or humanitarian intervention, for instance, has been a constant in analyses of NATO action) (Chivvis 2012–2013; Wheeler 2000; Williams 2011).

The foregoing suggests that important thematic continuities exist when looking at the Alliance (the episodes listed earlier, for example, all fall under the broad umbrella of NATO operations). Attention to such themes makes up a second set of NATO literature. Work in this vein is often highly specialised, looking at NATO's internal processes of transformation (its command structure, bureaucracy, military doctrine and modes of military cooperation) (Deni 2007; Hilde 2014, Meyer 2014), at the activities of a particular office (the NATO secretary general) (Hendrickson 2006) or at specific elements of NATO's combined defence (conventional and nuclear defence postures, ballistic missile defence, cyber defence, counterterrorism and so on) (Hunker 2013; Lindstrom 2013; Rühle 2013; Yost 2014: 31–122). Other work ranges more broadly, seeking to connect specialist themes (the formulation of NATO strategy) with particular actions (NATO operations) (Edström and Gyllensporre 2012; Odgaard 2014; Peterson 2011). Broader still is work which shows how an important set of activities has helped shape NATO's overarching development. Studies of enlargement, for instance, thus concern themselves with alliance bargaining (over the choice of countries deemed worthy of membership), leadership (agenda shaping by the US), impact (how the 'digestion' of new members has affected NATO politically and operationally) and strategic significance (not least the deleterious impact of the policy on relations with Russia) (Asmus 2002; David and Lévesque 1999; Goldgeier 1999; Hopkinson 2001; Yost 2014: 281–308). Enlargement, in this sense, has been viewed as on a par with NATO's increased operational tempo after the Cold War, giving the Alliance a refreshed 'sense of purpose' (at least up to the mid-2000s, at which point enlargement has slowed) in a shifting strategic context (Asmus 2002: 302–303).

Closely related to enlargement is the theme of partnership, a broadly conceived set of arrangements by which NATO has cooperated with non-members. Taken in the round, partnerships have been viewed as emblematic of NATO's ambition – in the 1990s as contributing 'to the construction of a peaceful political order in Europe as a whole' (Yost 1998: 91) and, since the 2000s, as part and parcel of NATO's commitment to 'cooperative security' on a global scale (Yost 2014: 200). The expansive nature of NATO's partnership initiatives has been seen as increasingly problematic (Flockhart 2013, 2014), but it is one specific part-nership – that with Russia – that has loomed largest in these discussions. In this connection, a whole sub-genre of literature has arisen, concerned *inter alia* with the historical ups and downs of the relationship (Forsberg and Herd 2015; Smith 2006); the impact (usually negative) of particular events such as NATO's Balkan interventions (Averre 2009) and the Crimea/Ukraine crisis (Kroenig 2015); Rus-sian reaction to NATO initiatives, enlargement most notably (Averre 1998; Ber-ryman 2010; Black 1999) and, finally, with what the state of the relationship tells us about NATO's place in the provision of pan-European security (Braun 2008).

Implicit (and often explicit) in these thematic treatments is an assumption that NATO's priorities are shaped by its leading members. Here, a third body of work looks at state preferences within NATO – at the debates these preferences engen-der and how far (and in what manner) such preferences are reconciled. A common view in this regard is that NATO is increasingly differentiated, split between the geostrategic priorities of its far-flung allies (Michta 2006). Enlargement (which has imported into the Alliance a group of states geopolitically fixed on Russia) and mission expansion (which means NATO has had to worry about problems as far apart as Afghanistan and the Baltic states) have both amplified this problem (Michta 2014). Of NATO's allies, the US, of course, looms largest. Here, work has considered how NATO sits within the broader framework of transatlantic cooperation and, related, how (or how far) NATO has shadowed US foreign pol-icy priorities (Andrews 2005; Hallams 2010, 2013; Sloan 2010; Webber 2009a). Important work has also been done on France (especially in light of its return to NATO's integrated military command) (*European Security* 2010), Germany (because of the country's geostrategic weight in Europe and unique position on the use of force) (Hyde-Price 2000: 136–171; Keller 2012), the UK (due to its close association with the US) (Auerswald and Saideman 2014: 116–127; David-son 2011) and NATO's middle powers and newer members (Edmunds 2003; Mat-láry and Petersson 2013; Zyla 2014).

National policies are often the subject of critique and prescription; indeed, this is a stock in trade of much policy-relevant literature, particularly in the US, where Washington's leadership of NATO is often part of broader assessments of US for-eign policy (Menon 2007: 53–100; Sherwood-Randall 2006). In the same manner, NATO itself has been subject to prescriptive analysis. Such analysis makes up a fourth strand of literature which, in turn, falls into two broad types of approach. First are those works which, although often critical of NATO, are concerned with recommending how the organisation might do things differently and more effec-tively. Highlights here include work on NATO's operations in Bosnia, Kosovo, Afghanistan and Libya; the pros and cons of enlargement and the NATO–Russia relationship.[4] Some work in this vein is very broad in scope. It examines NATO's overall portfolio of responsibilities and considers how this might be adjusted to keep the organisation fit for purpose as its external circumstances change (Berdal

2009; Croft, Howorth, Terriff and Webber 2000; Forster and Wallace 2001; Gordon 1997; Kashmeri 2010; Lindley-French 2007; Webber, Hallams and Smith 2014). A contrasting approach begins with a largely sceptical position on NATO's intentions. Whether in relation to particular activities (operations being a common concern) or NATO's broader remit, the view here is that the Alliance should be curtailed or even abolished due to its alleged bellicosity, subservience to US global ambition and subversion of international organisations such as the UN (Gowan 1999, 2010; Hallett 2007; McKinney 2012; Nazemroaya 2012).

Taken as a whole, it is clear that these four sets of literature – on episodes, themes, membership and prescriptions – make a significant contribution to our understanding of NATO. This work is historically informed, empirically rich, and policy focused. It is also significant in scale. Perhaps reflecting its centrality to US and European foreign policies, NATO is one of the most analysed and commented-upon international organisations of modern times, rivalled only by the EU in the range of work it has attracted.

NATO and IR theory

These gains notwithstanding, merit still attaches to the additional benefits to be had by looking at NATO with a theoretical sensibility. The work described earlier – representative of much of NATO scholarship – is essentially atheoretical in its concerns. However, NATO is not currently a theory-free zone. It has been susceptible to theoretical treatment in at least three ways, each operating at a different level of generality. A further small body of work, meanwhile, has ranged across all three of these levels in order to explore broad questions of NATO's underlying purpose and prospects. Before setting about our own endeavour, it is worth outlining the state of NATO theory by reference to this literature.

The first and most schematic type of treatment views NATO as nested within a broadly drawn, theoretically derived setting. This may entail a consideration of NATO and its relationship to international society or security governance (Cottey 2014; Webber 2011), but the best-known formulation is that of 'security community' – a group of states which enjoy 'dependable expectations of peaceful change' in their relations with one another (Adler and Barnett 1998: 30). Differences may exist in such a community, but, crucially, these are settled by ways other than war. This essentially empirical observation applies to North America and Western Europe most obviously, a 'pluralistic' security community in which cooperation is extensive but states still retain their sovereignty.[5] What makes the observation of theoretical interest is the notion that security cooperation is underpinned by 'shared identities, values, and meanings', something which gives rise to high levels of trust and reciprocity (Adler and Barnett 1998: 31). A common experience of democratic government at the domestic level and of institutional interaction at the international level, meanwhile, helps sustain this community over the long term. As the key institution of transatlanticism, NATO was at the heart of Karl Deutsch et al's (1957) original formulation of security community, and the Alliance has remained central to subsequent refinements of the concept, as well as being credited with identity and trust-building attributes in its own right (Sjursen 2004; Risse-Kappen 1995).

The theoretical premise of the Euro- Atlantic security community has been challenged by some in light of the deep disagreements which have bedevilled transatlantic relations since the 1990s. NATO by this view is of decreasing relevance and no longer 'the keystone upon which the transatlantic relationship has traditionally rested' (Cox 2005: 224). Others, however, have been more sanguine. Risse (2004: 220–226) has suggested that collective identity, dense interactions, 'strong institutionalisation' and 'enduring norms' – continue to sustain the Euro-Atlantic security community in general and NATO in particular (see also Gheciu 2011). Pouilot (2006), meanwhile, has argued that the fundamental property of this community remains unaltered – it is a community of peace between states. Disagreements occur (indeed, these may be more frequent as 'the intersubjective basis of the security community is being renegotiated'), but they are not resolved by force.

The second type of theoretical treatment has a more narrow focus, viewing NATO as indicative of some specific phenomenon of international life. Of obvious relevance here is alliance theory, which looks at how and why alliances are formed, managed and sustained. An emergent body of work here is concerned with the functional distinctions between organised alliances such as NATO and more loosely organised coalitions. Patricia Weitsman (2014), for instance, has argued that in war, there are both power-maximising and functional benefits to be had from alliances. These are benefits which accrue not just to the most powerful ally. NATO, in this sense, is effective because it serves the objectives of the US *and* other important allies. Of somewhat longer standing is the economic or public goods theory of alliances. The seminal work in this field was developed by reference to NATO, Olson and Zeckhauser (1966) arguing as far back as the mid-1960s that smaller allies will ride for free on the defence contributions of the larger. This proposition has been refined over the years to encompass intra-alliance risk sharing, patterns of defence spending under austerity, buy-in to defence collaboration and the decision calculus allies bring to major initiatives such as enlargement and operations (Hallams and Schreer 2012; Ivanov 2010; Lepgold 1998; Ringsmose 2010; Sandler and Hartley 1999). Mention should also be made of neo-realism, a general theory whose core concern with the balance of power (or threat) has a clear applicability to alliances. Alliances, by this view, arise because a set of states has a shared appreciation of a common danger. Once that danger attenuates, the alliance will, by logical extension, weaken or dissolve. Hence, the expectation that absent the Soviet Union and the Cold War, NATO would experience a growing incoherence and even court the possibility of disintegration (Walt 2000: 12–15; Williams 2013).

NATO has also been viewed as an 'institution' (in a manner distinct from the security community formulation earlier). The premise here is that conventional understandings of alliance as temporary, single-purpose and lacking organisation do not apply in NATO's case. NATO has, in fact, obtained a seeming permanence, developed a broad and fluid menu of functions and is home to a complex, well-established set of mechanisms that formulate and carry out policy. The latter, specifically, has been viewed as the key to its fortunes. For NATO's members, relying on the sunk costs, proven benefits and predictability of existing assets trumps possible alternative courses of action whether that be recourse to other (but unproven) bodies or the creation of new ones (McCalla 1996; Wallander 2000). NATO, by this view, is an institutional solution to the ongoing need for security cooperation among allies. States here are theoretically important, but so, too, are the formats in which they interact. For this reason, the approach is liberal rather than realist in its assumption that 'institutions matter'. Institutions bring benefits, functionally understood, and are something more than channels for states to simply pursue their own narrowly defined interests.

Finally, a third set of approaches uses a theoretical lens to explain particular NATO activities. Take, for instance, the case of enlargement. Alexandra Gheciu (2005: 5, 16–17) has sought to explain that process through a constructivist logic of 'international norm projection'. Here, NATO is attractive to post-communist states in East Central Europe because it is associated with a 'liberal democratic identity'. The Alliance, despite its material power, is thus perceived as friendly 'rather than [as] a source of threat'. Gheciu's rejection of 'rationalist' explanations (i.e., those which emphasise the instrumental benefits of enlargement) is shared by Ainius Lašas (2012: 9), who has suggested that enlargement is best explained (again with reference to constructivism) by 'historical-psychological legacies'. This is the collective guilt felt by NATO's existing membership toward its eastern neighbours – the consequence of 'crucial historical mistakes that left [those countries] behind the Iron Curtain for 50 years'. Enlargement has also been taken as the testing ground for other theoretically derived propositions: how NATO enlargement fosters trust and cooperation with members in waiting while degrading it with Russia (Kydd 2001); how enlargement promotes democracy among acceding and new members (Epstein 2005; Reiter 2001) and how it constitutes a process 'of state-crafting via the socialization' of 'political, military and functional elites' (Gheciu 2005: 3) in Central and Eastern Europe.

Another interesting case is NATO's relations with Russia. Here, Luca Ratti (2013: 273) has argued that the stuttering relationship is indicative of 'underlying diverging interests' best captured by a 'realist analytical framework'. Lionel Ponsard (2006), meanwhile, has combined a number of theoretical positions (realism, neo-realism, regime theory) and an analysis of identity to pinpoint the 'peculiarities' of NATO–Russia interaction and thus the possibilities of cooperation. Perhaps most innovatively, Vincent Pouliot (2010: 2) has developed a theory of 'practice'.[6] This suggests security community building between NATO and Russia has definite limits because of 'fierce symbolic power struggles' between the two sides. Their practice of diplomacy, in other words, is tainted by a mismatch in perceptions of status and position in the 'international security hierarchy'. NATO regards Russia from an assumed position of superiority, whereas Russia construes its international standing as higher than its resources and influence should allow. The upshot is a continuing inability to arrive at a shared sense of identity and only a rudimentary sense of shared interest.

The three theoretical approaches sketched out earlier usually stand apart. In some cases, however, different levels of theoretical concern have been brought together in service of a general assessment of NATO. This type of work takes two forms. The first deploys mainstream International Relations (IR) theories (usually realism, liberalism/institutionalism and constructivism) in order to address questions of NATO's long-term development. Work of this type was initially concerned with conjecturing whether NATO would survive the end of the Cold War (Hellmann and Wolf 1993). More than two decades on, it seeks to explain why NATO has indeed survived, referencing both NATO's multifaceted range of activities and multiple (even overlapping) understandings of NATO's character – as alliance, institution and community (Barany and Rauchhaus 2011; Webber, Sperling and Smith 2012). The second proceeds from a particular theoretical position as a way of getting at some fundamental logic of NATO's purpose. Sten Rynning (2005: 178), for instance, has argued that classical realism, with its emphasis on geopolitics, power and state interests, provides a compelling answer as to why 'NATO continues to exist'. The Alliance, he suggests, 'gathers (together) states sharing a particular status quo conception of the world and who have a geopolitical interest in protecting it'. Sireci and Coletta (2009: 58), similarly, have argued that in a world in which power and security are paramount, NATO still furnishes states with the fundamental resource of security from attack. With that basic need obtained, states are freed up to pursue other nationally specific security goals – many of which NATO also facilitates (access to legitimacy for the US or to collective resources for other allies). NATO is thus 'a brokerage house' for the pursuit of state autonomy. Utilising a quite different theoretical starting point, that of constructivism, a number of scholars have presented NATO as underpinned by values and a sense of shared identity. However, the logic of that assumption leads in different directions. Victoria Kitchen (2010: 26, 118–120), for instance, has argued that liberal values are a source of NATO's continuing vitality – the foundation of an ongoing commitment to transatlanticism (shared values), the premise of enlargement (the extension of values) and the basis of operations (the defence of values). Andreas Behnke (2013: 183–191), by contrast, has been much more downbeat. He has argued that NATO's 'continued ability to re-produce and re-present "the West" as a geo-cultural space [and . . .] security referent object' has been increasingly challenged by the proliferation of threats it has had to contend with. This is more than a functional challenge (making choices over how to allocate resources to multiple problems); it is also an ontological one (how NATO defines itself in a world it can no longer contain or even comprehend).

NATO has, then, been the subject of theoretical attention. But given its significance and standing as 'the world's most important security alliance since the days of the Second World War', it is a curiosity of IR scholarship that such work is still relatively underdeveloped (Neumann 2013: viii). Precisely because it has endured so long, has acquired unique features and is associated with the policies of the world's hegemonic security actor (the US) one would expect NATO to have given rise to a vibrant and theoretically driven dialogue among scholars. Sadly, this has not been the case.

Consider, by contrast, the study of the EU. This is a body which has given rise to an entire academic enterprise, a subject field that is both empirically rich *and* theoretically informed. To accommodate this work, the EU has spawned its own academic associations (the University Association of Contemporary European Studies and the European Union Studies Association) and specialist journals (*Journal of Common Market Studies, Journal of European Public Policy* and *European Union Politics*). There are no NATO-related equivalents. Further, and equally telling, study of the EU has prompted theoretical innovation as scholars have attempted to get to grips with the seemingly unique character of the European Union and its associated processes of integration. Although it is the case that federalism, neo-functionalism, liberal inter-governmentalism, supranational governance, consociationalism and new institutionalism are derived from 'a larger class of International Relations theories' (Schimmelfennig 2004: 75), their particular application to the EU has pushed these theories in interesting and otherwise unusual directions (Wiener and Diez 2009).

Although theoretical attention to the EU is readily understandable given that body's complexity, extensive policy outputs and unique blend of domestic and international politics, this does not render the comparison with NATO unfair. The Alliance, for different reasons, has also been of singular importance in European and transatlantic international relations and so the comparison is all that more telling. NATO's position in relation to academic IR and security studies is also an interesting case in point. The Alliance has been reasonably well covered in mainstream theorising (realism, liberalism and increasingly constructivism, as already indicated) but much less so in 'critical' perspectives. True, varieties of critical constructivism, which focus on practice and discourse, have paid some attention to NATO (see, for instance, reference to Behnke and Pouliet earlier)[7] but in other important ways NATO has been marginal – feminist IR, the 'Copenhagen school' of 'securitisation' and the 'Welsh school' of critical security studies have not engaged with NATO to any significant degree.[8] Equally, it would be hard to make the case that NATO has been the subject of much normative theorising. Prescription certainly has been much in evidence (as noted earlier), but work on NATO that addresses 'the moral dimensions of international relations' (Brown 1992: 3) tends to reference specific operations and activities (Gibbs 2009) rather than NATO's broader place in global order.

Overview

A single volume cannot alone make good these various shortcomings. What it can aim to do, however, is make a modest advance in the right direction. In undertaking that task, we take it as given that the application of theory is of scholarly benefit. Such an assumption is not, of course, straightforward – 'the definition, role and function of theory is one of the most highly contested issues' in the discipline of IR, Tim Dunne and others (2013: 406) have argued. The broad question of the utility of theory is one we turn to in the next chapter. But our starting position, one implicit in the survey earlier, is that theory is of benefit and that its standing in NATO scholarship is in need of improvement. In the chapters that follow, a number of explicitly theoretical treatments of NATO are therefore offered.

By way of introducing these, several points are worth bearing in mind. First, the volume makes no claim either to arbitrate between competing theoretical perspectives (to arrive at a winning theory) or to combine different perspectives in service of theoretical pluralism. Theoretical arbitration is usually seen as next to impossible and is rarely attempted (Reus-Smit and Snidal 2008). Pluralism, however, is increasingly fashionable (Checkel 2013). This volume takes a particular position in this regard; it is not pluralist in the sense of seeking to combine theories. Hence, although there are chapters on realism and constructivism, there is no treatment of realist constructivism. Pluralism of this sort is avoided, not because it is without merits, but because our principal concern is to offer space to different theoretical positions, which are best seen when presented alone and not in combination. The pluralism we do engage in, therefore, is akin to 'analytical eclecticism' involving the presentation of a diversity of perspectives (a theme elaborated upon in Chapter 2). This volume thus comprises analyses of NATO derived from mainstream or paradigmatic theories (varieties of realism, liberalism, institutionalism and constructivism) while also allowing room for more recently developed theoretical approaches (securitization, risk) and those grounded in middle-range theory (public goods, organisational learning). Further, allowance is given to dialogue between theories. Many chapters, for instance, proceed from the premise that neo-realism has been mistaken in its assumptions on NATO. This is a view derived, in large part, from a view that neo-realist claims made in the early 1990s (when the theory was of some influence) have not fared well. Chapter 3 by Adrian Hyde-Price brings neo-realism up to date and so is a useful balance to these arguments. Trine Flockhart's chapter, meanwhile, provides a constructivist take on NATO, and does so by juxtaposing it against the 'different focus [of] either realism and liberalism'. Frank Schimmelfennig, similarly, considers 'two major families' of institutionalist theory, contrasting rational institutionalism, on the one hand, with sociological or constructivist institutionalism on the other. Allowing for diversity and dialogue of this sort, the volume provides a conspectus of different interpretations of NATO and thus a tool on how to make sense of the organisation.

A second point concerns the analytical and historical terrain within which we are working. Here, the contributors proceed from the readily accepted notion that with the end of the Cold War NATO has undergone a fundamental and continuous process of change (of purpose, membership, capability generation, command structure and so on). In parallel, it has faced a multiplicity of crises – in the Balkans, Afghanistan and more recently, as noted earlier, in relation to Ukraine. These have tested NATO's internal cohesion and, for some observers, its very powers of survival. Such matters, empirically at least, are well covered in NATO scholarship elsewhere and are not reprised here. They are referred to in subsequent chapters only insofar as they illustrate matters of theoretical relevance. Our subject matter, in other words, is NATO *qua* NATO, and on that basis explicit theoretical perspectives are deployed to consider the conceptualisation, purpose and development of the Alliance. On a related note, because the present volume is theory driven, it makes no claim to historical comprehensiveness. The reader will learn a lot about what NATO has done since the end of the Cold War, but it is not the ambition of individual chapters or the book as a whole to present a history of the Alliance. Some chapters do range broadly over time, but some are narrower in scope. Gabi Schlag's chapter on securitisation and Michael Williams' on risk make persuasive arguments about NATO's character by focussing on the 1990s, NATO's first post–Cold War decade. James Sperling, meanwhile, focusses on a single episode – Operation Unified Protector in 2011 – in order to consider the usefulness of neo-classical realism.

Third, we are mindful that theoretical advance begs the question of policy relevance (Walt 2005). Ours is not a volume that seeks to engage directly with policy, but clearly we cannot ignore it, for in NATO's case shifts in policy have been profound. A number of the chapters which follow demonstrate the benefits and limits of theory in addressing these shifts. Jörg Noll and Sebastiaan Rietjens apply organisational learning theory to civil–military cooperation (CIMIC) to explain why NATO has found it so difficult to learn and institutionalise new concepts in operations. Jens Ringsmose refers to NATO as 'first and foremost a burden-sharing arrangement'; public goods theory, he contends, 'tells us something fundamental about how the Alliance works' and specifically how it deals with collective action problems when engaged in operations such as that in Afghanistan. James Sperling concludes in the case of NATO's Libya operation that neo-classical realism 'cannot claim to explain alliance behaviour, only the behaviour of individual states within one'. Frank Schimmelfennig shows from a sociological institutionalist perspective that 'flexibilisation' in NATO helps explain the Alliance's predisposition toward change and specifically its commitment to operations and enlargement. Other chapters, meanwhile, utilise theory in order to draw inferences about NATO policy in the round. Thus, according to Benjamin Pohl, liberal theory shows that NATO is not an actor but an 'arena' in which 'policy output is a compromise between the preferences of its member governments'. Gabi Schlag, by utilising securitisation theory, is able to demonstrate how NATO has come to adopt an 'unspecific, yet ambitious security agenda'. And Trine Flockhart asks how a 'constructivist approach can move from the abstract "world of theory" to the pragmatic "world of policy"'.

Fourth, we are aware also of the curse of many an edited book – the bringing together of chapters united by common themes but lacking in coherence. This problem we have avoided by giving each chapter a common brief: to present a particular theoretical position and then consider its utility when applied to analysis of NATO. Each contributor was encouraged in carrying out this task to consider a set of questions – What is NATO? What is NATO for? Who is NATO for? And whither NATO? Such consideration was not intended to determine how individual chapters were constructed. Indeed, a common format would have curtailed rather than opened up the analysis. That there is variation across chapters reflects the fact that some theories have less or more to say about these questions and may, in fact, be more concerned with others. Posing them did, at least, require the contributors to think about the relevance of a shared enquiry. We are hopeful that the book as a whole is successful in that endeavour.

Notes

1   This chapter considers literature written and published in English which, however
   regrettable, is the universal language of academic International Relations (IR). It also
   concentrates on academic writing (and so generally ignores think-tank pieces, editori-
   als and articles written by serving NATO officials). The logic here is clear given our
   subject matter. An assessment of a literature of theoretical significance is best done by
   surveying those sources in which theory is likely to be present or, where it is absent,
   that absence is itself of note.
2   On a smaller scale, NATO also intervened in Macedonia in 2001.
3   At its height in the first half of 2012, ISAF numbered 130,000 armed personnel drawn
   from all twenty-eight NATO members as well as twenty-two non-NATO partners.
   Twenty-two of twenty-eight NATO allies have sustained fatalities in Afghanistan, with
   losses falling particularly heavily upon the US, the UK, Canada, France, Germany,
   Italy and Denmark.
4   All these themes have already been touched on in summaries earlier, and much work
   already cited is also relevant here. For additional works that are more expressly prescriptive, see, on Bosnia, Gow (1997); on Kosovo, the literature summarised in Webber
   (2009b) and on Libya, Kuperman (2015). For enlargement, see Carpenter and Conry
   (1998). On NATO–Russia relations, see Hunter (1999) and Hunter and Rogov (2004).
5   An 'amalgamated security community', meanwhile, would be one in which states have
   formally merged. See Deutsch et al. (1957: 6).
6   For a similar argument which utilises a constructivist (rather than in Pouliot's case a
   Bourdieusian) approach, see Williams and Neumann (2000).
7   See also Williams (2007) and Hansen (2006).
8   Buzan, Wæver and de Wilde (1997); Booth (2007); Sjoberg (2010). Tellingly, the first
   two of these books does not contain NATO in its index. The third has just three short
   references.

References

[All web sources listed were last accessed 12 June 2015.]

Adler, E. and Barnett, M. (1998). 'A Framework for the Study of Security Communities',
   in Adler, A. and Barnett, M, (eds). *Security Communities*, Cambridge: Cambridge Uni-
   versity Press.
Allin, D. H. (2002). 'NATO's Balkan Interventions', *Adelphi Paper*, 347.
Andrews, D. M. (ed). (2005). *The Atlantic Alliance under Stress: US-European Relations
   after Iraq*, Cambridge: Cambridge University Press.
Asmus, R. D. (2002). *Opening NATO's Door: How the Alliance Remade Itself for a New
   Era*, New York: Columbia University Press.
Auerswald, D. P. and Saideman, S. M. (2014). *NATO in Afghanistan: Fighting Together,
   Fighting Alone,* Princeton: Princeton University Press.
Averre, D. (1998). 'NATO Expansion and Russian National Interests', *European Security*,
   7(1): 10–54.
Averre, D. (2009). 'From Pristina to Tskhinvali: The Legacy of Operation Allied Force in
   Russia's Relations with the West', *International Affairs*, 85(3): 575–592.
Barany Z. and Rauchhaus, R. (2011). 'Explaining NATO's Resilience: Is International
   Relations Theory Useful?', *Contemporary Security Policy*, 32(2): 286–307.
Barry, D. (2011). 'Libya's Lessons: The Air Campaign', *Survival*, 54(6): 57–65.
Behnke, A. (2013). *NATO's Security Discourse after the Cold War: Representing the West*,
   London: Routledge.

Berdal, M. (2009). 'NATO at 60', *Survival*, 51(2): 55–76.

Bergeron, J. (2014). 'Back to the Future in Wales', *The RUSI Journal*, 159(3): 4–8.

Berryman, J. (2010). 'Russia, NATO Enlargement and "Regions of Privileged Interests"', in Kanet, R. E. (ed). *Russian Foreign Policy in the 21st Century*, Houndmills, Basingstoke: Palgrave Macmillan.

Black, J. L. (1999). *Russia Faces NATO Expansion: Bearing Gifts or Bearing Arms?* Lanham: Rowman and Littlefield.

Booth, K. (2007). *Theory of World Security*, Cambridge: Cambridge University Press.

Braun, A. (ed). (2008). *NATO-Russia Relations in the Twenty-First Century*, London: Routledge.

Brown, C. (1992). *International Relations Theory: New Normative Approaches*, New York: Columbia University Press.

Burns, N. (2014). 'Three Critical Tests for NATO Leaders in Wales', *FT com*, 31 August at: www.ft.com/cms/s/0/26b10182–2f67–11e4–83e400144feabdc0.html#axzz 3cpN7wrf1.

Buzan, B. Wæver, O. and de Wilde, J. (1997). *Security: A New Framework for Analysis*, Boulder: Lynne Reinner.

Carpenter, T. G. and Conry, B. (1998). *NATO Enlargement: Illusions and Reality*, Washington D.C.: Cato Institute.

Chaudhuri, R. and Farrell, T. (2011). 'Campaign Disconnect: Operational Progress and Strategic Obstacles in Afghanistan, 2009–2011', *International Affairs*, 87(2): 271–296.

Checkel, J. T. (2013). 'Theoretical Pluralism in IR: Possibilities and Limits', in Carlsnaes, W. Risse, T. and Simmons, B.A. (eds). *Handbook of International Relations*, 2nd ed, London: Sage.

Chivvis, C. S. (2012–2013). 'Libya and the Future of Liberal Intervention', *Survival*, 54(6): 69–92.

Corterier, P. (1990). '*Quo Vadis* NATO?', *Survival*, 32(2): 141–156.

Cottey, A. (2004). 'NATO: Globalisation or Redundancy?', *Contemporary Security Policy*, 25(3): 391–408.

Cottey, A. (2014). 'NATO', in Sperling, J. (ed). *Handbook of Governance and Security*, Cheltenham: Edward Elgar.

Cox, M. (2005). 'Beyond the West: Terrors in Transatlantia', *European Journal of International Relations*, 11(2): 203–233.

Croft, S. Howorth, J. Terriff, T. and Webber, M. (2000). 'NATO's Triple Challenge', *International Affairs* 76(3): 495–518.

Daalder, I. H. and O'Hanlon, M. E. (2000). *Winning Ugly: NATO's War to Save Kosovo*, Washington D.C.: Brookings Institution Press.

David, C-P. and Lévesque, J. (eds). (1999). *The Future of NATO: Enlargement, Russia and European Security*, Montreal: McGill-Queen's University Press.

Davidson, J. W. (2011). *America's Allies and War: Kosovo, Afghanistan and Iraq*, Oxford: Oxford University Press.

Deni, J. (2007). *Alliance Management and Maintenance: Restructuring NATO for the 21st Century*, Aldershot: Ashgate.

De Santis, H. (1991). 'The Greying of NATO', *The Washington Quarterly*, 14(4): 51–65.

Deutsch, K. W., Burrell, S. A., Kann, R.A., Lee Jr., M., Lichterman, M., Lindgren, R. E., Lowenheim, F. L. and Van Read Wagenen, R. W. (1957). *Political Community and the North Atlantic Area: International Organization in the Light of Historical Expericence*, Princeton: Princeton University Press.

De Wijk, R. (1997). *NATO on the Brink of the New Millennium: The Battle for Consensus*, London: Brasseys.

Duffield, J. S. (1994–1995). 'NATO's Functions after the Cold War', *Political Science Quarterly*, 109(5):763–787.

Dunne, T. Hansen, L. and Wight, C. (2013). 'The End of International Relations Theory?', *European Journal of International Relations*, 19(3): 405–425.

Edmunds, T. (2003). 'NATO and Its New Members', *Survival*, 45(3): 145–166.

Edström, H. and Gyllensporre, D. (eds). (2012). *Pursuing Strategy: NATO Operations from the Gulf War to Gaddafi*, Houndmills, Basingstoke: Palgrave Macmillan.

Engelbrekt, K., Mohlin, M. and Wagnsson, C. (eds). (2014). *The NATO Intervention in Libya: Lessons from the Campaign*, London: Routledge.

Epstein, R. A. (2005). 'NATO Enlargement and the Spread of Democracy: Evidence and Expectations', *Security Studies*, 14(1): 63–105.

European Security (2010), 19(1), special issue on 'France's Return to NATO: Implications for Transatlantic Relations'.

Farrell, T. and Rynning, S. (2010). 'NATO's Transformation Gaps: Transatlantic Differences and the War in Afghanistan', *The Journal of Strategic Studies*, 33(5): 673–699.

Flockhart, T. (2013). 'NATO's Global Partnerships – A Haphazard Strategy?', in Hallams E., Ratti, L. and Zyla, B. (eds). *NATO beyond 9/11: The Transformation of the Atlantic Alliance*, Houndmills, Basingstoke: Palgrave Macmillan.

Flockhart, T. (ed). (2014). *Cooperative Security: NATO's Partnership Policy in a Changing World*, Copenhagen: Danish Institute for International Studies.

Forsberg, T. and Herd, G. (2015). 'Russia and NATO: From Windows of Opportunity to Closed Doors', *Journal of Contemporary European Studies*, 23(1): 41–57.

Forster, A. and Wallace, W. (2001). 'What Is NATO For?', *Survival*, 43(4): 107–122.

Gheciu, A. (2005). *NATO in the "New Europe": The Politics of International Socialization after the Cold War*, Stanford: Stanford University Press.

Gheciu, A. (2011). *Securing Civilization? The EU, NATO, and the OSCE in the Post-9/11 World*, Oxford: Oxford University Press.

Gibbs, D. N. (2009). *First Do No Harm: Humanitarian Intervention and the Destruction of Yugoslavia*, Nashville: Vanderbilt University Press.

Glaser, C. L. (1993). 'Why NATO Is Still Best: Future Security Arrangements for Europe', *International Security*, 18(1):5–50.

Goldgeier, J. M. (1999) *Not Whether But When: The US Decision to Enlarge NATO*, Washington, D.C.: Brookings Institution Press.

Goldstein, W. (ed). (1994). *Security in Europe: The Role of NATO after the Cold War*, London: Brasseys.

Gordon, M. R. (2014). 'Criticism over Afghan Pullout Expands', *International New York Times*, 6 June.

Gordon, P. H. (ed). (1997). *NATO's Transformation: The Changing Shape of the Atlantic Alliance*, Lanham: Rowman and Littlefield.

Gordon, P. H. and Shapiro, J. (2004). *Allies at War: America, Europe and the Crisis over Iraq*, New York: McGraw-Hill.

Gow, J. (1997). *Triumph of the Lack of Will: International Diplomacy and the Yugoslav War*, London: C. Hurst and Co.

Gowan, P. (1999). *The Global Gamble: Washington's Faustian Bid for Global Dominance*, London: Verso.

Gowan, P. (2010). *A Calculus of Power: Grand Strategy in the Twenty-First Century*, London: Verso.

Hallams, E. (2010). *The United States and NATO since 9/11: The Transatlantic Alliance Renewed*, London: Routledge.

Hallams, E. (2013). *A Transatlantic Bargain for the 21st Century: The United States, Europe, and the Transatlantic Alliance*, Carlisle: US Army War College, Strategic Studies Institute.

Hallams E. and Schreer, B. (2012). 'Towards a "Post-American" Alliance? NATO Burden Sharing after Libya', *International Affairs*, 88(2): 313–327.

Hallett, G. (2007). *European Security in the Post-Soviet Age: The Case against NATO*, York: William Sessions Ltd.

Hansen, L. (2006). *Security as Practice: Discourse Analysis and the Bosnian War*, London: Routledge.

Hellmann, G. and Wolf, R. (1993). 'Neorealism, Neoliberal Institutionalism, and the Future of NATO', *Security Studies*, 3(1): 3–43.

Hendrickson, R. C. (2006). *Diplomacy and War at NATO: The Secretary General and Military Action after the Cold War*, Columbia: University of Missouri Press.

Henriksen, D. (2007). *NATO's Gamble: Combining Diplomacy and Airpower in the Kosovo Crisis, 1998–1999*, Annapolis: Naval Institute Press.

Hilde, P. S. (2014). 'Lean, Mean Fighting Machine? Institutional Change in NATO and the NATO Command Structure', in Michta, A. A. and Hilde, P. S. (eds). *The Future of NATO: Regional Defence and Global Security*, Ann Arbor: University of Michigan Press.

Hodge, C. C. (2013). 'Full Circle: Two Decades of NATO Intervention', *Journal of Transatlantic Studies*, 11(4):350–367.

Hopkinson, W. (2001). 'Enlargement: A New NATO', *Chaillot Paper*, 49, October.

Hunker, J. (2013.) 'NATO and Cyber Security' in Herd, G. P. and Kriendler, J. (eds). *Understanding NATO in the 21st Century: Alliance Strategies, Security and Global Governance*, London: Routledge.

Hunter, R. E. (1999). 'Solving Russia: Final Piece in NATO's Puzzle', *The Washington Quarterly*, 23(1): 115–134.

Hunter, R. E. and Rogov, S. M. (2004). *Engaging Russia as Partner and Participant: The Next Stage of NATO-Russia Relations*, Santa Monica: RAND Corporation.

Hyde-Price, A. (2000). *Germany and European Order: Enlarging NATO and the EU*, Manchester: Manchester University Press.

Ivanov, I. D. (2010). 'The Relevance of Heterogenous Clubs in Explaining Contemporary NATO Politics', *Journal of Transatlantic Studies*, 8(4): 337–361.

Kaufman, J. P. (2002). *NATO and the Former Yugoslavia: Crisis, Conflict and the Atlantic Alliance*, Lanham: Rowman and Littlefield.

Kamp, K-H. (2014). 'Five Long-term Challenges for NATO beyond the Ukraine Crisis', *NDC Research* Report, July.

Kashmeri, S. A. (2010). *NATO 2.0: Reboot or Delete?* Washington, D.C.: Potomac Books.

Kaufman, J. P. (2002). *NATO and the Former Yugoslavia: Crisis, Conflict and the Atlantic Alliance*, Lanham: Rowman and Littlefield.

Kay, S. (1998). *NATO and the Future of European Security*, Lanham: Rowman and Littlefield.

Keller, P. (2012). 'Germany in Europe: The Status Quo Ally', *Survival*, 54(3): 95–110.

Kitchen, V. M. (2010). *The Globalisation of NATO: Intervention, Security and Identity*, London: Routledge.

Kroenig, M. (2015). 'Facing Reality: Getting NATO Ready for a New Cold War', *Survival*, 57(1): .49–70.

Kuperman, A. J. (2015). 'Obama's Libya Debacle: How a Well-Meaning Intervention Ended in Failure', *Foreign Affairs*, 94(2): 66–77.

Kydd, A. (2001). 'Trust Building, Trust Breaking: The Dilemma of NATO Enlargement', *International Organisation*, 55(4): 801–828.

Lambeth, B. S. (2001). *NATO's Air War for Kosovo: A Strategic and Operational Assessment*, Santa Monica: RAND Corporation.

Lašas, A. (2012). *European Union and NATO Expansion: Central and Eastern Europe*, Houndmills, Basingstoke: Palgrave Macmillan.

Latawski, P. and Smith, M. A. (2003). *The Kosovo Crisis and the Evolution of Post-Cold War European Security*, Manchester: Manchester University Press.

Lepgold, J. (1998). 'NATO's Post-Cold War Collective Action Problem', *International Security*, 23(1): 78–106.

Levine, R. A. (ed). (1992). *Transition and Turmoil in the Atlantic Alliance*, New York: Crane Russak.

Lindley-French, J. (2007). *The North Atlantic Treaty Organisation: The Enduring Alliance*, London: Routledge.

Lindstrom, G. (2013). 'NATO: Towards an Adaptive Missile Defence', in Herd, G. P. and Kriendler, J. (eds). *Understanding NATO in the 21st Century: Alliance Strategies, Security and Global Governance*, London: Routledge.

Lunn, S. (1992). 'The Future of NATO', in O. Pick. (ed). *The Cold War Legacy in Europe*, London: Pinter Publishers.

Martin, P. and Brawley, M. R. (eds). (2000). *Alliance Politics, Kosovo and NATO's War: Allied Force or Forced Allies?* Houndmills, Basingstoke: Palgrave.

Mátlary, J. H. and Petersson, M. (eds). (2013). *NATO's European Allies: Military Capability and Political Will*, Houndmills, Basingstoke: Palgrave Macmillan.

Mattelaer, A. (2011–2012). 'How Afghanistan Has Strengthened NATO', *Survival*, 53(6): 127–140.

McCalla, R. B. (1996). 'NATO's Persistence after the Cold War', *International Organisation*, 50(3): 445–475.

McInnes, C. (1995). 'The Future of NATO', in C. Bluth et al (eds), *The Future of European Security*, London: Dartmouth Publishing Company.

McKinney, C. (ed) (2012). *The Illegal War on Libya*, Atlanta: Clarity Press.

Medcalf, J. (2008). *Going Global or Going Nowhere? NATO's Role in Contemporary International Security*, Oxford: Peter Lang.

Menon, R. (2007). *The End of Alliances*, Oxford: Oxford University Press.

Meyer S. (ed). (2014). *NATO's Post-Cold War Politics: The Changing Provision of Security*, Houndmills, Basingstoke: Palgrave Macmillan.

Michta, A. A. (2006). *The Limits of Alliance: The United States, NATO and the EU in North and Central Europe*, Lanham: Rowman and Littlefield.

Michta, A. A. (2014). 'Introduction: Regional Versus Global Priorities – Can NATO Get the Balance Right?', in Michta, A. A. and Hilde, P. S. (eds). *The Future of NATO: Regional Defence and Global Security*, Ann Arbor: University of Michigan Press.

Moore, R. R. (2007). *NATO's New Mission: Projecting Stability in a Post-Cold War World*, Westport: Praeger Security International.

NATO. (2014). 'Wales Summit Declaration', NATO Press Release (2014) 120, 5 September at: www.nato.int/cps/en/natohq/official_texts_112964.htm.

Nazemroaya, M. D. (2012). *The Globalisation of NATO*, Atlanta: Clarity Press.

Neumann, I. B. (2013). 'Series Editor's Preface' to Behnke, A. *NATO's Security Discourse after the Cold War: Representing the West*, London: Routledge.

Niblett, R. (2014). 'A Chance to Regroup for NATO', *The World Today*, August–September: 30–31.

Noetzel, T. and Schreer, B. (2009). 'NATO's Vietnam? Afghanistan and the Future of the Atlantic Alliance', *Contemporary Security Policy*, 30(3): 529–547.

Odgaard, L. (ed) (2014). *Strategy in NATO: Preparing for an Imperfect World*, Houndmills, Basingstoke: Palgrave Macmillan.

Olson, M. and Zeckhauser, R. (1966). 'An Economic Theory of Alliances', *Review of Economic Statistics*, 48(3): 266–279.

Peterson, J. W. (2011). *NATO and Terrorism: Organisational Expansion and Mission Transformation*, New York: Continuum.

Pond, E. (2004). *Friendly Fire: The Near-Death of the Transatlantic Alliance*, Washington, D.C.: Brookings Institution Press and Pittsburgh: European Union Studies Association.

Ponsard, L. (2006). *Russia, NATO and Cooperative Security: Bridging the Gap*, London: Routledge.

Pouliot, V. (2006). 'The Alive and Well Transatlantic Security Community: A Theoretical Reply to Michael Cox', *European Journal of International Relations*, 12(1): 119–127.

Pouliot, V. (2010) *International Security in Practice: The Politics of NATO-Russia Diplomacy*, Cambridge: Cambridge University Press.

Rasmussen, A. F. (2014). Press Conference of the NATO Secretary General, 1 September at: www.nato.int/cps/en/natohq/opinions_112238.htm.

Ratti, L. (2013). 'NATO-Russia Relations after 9/11: New Challenges, Old Issues', in Hallams E., Ratti, L. and Zyla, B. (eds). *NATO beyond 9/11: The Transformation of the Atlantic Alliance*, Houndmills, Basingstoke: Palgrave Macmillan.

Reiter, D. (2001). 'Why NATO Enlargement Does Not Spread Democracy', *International Security*, 25(4): 41–67.

Reus-Smit, C. and Snidal, D. (2008). 'Between Utopia and Reality: The Practical Discourses of International Relations', in Reus-Smit, C. and Snidal D. (eds). *The Oxford Handbook of International Relations*, Oxford: Oxford University Press.

Ringsmose, J. (2010). 'NATO Burden-Sharing Redux: Continuity and Change after the Cold War', *Contemporary Security Policy*, 31(2): 319–338.

Risse, T. (2004). 'Beyond Iraq: The Crisis of the Transatlantic Security Community', in Held, D. and Koenig-Archibugi, M. (eds). *American Power in the Twenty-First Century*, Oxford: Polity.

Risse-Kappen, T. (1995). 'Collective Identity in a Democratic Community: The Case of NATO', in Katzenstein, P. (ed).*The Culture of National Security: Norms and Identity in World Politics*, New York: Columbia University Press.

Rühle, M. (2013). 'NATO and Nuclear Weapons' in Herd, G. P. and Kriendler, J. (eds). *Understanding NATO in the 21st Century: Alliance Strategies, Security and Global Governance*, London: Routledge.

Rumer, E. (2014). 'Time for NATO to Look Inward', European Leadership Network, 8 July at: www.europeanleadershipnetwork.org/time-for-nato-to-look-inward_1622.html.

Rynning, S. (2005). *NATO Renewed: The Power and Purpose of Transatlantic Cooperation*, New York: Palgrave Macmillan.

Rynning, S. (2012). *NATO in Afghanistan: The Liberal Disconnect*, Stanford: Stanford University Press.

Sandler T. and Hartley, K. (1999). *The Political Economy of NATO: Past, Present, and into the 21st Century*, Cambridge: Cambridge University Press.

Schimmelfennig, F. (2004). 'Liberal Intergovernmentalism', in Wiener, A. and Diez, T. (eds). *European Integration Theory*, Oxford: Oxford University Press.

Schulte, G. L. (1997). 'Former Yugoslavia and the New NATO', *Survival*, 39(1): 19–42.

Sherwood-Randall, E. (2006). 'The Case for Alliances', *Joint Forces Quarterly*, 43(4): 54–59.

Siegel, S. N. (2009). 'Bearing Their Share of the Burden: Europe in Afghanistan', *European Security*, 18(4): 461–482.

Sireci, J. and Coletta, D. (2009). 'Enduring without an Enemy: NATO's Realist Foundations', *Perspectives*, 17(1): 57–82.

Sjoberg, L. (ed). (2010). *Gender and International Security: Feminist Perspectives*, London: Routledge.

Sjursen, H. (2004). 'On the Identity of NATO', *International Affairs*, 80(4): 687–703.

Sloan, S. R. (ed). (1989). *NATO in the 1990s*, Washington, D.C.: Pergamon-Brasseys.

Sloan, S. R. (2010). *Permanent Alliance? NATO and the Transatlantic Bargain from Truman to Obama*, New York: Continuum.

Smith, M. A. (2006). *Russia and NATO since 1991: From Cold War through Cold Peace to Partnership?* London: Routledge.

Sperling, J. and Webber, M. (2009). 'NATO: From Kosovo to Kabul', *International Affairs*, 85(3): 491–512.

Sperling, J. and Webber, M. (2012). 'NATO's Intervention in the Afghan Civil War', *Civil Wars*, 14(3): 344–372.

Thies, W. (2009). *Why NATO Endures*, Cambridge: Cambridge University Press.

Wallander, C. A. (2000). 'Institutional Assets and Adaptability: NATO after the Cold War', *International Organisation*, 54(4): 705–735.

Walt, S. M. (2000). 'NATO's Future (in Theory)', in Martin. P. and Brawley, M. R. (eds). *Alliance Politics, Kosovo, and NATO's War: Allied Force or Forced Allies?* New York: Palgrave.

Walt, S. M. (2005). 'The Relationship between Theory and Policy in International Relations', *Annual Review of Political Science*, 8: 23–48.

Webber, M. (2009a). 'NATO: The United States, Transformation and the War in Afghanistan', *British Journal of Politics and International* Relations, 11(1): 46–63.

Webber, M. (2009b). 'The Kosovo War: A Recapitulation', *International Affairs*, 85(3): 447–460.

Webber, M. (2011). 'NATO: Within and Between European International Society', *Journal of European Integration*, 33(2): 139–158.

Webber, M. (2012). 'NATO's Post-Cold War Operations in Europe', in Sperling, J. and Papacosma, S. V. (eds). *NATO after Sixty Years: A Stable Crisis*, Kent: Kent State University Press.

Webber, M. Hallams, E. and Smith, M.A. (2014). 'Repairing NATO's Motors', *International Affairs*, 90(4): 773–793.

Webber, M., Sperling, J. and Smith, M. A. (2012). *NATO's Post-Cold War Trajectory: Decline or Regeneration?* Houndmills, Basingstoke: Palgrave Macmillan.

Weitsman, P. A. (2014). *Waging War: Alliances, Coalitions, and Institutions of Interstate Violence*, Stanford: Stanford University Press.

Wheeler, N. J. (2000). *Saving Strangers: Humanitarian Intervention in International Society*, Oxford: Oxford University Press.

Wiener, A. and Diez T. (eds). (2009). *European Integration Theory*, 2nd ed, Oxford: Oxford University Press.

Williams, M. C. (2007). *Culture and Security: Symbolic Power and the Politics of International Security*, London: Routledge.

Williams, M. C. and Neumann, I. B. (2000). 'From Alliance to Security Community: NATO, Russia, and the Power of Identity', *Millennium: Journal of International Studies*, 29(2): 357–387.

Williams, M. J. (2011). *The Good War: NATO and the Liberal Conscience in Afghanistan*, Houndmills, Basingstoke: Palgrave Macmillan.

Williams, M. J. (2013). 'Enduring but Irrelevant? Britain, NATO and the Future of the Atlantic Alliance', *International Politics* 50(3): 360–386.

Wolfson, A. (2014). 'Russian Resurgence Has Blindsided NATO', *Standpoint*, July-August: 32–35.

Yost, D. (1998). *NATO Transformed: The Alliance's New Roles in International Security*, Washington, D.C.: United States Institute of Peace Press.

Yost, D. (2014). *NATO's Balancing Act*, Washington, D.C.: United States Institute of Peace Press.

Zyla, B. (2014). *Sharing the Burden? NATO and Its Second-Tier Powers*, Toronto: University of Toronto Press.

2 Theorising NATO

Adrian Hyde-Price

Opening up space for theoretical debate

This volume seeks to open up space for theoretical reflection and analysis of NATO – Europe's most important security provider, and one of the central institutional pillars of the European security system. This is a topic that has received surprisingly limited attention by International Relations (IR) scholars, let alone other social theorists. As pointed out in the previous chapter, much of the scholarship on the Alliance is descriptive, empirically focused and policy-prescriptive. And although NATO has been the subject of some theoretical attention, such efforts have failed to accumulate into a coherent and informed understanding of the nature of the Alliance or its place in the international security system.

The individual contributions which follow reflect upon a variety of theoretical positions. Given their individual merits, common themes and collective focus, they provide a starting point and a stimulus for theoretical work on NATO comparable to that which has occurred in European integration studies. As a preliminary to them, this chapter makes the case (already alluded to in Chapter 1) for theory as such – in general in the discipline of IR, and in particular by reference to NATO.

Why theorise NATO?

Before beginning to reflect on *how* we theorise NATO, it is important to remind ourselves *why* we should theorise NATO. What are the roles and purposes of theory? What are its utility and its benefits? And what are its limitations? 'Social science theories', John Mearsheimer has written, 'are often portrayed as the idle speculations of head-in-the-cloud academics that have little relevance to what goes on in the "real world"'. As Mearsheimer (2001: 8–9) points out:

> In this view, theory should fall almost exclusively within the purview of academics, whereas policymakers should rely on common sense, intuition, and practical experience to carry out their duties.
>
> This view is wrongheaded. In fact, none of us could understand the world we live in or make intelligent decisions without theories. Indeed, all students and practitioners of international politics rely on theories to comprehend their

surroundings. Some are aware of it and some are not, some admit it and some do not; but there is no escaping the fact that we could not make sense of the complex world around us without simplifying theories.

Theory serves a number of essential purposes in academic research and the discipline of IR. First and foremost, theory makes it easier to grasp the modern world by simplifying complexity and outlining 'feasible avenues of enquiry' – what has been termed the 'keep it simple' doctrine (Jorgensen 2010: 8). Theories, Hans Morgenthau (1993: 3) argued, are used to 'bring order and meaning to a mass of phenomena without which [these] would remain disconnected and unintelligible' (see also Ashe et al. 1999: viii). They serve to simplify, abbreviate and abstract reality. This may mean sacrificing rich empirical detail and descriptive accuracy, but in return one obtains breadth and thus an ability to explain at a general level. Theories thus provide mental maps with which to navigate a complex and multifaceted world. 'Theory exists', Carl von Clausewitz (1989: 141) argued, 'so that one need not start afresh each time sorting out the material and ploughing through it, but will find it ready to hand and in good order'.

Second, theory is an essential guide for empirical research. Theories identify criteria for selecting 'relevant' facts and specifying causal mechanisms. As Hans Morgenthau noted (cited in Aron 2003: 2), 'theory requires that the criteria for selection of problems for intensive study be made explicit. It is not always recognised that whenever a particular problem is selected for study and analysis in some context or other, there is practically always a theory underlying the choice'. Without theories, we have no guide as to the appropriate actors, structures or interactions to investigate, and our analytical narratives will lack coherence and clarity. 'How do we decide which factors to include in our narratives and which to exclude?' Colin Wight (2006: 288) has written. 'Theory provides the answer. Theory is suggestive of the elements we deem important to the explanation of any given event. Different theories will explain the same events differently'.

Third, theory can provide an excellent tool to 'challenge prejudices, traditional world views or conventional wisdom' (Jorgensen 2010: 8). Theoretically informed analysis is a powerful tool with which to challenge politically expedient reasoning and unsound policy, and provides a means by which to evaluate policy initiatives. It is thus the scientific and analytical foundation for 'speaking truth to power'. A good example in this regard is John Mearsheimer and Stephen Walt's (2003) theoretically based critique of the 2003 Iraq war, which challenged the faulty logic on which the Bush administration had based its invasion of the country. Theory thus provides a basis for challenging the common sense assumptions of policy makers, thereby opening up space for critical debate.

Fourth, theoretical reflection is necessary to summarise and synthesise the findings of empirical studies, and so contribute to cumulative knowledge – a primary goal of all academic study and the basis for developing IR as a distinct academic discipline (Jorgensen 2010: 8). Without theories, we are left with a plethora of empirical findings based on different independent variables that cannot be integrated into a more overarching explanation. As Mearsheimer and Walt

(2013: 444–445) have argued, 'simplistic hypothesis testing' that is not driven by well-crafted theory produces a mass of empirical findings that do not contribute to cumulative knowledge, and is susceptible to 'poor data quality, selection bias, vague conceptualisations, lack of cumulation, and other problems'.

Finally, good theory can profoundly and irrevocably alter the way in which we view the world and our place in it. Examples of this include Newton's theory of gravity or Darwin's theory of evolution. By changing the way we understand the world, theoretical innovation can pave the way for further scientific and societal discoveries, and contribute to progress in an academic discipline. Without good theory, therefore, our knowledge and understanding of a subject under observation, be it objects in motion, the evolution of species or, indeed, the development of a body such as NATO, will remain patchy, incomplete and fragmented.

The nature of theory

Within IR, there is a variety of different forms and types of theory. The most widespread and influential is 'explanatory theory', which seeks to explain events by identifying causal relationships. A very different approach is 'normative theory', which draws upon the ethical insights of political philosophy to address the 'normative dimensions of international relations' (Brown 1992: 2; see also Caney 2005 and Hyde-Price 2009). An example is the very rich debate on humanitarian military intervention, driven in part by NATO's interventions in Bosnia and Kosovo (Chatterjee and Scheid 2003; Holzgrefe and Keohane 2003; Pattison 2010). A third approach is critical theory, which seeks to critique existing inequalities of power, wealth and influence, and which includes an explicit commitment to emancipatory projects (Booth 2007; Cox 1987; Gill 1993; Rosenberg 1994). Often juxtaposed to explanatory theory, critical theory does, in fact, share some common ground with its more established counterpart (in critiquing global inequalities, for instance, critical theory will base its analysis on an examination of the causal factors that first generate these inequalities) (Dunne, Hansen and Wight 2013). The two part company, however, in that many critical theorists have explicitly questioned what are seen as 'positivist' understandings of epistemology and knowledge creation, and have sought to develop 'anti-foundational' and 'post-positivist' approaches. Such a position provides a bridge to the fourth and final type of theoretical analysis. This category embraces a disparate group of 'interpretive' and 'constitutive' theories, rooted in post-positivist ontologies and epistemologies (Campbell 1998; Der Derian and Shapiro 1989; Peterson 1992; Pettman 1996; Walker 1993; Weber 1995;). Given the proliferation of these approaches and their profound differences with explanatory theory, the biggest divide within contemporary IR is largely between these post-positivist approaches and what is usually (but incorrectly) termed 'positivist' theories (Patomäki and Wight 2000; Wight 2002). As David Lake has noted, 'there is a real and emerging divide in the field of International Relations between positivists and post-positivists [. . .] Two communities are developing with different cultures, practices and languages that render conversation and interchange difficult and fraught with misunderstanding' (Lake 2013: 577–578).

Despite these differences, there is at least a broad consensus that theory involves simplification, abstraction and generalisation. 'At a very basic level', it has been noted, 'the different theoretical schools in IR are at least in agreement that theories should be understood as abstractions from a complex reality and that they attempt to provide generalisations about the phenomena under study' (Dunne, Hansen and Wight 2013: 407). Theories provide a means of going beyond mere description and categorisation of events and aim to explain or understand *why* such events happened and *why* they are significant. 'The difference between an empirical and a theoretical interpretation of international relations', Raymond Aron (2003: 2–3) has written, 'is comparable to the difference between a photograph and a painted picture. [. . .] The photograph shows everything that can be seen by the naked eye. The painted portrait does not show everything that can be seen by the naked eye, but it shows something the naked eye cannot see: the human essence of the person who is portrayed' (Aron 2003: 2–3).

Theory building

Theory building itself involves two important steps. The first is to specify the object of study (the domain of enquiry). The second is the process of theorising itself (the practice of theoretical production). The first step is essential because theories, by their very nature, are designed to explain or understand a particular set of phenomena. Theories do not seek to explain everything, but rather, to elucidate a few matters of consequence. 'No matter what the subject', Kenneth Waltz (1979: 2–3) argued, 'we have to bound the domain of our concern, to organise it, to simplify the materials we deal with, to concentrate on central tendencies, and to single out the strongest propelling forces'.

Theoretical production, meanwhile, involves a number of distinct tasks. The first is to define the key terms and concepts with which to categorise data and map the relevant domain. 'The primary purpose of any theory', Clausewitz (1989: 132) argued, 'is to clarify concepts and ideas that have become, as it were, confused and entangled. Not until terms and concepts have been defined can one hope to make any progress in examining the question clearly and simply and expect the reader to share one's views'. Indeed, Stefano Guzzini (2013: 535) has recently argued that 'concepts are co-constitutive of theories', and hence we should think of theory less as a set of cookbooks and more as an 'unfinished dictionary', with conceptual analysis holding centre stage in all modes of theorising.

Broadly speaking, theorists fall into one of two camps when it comes to conceptual definition: 'lumpers' or 'splitters'. These terms come from Charles Darwin, who made this distinction in a letter written to his close friend and fellow botanist Joseph Hooker in 1857 (Endersby 2009). Darwin argued that 'splitters' were those who sought to create ever more precise definitions, rigorously defined categories and discrete classifications, whereas the 'lumpers' sought to reduce the number of categories by identifying broad similarities between larger numbers of cases. Splitters, in other words, tend to focus on individual trees, whereas lumpers prefer to see the wood as a whole and are keen to generalise. Theoretical analysis of

NATO can be categorised in similar terms: the splitters would prefer to see NATO as a *sui generis* alliance with highly specific features that eludes explanation by conventional IR theories and which, therefore, requires its own theoretical tools of analysis. The lumpers, on the other hand, would see NATO as an international organisation or security community comparable to others and, therefore, amenable to analysis within established categories and concepts of IR theory. Thus, specifying the conceptual categories relevant to understanding NATO already implies certain theoretical assumptions and approaches.

The second task of theoretical production is the identification of key variables and through this the selective sifting of empirical data. Most theories are based on the principle of 'Occam's razor',[1] which stipulates that *entia non sunt multiplicanda praeter necessitatem* ('bodies should not be multiplied except when necessary'). Occam's razor leads most social scientists to build elegant and parsimonious theoretical models that minimise the number of explanatory variables employed (Burnham, Gilland, Grant and Leyton-Henry 2004: 4). Typically, social science entails specifying what needs to be explained (the dependent variable) and then identifying the few key (or independent) variables that account for the phenomena under investigation, taking account in turn of other factors (intervening variables) that might affect the causal relationship. By focusing on a specific research puzzle or issue, theories aim to shed light on a few important aspects of behaviour. Explanatory theory in particular is thus based on the principle of 'maximizing leverage', or 'explaining as much as possible with as little as possible' (King, Keohane and Verba 1994: 29). Maximising leverage is 'one of the most important achievements of all social science'. The primary way to do this is to 'evaluate as many observable implications of [one's] theory as possible' (King, Keohane and Verba 1994: 29). Leverage increases with the level of abstraction and generality of a scientific proposition, rather than by examining specific and context-dependent case studies (Yin 1984).

The third and most demanding task is to develop a theoretical explanation for the processes or events under investigation. This requires inspiration and, more often than not, a high degree of lateral thinking, for as Albert Einstein noted, in pure research 'imagination is more important than knowledge'.[2] Kenneth Waltz also noted that no theory can be created 'unless at some point a brilliant intuition flashes, a creative idea emerges' (Waltz 1979: 9). Mearsheimer and Walt have argued that one of the reasons for the rise of 'dreary hypothesis-testing' in place of theory building and development is that 'theoretical fertility depends primarily on individual creativity and imagination'. IR departments find it difficult to 'teach people to be creative', and hence focus on inculcating graduate students with a set of methodological tools with which to produce a competent thesis. 'Developing or refining theory is more time-consuming and riskier as it requires deeper immersion in the subject matter and the necessary flash of inspiration may never occur' (Mearsheimer and Walt 2013: 446).

In one of the most influential books on how to 'think theoretically', James Rosenau and Mary Durfee (1995: 178) argue that if one wishes to proceed from 'passive observer of world politics to that of an active theorist', then it is important to have some guidelines about how best to make that journey. They make a number of suggestions, the most important of which are as follows. First, in order to think theoretically, one must assume that human affairs manifest some underlying patterns of ordered behaviour rather than being the product of random, arbitrary and contingent fate. From this follows the second key principle: to think theoretically, one must be predisposed to ask about every event or observed phenomenon, 'of what is this an instance?' Third, thinking theoretically means that one must be prepared to sacrifice detailed descriptions for broad observations. In other words, one must be willing to see the wood from the trees and not to become captivated by the 'ephemera of events'.[3] One must also be genuinely puzzled about international politics and willing to think flexibly and creatively ('playfully' is the phrase they use) about them. Finally, one must be tolerant of ambiguity, concerned about possibilities, distrustful of absolutes and, of course, most importantly of all – one must be constantly ready to be proven wrong (Rosenau and Durfee 1995: 178–190).

Picking up on this last point, Michael Doyle (1997: 37) has suggested that Arnold Wolfers 'wrote what should be a credo for the international political theorist':

> If there is any difference between today's political scientist and his predecessors (the classical political theorists) – who, like himself, were confronted with such problems as alliance policy, the balancing of power, intervention in the affairs of other countries, and the pursuit of ideological goals – one would hope it might lie in a keener realization of the controversial and tentative nature of his reply, in a greater effort to consider alternative answers, and in a more conscious attempt to remain dispassionate and objective.
>
> (Wolfers 1962: 237)

Theory's limits: *caveat emptor*!

Before discussing how best to theorise a complex, multidimensional institution like NATO, two caveats concerning the limitations of theoretical enquiry are in order. The first is that theory is not an alternative to empirical research, data collection and hypothesis testing, but their necessary corollary. There is a fundamental limit to the role of theoretical speculation in the social world, Colin Wight (2006: 294–295) has argued, and 'there is simply no theoretical substitute for empirical research'. Wight therefore advocates 'the development of theoretically informed accounts which are then put to the epistemological sword'. Carl von Clausewitz (1989: 61) put this somewhat more elegantly in his preface to *On War*. 'Analysis and observation, theory and experience', he insisted, 'must never distain or exclude each other; on the contrary, they support each other'. When the thread of theoretical reflections 'became too thin', he noted,

> I have preferred to break it off and go back to the relevant phenomena of experience. Just as some plants bear fruit only if they don't shoot up too high,

so in the practical arts the leaves and flowers of theory must be pruned and the plant kept close to its proper soil – experience.

The second caveat is that theoretical analysis alone cannot provide final and definitive answers to the questions posed at the start of this project. What is NATO? What is NATO for? Who is NATO for? And whither NATO?

The idea that the role of theory is to settle questions once and for all – to reach conclusions – is fundamentally mistaken, the product of a misreading of the nature of science and a misapplication of this misreading to the social sciences.

(Brown quoted in Jorgensen 2010: 33)

A complex empirical puzzle like NATO is not explicable by any one theory alone: consequently, there can be no simple thing as a general theory of NATO that can fully explain its nature, role, function and purpose.

For this reason, the existence of a variety of different theoretical perspectives and approaches, each with their own ontologies and epistemologies, provides a healthy environment within which theoretical analysis of NATO can flourish (Dunne, Hansen and Wight 2013). The idea that the purpose of debate between competing theories and paradigms is to reach a final victor for one theory over several others is fundamentally wrong. Theoretical debates are not gladiatorial contests to the death, but the sign of a healthy exchange of views and perspectives among a community of scholars within a discipline. Such debates – sometimes scorned and dismissed as 'paradigm wars' – can aid conceptual precision and logical coherence, and without them, the discipline would fracture into separate and discrete schools of thought. 'A discipline debating the merits of competing paradigms', Colin Elman and John Vasquez (2003: 303; see also Herman 1998) have argued,

is a community of scholars engaged in each other's work, still keeping an open mind, and learning from each other. We would think that such a community of scholars would also more quickly uncover their mistakes and illusions than one that devolved into a community of like-minded people.

The discipline of IR is, therefore, best conceived as a 'conversation' in the sense that this term was used by Michael Oakeshott (1991). A conversation, Oakeshott argued, consists of many different voices, reflecting different sorts of knowledge, all of which may potentially have something of value to contribute. Conversations may be dominated for a time by one voice and one idiom of knowledge, but others can also make a contribution. For a time, some voices may be heard more than others, but if a conversation is to be sustained and have value for its participants, it cannot be a monologue, or even a dialogue. This means that there must be space for many different theories and approaches; the predominance of any one tradition would present a danger to intellectual creativity and theoretical advancement.

It also means that in terms of the conversation of IR, theoretical debate will serve, not to arrive at one single 'truth', but to clarify concepts, expose logical inconsistencies and improve analytical quality. As Clifford Geertz (cited in Jorgensen 2010: 33) has argued, theoretical debate contributes to an academic discipline 'less by a perfection of consensus than by a refinement of debate'. Theory, in other words, is a form of ceaseless intellectual exploration, such that, to cite T. S. Elliot, 'the end of our exploring shall be to arrive where we started, and know the place (as if) for the first time'.

NATO the elephant

Theoretical analysis and reflection on NATO should be geared toward clarifying and elucidating key features of the Alliance, thus making us aware of characteristics and aspects that we might otherwise have overlooked, underestimated or ignored.

The need for theoretical pluralism, as well as a vibrant academic conversation on NATO, arises from the complex and multifaceted nature of the Alliance itself. NATO presents scholars with a complex empirical puzzle: different theories can illuminate and elucidate certain aspects of this puzzle, but not others. No one theory can do more than explain certain specific aspects of NATO's nature, purpose, character and future. The problem of the limited explanatory power of any one theory is well illustrated by Donald Puchala's (1972: 267) retelling of the parable of the blind men and the elephant:

> Several blind men approached an elephant and each touched the animal in an effort to discover what the beast looked like. Each [. . . having] touched a different part of the large animal [. . .] concluded that the elephant had the appearance of the part he had touched.

The upshot was an absence of agreement on the nature of the elephant, although each man individually was convinced he understood the animal's physical character. NATO is an elephant, and like an elephant, it eludes simple categorisation or general theoretical explanation. Attempts to develop general theories tend to fall victim to one of three errors: reductionism, subsumption or empiricism. Reductionism involves reducing the whole to the study of its parts;[4] subsumption involves indiscriminately lumping particular cases under the heading of a more general phenomenon (Jessop 1982: 212); and empiricism rests on the 'inductivist illusion' that knowledge comes from the accumulation of ever more data.[5]

Given the problems parsimonious and reductionist theories have in understanding and explaining an elephant (or complex phenomenon) like NATO, scholars have proposed a number of alternative research strategies that seek to avoid putting all one's theoretical eggs in one basket. One such is 'perspectivism', which suggests utilising a variety of different theoretical perspectives to shed light on an empirical puzzle from a number of different angles. This assumes that there are no serious underlying ontological or epistemological reasons why different theoretical perspectives cannot be compared and contrasted (Burnham, Gilland, Grant and Leyton-Henry 2004: 23). Another is to synthesise different theories – a call frequently made to overcome the divide between realism's 'children of darkness' and liberalism's 'children of light' (Niebuhr 1986: 166–67).[6] More recently, the notion of theoretical 'eclecticism' has generated considerable interest and garnered a swathe of enthusiastic adherents.[7] This approach argues that the empirical puzzle should determine the choice of theoretical assumptions and analytical strategies, and that 'problem driven research' is best served by integrating the insights and research tools of a variety of theories and paradigms. 'Analytical eclecticism', Peter Katzenstein and Noburo Okawara (2001: 184–185; see also Sil and Katzenstein 2010) have argued, 'highlights different layers and connections that parsimonious explanations conceal' and is 'attuned to empirical anomalies that analytical parsimony slights'. Eclecticism also 'protects us from taking as natural paradigmatic assumptions about the world' and 'protects us, imperfectly to be sure, from the inevitable failings of any one paradigm, unfounded expectations of what is natural, and the adoption of flawed policies that embody those very expectations. Theory and policy are both served better by eclecticism, not parsimony'.

Eclecticism, perspectivism and synthesis are not without their critics and pose some distinctive challenges of their own. Max Weber (cited in Patomäki and Wight 2000: 214–215) was an early critic of theoretical synthesis, arguing in 1904 that one should 'struggle relentlessly against the self-deception which asserts that through the synthesis of several party points of view [. . .] practical norms of scientific validity can be arrived at'. In a similar vein, Rosenau and Durfee have argued that a clear theoretical focus is essential to bring clarity and coherence to a mass of empirical detail. Although recognising that a single paradigmatic commitment involves the dangers of 'combative instincts' and risks leaving scholars 'entrapped in a conceptual jail of one's own making', they argue that:

> without a self-conscious paradigmatic commitment, one is destined for end-less confusion, for seeing everything as relevant and thus being unable to tease meaning out of the welter of events, situations, trends, and circum-stances that make up international affairs at any and every moment in time. Without a readiness to rely on the interlocking premises of a particular para-digm, our efforts at understanding would be, at best, transitory, and at worst they would be arbitrary, filled with gaping holes and glaring contradictions.
>
> (Rosenau and Durfee 1995: 6–7)

One obvious problem with eclecticism, synthesis and perspectivism is that they are parasitic intellectual activities. They are only possible because of the efforts of those working in distinct paradigms or theoretical traditions, who contribute to cumulative knowledge on the basis of a distinct tradition of enquiry, and who specify the underlying assumptions upon which their choice of analytical strategies is premised. As Guzzini (2013: 531) notes, eclecticism thus represents more of an uneasy 'truce' in the inter-paradigm debates rather than their end.

Eclecticism is not, therefore, an alternative to inter-paradigm debates; on the contrary, vibrant inter-paradigm debates are a prerequisite for theoretical eclecticism, perspectivism and synthesis.

A more substantive problem is that a poorly conceived 'pick 'n mix' approach to different theories risks generating incommensurate findings that do not contribute to cumulative knowledge or to a more rounded multi-causal and multi-variate explanation. Yosef Lapid (2003: 131) has warned of the dangers of a 'flabby pluralism' (2003: 131), and Christian Reus-Smit (2013) has argued that analytical eclecticism risks being coloured by unstated epistemological and ontological assumptions, and cannot therefore generate the practical knowledge it is designed to produce. Even an enthusiast of eclectic mid-range theory such as David Lake (2013: 579) has noted that seeking to combine paradigms divided by epistemology and ontology will only result in 'a pabulum of inconsistent approaches or profound frustration from dealing with incommensurate facts and "explanations" '.

Theoretical construction and the method of articulation

Despite these caveats, there is no alternative to theoretical pluralism and some form of analytical eclecticism when confronted by an elephant like NATO. The Alliance, like the international system within which it is embedded, is stratified into various layers and domains that require different concepts, assumptions and principles of explanation. No one theory can do more than elucidate a particular aspect or dimension of the empirical puzzle posed by the complex and multifaceted nature of this particular beast. However, if theorists of NATO are to avoid the problems of flabby pluralism, incommensurate data and divergent ontological premises, the task of constructing more eclectic and holistic theoretical tools must be approached with caution. Different modes of analysis must be carefully 'articulated' together so they form a coherent and logically consistent whole, paying particular attention to their underlying ontological and epistemological assumptions. Theoretical analysis of NATO must therefore be 'conscious and explicit about the underlying assumptions upon which its choice of analytical strategies is premised and more sensitive to the trade-offs necessarily entailed in any choice of foundational premises' (Hay 2002: 1).

Social scientists, in other words, should devote considerable energy to the process of theory construction and focus on the requirements of building analytical models. As Bob Jessop (1982: 29) has argued, the explanation of complex empirical problems involves a synthesis of many different determinants and the 'articulation of quite different principles of explanation and modes of analysis'. Jessop has proposed the 'method of articulation' as a route to theory construction. This involves a form of theoretical eclecticism that seeks to integrate different causal mechanisms and theoretical explanations within a coherent framework. In ontological terms, Jessop (1990: 11) argues,

the need for the method [of articulation] is implied in the non-necessary interaction of different causal chains to produce a definite outcome whose own necessity originates only in and through the contingent coming together of these causal chains in a definite context.

Epistemologically, he argues, an analysis of events and phenomena 'requires us to combine concepts, assumptions and principles of explanation from different theoretical systems and to relate them to a given, theoretically defined explanandum':

> In turn, this implies that the appropriate methodology for theory construction is one based on a dual movement: from abstract to concrete along one plane of analysis; and, secondly, from simple to complex through the differential articulation of different planes of analysis of the real world. By combining these two forms of theoretical development, increasingly adequate explanations are generated.
>
> (Jessop 1990: 11)

This dual process – of conceptual definition moving from the abstract to the concrete, and of analysis that involves developing more complex causal explanations – is essential for our present purposes given the complex character of NATO the elephant. The Alliance has a number of distinct roles and an intricate, multi-faceted institutional structure; it has political as well as military functions, and is deeply embedded in a distinctive normative, cultural and ideational framework, from which it derives its legitimacy and identity as an organisation. NATO operates across different levels of analysis (system, state and the domestic) and cannot therefore be understood by drawing upon the resources of any one theoretical approach in IR or comparative politics. NATO is also shaped by both material and ideational factors, and is rooted in a number of distinct 'sources of social power' (political, military, economic and ideological), with each of these generating domains or sectors of social life with their own structural properties, actors and dynamics (Mann 2010).

The complex phenomenon that is NATO can only be understood and explained by a process of theoretical articulation, drawing on different methodological approaches, principles of explanation and modes of analysis. Different theories can illuminate and elucidate certain aspects of this puzzling beast, but not others. We need to draw upon different theories and approaches in order to explain the multiple levels and domains within which NATO is situated.

Indeed, the international and domestic political systems are all highly stratified, and there are 'relatively enduring structures of society' and 'hidden layers' which are not reducible to 'observations of individual behaviour or a hermeneutic study of intentions and actions'. The task of the social sciences, Colin Wight (2006: 60) has argued, is to uncover these hidden layers and the 'unobservable nature of social entities, such as rules, roles, relations and meanings', and to provide theoretical and analytical tools with which to empirically investigate the 'real and relatively enduring set of structural properties that exert effects and which can be the subject of scientific inquiry'. Drawing on critical realism, he advocates an 'emergent ontology' similar to that of Bob Jessop which rejects all reductive explanations in preference for an approach that draws on a range of different theories:

> The laws discovered and identified at one level are irreducible to those at other levels. Each level has its own emergent powers that, although rooted in, emergent from and dependent upon other levels, cannot be explained by explanations based at the more fundamental levels. The emergent levels, then, have powers and liabilities unique to that level. . . . Scientific progress is a process where our knowledge of nature is deepened and underlying each mechanism, or level, there are always other levels waiting to be explained.
>
> (Wight 2006: 36)

Future directions for theorising NATO

The contributions to this volume provide an excellent overview of the richness and diversity of theoretical inquiry into NATO and transatlantic security cooperation, and indicate the potential for developing complex multi-causal analytical models. Looking beyond the existing inter-paradigm debates, however, it is also evident that the debate on NATO would benefit from drawing on a wide range of sources for theoretical innovation and renewal. Some of the requirements for theoretical advancement have been identified earlier: the ability to go beyond reductionism and integrate both systems-level and domestic factors in the analysis, a clearer understanding of the ontological status of agents and structures in the transatlantic alliance and an approach that gives due weight to both material and ideational factors in the shaping of NATO security policy.

The starting point for theorising NATO is ontology. 'Ontology', Robert Cox (cited in Wight 2006: 3) has argued, 'lies at the beginning of any enquiry'. Ontology deals with the dramatis personae of the political arena, such as social collectivities, classes, groups, states, nations, international organisations, systems, and so on. Political ontology is thus 'intimately associated with adjudicating the categories to which legitimate appeal might be made in political analysis' (Hay 2006: 2). Ontological differences underlie the debate between differing theoretical perspectives on transatlantic security cooperation given disputes over which actors – states, sub-state actors or NATO itself – play the determining role in shaping policy. 'Differing theories all have their own proposed ontology', Colin Wight (2006:4) argues:

> All theories suggest key variables, factors, units and processes, just as all political accounts of the social world contain within them accounts of why and how the world is the way it is, and through a critique of this world how it might be improved.

In terms of theorising NATO, one particularly promising ontological perspective is that which combines 'depth ontology' with a theory of 'emergence'. Such a perspective offers a way of avoiding reductive explanations and generating an analytical framework that integrates domestic and international levels – avoiding the one-dimensional approaches of theories such as liberalism and realism. Rejecting reductionism, Wight argues,

> legitimates a distinct realm of human activity at the level of the international, as well as demonstrating how this realm cannot be studied in a manner that assumes its isolation from other realms located both horizontally and vertically in relation to it.
>
> (Wight 2006: 37)

Depth ontology presupposes that there are structures, agents and mechanisms that operate and exist independently of our ability to know or manipulate them. It also implies that social reality is stratified into a number of distinct levels, and that each level has its own distinctive structures and dynamics that are irreducible to those operating at other levels. This is where depth ontology needs to be combined with a theory of emergence that recognises that the structural properties that operate at one level or in one domain are not reducible to those at others and that each has its own emergent laws, logics and characteristics.

Greater clarity about the underlying ontology of NATO is also essential for making sense of the agent–structure problem, which continues to bedevil theories of the Alliance. Does NATO possess agency itself, or is it simply an arena upon which other actors (notably states) interact and compete? What the agent–structure problem certainly highlights, Colin Wight notes, is:

> the impossibility of maintaining the disciplinary boundary between domestic and international politics . . . when viewed from an agent-structure perspective the distinction between domestic and international structures seems untenable and agents are seen to be located within a plurality of structural constraints and enablements, some domestic, some international.

International political agents are thus 'subject to systemic, regional, domestic, bureaucratic and micro-interactional structure. All these various levels of structure impinge upon the identities, interests and options of agents and thus play an influential role in international politics' (Wight 2006: 292).

Understanding the distinctive nature of NATO as an international security actor thus involves recognising the extent to which agents are 'situated actors' within structures that are themselves 'strategically selective' (Hyde-Price 2007). The mutually constitutive relationship between agents and structures, which is implicit in this conception of 'situated actors' and 'strategically selective' structures, has been developed by Bob Jessop (2008) in his 'strategic-relational approach' (SRA). Premised upon a critical realist philosophy of social science, SRA 'adopts a dialectical approach to the material and discursive interdependence of structure and strategy and their co-evolution'. Although its origins lie in debates on state theory, 'as the SRA has developed, its principal concepts and arguments have been disentangled from the immediate theoretical and historical contexts in which they were developed' in an effort 'to make them more generally applicable'. Jessop himself has called on others 'to take up the challenge to develop the strategic-relational approach in their own fashion and their own fields' (Jessop 2008: 22, 16, 245), a challenge for which NATO and transatlantic security cooperation is eminently suitable.

SRA offers a particularly useful way of conceptualising the ontological status of NATO as an international security actor. Is NATO an 'actor', a subject with its own autonomous identity and agential power, as some accounts imply? Or is it simply a 'thing' that is used and manipulated in instrumental ways by other actors (i.e., its member states)? SRA would suggest that it is neither a unified subject nor an inanimate instrument or thing captured and used by others. Rather, it is a complex institutional terrain which structures and patterns the interactions of agonistic social and political forces. To use more abstract terminology, NATO is a material embodiment of social relations, a 'form-determined condensation of the changing balance of forces'. The institutional terrain of the Alliance does not provide a neutral space or a 'level playing ground' for this process of political competition because its structures (themselves the condensed outcome of previous interactions) privilege certain interests and political strategies rather than others (notably, perhaps, those of the United States). They are therefore 'strategically selective' in the sense that they have a

> specific, differential impact on the ability of various political forces to pursue particular interests and strategies in specific spatio-temporal contexts – capacities that always depend for their effectiveness on links to forces and powers that exist and operate beyond [NATO's] formal boundaries.
>
> (Jessop 2002: 40)

The dependence of NATO on capacities beyond its formal boundaries (that is, on military capacities possessed by member states) implies that the Alliance cannot be conceptualised outside of the wider pattern of international social relations within which it is embedded – particularly the wider transatlantic relationship. In the same way as the state cannot be theorised without a corresponding theory of society, NATO cannot be theorised without a theory of the transatlantic liberal order within which it is situated and embedded (Gilpin 1981: 15). In terms of SRA, therefore, NATO can be conceived as neither a unified subject nor a neutral instrument, but an asymmetrical institutional terrain on which various actors contest control over the Alliance's institutional apparatus and its distinctive capacities (Jessop 2008: 31).

Depth ontology and SRA provide some useful pointers to new directions for theorising NATO, but there is one final issue that needs to be addressed as part of a more fundamental rethinking of the nature of NATO and transatlantic security relations. This is the key issue of the relationship between material structures, ideas and institutions (Hyde-Price 2008). As Jessop (2008: 48–49) argues, ideas are central to 'any adequate understanding of the relationship between agent and structure': those who 'are able to provide the cognitive filters, such as policy paradigms, through which actors interpret the strategic environment' consequently have significant power. As a result, a more eclectic theoretical approach to NATO must involve recognising the key role played by both discursive and material aspects of social reality in shaping the transatlantic alliance. To do so, a discursive–materialist analysis of transatlantic security relations must go beyond the ontological dualism found in the increasingly barren exchanges between realists and constructivists. Whereas realists have tended to see ideas as reducible to ultimately determining material factors, constructivists have rejected this and accorded ideas an independent causal role in political explanation. As Colin Hay (2006: 93) argues,

> whilst it is important not simply to reduce the ideational to a reflection, say, of underlying material interests, it is equally important not to subscribe to a voluntarist idealism in which political outcomes might be read off, more or less directly, from the desires, motivations, and cognitions of the immediate actors themselves.

This points to a more nuanced understanding of the complex interaction between material and ideational factors in the international system, as well as a view of international political outcomes as 'neither a simple reflection of actors' intentions and understandings nor of the contexts which give rise to such intentions and understandings' (Hay 2006: 93). Instead, outcomes can be conceptualised as the result of 'the impact of the strategies actors devise as means to realise their intentions upon a context which favours certain strategies over others and does so irrespective of the intentions of the actors themselves' (Hay 2006: 93). In other words, an international outcome like the transatlantic security alliance is neither the result merely of the balance of power and the structural logic of material factors, nor can it be attributed to the ideational preferences of individual member states (Hyde-Price 2013). Rather, it can only be adequately explained by a process of theoretical articulation that draws on a variety of analytical strategies and principles of explanation, based on explicit ontological premises and a more nuanced understanding of the relationship between agents, structures and ideas.

Notes

1   Named after the Franciscan monk, William of Occam (1284–1349).
2   Einstein remarked that in 1905, the year in which he produced five papers that transformed the elemental science of physics, 'a storm broke loose in my mind'.
3   However, a word of caution is called for here: as King, Keohane and Verba (1994: 10) note, 'Human beings are very good at recognizing patterns but are not very good

at recognising nonpatterns. (Most of us even see patterns in random ink blots!)'. For this reason, they argue, it is important to retain a healthy dose of scepticism about the claims of any theory's explanatory power, a point also underlined by Rosenau and Durfee (1995: 189).

4   'With a reductionist approach, the whole is understood by knowing the attributes and the interactions of its parts [. . .] Essential to the reductionist approach, then, is that the whole shall be known through the study of its parts' (Waltz 1979: 18–19; see also Jessop 1982: 212).

5   'The "inductivist illusion", as structural anthropologist Lévi-Strauss terms it, is the belief that truth is won and explanation achieved through the accumulation of more and more data and the examination of more and more cases' (Waltz 1979: 4).

6   On theoretical synthesis, see Moravcsik (2003), Kratochwil (2003) and Wight (2006: 42–43). On a synthesis of liberalism and realism, see Baldwin (1993), Hoffmann (1998: 54–56), Donnelly (2000: 196–98) and Hall (1996: 30–32).

7   Eclectic theory 'represents the future of International Relations – not a new future, since it already has a long history, but the future nonetheless' (Lake 2013: 572).

References

Aron, R. (2003). *Peace and War: A Theory of International Relations*. New Jersey: Transaction Publishers.

Ashe, F. Finlayson, A. Lloyd, M. MacKenzie, I. Martin J. and O'Neill, S. (1999). *Contemporary Social and Political Theory: An Introduction*. Buckingham: Open University Press.

Baldwin, D. (1993). 'Neoliberalism, Neoliberalism, and World Politics', in Baldwin, D. (ed). *Neorealism and Neoliberalism*. New York: Columbia University Press.

Booth, K. (2007). *Theory of World Security*. Cambridge: Cambridge University Press.

Brown, C. (1992). *International Relations Theory: New Normative Approaches*. New York: Columbia University Press.

Burnham, P. Gilland, K. Grant, W. and Leyton-Henry, Z. (2004). *Research Methods in Politics*. London: Palgrave, 2004.

Campbell, D. (1998). *Writing Security: United States Foreign Policy and the Politics of Identity*, rev ed. Manchester: Manchester University Press.

Caney, S. (2005). *Justice Beyond Borders: A Global Political Theory*. Oxford: Oxford University Press.

Chatterjee D. and Scheid, D. (eds). (2003). *Ethics and Foreign Intervention*. Cambridge: Cambridge University Press.

Clausewitz, C. von. (1989). *On War*, edited and translated by Howard, M and Paret, P., Princeton: Princeton University Press.

Cox, R. (1987). *Production, Power and World Order: Social Forces in the Making of History*. New York: Columbia University Press.

Der Derian, J. and Shapiro, M. (eds). (1989). *International/Intertextual Relations: Postmodern Readings of Modern Politics*. Lexington: Lexington Books.

Donnelly, J. (2000). *Realism and International Relations*. Cambridge: Cambridge University Press.

Doyle, M. (1997). *Ways of War and Peace Realism, Liberalism and Socialism*. New York: W. W. Norton and Company.

Dunne, T. Hansen, L. and Wight, C. (2013). 'The End of IR Theory?', *European Journal of International Relations*, 19(3): 405–425.

Elman, C. and Vasquez, J. (2003). 'Closing Dialogue', in Vasquez, J. and Elman, C. (eds). *Realism and the Balancing of Power: A New Debate*. New Jersey: Prentice Hall.

Endersby, J. (2009). 'Lumpers and Splitters: Darwin, Hooker, and the Search for Order', *Science*, 326 (11 December): 1496–1499.

Gill, S. (ed). (1993). *Gramsci, Historical Materialism and International Relations*. Cambridge: Cambridge University Press.

Gilpin, R. (1981). *War and Change in World Politics*. Cambridge: Cambridge University Press.

Guzzini, S. (2013). 'The Ends of International Relations Theory: Stages of Reflexivity and Modes of Theorising', *European Journal of International Relations*, 19(3): 521–541.

Hall, J. (1996). *International Orders*. London: Polity.

Hay, C. (2002). *Political Analysis: A Critical Introduction*. London: Palgrave.

Hay, C. (2006). 'Political Ontology', in Goodwin, R. and Tilly, C. (eds). *The Oxford Handbook of Contextual Political Analysis*. Oxford: Oxford Handbooks Online.

Hoffmann, S. (1998) 'Beyond Realism and Idealism in International Politics', in Hoffmann, S. (ed). *World Disorders: Troubled Peace in the Post-Cold War Era*. Lanham: Rowman and Littlefield Publishers.

Holzgrefe, J. and Keohane, R. (eds). (2003). *Humanitarian Intervention: Ethical, Legal and Political Dilemmas*. Cambridge: Cambridge University Press.

Hyde-Price, A. (2007) *European Security in the Twenty-First Century: The Challenge of Multipolarity*, London: Routledge.

Hyde-Price, A. (2008). 'A "Tragic Actor"? A Realist Perspective on "Ethical Power Europe"', *International Affairs*, 84(1): 49–64.

Hyde-Price, A. (2009). 'Realist Ethics and the "War on Terror"', *Globalisations*, 6(1): 23–40.

Hyde-Price, A. (2013). 'Neither Realism nor Liberalism: New Directions in Theorising EU Security Policy', *Contemporary Security Policy*, 34 (2): 397–408.

Jessop, B. (1982). *The Capitalist State*. Oxford: Martin Robertson.

Jessop, B. (1990). *State Theory: Putting the Capitalist State in its Place*. Cambridge: Polity Press.

Jessop, B. (2002). *The Future of the Capitalist State*. Cambridge: Polity.

Jessop, B. (2008). *State Power: A Strategic-Relational Approach*. Cambridge: Polity.

Jorgensen, K. (2010). *International Relations Theory: A New Introduction*. London: Palgrave Macmillan.

Katzenstein, P. and Okawara, N. (2001). 'Japan, Asian-Pacific Security, and the Case for Analytical Eclecticism', *International Security*, 26(3): 153–185.

King, G. Keohane, R. and Verba, S. (1994). *Designing Social Inquiry. Scientific Inference in Qualitative Research*. Princeton: Princeton University Press.

Kratochwil, F. (2003). 'The Monologue of "Science"', *International Studies Review* 5(1): 124–128.

Lake, D. (2013). 'Theory Is Dead, Long Live Theory: The End of the Great Debates and the Rise of Eclecticism in International Relations', *European Journal of International Relations*, 19(3): 567–587.

Lapid, Y. (2003). 'Through Dialogue to Engaged Pluralism: the Unfinished Business of the Third Debate', *International Studies Review* 5(1): 128–153.

Mann, M. (2010) *The Sources of Social Power: Volume One*, new edition. Cambridge: Cambridge University Press.

Mearsheimer, J. (2001). *The Tragedy of Great Power Politics*. New York: W.W. Norton and Company.

Mearsheimer, J. and Walt, S. (2003). 'An Unnecessary War', *Foreign Policy*, (January/February): 51–59.

Mearsheimer, J. and Walt, S. (2013). 'Leaving Theory Behind: Why Simplistic Hypothesis Testing Is Bad for International Relations', *European Journal of International Relations*, 19(3): 427–457.

Moravcsik, A. (2003). 'Theory Synthesis in International Relations: Real Not Metaphysical', *International Studies Review*, 5(1): 131–136.

Morgenthau, H. (1993). *Politics Among Nations: The Struggle for Power and Peace*, brief edition, revised by Kenneth Thompson. New York: McGraw-Hill.

Niebuhr, R. (1986). 'The Children of Light and the Children of Darkness', in Brown, R. (ed). *The Essential Reinhold Niebuhr: Selected Essays and Addresses*. New Haven: Yale University Press.

Oakeshott, M. (1991). 'The Voice of Poetry in the Conversation of Mankind', in *Rationalism in Politics and Other Essays*, new and expanded edition. Indianapolis: Liberty Press.

Patomäki, H. and Wight, C. (2000). 'After Postpositivism? The Promises of Critical Realism', *International Studies Quarterly*, 44(2): 213–238.

Pattison, J. (2010). *Humanitarian Intervention and the Responsibility to Protect: Who Should Intervene?* Oxford: Oxford University Press.

Peterson, S. (ed). (1992). *Gendered States: Feminist (Re)Visions of International Relations Theory*. London: Lynne Rienner.

Pettman, J. (1996). *Worlding Women: A Feminist International Politics*. London: Routledge.

Puchala, D. (1972). 'Of Blind Men, Elephants and International Integration', *Journal of Common Market Studies*, 10(3): 267–284.

Reus-Smit, C. (2013). 'Beyond Metatheory: The Contours of Analytical Eclecticism', *European Journal of International Relations*, 19(3): 609–626.

Rosenau, J. and Durfee, M. (1995). *Thinking Theory Thoroughly: Coherent Approaches to an Incoherent World*. Boulder: Westview Press.

Rosenberg, J. (1994). *The Empire of Civil Society. A Critique of Realist Theory of International Relation*. London: Verso.

Sil, R. and Katzenstein, P. (2010). 'Analytical Eclecticism in the Study of World Politics: Reconfiguring Problems and Mechanisms across Research Traditions', *Perspectives on Politics* 8(2), 411–431.

Woods, N. (1996) 'The Uses of Theory in the Study of International Relations', in Woods, N. (ed). *Explaining International Relations Since 1945*. Oxford: Oxford University Press.

Walker, R. (1993). *Inside/Outside: International Relations as Political Theory*. Cambridge: Cambridge University Press.

Waltz, K. (1979). *Theory of International Politics*. Reading: Addison-Wesley

Weber, C. (1995). *Simulating Sovereignty: Intervention, the State, and Symbolic Exchange*. Cambridge: Cambridge University Press.

Wight, C. (2002). 'Philosophy of Social Science and International Relations', in Carlsnaes, W. Risse, T. and Simmons, B. (eds). *Handbook of International Relations*. London Sage.

Wight, C. (2006). *Agents, Structures and International Relations: Politics as Ontology.* Cambridge: Cambridge University Press.

Wolfers, A. (1962). *Discord and Collaboration: Essays in International Politics*, Baltimore: Johns Hopkins University Press.

Yin R. (1984) *Case Study Research: Design and Methods.* London: Sage.

3 NATO and the European security system

A neo-realist analysis

Adrian Hyde-Price

This chapter offers an analysis of NATO rooted in neo-realist (or 'structural realist') international theory. It situates the Alliance in the context of the changing structural dynamics of the European security system. More specifically, it argues that the evolution of NATO since the end of Cold War bipolarity is inexplicable without reference to two key trends in the distribution of relative power capabilities in Europe: the continuing primacy of American power (albeit challenged by a resurgent Russia) and the process of 'continental drift' which has characterised transatlantic relations since the end of East–West conflict.

The chapter begins with a brief overview of the main tenets of neo-realist theory. It then examines the evolution of NATO in the wake of Cold War bipolarity and considers the dilemmas and ambiguities surrounding the Alliance's role in the late 1990s and early twenty-first century. The analysis presented here reflects a distinctly Euro-centric perspective on international politics. The central argument is that the European security system – with NATO at its core – is being refashioned by the confluence of two distinct power configurations: global unipolarity and regional multipolarity in Europe (Hyde-Price 2007: 41–43). In this context, the United States (US) has used NATO as an instrument for enhancing its primacy in the international system, and NATO collectively has sought to take advantage of the changed balance of power in pursuit of opportunistic power maximisation. NATO's preservation at the Cold War's end and its utilisation subsequently reflects a strategy of 'offensive dominance' through which the US has pushed for 'a revision of the status quo [in Europe] in its own favour' (Monteiro 2014: 189).

Most American realists have argued that NATO is destined to wither and die in the post–Cold War world. From a 'defensive realist' perspective, Kenneth Waltz (1993: 76) famously suggested shortly after the Cold War had concluded that 'NATO's days might not be numbered, but its years are'. Similarly, John Mearsheimer (2001a: 47), the doyen of 'offensive realism', has argued that 'the most likely scenario in Europe is an eventual American exit'. The neo-realist analysis presented here draws on the deductive logic of offensive realism, but differs from Mearsheimer by arguing that the strategic interests of the US are not best served by withdrawing from Europe (or, indeed, other regions). For an offensive realist, Mearsheimer has a curiously passive understanding of US grand strategy. He assumes that as a regional hegemon in North America, the US will disengage from other regions and adopt a 'buck-passing' strategy, intervening as an 'off-shore balancer' only as a last resort. This chapter argues, however, that the competitive logic of international anarchy provides powerful incentives for a unipolar *hyperpuissance* to pursue an active, interventionist and assertive foreign policy designed to consolidate international primacy, impede the emergence of potential rivals, cause trouble in other great powers' backyards and maximise its own power and influence in regions of strategic or economic importance.

In this light, NATO offers the US a valuable and important instrument with which it can exert influence in Europe, set limits to the emergence of an independent and autonomous EU security and defence policy and build alliances around American leadership for addressing shared security concerns. At the same time, the fundamental shift in the distribution of relative power capabilities that took place as a result of the collapse of the Soviet Union and communist eastern Europe has presented NATO members collectively with the opportunity to play a more active and assertive role in the post-communist East. This changed structural environment has, in other words, created the conditions in which NATO member states, led by the US, have been able pursue a relatively low-cost and risk-free strategy of collective power maximisation – in line with the deductive logic of neo-realist theory.

This power maximisation strategy has had two elements. The first has been the enlargement of NATO to incorporate former communist states. Rejecting more inclusive approaches to a post–Cold War security architecture, NATO member states – led by the US and a newly reunited Germany – embarked on a policy of expansion during the 1990s. In March 1999, three former Warsaw Pact allies of the Soviet Union (Poland, the Czech Republic and Hungary) were formally brought into NATO. The Alliance has gone on to extend this process on two further occasions. In 2004, a 'big bang' enlargement saw seven new members join NATO (including the three Baltic states, which had been formerly part of the Soviet Union) and in 2009, the Alliance incorporated for the first time states in the Balkans (Albania and Croatia). Macedonia, Montenegro and Bosnia-Herzegovina, meanwhile, remain on track for accession via official Membership Action Plans. At the Bucharest summit in 2008, in a move that inflamed Russian opinion, NATO signalled its intention to incorporate Ukraine and Georgia, albeit at an unspecified point in time.

The second element of NATO's power maximisation strategy has been regional military crisis management (termed 'non-Article Five crisis response operations' in the 1999 NATO Strategic Concept) as an instrument for collective milieu shaping. Initially focused on the Balkans (Bosnia, Croatia, Kosovo and Macedonia), NATO's role in crisis management has since included major operations in both Afghanistan and Libya. All these operations have given rise to controversy – but it was Operation Allied Force (OAF) that was to prove a historic watershed in relations with Russia, signalling as it did an offensive military operation against a sovereign state (the Federal Republic of Yugoslavia) in Europe in the teeth of complaints not just from Russia, but also China, India and other regional powers (Averre 2009).

As Russian power began to recover in the first decade of the twenty-first century (with more effective political leadership, export-led economic growth and increased military expenditure), security competition with the Euro-Atlantic community steadily intensified in areas of geostrategic rivalry such as Eastern Europe and the Caucasus. The Georgian conflict in 2008 was the first clear indication that Russia was prepared to challenge the US and NATO for influence in areas it considered vital to its national security (Asmus 2010). With the subsequent conflict in Ukraine and the annexation of Crimea, it is evident that Russia is willing and able to use coercive military power to change the territorial status quo in Europe – as NATO did previously in Kosovo. In this new geopolitical context, NATO's role and purpose are likely to change again, given that the configuration of power relations in Europe no longer favours a power maximisation strategy. In this context, NATO has rediscovered its former function as a means of ensuring Article Five security guarantees for those member states (the Baltics and Poland particularly) living in the shadow of a resurgent and recidivist Russia (Simon 2014).

In terms of the four key questions around which this book is organised, therefore, neo-realism provides a clear and distinctive voice, reflecting its elegant and parsimonious theoretical precepts. To the question, '*what is NATO?*' neo-realism would maintain that the Alliance is an inter-state organisation that serves as a vehicle or instrument through which member states pursue their interests, rather than an independent actor in its own right. To the question '*what is NATO for?*' two answers might be elicited. For the US, NATO is about both power and security maximisation; for NATO's other members, priority is accorded to the latter function, not the former. If its member states (the US included) view their security environment as largely benign, NATO can also serve as a vehicle for collective milieu shaping and the pursuit of second-order normative concerns (intervention in the Balkans, although premised on power maximisation, also served to promote humanitarian goals). With regard to the question, '*who is NATO for?*', neo-realism would suggest it is for its member states, particularly its largest – above all the US, which played a central role in creating the liberal international order after World War II of which NATO is part. Finally, in response to the question '*whither NATO?*' neo-realism would suggest that the key factor shaping the future evolution of the Alliance is the changing constellation of international power, particularly in the Euro-Atlantic region. At the same time, neo-realism notes that as a result of the changing balance of power between Europe and the US, and the consequent process of continental drift, the bonds that have connected the two sides of the Atlantic are becoming ineluctably looser and weaker. This means that NATO is likely to be less cohesive – and therefore less effective – as the twenty-first century unfolds.

Neo-realist theory

Before examining the main thrust of a neo-realist analysis of NATO, it is necessary to begin by outlining the key assumptions and propositions of neo-realist international theory. Realism is a broad church that emphasises the constraints on human progress and the inherent tragedy of international politics. Whereas classical realism explains international politics in terms of human nature and the domestic character of states (Morgenthau 2005: 3–11), neo-realism focuses on the structural pressures that 'shape and shove' the behaviour of states in the international system. Neo-realism is also an explicitly parsimonious theory that seeks to provide elegant theoretical explanations to the 'big questions' of international politics, such as the causes of war and the conditions of peace.

Within neo-realism, there are important differences of emphasis. The theory outlined here draws on the insights first and foremost of Kenneth Waltz (the original source of neo-realism), often referred to as 'defensive realism' (an approach shared by scholars such as Stephen Van Evera and Barry Posen). This position has been challenged, however, by the 'offensive realism' of John Mearsheimer.[1] The distinction between these two schools is important in what follows where it is suggested that states trade off between security (defensive) and power (offensive) maximisation according to circumstance. Such a distinction illustrates that neo-realist theory is not a set of shibboleths set in stone. Rather, it is an analytical tool for 'turning the soil of ignorance' to use Michael Oakshott's (2004: 69) phrase. Neo-realism goes beyond mere description of the ephemera of events. By analysing the structural distribution of relative power capabilities shaping the Euro-Atlantic region, it offers a parsimonious theory for elucidating the underlying systemic pressures shaping the evolution of the NATO alliance.

Core assumptions

Neo-realist analysis is based on a set of core assumptions, from which a series of general propositions can be derived (Mearsheimer 2001b: 30; Waltz 1995: 72). These core assumptions are as follows:

1. International systems are anarchic

Neo-realism depicts the international system as anarchic – a domain without a sovereign. For this reason, it is also a self-help system: states must look to their own security and survival in what is a competitive realm. Security competition is pervasive, and although a relatively rare occurrence, there is always the risk that security competition could give rise to war.[2] In essence, neo-realism suggests that the primary roots of conflict and war lie not in the domestic character of individual states or regimes, or in human nature, but in the structure and dynamics of the international system itself (Waltz 1959).

2. States are the primary international actors

Realists, like Marxists, emphasise the importance of groups, not individuals, in human history (Carr 2001: 91). International politics is characterised by competition between rival political groups, the most important of which is the state. The modern nation-state is 'the human group of strongest social cohesion, of most undisputed central authority and of most clearly defined membership'. Since the seventeenth century, therefore, it has been 'the most absolute of all human associations' (Niebuhr 2013: 83). States, especially the great powers, establish the context and define the rules for other actors, including international organisations like NATO, the EU, the UN, the Organisation for Security and Co-operation in Europe (OSCE) and so on. International organisations are not actors in their own right, but they can function at times as vehicles for the collective interests of their most powerful member states. As Waltz (1979: 94) notes,

> 'states set the scene in which they, along with non-state actors, stage their dramas or carry on their humdrum affairs. Though they may choose to interfere little in the affairs of non-state actors for long periods of time, states nevertheless set the terms of the intercourse.

3. States are functionally similar

In hierarchical systems, units become functionally differentiated. In anarchic systems, however, units remain functionally similar. States develop similar institutional features as a consequence of systemic influences. 'Since [neo-realist] theory depicts international politics as a competitive system', Waltz (1979: 128) argues, 'one predicts more specifically that states will display characteristics common to competitors: namely, that they will imitate each other and become socialised to their system'. Functional similarity also means that all states, particularly great powers, seek to maintain a balanced portfolio of capabilities across the three main dimensions of power: military power, economic power and power over opinion (Carr 2001: 102). One important consequence of this is that all great powers have some offensive military capability, 'which gives them the wherewithal to hurt and possibly destroy each other' (Mearsheimer 2001b: 30).

4. States are rational, unitary actors

For the purposes of theory, neo-realism assumes that states are unitary actors capable of acting consciously, reflexively and strategically on the basis of a rational calculation of the costs and benefits of alternative courses of action. Clearly, this is not descriptively true. Since Graham Allison's (1971) pioneering work on foreign policy decision making, it is widely accepted that states are characterised by institutional polyphony and that rationality is 'bounded'.[3] However, explaining the regularities and repetitions of international politics involves abstracting and simplifying domestic political processes. Allison's work sought to explain specific foreign policy decisions (American and Soviet actions during the Cuban missile crisis); neo-realism seeks to explain the broad patterns of international politics and state behaviour over time. Consequently, it makes the assumption that states act purposely to realise their interests and preferences, and monitor the results of their actions in order to adjust or revise strategic choices. Over time, therefore, states engage in a process of 'strategic learning' and become more acquainted with the opportunities and constraints of the structural context within which they operate.[4] States, it is assumed, 'are able not just to perceive systemic-level constraints but also to formulate and to execute measures in response to them' (Grieco 1997: 166). They 'consider the preferences of other states and how their behaviour is likely to affect the behaviour of those other states, and how the behaviour of those other states is likely to affect their own strategy for survival' (Mearsheimer 2001b: 31). As Robert Keohane (1986: 167) notes, the rationality assumption is the crucial link between system structure and actor behaviour, 'which enables the theorist to predict that leaders will respond to the incentives and constraints imposed by their environment'.

Propositions

On the basis of these assumptions, a set of five propositions can be inferred about the dynamics of the international system and the motor forces driving states' interaction with other states.

1. Security competition in a self-help system

International anarchy, coupled with the constant shadow of war and conflict, generates pervasive security competition. In the absence of international government, states must rely for their survival and security on their own resources, or on those of their allies (Walt 1987). The level of security competition varies according to the structural distribution of power in the system, but it can never be eradicated. Fear is pervasive, and trust is a scarce commodity. In this context, cooperation is difficult, though not impossible, to achieve, and those institutions that are created to this end have limited autonomy. According to Mearsheimer (1994–1995: 334) institutions 'are based on the self-interested calculations of the great powers, and they have no independent effect on state behaviour'. Consequently, the international organisations which comprise Europe's dense institutional architecture can be regarded as intervening variables which occasionally modify the behaviour of states, but which have a marginal impact on the structural dynamics of the European security system itself.

2. Security and power maximisation

In anarchic, self-help systems, security is the primary concern of states. At the very least, therefore, states must act as 'defensive positionalists', seeking to maintain their position in the pecking order of great powers (Grieco 1993a: 138). But there are also strong incentives for states, especially great powers, to think more aggressively about maximising their power so as to be able to eliminate or neutralise all potential rivals and establish hegemony over one's region (Carr 2001: 104–105; Mearsheimer 2001b: 33–34). States must seek to preserve their power relative to their potential enemies and competitors: if they can strengthen their relative position, so much the better. Systemic pressures, in other words, mean that all states are security maximisers, but they also have a rational interest in maximising their relative power because this is the ideal way to guarantee survival in the long term.

That said, not all states seek to aggressively maximise power. Some may not be strong enough to do so; others might lack the opportunity by virtue of their geopolitical location. Some powerful states, meanwhile, might eschew an overt power maximisation strategy, fearful that it might provoke a hostile counter-balancing coalition or pre-emptive strike on the part of a rival. Realism assumes that states are rational actors, and thus when power maximisation strategies appear to be counter-productive, states will focus on security maximisation instead until more favourable opportunities present themselves. In certain circumstances, therefore, states will behave more like defensive positionalists rather than power maximisers, seeking to maintain their position within the system. All the while, however, these states – if they are behaving rationally – will be constantly on the lookout for opportunities to increase their relative power, and when faced with such occasions, they will act opportunistically to do so (Labs 1997; Mowle 2004: 21–22). In this sense, states will instinctively employ a marginal utility calculus, weighing up the expected costs and perceived benefits of pursuing power maximisation (Snyder 2002: 172).

3. Relative gains

Neo-realism posits that states focus on relative gains and argues that this places limits on cooperative ventures. States are concerned about their position in the international system relative to their main rivals and potential enemies. A state will, therefore, only engage in cooperation if it is likely to gain as much or more than its peer equivalents. This is particularly true of great powers; small powers can be more relaxed (they are less engaged in a competition for influence), and so are more content with absolute gains.[5] Nonetheless, realists recognise that under some conditions, great powers, too, may relax their concern with relative gains. This tends to occur in situations where security competition is muted or weak and where states do not face an immediate inter-state threat. According to Waltz (1979: 195), '[a]bsolute gains become more important as competition lessens'. Such circumstances, however, tend to be temporary, and great powers will rarely rest content with absolute gains for long (Grieco 1993b).

4. Milieu shaping

The overriding concern of states with security and survival means they will use their material power capabilities to not only exert direct influence over other actors, but also to shape the external environment within which they operate. The ability to exert such influence is a luxury enjoyed by few states, however. Those with sufficient resources will pursue what Arnold Wolfers (1962: 73–75) several decades ago termed 'milieu goals' in an effort to shape the material and strategic context within which their policy choices are framed.

Waltz (1979: 209) noted that all states face four common problems: poverty, pollution, population growth and proliferation. Today, one can add at least two more: international terrorism and failed states. Waltz argues that system-wide management tasks are more likely to be undertaken by great powers because they have a greater stake in the stability of the system and because they have the capabilities to take on special responsibilities: '[u]nits having a large enough stake in the system will act for its own sake, even though they pay unduly in doing so' (Waltz 1979: 198). This is not the result of an altruistic and idealist concern to serve the common good, but rather a function of what can be seen as a form of 'enlightened self-interest' driven by strategic and security interests. The problem, however, is how the required management or governance of the international system can be achieved in the absence of a central authority. Who will incur the costs of addressing common problems given concerns about relative gains? How can the 'free-rider' problem be overcome? Will major powers allow any one of their number to take the lead in addressing common problems if that state thereby accrues political or other benefits?

5. Second-order concerns

Neo-realists recognise that states are not only motivated by security and power maximisation. They also pursue a range of moral and ethical concerns reflecting their distinct political values – from protecting the environment to international human rights.[6] Realists are not so blinkered and one-dimensional in their thinking as to assert that states are only motivated by an insatiable lust for power. Even 'offensive realists' such as Mearsheimer (2005: 142) recognise that there is 'a well-developed and widely accepted body of idealist or liberal norms in international politics' and that 'most leaders and most of their followers want their state to behave' in conformity with 'these general principles'. But realists maintain that such norms are 'second order' to more fundamental national interests. Few states – and, certainly, few states that wish to survive in the competitive realm of international politics – will act on ethical or normative principles when these conflict with what they perceive to be their vital interests (Hyde-Price 2008).

The propositions outlined here are at a level of generality that is often seen as a weakness of neo-realism. That criticism will be addressed in the concluding section later, but for now it is worth pointing out that these propositions are, nonetheless, relevant to NATO. Taken together, they suggest that the Alliance is subordinate to the interests of its members, the US in particular, and is an instrument through which power and security-maximising strategies can be pursued. In the two sections that follow, the logic of neo-realism is explored in the context of NATO through two distinct arguments. The first is that the US has exerted an extraordinary influence on the Alliance; this has ensured NATO's ongoing development in the absence of the balance of power logic which sustained it during the Cold War. The Waltzian argument, which simply views NATO as a form of balancing behaviour, is thus incomplete. Second, although states are mindful of relative gains, in alliance formats they are still able to sustain a modicum of cooperation. This is a process promoted by great power leadership and a meeting of interests on certain core concerns (no NATO state, for instance, with the highly qualified exception of France, regards any other institutional configuration as an alternative to the Alliance in providing for European security). Yet, alliance discipline remains problematic when the source of common interest is fluid. During the Cold War, NATO's cohesion was sustained by the common appreciation of the danger posed by the Warsaw Pact (and even then there were disagreements over strategy). In the post–Cold War period, the sources of danger have multiplied. Balancing, in other words, is less compelling, and so alliance cohesion has weakened.

NATO in a unipolar world

The relevance of neo-realism's deductive logic for understanding NATO's role in international politics can be seen from an analysis of the broad patterns of security relations in the post–Cold War era. The end of bipolarity left a huge question mark over an alliance designed originally, in the words of its first Secretary General Lord Ismay, to 'keep the Russians out, the Americans in, and the Germans down' (cited in Andrews 2005: 61). In the immediate post–Cold War years, NATO was seen by many of its members as serving three purposes: providing an insurance against future recidivism in Russia, acting as the principal forum for transatlantic relations and serving as a multilateral constraint on a reunified Germany (Hyde-Price 1991: 120–122). Yet as the 1990s progressed, it became increasingly apparent that these roles were no longer appropriate for the changed security agenda. Russia's precipitate military decline made a high-intensity war a distant prospect, and the issue with Germany was not curbing nascent militarism and hegemonic ambitions, but rather encouraging its transformation from a security consumer to a security provider. NATO's utility as a forum for transatlantic dialogue also declined, primarily because of the growing divergence in US and European approaches to global order (Kamp 2005: 8).

The attenuation of Soviet and then Russian power meant few in North America or in Europe were willing to justify NATO's existence by reference only to the organisation's Article Five security guarantee. Other proposals, therefore, were put forward to the effect that the Alliance could act as the institutional foundation for a more cooperative form of 'common security' with the Russians and East Europeans (using the newly created Euro-Atlantic Partnership Council and the NATO–Russia Permanent Joint Council[7]) or that it might serve as an instrument of security governance, involving defence-sector transformation and functional military cooperation (through the mechanism of the Partnership for Peace programme) (Donnolly 1997; Williams 1996). Neither proposal, however, offered to NATO the clarity of purpose it had enjoyed during the Cold War when it developed, in effect, as a manifestation of bipolar competition. It was, therefore, no surprise that Waltz (1993: 76), whose analyses of international politics was premised on a logic of balancing, came to suggest that NATO would inevitably become redundant.

What Waltz failed to recognise, however, was that NATO was not conjured up simply to reflect the balance of power; its direction and purpose have also been the consequence of great power leadership. Hence, it could continue to play an important role at the behest of the US (and, to a lesser degree, the European powers) in a context of global unipolarity and regional multipolarity in Europe. Thus, rather than fading into oblivion, NATO has survived insofar as it continues to serve the purpose of bolstering US power and influence. By the mid-1990s, such an assumption was, in fact, explicit in US foreign policy (Department of Defence 1997: 58). Rather than allowing NATO to wither on the vine, the Clinton administration pursued a twin-track policy: on the one hand, opening the Alliance up to new members from East Central Europe, which served to extend US influence into Russia's former sphere of influence, and on the other, orientating the strategic rationale of NATO towards non–Article Five 'crisis response operations', thereby ensuring allied participation in US-led and directed military crisis management (Chollet and Goldgeier 2008: 117, 122–134).

Commensurate with this approach, NATO undertook its first major intervention in 1995 during Operation Deliberate Force in Bosnia. It subsequently provided the military infrastructure for peace-support operations (IFOR/SFOR) within the framework of the Dayton Accords negotiated by US Assistant Secretary of State Richard Holbrooke. NATO's most significant military operation in the 1990s, however, was during the war over Kosovo in 1999. Here, the NATO air campaign, OAF, was significant in a number of respects. We have already noted how the mission marked a break in relations with Russia. But four other consequences stand out. First, OAF was conducted without an explicit UN Security Council mandate; the NATO powers on the Security Council – the US, France and the UK – regarded the legitimacy accorded to the operation by NATO's own decision-making authority, the North Atlantic Council, as of sufficient weight to compensate for the lack of UN approval (Haines 2009: 479). Second, it demonstrated the capabilities of the American military and the weakness of their European counterparts. Third, European unease with the US conduct of the military campaign led to the development of the Common Security and Defence Policy (CSDP), which aimed to make available capabilities for autonomous military crisis management by EU member states. Finally, it led to US disillusionment with the idea of conducting military operations through a multilateral decision-making framework, and so strengthened unilateralist instincts in Washington (Bozo 2003).

Throughout this period, the US faced a number of dilemmas in its policy towards the Alliance. On the one hand, it sought to use enlargement to strengthen its influence in Europe and to win new allies in the post-communist East. On the other hand, it wanted to move NATO away from collective defence towards out-of-area military crisis management. The problem here was that the new members were primarily interested in NATO as a means to access a US security guarantee via Article Five of the North Atlantic Treaty; they were much less keen on assuming responsibilities for non–Article Five crisis response operations (Jacoby 2005). Thus, whereas the US feared 'entrapment' in conflicts peripheral to its core interests, the new NATO members worried about 'abandonment' by their American protector – a contemporary version of the old transatlantic dilemma of extended deterrence (Snyder 1984). At the same time, the US faced another dilemma in responding to European aspirations for a 'Europeanisation' of NATO and the strengthening of an autonomous European capacity for crisis management. These initiatives were potentially a means to enhance burden sharing across the Atlantic, but they also gave rise to the possibility of a dilution of American leadership in European security. Consequently, throughout the 1990s, Washington was highly ambivalent about both CSDP and NATO's own efforts toward a European defence 'pillar' – the European Security and Defence Identity (EDSI) (Clarke and Cornish 2002).

The terrorist attacks of September 11, 2001, led to a further evolution in the role of NATO. For the first time in its history, the Alliance invoked Article Five. Although the Bush administration welcomed the diplomatic solidarity symbolised by this decision, it was initially wary of its implications for America's freedom to pursue its 'war on terror' on its own terms. US Secretary of Defence Donald Rumsfeld's insistence that the 'mission must determine the coalition' meant that America's NATO allies were initially given little say in shaping Operation Enduring Freedom (OEF). European military participation in Afghanistan only began in November 2001, and was conducted through Central Command (CENTCOM), not SHAPE (Rumsfeld 2011: 354–355). NATO subsequently took command of the International Security Assistance Force (ISAF) in Kabul in August 2003, but avoided engaging in combat operations in the south and west of the country against remnants of the Taliban and al Qaeda. America's European allies were initially keen to keep ISAF separate from OEF in order to minimise risks to their troops (Dempsey and Cloud 2005; Gordon 2006: Pfaff 2006).[8] In December 2005, however, they agreed to extend NATO operations to the whole of Afghanistan, but only after receiving guarantees that they would have a say in the treatment of enemy combatants (Dempsey 2005; Gall 2006; *The Economist* 2005). The ISAF mission in Afghanistan would subsequently become the most challenging and difficult expeditionary operation in the Alliance's history (Rynning 2012), and one which (at least in scale) is unlikely to be repeated in the foreseeable future (particularly given Russian recidivism in Eastern Europe and the Baltic Sea region, which is pushing NATO to refocus its attention on its eastern flank). Yet whatever the challenges NATO has faced in Afghanistan, it remains ensconced in the country. Operation Resolute Support succeeded ISAF in January 2015 as a non-combat mission to support the Afghan National Security Forces. The mission priorities, as with ISAF, reflect the strategic interests first and foremost of the US. Contributions to the force, as well as its command structure, are also dominated by the American military.

As this account of NATO's recent history suggests, NATO's years do not seem to be numbered at all. To some degree, its persistence reflects institutional inertia: once institutions have acquired organisational assets, they tend to define new roles for themselves (Wallander 2000). But this is only part of the story. More importantly, the Alliance has been partially reconfigured in the light of the changed post–Cold War political and strategic interests of the US, first in the Balkans and then in Afghanistan. Through enlargement, the US has extended its influence in Europe. NATO's persistence as the principal military body on the continent, meanwhile, ensures an ongoing US impact on Europe's militaries through joint training, multi-national exercises and interoperability with US military standards (Deni 2014).

NATO's story in the post–Cold War period is not, however, only about the US. Although NATO is clearly a vehicle of US influence, other powers also see their interests served by the Alliance – both because they are willing to succumb to US leadership and because NATO offers distinct advantages of its own as an instrument for milieu shaping and second-order normative concerns. In Libya, for example, NATO provided the institutional vehicle for France and the UK to lead a UN-sanctioned military intervention, with the US on this occasion offering space to the Europeans 'to take the military lead' in relation to what was regarded as 'a mainly European problem' (Michaels 2013: 205).

More recently, as Russia has recovered some of its old strength – and much of its old belligerence – NATO has refocused strategic attention on developments in its eastern flank, where the shifting power balance has allowed Russia to reassert its former great power role. The announcement at NATO's 2014 Wales summit of the Very High-Readiness Joint Task Force and the Readiness Action Plan (RAP) indicated German and British (and not just American) commitment to the common defence, as well as giving weight to the concerns of new NATO members such as Poland and the Baltic states.

Continental drift and the loosening of transatlantic security relations

Shifts in the global power configuration have also affected transatlantic relations, resulting in a fraying of the ties that once created a strong sense of transatlantic community. The transformation of NATO in the 1990s, from a central pillar of Europe's security architecture concerned with collective territorial defence to an instrument of coalitional coercive diplomacy and military crisis management, reflected broader developments in transatlantic relations during this period. The primary effect of the end of bipolarity was to remove the central plank of post-war transatlantic relations – institutionalised security cooperation in the face of a common threat. The result was to 'de-link' security, trade and political relations, generating continental drift and a consequent fracturing of US–European relations (Daalder 2001). A much more complex and differentiated pattern of cooperation and rivalry between the US and individual European states thus emerged, something, in turn, reflected in the changing role and character of NATO.

Elements of this trend were all too evident during the Balkan conflicts. NATO heroically held together over Bosnia and Kosovo, but it was clear that the diplomatic and military effort in both cases was the product of American leadership, a leadership which gave rise to all sorts of charges in the US of European weakness and vacillation (Dunn 2009: 542–544).

More alarming was the dispute which unfolded in NATO over the march to war in Iraq in 2003. Described as marking 'the end' of NATO by one analyst (Kupchen 2003) and even by the NATO secretary general as indicative of an Alliance 'in disarray' (cited in Webber, Sperling and Smith 2012: 12), NATO would nonetheless survive the crisis. That it was a US-led coalition which intervened in Iraq and not NATO as such, however, was the lasting legacy. The UK, Denmark, Poland, Portugal and Spain joined the US in the fateful intervention. France and Germany were adamantly opposed.

NATO would subsequently also go on to mount a truly allied effort in Afghanistan and, further, would demonstrate solidarity over support measures for its eastern allies consequent upon the Ukraine crisis. However, Iraq illustrated a trend that has run in parallel with these ongoing expressions of alliance unity – namely, a fraying of trust and a decline in deference to the US (Washington, as noted earlier, exercises ongoing leadership in NATO, but this is not beyond question among its allies in Europe and, indeed, Canada).

Transatlantic relations are now increasingly characterised by multiple and differentiated bilateralism on a hub-and-spokes basis. Washington enjoys close relations with a number of traditional 'Atlanticist' countries such as the UK, the Netherlands, Denmark and Norway. It has also courted new allies in Central and Eastern Europe – most importantly Poland, America's 'new model ally' (Dunn 2003). France has long been America's fiercest critic within NATO, but even so, Paris and Washington have worked closely on specific foreign policy issues (such as Libya, Lebanon, Syria and India) (Haglund 2010). The biggest US sceptic in NATO since 2012 has been Turkey, which has shown a reluctance to conform to US policy preferences over Syria and Russia (*International New York Times* 2015).

The most important European country from Washington's perspective, however, remains Germany – the most powerful EU member state, and the pivot of the European balance of power. The US has consistently sought closer relations with Germany: it firmly supported unification, and also offered Bonn a privileged strategic relationship as 'partners in leadership' in May 1989 (Denison 2001: 160). This offer was not taken up at the time, but relations between Germany and the US remained close throughout the 1990s. Chancellor Gerhard Schröder's decision to join France and Russia in opposing the Iraq war led to a pronounced cooling of relations (Haftendorn and Kolkmann 2004; Zimmermann 2005). However, with the formation of a grand coalition under Angela Merkel in November 2005, there were renewed efforts to establish a privileged strategic partnership with Europe's *Zentralmacht*.[9] But relations between Berlin and Washington still have their ups and downs. The Edward Snowdon revelations over the operations of the US National Security Agency included information that Chancellor Merkel's phone had been bugged for over ten years. In July 2014, the German authorities requested that the CIA station chief in Berlin leave the country over allegations of spying (Smale, Mazzetti and Sanger 2014).

Transatlantic drift has also been evident in the reduction of America's military footprint in Europe. The overall number of US troops has been markedly reduced, and base closures in Western Europe have been increasing as the American 'rebalance' to Asia takes shape. At the end of the Cold War, the US troop presence amounted to some 213,000 personnel; by mid-2013 this had been reduced to just 64,000. Plans announced in January 2015 envisaged the removal of further American personnel from some fifteen bases across the UK, Germany and Portugal. This does not presage a complete American military disengagement from the continent. Indeed, US force rotations to Eastern Europe in the wake of the Ukraine crisis mean that the total number of personnel has remained stable despite the cuts of 2015. It does signal a strong belief in Washington, however, that the Europeans should do more for their own security and defence, and take on a greater role in safeguarding international peace and security. In the wake of the Ukraine crisis, the US has signalled both a willingness to provide reassurance for NATO's geostrategically vulnerable members in Eastern Europe and the Baltics, and a desire for NATO's European members to honour their commitments to spend more on their armed forces and shoulder more of the burden of common defence. These demands have multiplied as European defence cuts have accelerated in the wake of the global financial crisis in 2008 (Carpenter 2014). This is only likely to accelerate the trend toward multiple bilateralism already noted. The commitments entered into by NATO at its 2014 Wales summit – to increase defence spending and to pursue measures in support of the defence of its eastern members – are not shared with equal enthusiasm among all allies. Following the summit, most NATO states promptly instituted further cuts (including the big spenders France, Germany and the UK), whereas those closest to Russia – Poland, the Baltic states, Romania and Norway – registered modest increases (Raynova and Kearns 2015). In an age of fiscal austerity, the pressure is to cut defence expenditure, not raise it; equally, the RAP and related commitments may simply go the way of the ISAF effort in Afghanistan – with some allies raising caveats and excuses for shifting the burden of the campaign effort to others. The US retains the desire (and the capacity) to lead NATO's defence, but the Europeans, by and large, still lean 'in the inverse direction'. The allies have lost the 'the ability to speak the same language of defence' and the response to the Ukraine crisis in 2014 is not guaranteed to return NATO to the 'good old days' of Cold War unity (Rynning 2014: 1393).

Conclusion: the strengths and weaknesses of neo-realism

As a means of theoretical analysis, neo-realism offers a powerful set of tools for elucidating some of the key aspects of NATO's role in European security and the wider international system. Kenneth Waltz's great achievement was to develop a parsimonious and deductive theory that established neo-realism as a distinctive research paradigm able to generate cumulative knowledge. 'The contribution of the realist paradigm to the development of a scientific study of international relations', John Vasquez (1998: 39) has written,

> has been, first, to point out that science must be empirical and theoretical, not normative and narrowly historical, and second, to provide a picture of the

world (i.e. a paradigm) which has permitted the field to develop a common research agenda and to follow it systematically and somewhat cumulatively.

With his seminal text *Theory of International Politics*, Waltz produced a 'Copernican revolution' in international political theory by

> showing how much of states' actions and interactions, and how much of the outcomes their actions and interactions produce, can be explained by forces that operate at the level of the system, rather than at the level of the units.
>
> (Waltz 1979: 69)

Neo-realism's theory of international politics is based on the conviction that there is an underlying order in human affairs that gives rise to patterned behaviour. It provides a sophisticated set of analytical tools for identifying these broad patterns, above all, the systemic causes of conflict and competition. Realists draw a distinction between the domestic and international realms on the grounds that the former is organised hierarchically and the latter anarchically. Having specified the domain to which the theory applies (the international system), neo-realism focuses on the distribution of relative power capabilities as the primary independent variable which shapes the recurrent patterns of international politics and the behaviour of the system's primary units. Neo-realism elucidates not simply the broad outcomes of international politics (war and peace, the formation of power balances), but also the grand strategies of the system's most important actors – the great powers. The development of systemic theory thus continues to offer fruitful avenues for analysing the dynamics of international politics – including, in this case, the changing role of NATO in the European security system.

But neo-realism's greatest strength is also its greatest weakness. The theory's parsimony and elegance give it considerable explanatory power, but provide only a broad-brush approach to international politics. Neo-realism deals primarily with recurrent patterns and general trends, and lacks explanatory power when confronted with more narrowly focused research puzzles.[10] It therefore washes out much of the detail and nuance that gives the study of international politics its abiding interest for scholars and students. Moreover, in some cases, particularly in contexts of multipolarity, a structural analysis is indeterminate in terms of predictive behaviour and can therefore shed only limited light on outcomes and behaviour (Wohlforth 2002: 251). As a tool for analysing NATO, neo-realism focuses on the role played by the logic of anarchy and considerations of power in the strategic calculations of states. It can explain the broad patterns of cooperation and conflict in contemporary Europe and transatlantic relations, but cannot elucidate the tactical calculations of individual states when they consider specific policy issues, such as, military intervention in Iraq, Libya and Afghanistan; the future of NATO's nuclear deterrent; or commitment to the RAP.

Neo-realist international theory is thus a *necessary* but not *sufficient* tool for analysing NATO's post–Cold War role. A structural analysis identifies the broad systemic pressures which have shaped NATO and which continue to underpin the institutional architecture of the European security system. Most significantly, NATO's evolution has been shaped by the fall and subsequent re-assertion of Russia. The precipitous decline of Russian power in the 1990s allowed NATO (at the initiative of the US) to engage in collective milieu shaping in the Balkans and to embark upon a bold policy of enlargement. Russia's re-emergence as a great power under President Putin – evident in the war with Georgia in 2008 and, more recently, the annexation of Crimea and destabilisation of eastern Ukraine – has led NATO to focus on its vulnerable eastern flank and to de-emphasise expeditionary operations in far-flung lands.

But if we wish to go beyond these broad systemic pressures and try to make sense of the detailed decision-making processes behind NATO policies, we must supplement a structural analysis with more fine-grained and narrowly focused theories. These supplementary theories can help evaluate the significance of important intervening variables, such as strategic culture or idiosyncratic domestic contexts, which modify or impede the effects of the independent variable (the structural distribution of power). Nonetheless, when seeking to understand a complex and multifaceted issue such as the NATO alliance, neo-realism provides an illuminating vantage point – a 'powerful flashlight in a dark room'. Neo-realism 'cannot illuminate every nook and cranny [but] most of the time it is an excellent tool for navigating through the darkness (Mearsheimer 2001b: 11). Neo-realism, Charles Glaser (2003: 275) has suggested, 'is a rational, parsimonious theory' which can provide the starting point for progressively more complex and multi-level research. In NATO's case, it offers meaningful propositions, two of which stand out from our analysis earlier – first, that the Alliance is subject to the calculations of its powerful members (the US most notably) and second, that in the absence of a powerful external threat, internal cohesion has weakened.

Notes

1 For a clear and concise exposition of the main differences between defensive and offensive realism, see Mearsheimer (2006). On 'second generational' defensive realism, see Glaser (2003).

2 This state of affairs was well articulated by Thomas Hobbes (1991): 89–90. 'For as the nature of Foule weather, lyeth not in a showre or two of rain; but in an inclination thereto of many dayes together: So the nature of War, consisteth not in actual fighting; but in the known disposition thereto, during all the time there is no assurance to the contrary'.

3 See also Waltz (1979: 119), who freely admits that 'states are in fact not unitary, purposive actors'.

4 This understanding of agents is similar to the 'critical realism' of Roy Bhaskar and the 'strategic-relational approach' of Bob Jessop. See Hay (2002: 126–134).

5 Defined as a benefit which is judged in its own terms and not by reference to how it compares with the benefits accorded to other states.

6 As Waltz (1967: 15–16) notes '[i]f the preservation of the state is not in question, national goals easily fluctuate between the grandiose and the frivolous'.

7 That body created in 1997 was succeeded in 2002 by the NATO–Russia Council.

8 By 2006, ISAF had approximately 11,000 troops under its command, compared with the 20,000 troops in the US-led force engaged in OEF.

9 America's new partnership with Germany was symbolised by President's Bush's claim
to have 'glimpsed into [the] soul' of Chancellor Angela Merkel – echoing his claim to
have gained an insight into the soul of Vladimir Putin. See *New York Times* (2006).
10 As Wohlforth (2004: 234) has noted, '[a] theory that seems to apply everywhere all
the time is likely to be of little practical utility. Any theory worth its salt is likely to be
wrong about some things and simply inapplicable to others'.

References

[All web sources listed were last accessed 12 June 2015.]

Allison, G. (1971). *Essence of Decision: Explaining the Cuban Missile Crisis*, Boston:
Little, Brown and Company.
Andrews, D. M. (2005). 'The United States and Its Atlantic Partners', in Andrews, D. M.
(ed). *The Atlantic Alliance under Stress: US-European Relations after Iraq*, Cambridge:
Cambridge University Press.
Asmus, R. D. (2010). *A Little War that Shook the World: Georgia, Russia and the Future of
the West*, New York: Palgrave Macmillan.
Averre, D. (2009). 'From Pristina to Tskhinvali: The Legacy of Operation Allied Force in
Russia's Relations with the West', *International Affairs*, 85(3): 575–592.
Bozo, F. (2003). 'The Effects of Kosovo and the Danger of Decoupling', in Howorth, J. and
Keeler, J.T.S. (eds). *Defending Europe: The EU, NATO and the Quest for Autonomy*,
New York: Palgrave.
Carpenter, T. G. (2014). 'Hagel's Futile Quest for NATO Burden Sharing', *The National
Interest*, 4 March, at: http://nationalinterest.org/commentary/hagel%E2%80%99s-futile-
quest-nato-burden-sharing-9991.
Carr, E. H. (2001). *The Twenty Years' Crisis*, 2nd ed, New York: Palgrave.
Chollet, D and Goldgeier, J. (2008). *America between the Wars – from 11/9 to 9/11 – the
Misunderstood Years between the Fall of the Berlin Wall and the Start of the War on
Terror*, New York: Public Affairs.
Clarke, M and Cornish, P. (2002). 'The European Defence Project and the Prague Summit',
International Affairs, 78(4): 777–788.
Daalder, I. (2001). 'Are the United States and Europe Heading for Divorce?', *International
Affairs*, 77(3): 553–567.
Dempsey, J. (2005). 'Rice and NATO to Set Rules for Afghan Force: Dutch Demand
Assurance Against Torture', *International Herald Tribune*, 8 December.
Dempsey, J and Cloud, D. (2005), 'Europeans Balking at New Afghan Role', *International
Herald Tribune*, 14 September.
Deni, J. (2014). 'Maintaining Transatlantic Strategic, Operational and Tactical Interoper-
ability in an Era of Austerity', *International Affairs*, 90(3): 583–600.
Denison, A. (2001). 'German Foreign Policy and Transatlantic Relations Since Unifica-
tion', in Webber, D. (ed). *New Europe, New Germany, Old Foreign Policy?* London:
Frank Cass.
Department of Defence. (1997). *Report of the Quadrennial Defence Review* at: www.dod.
mil/pubs/qdr/.
Donnolly, C. (1997). 'Defence Transformation in the New Democracies: A Framework for
Tackling the Problem', *NATO Review*, 45(1): 15–19.
Dunn, D. H. (2003). 'Poland: America's New Model Ally', in Zaborowski, M. and Dunn,
D. H. (eds). *Poland: A New Power in Transatlantic Security*, London: Frank Cass.

Dunn, D. H. (2009). 'Innovation and Precedent in the Kosovo War: The Impact of Operation Allied Force on US Foreign Policy', *International Affairs*, 85(3): 531–547.

Gall, C. (2006). 'NATO Takes up Challenge in Afghanistan's South', *International Herald Tribune*, 5 May.

Glaser, C. (2003). 'The Necessary and Natural Evolution of Neorealism', in Vasquez, J. A. and Elman, C. (eds). *Realism and the Balancing of Power: A New Debate*, New Jersey: Prentice-Hall.

Gordon, P. (2006). 'Back Up NATO's Afghanistan Force', *International Herald Tribune*, 7–8 January.

Grieco, J. (1993a). 'Anarchy and the Limits of Cooperation: A Realist Critique of the Newest Liberal Institutionalism', in Baldwin, D. (ed). *Neorealism and Neoliberalism: The Contemporary Debate*, New York: Columbia University Press.

Grieco, J. (1993b). 'Understanding the Problem of International Cooperation: The Limits of Neo-Liberal Institutionalism and the Future of Realist Theory', in Baldwin, D. (ed). *Neorealism and Neoliberalism: The Contemporary Debate*, New York: Columbia University Press.

Grieco, J. (1997). 'Realist International Theory and the Study of World Politics', in Doyle, M. and Ikenberry, J. (eds). *New Thinking in International Relations Theory*, Boulder: Westview Press.

Haftendorn, H and Kolkmann, M. (2004). 'Germany in a Strategic Triangle: Berlin, Paris, Washington . . . and What about London?, *Cambridge Review of International Affairs*, 17(3): 467–80.

Haglund, D. G. (2010). 'Happy Days Are Here Again? France's Reintegration into NATO and Its Impact on Relations with the USA', *European* Security, 19(1): 123–142.

Haines, S. (2009). 'The Influence of Operation Allied Force on the Development of the *Jus Ad Bellum*', *International Affairs*, 85(3): 477–491.

Hay, C. (2002). *Political Analysis: A Critical Introduction*, Houndmills, Basingstoke: Palgrave Macmillan.

Hobbes, T. (1991). *Leviathan*, edited by Tuck, R,. Cambridge: Cambridge University Press.

Hyde-Price, A. (1991). *European Security Beyond the Cold War: Four Scenarios for the Year 2010*, London: Sage.

Hyde-Price, A. (2007). *European Security in the Twenty-first Century: The Challenge of Multipolarity*, London and New York: Routledge.

Hyde-Price, A. (2008). '"Praise the Lord and Pass the Ammunition"!: A Realist Response to Isaiah's Irenic Vision', in Cohen, R. and Westbrook, R. (eds). *Isaiah's Vision of Peace in Biblical and Modern International Relations*, Houndmills, Basingstoke: Palgrave.

International New York Times. (2014). Editorial 'Turkey's Drift from NATO', 16 March.

Jacoby, W. (2005). 'Military Competence versus Policy Loyalty: Central Europe and Transatlantic Relations', in Andrews, D. M. (ed). *The Atlantic Alliance Under Stress: US-European Relations after Iraq*, Cambridge: Cambridge University Press.

Kamp, K-H. (2005). 'The Need to Adapt NATO's Strategic Concept', in Dufourcq, J. and Masala, C. (eds). *Security Strategies and Their Implications for NATO's Strategic Concept*, Rome: NATO Defence College.

Keohane, R. O. (1986). 'Theory of World Politics: Neorealism and Beyond', in Keohane, R. O. (ed). *Neorealism and its Critics*, New York: Columbia University Press.

Kupchan, C. (2003). 'The Atlantic Alliance Lies in the Rubble', *Financial Times*, 9 April.

Labs, E. J. (1997). 'Beyond Victory: Offensive Realism and Why States Expand Their War Aims', *Security Studies*, 6(4): 1–49.

Mearsheimer, J. J. (1994–1995). 'A Realist Reply', *International Security*, 20(1): 82–93.

Mearsheimer, J. J. (2001a). 'The Future of the American Pacifier', *Foreign Affairs*, 80(5): 46– 61.

Mearsheimer, J. J. (2001b). *The Tragedy of Great Power Politics*, New York: W. W. Norton and Co.

Mearsheimer, J. J. (2005). 'E. H. Carr vs. Idealism: The Battle Rages On', *International Relations*, 19(2): 139–152.

Mearsheimer, J. J. (2006). 'Conversations in *International Relations*: Interview with John J. Mearsheimer (Part 1)', *International Relations*, 20(1): 105–123.

Michaels, J. H. (2013). 'A Model Intervention? Reflections on NATO's Libya "Success"'', in Hallams E. Ratti, L. and Zyla, B. (eds). *NATO beyond 9/11: The Transformation of the Atlantic Alliance*, Houndmills, Basingstoke: Palgrave Macmillan.

Monteiro, N. P. (2014). *Theory of Unipolar Politics*, Cambridge: Cambridge University Press.

Morgenthau, H. J. (2005). *Politics among Nations: The Struggle for Power and Peace*, seventh edition revised by Thompson, K. W. and Clinton, W. D. Boston: McGraw-Hill Education.

Mowle, T. (2004). *Allies at Odds? The United States and the European Union*. Houndmills, Basingstoke: Palgrave.

New York Times (2006), 'Bush again Glimpses a Leader's Soul', 6 May, at: www.nytimes. com/2006/05/07/world/europe/07iht-merkel.html?_r=0.

Niebuhr, R. (2013). *Moral Man and Immoral Society: A Study in Ethics and Politics*, 2nd ed, Louisville: Westminster John Knox Press.

Oakeshott, M. (2004). *What Is History and Other Essays*, Exeter: Imprint Academic.

Pfaff, W. (2006). 'NATO's Future on the Line', *International Herald Tribune*, 12 January.

Raynova, D. and Kearns, I. (2015), 'The Wales Pledge Revisited: A Preliminary Analysis of 2015 Budget Decisions in NATO Member States', *Policy Brief*, European Leadership Network, at: www.europeanleadershipnetwork.org/medialibrary/2015/02/20/04389e1d/ELN%20NATO%20Budgets%20Brief.pdf.

Rynning, S. (2012). *NATO in Afghanistan: The Liberal Disconnect*, Stanford: Stanford University Press.

Rynning, S. (2014). 'The Geography of the Atlantic Peace: NATO 25 Years after the Fall of the Berlin Wall', *International Affairs*, 90(6): 1383–1401.

Rumsfeld, D. (2011). *Known and Unknown: A Memoir*, New York: Sentinel.

Simon, L. (2014). '"Back to Basics" and "Out of Area"'', *The RUSI Journal*, 159(3): 14– 19.

Smale, A., Mazzetti, M. and Sanger, D. E. (2014). 'Berlin Expels American Spy Chief as Strains Grow', *International New York Times*,1 July.

Snyder, G. (1984), 'The Security Dilemma in Alliance Politics', *World Politics*, 36(4): 461–495.

Snyder, G. (2002). 'Mearsheimer's World – Offensive Realism and the Struggle for Security', *International Security*, 27(1): 149–173.

The Economist (2005). 'Afghanistan: Southward, Ho!', 5 November.

Vasquez, J. (1998). *The Power of Power Politics: from Classical Realism to Neotraditionalism*, Cambridge : Cambridge University Press.

Wallander, C. A. (2000). 'Institutional Assets and Adaptability: NATO after the Cold War', *International Organisation*, 54(4): 705–735.

Walt, S. (1987). *The Origins of Alliances*, Ithaca: Cornell University Press.

Waltz, K. N. (1959). *Man, the State and War: A Theoretical Analysis*, New York: Columbia University Press.

Waltz, K. N. (1967). *Foreign Policy and Democratic Politics: The American and the British Experience*, Boston: Little Brown.

Waltz, K. N. (1979). *Theory of International Politics*, Reading: Addison-Wesley.

Waltz, K. N (1993). 'The Emerging Structure of International Politics', *International Security*, 18(2): 44–79.

Waltz, K. (1995). 'Realist Thought and Neorealist Theory', in Kegley, C. (ed). *Controversies in International Relations Theory. Realism and the Neoliberal Challenge*, New York: St. Martin's Press.

Webber, M. Sperling, J. and Smith, M. A. (2012). *NATO's Post-Cold War Trajectory: Decline or Regeneration?* Houndmills, Basingstoke: Palgrave Macmillan.

Williams, N. (1996), 'Partnership for Peace: Permanent Fixture or Declining Asset?', *Survival*, 38(1): 98–110.

Wohlforth, W. (2002). 'Measuring Power – and the Power of Theory', in Vasquez, J. A. and Elman, C. (eds). *Realism and the Balancing of Power: A New Debate*, New Jersey: Prentice-Hall.

Wohlforth, W. (2004). 'Revisiting Balance of Power Theory in Eurasia', in Paul, T. V., Wirtz, J. J. and Fortmann, M. (eds). *Balance of Power: Theory and Practice in the 21st Century*, Stanford: Stanford University Press.

Wolfers, A. (1962). *Discord and Collaboration: Essays in International Politics*, Baltimore: Johns Hopkins University Press.

Zimmermann, H. (2005). 'Security Exporters: Germany, the United States and Transatlantic Cooperation', in Andrews, D. M. (ed). *The Atlantic Alliance under Stress: US-European Relations after Iraq*, Cambridge: Cambridge University Press.

4 Neo-classical realism and alliance politics

James Sperling[1]

Prominent neo-realists predicted that NATO would enter into terminal decline with the end of the Cold War and dissolution of the Soviet Union (Waltz 1993: 75–76) or that a recalibration in the balance of power would trigger NATO's eventual decline as Europe engaged in the hard or soft balancing of American power (Paul 2005; Posen 2006). Yet neither outcome has materialised. A structural account of the Alliance is thus arguably a flawed one. What is needed instead is a robust theory of comparative foreign policy that conjoins both systemic and unit-level variables. Neo-classical realism (NCR) is just such a theory: it preserves the neo-realist emphasis on international structure as the primary determinant of state action, but introduces unit-level characteristics as intervening variables in order to explain variations in national policies crafted in response to the same threat complex and structure of power.

NATO military operations since the end of the Cold War have provided a rich empirical field for understanding the ability of the Alliance to meet the challenge of regional security and stability within and outside Europe; it has also presented analysts with asymmetries of participation in those operations. Operation Unified Protector (OUP), the NATO mission in Libya in 2011, is an indicative case in this regard. OUP highlights three distinct features relevant to NATO: first, it was an out-of-area expeditionary operation, an example of NATO's most important operational responsibility other than collective defence; second, OUP revealed divergent national interests and definitions of threat; and, third, it seemed to indicate a long-term deterioration of Alliance cohesion.

The Libyan crisis, and NATO's role in it, represents a paradox of sorts for the Alliance. The decision to embark upon OUP underlined NATO's commitment to regional stability along Europe's perimeter. Having commenced the operation, NATO saw it through seemingly successfully. The mission's immediate operational objectives were realised and NATO could claim to have demonstrated its strategic utility, especially when compared to the European Union (EU), which was largely absent during the crisis (Daalder and Stravidis 2012; Rasmussen 2011; Vasalek 2012; Wilson 2011).[2] Yet these positives were offset by a crisis of participation as some important allies refused to take part, a state of affairs that diluted the sense of NATO resolve and revived the idea that NATO was prone to internal dysfunction (Webber, Sperling and Smith 2012: 9–10).

This paradox is worth investigating. And a theory of comparative foreign policy such as NCR ought to be helpful here in explaining how national expectations helped determine NATO's political priorities in the Libyan case while also accounting for the vexatious alliance politics which attended the intervention. NCR, in this sense, offers a means to examine alliance politics as an expression of national foreign policy choices. It permits the view that NATO may be different things to different states, while still being effective as a military alliance. NATO, in other words, performs overlapping functions for each member state and so is able to mitigate the disparate, even conflicting, expectations that each brings to an issue. To pursue this line of analysis, the positions of five NATO member states – Canada, France, Germany, Italy and the UK – will be considered.

Neo-classical realism: claims, assumptions and logic

The analytical power of NCR is located in its two distinguishing characteristics. First, it is system dominant and retains the parsimony ascribed to neo-realism and classical realism; and second, it integrates unit-level characteristics as intervening variables for understanding responses to systemic continuity and change. The recourse to the unit (or state) level, it is claimed, means that NCR avoids the determinism of neo-realism, bypasses the level of analysis problem, explains national foreign policy choice under conditions of uncertainty and captures the tension between systemic necessity and domestic choice.[3] Further, NCR augments classical realism with three supplementary assumptions. First, a positive shift in a state's relative power encourages, even compels, the state concerned to pursue more ambitious milieu-shaping foreign policies (Zakaria 1999: 42). Second, the direction of policy in such cases will be indeterminate because policy is the outcome of perceptions, beliefs and interests held by national foreign policy elites. These subjective factors operate within a certain range of possibilities (subject to national security cultures, for instance), but they are not so narrow as to preclude reliable accounts of how policy is likely to unfold (Talliaferro 2000–2001: 141–42). Third, and related, unit-level characteristics can be said to establish the range of domestically sustainable policies and the milieu goals sought (Bulmer, Jeffery and Paterson 2000: 124).

On this basis, the analytical logic of NCR may be summarised as follows: exogenous shifts in the relative distribution of power (the independent variable) are refracted through domestically derived constraints and opportunities (the intervening variables) that generate idiosyncratic foreign policies (the dependent variable).[4] The robustness of this logic is contingent, therefore, upon the clarity or ambiguity of external threats and thus the appropriate policy response to them. Although NCR accords primacy to systemic shifts in power (or constellations of threat) as the sole independent variable, there is a considerable divergence about the relevant unit-level or intervening variable(s). Gideon Rose (1998: 157–168) has identified four general categories of unit-level variable: the direct and indirect material interests of states; state strength defined as the net power resources at the disposal of a national government *and* the government's extraction and mobilisation capabilities; the domestic political context, including both its structural (constitutional form) and temporal (electoral cycle) components; and the proscriptions and prescriptions of the national security culture.[5] The precise content of those unit-level characteristics and the weight ascribed to each remains contested, however, in the NCR literature.

With a few exceptions (Cladi and Webber 2011; Dueck 2009; Ratti 2006; Rynning 1998, 2005), neo-classical realists have been preoccupied more with patterns of alliance formation or the emergence of great powers than with intra-alliance debate or participation in expeditionary military operations. That said, NCR is a potentially powerful framework for understanding the more prosaic aspects of alliance politics, particularly where there is ambiguity over the appropriate policy response to a generally agreed upon security threat. The Libyan intervention met this condition: no NATO member state had any real doubt that the crisis in Libya posed an imminent threat to stability in the Mediterranean basin. But there was deep disagreement on how to best mitigate it.

Neo-classical realism: four propositions about the Libyan intervention

The introductory chapter posed four questions about the Alliance: What is NATO? What is NATO for? Who is NATO for (and, related, what are the barriers to preference aggregation in NATO)? And whither NATO (in other words, why does NATO endure)? Four propositions derived from NCR provide the starting point for theoretically informed answers to those questions.

Any variant of realism *assumes* that NATO was a response to the Soviet–American competition for European hegemony and functioned to preserve the postwar status quo (Liska 1977). When extended to the post–Cold War period, this assumption yields the following proposition for answering the question: What is NATO?

> *Proposition 1*: NATO remains the preferred mechanism of its members for maintaining European stability and managing change, particularly disturbances in the regional milieu.

This proposition captures the NCR claim that alliance coherence is positively correlated with convergent assessments of security defined in terms of threats (Walt 1987) or interests (Schweller 2004). NATO's character, by this thinking, lies in its military function; it is an alliance of states whose core competence is the provision of aggregated security. Emphasis here on NATO's inter-governmental aspect stands separate from the liberal or constructivist positions that NATO has an institutional or social character.

The second question presumes both continuity and change. Continuity because the underlying task of collective defence remains NATO's uncontested *raison d'etre*; and change because each non–Article Five contingency progresses the Alliance's ancillary collective security role (Webber, Sperling and Smith 2012: 47–88). NCR posits that the evolution of the Alliance, from collective defence to collective security necessarily reflects perceived shifts in the post–Cold War structure of power and the threat environment.[6] We should expect that flux in the international environment will affect national perceptions of the structure of power, critical threats to national security and the geographic sources of those threats – all of which will test Alliance coherence. This expectation generates a second proposition:

> *Proposition 2*: The greater the divergence of national milieu goals or perceptions of threat in a period of flux or crisis, the more likely NATO will function as an institutional nexus for shifting coalitions of the willing.

This proposition is complemented by a corollary: as the extraction and mobilisation capacity of states declines, intra-alliance conflict over the purpose of NATO, and the level of commitment to allied military interventions, will be aggravated.[7]

NCR assumes that alliances serve national security interests and so generates a robust proposition about the expression and aggregation of national preferences that strengthen, sustain, or weaken such a collective endeavour. National security policies arise from the interaction of interdependent unit-level variables – the perceived implications of shifting threats or challenges to the regional milieu, the level of government autonomy from the domestic political context and the proscriptions and prescriptions of the national security culture (Rose 1998). These variables generate a third proposition for addressing the issue of preference aggregation and, by extension, the question of who NATO is for:

> *Proposition 3*: The greater the alignment of intra-alliance domestic political processes and perception of threat, the more likely will national preferences be successfully aggregated within an alliance and the lower the risk of defection from it (Lobell 2009: 64–66).

Three specific corollaries arise from this proposition. First, the greater the agreement on the perception of the external environment across national foreign policy elites, the lower the barrier to collective action will be (Ratti 2006: 101; Taliaferro 2009: 64–65). Second, joint action within an alliance will be facilitated when governments enjoy both a high degree of structural autonomy from the domestic political process and a low level of political vulnerability (Lobell, Ripsman, and Talliaferro 2009: 281). Third, the greater the overlap of security cultures, particularly in relation to role conceptions vis-à-vis the Alliance,[8] the greater the extent of agreement on the ends and purposes of NATO.

The final question – why does NATO endure? – points toward an aggregation of the national calculations of interest that have shaped the Alliance's evolution. NCR focuses our attention, first and foremost, on a relatively simple question: Have changes in the distribution of power or threat constellation been significant enough to alter the shared understanding of NATO's role or utility as a military alliance? The palpable shift in the operational mission of the Alliance – from territorial defence to expeditionary military operations serving inherently ambiguous milieu goals – has diminished the utility of system-level explanations for NATO's persistence (Dueck 2009: 148). NCR, then, generates a fairly straightforward proposition about NATO's future:

> *Proposition 4*: The greater the congruence of national threat assessments and preferred responses for meeting them, the greater NATO's durability and cohesion will be.

This proposition is unlikely to yield anything other than tentative conclusions about NATO's future, but operations such as OUP at least provide a point of departure for considering NATO's trajectory.

The Libyan crisis and Operation Unified Protector

OUP marked NATO's first coercive mission in the southern Mediterranean littoral – an air and sea campaign of seven months' duration aimed ostensibly at the protection of Libyan civilians but which soon evolved into a campaign to unseat Libya's long-time ruler Muammar al-Qaddafi (Kuperman 2013). Three allies – Canada, France and the UK – were fully committed military participants in OUP from the outset. France and the UK were also instrumental diplomatically in the generation of United Nations Security Council Resolution (UNSCR) 1973 on the Libyan crisis. Italy, by contrast, was a less-than-enthusiastic participant. The Berlusconi government initially restricted Italian fighter aircraft to non-combat roles, although it did commit naval forces to support the NATO arms embargo and provided seven airbases critical to allied operations. Germany, meanwhile, not only abstained during the Security Council vote on UNSCR 1973, but also removed from NATO command all German air and naval forces operating in the Mediterranean once OUP commenced.

The Libyan intervention diverged from NATO operations of the post–Cold War period in that it was European (not American) led and executed by a relatively small coalition of the willing straddling NATO and regional states. The NATO allies established three prerequisites for intervention in February 2011: a demonstrable need for action, a clear legal mandate for an intervention and firm regional support. The latter was provided when the League of Arab States called upon the international community to impose a no-fly zone over Libya and a small number of Arab states pledged token contributions to such an operation. The demonstrable need for action, meanwhile, had two components: first, the Qaddafi regime's threat to slaughter the citizens of Benghazi would have crossed, if carried out, the threshold of a gross violation of international norms and law;[9] and second, only the NATO powers possessed the expeditionary capabilities and political will to intervene with any prospect of success. UNSCR 1973 finally provided the legal basis for the intervention in response to 'serious violations of human rights and international humanitarian law' (United Nations 2011) and represented the first ever invocation of the 'responsibility to protect' against 'the wishes of a functioning state' (Bellamy and Williams, 2011: 825).

UNSCR 1973 had four components. The first permitted UN member states 'acting nationally or through regional organisations' (i.e., NATO) 'to take all necessary measures [. . .] to protect civilians and civilian populated areas under threat of attack'. The second established a no-fly zone over Libyan airspace and permitted states 'to take all necessary measures to enforce compliance'. The third authorised a naval and aerial arms embargo on the Qaddafi regime. The final component strengthened pre-existing economic sanctions with a comprehensive asset freeze. The resolution explicitly prohibited 'a foreign occupation force of any form on any part of Libyan territory', a provision that eased parliamentary approval throughout the Alliance since it proscribed any 'boots on the ground' that could escalate into another Iraq or Afghanistan.

President Nicolas Sarkozy ordered the first French combat sortie against Libyan government positions around Benghazi on 19 March 2011, before the conclusion of the Paris emergency summit on implementing UNSCR 1973. On 20 March 2011, the US launched Operation Odyssey Dawn (OOD) (along with parallel French, British and Canadian operations).[10] The US assumed an outsized share of the initial combat operations and reportedly fired 159 Tomahawk cruise missiles at Libyan targets by 22 March, effectively neutralising Libyan air defences and grounding the Libyan air force. There was a brief internal debate over the subordination of national operations to a unified NATO command. France and Turkey maintained that another NATO intervention in the Arab world would (eventually) undermine the legitimacy of the entire operation, whereas Canada, Denmark, Italy, Norway, the US and UK insisted that the operation be transferred to NATO (Frefel, Hecking and Zepelin 2011; Spiegel and Hollinger 2011; Strauss 2011). In the end, France and Turkey agreed to this position, but President Sarkozy (cited in Pop 2011) was probably correct in his assessment that the coalition enforcing UNSCR 1973 'is principally a political one, while the command structure will be in the hands of NATO'.

The US combat role declined rapidly once NATO assumed the initial tasks of enforcing the arms embargo (23 March 2011) and the no-fly zone (24 March 2011), and then of protecting the civilian population under threat of attack (29 March 2011). After 4 April, the US reduced its role to the provision of critical enabling capabilities (intelligence and surveillance, logistics, search and rescue, strategic lift and aerial refuelling) (Global Security 2012). By the time OUP concluded on 31 October 2011, Canada, France, Italy and the UK had accounted for 58 per cent of the 9,700 strike sorties and 70 per cent of the 26,500 sorties overall.[11] Moreover, Canada, France, Italy and the UK contributed seventeen of the twenty-eight non-US naval combat and support vessels that were committed to the maritime arms embargo after 30 March. Those same states also provided eighty-one (of ninety-four) non-US NATO combat aircraft, nine (of eleven) tankers capable of aerial refuelling, twenty-five (of twenty-six) transport aircraft and approximately twenty Tiger and Apache attack helicopters (Global Security

2011a, 2011b). The US, however, remained central. It was American enabling capabilities and its resupply of NATO allies with precision-guided munitions that ultimately made possible OUP's success (*The Economist* 2011b: 55; Global Security 2012).

The controversy over participation within the Alliance went far beyond chronic debates about burden sharing. Only fourteen NATO allies made any direct military contribution (Belgium, Bulgaria, Canada, Denmark, France, Greece, Italy, the Netherlands, Norway, Romania, Spain, Turkey, the UK and the US) and five of those states (Bulgaria, Spain, Greece, Romania and Turkey) refrained from a combat role, with Italy only assuming one reluctantly in late April 2011. Even more troubling was the stance of allies such as Germany and Poland, two states with significant military capabilities, who refused to take part. This crisis of participation reflected very different national assessments of the requirements of regional stability with respect to both means and ends.

Foreign policy choice

As noted earlier, the analytical logic of NCR posits that exogenous shifts in the relative distribution of power (the independent variable) are refracted through domestically derived constraints and opportunities (the intervening variables) that explain national foreign policies (the dependent variable). What needs to be explained is the variation in the British, Canadian, French, German and Italian responses to UNSCR 1973 and the differing levels of willingness to contribute to OUP. This is all the more interesting because, unlike the crisis generated by the 2003 Iraq war, the fundamentals of the situation were uncontroversial. The Libyan operation was a UN-mandated and NATO-led mission, and there was agreement on the threat the Qaddafi regime posed to regional stability. What, then, accounts for these divergent national responses?

Independent variable

Post–Cold War shifts in the global and regional balances of power established a range of viable national foreign policy options. The end of the Cold War marked a sudden shift to unipolarity as the US emerged as the unchallengeable superpower (Wohlforth 1999). Europe's relative power also appeared on the rise. In the 1990s, European gross domestic product (GDP) as a share of global GDP was only slightly lower than that of the US, as were the quantity and quality of European military capabilities.

A second major shift, the rise of China, emerged at the turn of the millennium and had been consolidated by the first decade's end. China's emergence as a manufacturing power, increasingly critical role as creditor to the West, rapid military modernisation and ambition to acquire a deep-water maritime capability has effectively ended the 'unipolar moment' and now threatens America's strategic dominance in the Pacific. This second shift is responsible for the Obama administration's redeployment of US military assets to the Asia-Pacific region and strategic retreat from Europe, a process delayed, but not reversed, by the Ukraine crisis (Webber 2015).

Developments within Europe amplified these systemic shifts in the structure of power. After the Cold War, the US expected its allies to play a larger role in promoting order and stability along Europe's eastern and southern peripheries. Europe simultaneously claimed the prerogative to do so, first within the NATO-sponsored European Security and Defence Identity (ESDI) and subsequently through the EU's Common Security and Defence Policy. Yet, the transition from territorial defence to milieu-shaping security policies reduced the cohesion and purpose of NATO. There is often disagreement on those regions critical to NATO and on the appropriate instruments for sustaining stability. Moreover, regional instability presents each ally with asymmetrical risks and vulnerabilities.

Germany's emergence as the dominant Eurozone economy represents a further major shift in the regional constellation of power. The contemporary German foreign policy elite lacks the same instinctive Atlanticism of the post-war leadership. It has thus placed German economic power in the service of a narrowly defined and articulated national interest – a trend that has carried over into security policy rendering it a less compliant security partner.

What do these shifts in the global and regional structures of power imply? First, Europeans have undertaken regional milieu shaping consistent with European values and interests. Europe's rising vulnerability to disorder in the Mediterranean basin in particular has compelled the European allies to adopt a more assertive foreign policy agenda and seek primary responsibility for regional order. Second, the end of bipolarity has decreased significantly the costs of defecting from US policy preferences or adopting policies that frustrate US objectives. And third, Chinese assertiveness has led the Americans to recalibrate the strategic importance ascribed to Europe and downgrade American responsibility for secondary strategic challenges in South East Europe and the Mediterranean. Alongside this, Europe's relative power has declined as China's has risen. Alongside European wariness of the American global security agenda, particularly in Asia, this has expressed itself in a European reluctance to pursue an American agenda of NATO globalisation.

These developments have had three major consequences for the Alliance. First, alliance cohesion – between North America and Europe or within Europe itself – is no longer guaranteed by a commonly acknowledged existential threat to allied security. Second, cohesion has been strained by the ability and willingness of some European states to disagree publically with the US on those occasions where they hold divergent perceptions or imperfectly overlapping definitions of what constitutes a common strategic threat *and* the optimal method for addressing it. Third, shifts in power have transformed NATO into a voluntary alliance, and it is likely as not to evolve into a permanent coalition of the willing on matters falling outside Article Five.[12] But these shifts in power, and their consequences, cannot alone explain the patterns of national (and by aggregation, collective) behaviour within NATO. Explanation here also requires the consideration of unit-level intervening variables.

Intervening variables

(i) Material interests

Three direct and indirect material interests may have shaped the policies of NATO allies. First, pundits and politicians, particularly in Germany and France, posited a causal connection between Libyan intervention and the desire to secure national oil and gas supplies.[13] Italy, which imported just over 20 per cent of its oil and natural gas imports from Libya, was most vulnerable to a supply disruption (Frappi and Varvelli 2010: 111–112; Miranda 2012: 11). None of the other NATO states under consideration, however, imported more than 1 per cent of its natural gas supplies from Libya; although France did import 16 per cent of its oil from the country, and the figures for Germany and the UK were 7.7 per cent and 8.5 per cent, respectively (IEA 2011). High German dependence on the Russian Federation for oil and gas supplies, meanwhile, may have influenced policy towards Libya.[14] At a minimum, the material interests of Italy and Germany in particular indicated a cautious approach to the Libyan crisis: the Qaddafi regime possessed the virtue of guaranteeing Italy a stable supply of oil and natural gas, whereas Germany was cognizant that a diplomatic crisis could lead to a disruption of Russian energy supplies.

By contrast, no ally's bilateral investment and trading relationship with Libya crossed the threshold of a critical national interest. Libya accounted for less than 1 per cent of NATO allies' total exports, with the exception of Germany (3.34 per cent) (Eurostat 2012a). These states' investment position in Libya was similarly marginal (less than 1 per cent of total foreign direct investment [FDI]) (OECD 2012). Libyan FDI was also inconsequential – at its highest in Italy where it still only accounted for 1.67 per cent of total FDI in the country (OECD 2012).

A German interest in currying favour with Brazil, Russia, India and China (BRIC) has been identified as the rationale for casting an abstention on UNSC Resolution 1973 (Guérot 2012: 10; Hacke 2011: 53; Ischinger 2012: 53). Compared with the other NATO allies, Germany does enjoy deeper trade and financial relations with BRIC, accounting for 13 per cent of total German exports, almost double that of the next closest ally (France with 6.7 per cent), and it is the fastest growing market for German manufactures. Allied direct investment in BRIC falls within a relatively low range, but Germany has the largest European stake. Yet despite German economic interest in BRIC, it is highly doubtful that Berlin's abstention on UNSCR 1973 was shaped by mercantile interests. The existing pattern of trade within the Atlantic economy should, if Germany were driven by economic considerations, have yielded a German vote *for* the resolution: the EU, the US and Canada are, after all, home to 83 per cent of German FDI and together purchase 66 per cent of total German exports goods and services (Eurostat 2012a).

The fear of mass migration and internal displacement of Libyan citizens and resident North Africans, meanwhile, played into the dominant narrative explaining French and Italian foreign policy (Miranda 2012: 13; Moens 2012: 153). Italian Foreign Minister Franco Frattini expressed the Italian fear of a 'biblical exodus' of unwanted refugees landing on Italian shores (Squires 2011). That fear was seemingly realised when 26,000 Tunisians landed at the Italian port of Lampedusa between January and March 2011. And although the 300,000 to 1 million North African refugees expected to flood Italy failed to materialise, the potential for uncontrolled migration was real. By mid-May 2011, an estimated 330,000 Libyans were internally displaced and 790,000 Libyans and foreign workers had fled to neighbouring countries (Canada, Parliament 2011b: 1150, 1210). France was similarly preoccupied with the potential flood of refugees from the region, although the threat was less immediate (and lower in scale) and so a less compelling rationale for an intervention.

(ii) Extraction and mobilization

Constraints on a government's extraction and mobilisation capabilities are likely to diminish an ally's ability and willingness to undertake or to sustain an expeditionary operation (Dueck 2009; Schweller 2009). It is difficult to determine the precise impact this variable has on a state's decision to intervene at a point in time, but resource constraints became manifest during OUP and indicate a structural barrier to future NATO expeditionary operations.

Western governments enjoy a high degree of latitude in extracting resources from society: general government expenditure as a share of GDP for the countries under consideration ranges from almost 57 per cent in France to 44 per cent in Canada (Eurostat 2012b; World Bank 2012). Three factors constrain resource extraction and mobilisation, however, for foreign policy purposes: the concurrent fiscal crises and the prolonged recession arising from the meltdown of the global financial system in 2008, the unwillingness of electorates to tolerate cuts in social welfare programmes to sustain or increase defence expenditures and unsustainable levels of central government debt. Canada and Germany enjoy a 'debt cushion'; France, Italy and the UK do not. And although that placed these three states in a more exposed position, by 2011 all five states considered here were embarking upon cuts to national defence budgets (Baldwin 2013).

Fiscal constraints limit the number of deployable and sustainable troops, as well as the acquisition of additional force projection capabilities (Heisbourg 2012: 30–33). Italian and British operations were both circumscribed by budgetary exigencies during OUP: the Italians were forced to remove the aircraft carrier *Garibaldi* from operations; British budget cuts forced the premature removal of three Nimrod surveillance aircraft from in-theatre service; and France, Italy and UK quickly expended already low stocks of precision-guided munitions (Harding 2011).

(iii) Domestic political context

As noted earlier, the domestic political context has two aspects: constitutional provisions enabling or constraining military interventions, and the dynamics of the domestic political system.

The constitutional freedom of action to commit troops to combat operations varies widely among the NATO allies. France and Germany occupy two ends of the spectrum in this respect. The French president does not require parliamentary approval to commit French forces and need only inform the National Assembly and the Senate of the decision to do so. German constitutional law, by contrast, requires a UN-mandate legitimising the use of force and parliamentary approval of any troop commitment or change in the level or type of commitment to an operation. A legal challenge in the *Bundesverfassungsgericht* (Federal Constitutional Court) is also possible for any aspect of an operation falling outside a parliamentary mandate. Canadian and British prime ministers have a relatively free hand in committing troops, although sustaining that commitment requires a parliamentary majority, a near certainty when single-party majority governments are in power. Italy, too, requires parliamentary approval for participation in expeditionary operations, although chronic coalition turbulence slows the decision-making process and consequently reduces the expectation of a timely direct Italian contribution to an allied operation.

In the Italian case, coalition negotiations between Berlusconi's ruling *People of Freedom party* and Umberto Bossi's *Northern League* contributed to the initial non- participation of the Italian air force in combat missions (Croci and Valigi 2012). Interestingly, a coalition government in the UK and a minority government in Canada neither prevented nor impeded the decision to enforce UNSCR 1973. The German government, meanwhile, faced a more stringent set of political and constitutional constraints. Although the UNSC vote was not subject to parliamentary approval, the absence of a Bundestag mandate to participate in OOD or OUP required the government to withdraw German warships from the nearby Operation Active Endeavour and to suspend German crews from airborne early warning and control systems (AWACs) patrolling the Mediterranean. The redeployment of German AWAC crews to Afghanistan, meanwhile, was only possible because it did not exceed the Bundestag-mandated troop ceiling for ISAF (Westerwelle 2011: 1179).[15]

Public opinion, the electoral cycle and the vulnerability of the government of the day constitute the dynamic aspects of the domestic political process. Support for the intervention varied by country (although there was general sympathy for Responsibility to Protect as a foreign policy principle).[16] Sixty-three per cent of the French public opposed the idea of intervening in Libya before UNSCR 1973. But once Operation Harmattan commenced, a majority of the French public supported the intervention (support ranged between 52 per cent and 73 per cent in eight polls and only dipped under 50 per cent once in a June 2011 poll) (Ifop 2011: 4–5). Popular support for the operation in the UK, meanwhile, remained over 50 per cent between April and August 2011 in five separate polls, only to fall below 50 per cent in two polls conducted on 20–21 March 2011 and August 2011 (YouGov 2011a, 2011b). A July poll in Canada found that only 41 per cent of Canadians approved of the operation and 33 per cent disapproved (Abacus Data 2011), although one month earlier 70 per cent of Canadians had been supportive (IPSOS 2011a: 4). Italian support for the intervention fluctuated: in one poll a majority approved of the operation, whereas in two others 60 per cent disapproved (IPSOS MORI 2011: table 1; IPSOS 2011b; Ifop 2011: 4–5). The German electorate assumed the most paradoxical position on the operation: in March and April, a majority of the public approved the government's abstention on UNSC Resolution 1973 and non-participation in OUP, but nonetheless welcomed in principle NATO's intervention (ARD 2011a: 18, 2011b).

The electoral cycle did not play a particularly important role in Canadian, British or Italian policy calculations. It did figure prominently, however, in press reports and parliamentary debates seeking to explain the policy positions assumed by the French (Ash 2011; Stephens 2011) and German governments (Bertram 2011; Joffe 2011; Maull 2012: 35). French President Sarkozy's advocacy of military intervention plausibly reflected two electoral calculations: first, a desire to bolster his prospects in the April 2012 presidential election, and second, the need to boost the prospects of the center-right coalition in the September 2011 Senate elections. Yet despite the success of OUP, the Senate elections produced a centre-left coalition, and Sarkozy lost the presidency seven months later.

In Germany, the opposition Social Democrats' foreign policy spokesman Rolf Mützenich claimed that policy on Libya was driven by the coalition's electoral calculations for the spring 2012 elections in five German *Länder* (Germany, Deutscher Bundestag 2011b: 11139–11140). If the coalition of the Christian Democratic Union (CDU) and the Free Democratic Party (FDP) were to lose those elections, it threatened a blocking majority in the Bundesrat – a not inconsiderable concern given the nature of German federalism. It was generally assumed that German participation in OUP would guarantee a poor electoral showing for the governing coalition. As it turned out, the CDU and FDP suffered electoral defeats in each of the *Landtag* elections that had more to do with local issues than with foreign policy (Olsen 2012: 119–121).

As for government vulnerability, this has three aspects: the susceptibility of a government to a vote of no confidence, the size of the parliamentary majority enjoyed by the governing party or coalition and the stability of the governing coalition. The constitutional status of the French president and the governing centre-right coalition in the French National Assembly left the French government immune from a vote of no confidence, at least until July 2011 when the government was required to seek a parliamentary mandate to continue the mission (which it won with a large majority). The Conservative–Liberal Democratic coalition in the UK marked a departure from the post-war norm of single-party majority governments. Consensus on policy towards Libya within the Conservative–Liberal coalition (as well as between the government and opposition), however, rendered a no-confidence motion moot. In Germany, the constitutional barrier to a successful constructive vote of no confidence is so high that even had Germany participated in OUP, a successful challenge to any government policy would have been remote at best.

The Berlusconi and Harper governments (in Italy and Canada, respectively) were most vulnerable to a vote of no confidence and loss of a working parliamentary majority. The Italian case is the most difficult to disentangle due to the rhetorical posturing that occurs during foreign policy debates (Croci 2005, 2008). There were tensions within the coalition, particularly between Berlusconi and Bossi. Osvaldo Croci and Marco Valigi (2012: 213) claim that the Lega Nord's scepticism towards expeditionary operations 'turned into opposition when the government decided to participate in the enforcement of the "no-fly zone plus"' in late April. Nonetheless, the Chamber of Deputies continued to support Italy's participation in OUP. The minority Conservative government of Stephen Harper, in committing Canada to an enforcement of UNSCR 1973, was the most vulnerable to a parliamentary revolt. Despite the Canadian House of Commons' unanimous approval of Operation Mobile on 21 March, the Harper government fell on 25 March after a successful vote of no confidence on an unrelated matter (CBCnews 2011).

(iv) National security cultures

National security culture is the lens through which national authorities view the structural position of the state in the international system (Katzenstein 1996; Kirchner and Sperling 2010). It explains national policy positions by reference to four interrelated components: a nation's self-ascribed role in the international system (Krotz and Sperling 2011: 307); the foreign policy elite's subjective understanding of the purposes of foreign policy that justify the expenditure of blood and treasure; the instrumental preferences of national electorates and elites in the execution of policy; and the interaction preference for unilateral, bilateral or multilateral action both within and outside of formal institutions. The marginal differences in NATO member-state security cultures had significant consequences for their readiness to commit forces to OUP.[17]

The Canadian political debate on Libya centered almost entirely on the moral imperative of enforcing UNSC Resolution 1973; references to the Canadian national interest or a specific threat to Canadian security were largely absent. Minister of Defence Peter McKay stated that Canada was 'compelled to intervene, both in moral duty and by duty of NATO and the United Nations, which [. . .] are two institutions that we helped found' (Canada, Parliament 2011a: 1540). The moral obligation was embedded in the long-standing Canadian self-conception as a leading contributor to UN peacekeeping missions and was derived from Canada's role as progenitor of the concept of Responsibility to Protect (Canada, Parliament 2011a: 1555). This self-conception was shared across the entire Canadian political spectrum.[18] Canada's role as a close ally of the US also affected the decision.[19] Hence, Defence Minister McKay claimed that if Canada were to abstain from participation, it 'would undermine the credibility of the Alliance' (Canada, Parliament 2011b: 1140).

Minister of Foreign Affairs John Baird noted that Canadians as a rule 'oppose the use of lethal force' or a reliance on 'military action to resolve the problems of the international community' (Canada, Parliament 2011b: 1025). However, once it became clear that the economic sanctions mandated by UNSC Resolution 1970 had failed to modify the Qaddafi regime's behavior, there was no hesitation in committing Canadian armed forces. As the operation progressed, parliamentarians also placed greater emphasis on providing the technical and financial resources needed to support democracy in Libya post-Qaddafi.[20]

As a middle-sized power, multilateralism has been a necessity rather than a choice for Canada. But the Canadian multilateral impulse has less to do with never acting alone than with promoting international governance underpinned by the rule of law and collective action. Multilateralism legitimised Canadian participation in OOD and OUP. Here, the importance of the UN mandate cannot be overstated; the successful implementation of Responsibility to Protect was considered an essential building block for a law-governed international system (Fitz-Gerald 2012: 215; Macnamara 2012: 49–52). This position even qualified the Canadian obligation to NATO. Canada, Paul Dewar MP argued, ought not to 'support unilateral actions by NATO [or] to involve itself [in such conflicts] without the support of the UN' (Canada, Parliament 2011b: 1105).

Turning to the UK, its self-ascribed foreign policy role blends leadership in the Alliance with fidelity to American policy preferences. The 'special relationship' was on full display during the Libyan crisis, although that crisis also brought about a full flowering of Anglo-French security and diplomatic cooperation. Two other aspects of the British role conception are particularly relevant. The first was the UK's assumption that it occupied a leading position in the international system and so had a special responsibility to enforce international law. Prime Minister Cameron observed in this connection that 'if we will the end, we should also will the means to that end' (United Kingdom – House of Commons 2011a: 629).[21] The second reflected a narrower concern with regional order and interest in preventing Libya's re-emergence as a pariah state along Europe's periphery (United Kingdom, House of Commons 2011a: 616; 2011b: 711; see also Blitz 2011: 5; Jackson 2011).[22]

The British solution to the upheaval in Libya in late February 2011 included an acceptance of military action (Cameron 2011: 5; Parker and Blitz 2011: 6). This willingness to use force was met with some reservations during the initial House of Commons debates on Libya. John McDonnell (Labour) believed that 'another military interventions in a Muslim country would harm British interests over the long term' (United Kingdom, House of Commons 2011a: 624); Rory Stewart (Conservative) feared that participation in OUP would overcommit British forces and delegitimise British purpose (United Kingdom, House of Commons 2011c: 741–42); and Caroline Lucas (Green) lamented that Britain had not yet framed the use of force with 'clear principles [. . .] as independent of self-interest as we can possibly make them' (United Kingdom, House of Commons 2011c: 776). Sir Malcolm Rifkind (Conservative) and Sir Menzies Campbell (Liberal Democrat), however, represented the majority view of Parliament that the intervention was legitimate under international law and morally justified (United Kingdom, House of Commons 2011b: 724–725).

Prime Minister Cameron and Leader of the Opposition Miliband insisted that any military intervention in Libya ought to enjoy broad international support. That threshold was met when the Arab League requested the international community impose a no-fly zone on Libya. Jordan and Lebanon agreed to join France and the UK as co-sponsors of UNSCR 1973, and three African states on the Security Council supported the resolution (United Kingdom, House of Commons 2011a: 612 and 718). Cameron also required that France and the US, along with the UK, serve as the core members of any multilateral military operation, but expressed a reflexive preference for US leadership (United Kingdom, House of Commons 2011a: 616). When the Obama administration decided to demure, the British then insisted that the operation be NATO led. The rationale here was both pragmatic and diplomatic: NATO possessed a 'tried and tested machinery' for coordinating a multinational operation; it also provided an institutional framework enabling the meaningful participation of non-NATO states in the operation (United Kingdom, House of Commons 2011b: 711; United Kingdom, Press Office 2011).

In the case of Italy, the Libyan crisis revealed three essential elements of the country's self-ascribed role as a security actor. First was the view that Italy stands as a Mediterranean power with an attendant responsibility for regional leadership.[23] Second, Italy viewed itself as a loyal NATO member and ally of the US. Foreign Minister Frattini and Defence Minister La Russa both underscored Italy's 'absolute loyalty' to a US-led operation (Italy, Senato della Repubblica 2011: 7, 9). Third, the Italians emphasised their humanitarian orientation, a role derived from Italy's legacy as a colonial power, defeat in the Second World War, and, as Senator Emma Bonio observed, a lack of credibility as a stand-alone military actor (Italy, Senato della Repubblica 2011: 18).[24]

The Italians also attached great importance to the observation and strengthening of international law. Unlike the Canadians and British, the Italians lacked a preoccupation with the importance of Responsibility to Protect. Instead, Italian politicians focused on a duty to uphold Security Council resolutions as an enduring principle of international law (Italy, Senato della Repubblica 2011: 5, 9, 11, 20, 21).

On balance, the Italian conception of the purposes to which power should be put were material rather than ideational. Foreign Minister Frattini expressed concern not only over the Qaddafi regime's excesses in suppressing protests, but also the adverse consequences of an assertion of radical Islam in Cyrenaica or the partition of Libya (Italy, Ministry of Foreign Affairs 2011a). Italian offers of assistance reflected primarily regional objectives: stabilising Libya and stemming a potential flood of unwanted refugees (*The Economist*: 2011a).

The preferences of Italian security culture have generally reflected those of a 'civilian power' (Foradori and Rosa 2007). The desire to avoid military instruments initially limited Italian participation in OUP. Italian parliamentarians acknowledged the important role of military force in preventing a 'blood bath' in Benghazi, but were nonetheless more comfortable extolling the virtues of humanitarian aid.[25] Before and during OUP, Foreign Minister Frattini emphasised Italy's humanitarian role and advocated a Mediterranean Marshall Plan to support regional democratization and stability (Frattini 2011: 8; Italy, Ministry of Foreign Affairs 2011a: 4; 2011b: 1–2; 2011c: 1).

A commitment to institutionalised multilateralism is also integral to Italian national security culture (Foradori and Rosa 2007, 2010; Miranda 2011: 5). This commitment is instrumental insofar as the erosion of multilateralism would limit Italian influence inside and outside Europe (ISPI 2011: 1). The strong preference for institutionalised multilateralism divides the Italian foreign policy elite between those voicing a rhetorical preference for the EU and those preferring NATO as the fulcrum of Italian security policy (Croci 2008; Miranda 2011: 4). Reflecting this division, the Italians initially called for a 'Goldilocks' solution – a joint EU–NATO operation – but insisted that it be NATO led when the EU could only agree on a post-conflict role (EUFOR Libya) (Italy, Senato della Repubblica 2011: 7).[26]

As for France, independence, autonomy and European leadership define its security culture (Irondelle and Besancenot 2010: 22–25; Krotz and Sperling 2011: 308–10, 315). In the National Assembly, Christian Jacob of the Union pour un Mouvement Populaire (UMP), for example, extolled France's diplomatic and military leadership role; François Bayrou of the Mouvement Démocrate claimed that France had emerged as a 'diplomatic power' over Libya; and Defence Minister Gerard Longuet underscored the joint Anglo-French leadership of OUP (France, Assemblée nationale 2011b: 1882, 1887; Longuet 2011: 6351). French leadership, in turn, was seen as 'inspired by the values of the Republic and a respect for human rights' and legitimised by virtue of France's historic role since the revolution as the 'standard bearer of universal values'.[27]

France, like most Western nations, relies upon international law as a mechanism to justify national policy and galvanise collective action, but that reliance is extrinsic, not intrinsic, to its national security culture (Tardy 2007). The legitimising power of a UN mandate did feature in National Assembly and Senate debates on Libya in March 2011. The principle of Responsibility to Protect was similarly cited as a justification for action by a number of political actors spanning the political spectrum. Deputy François Sauvadet (Nouveau Centre) stated that no less was at stake than protecting a 'global order in the service of freedom';[28] Deputy Renaud Muselier (UMP) underscored the importance of Responsibility to Protect as a pillar of international law (France, Assemblée nationale 2011b: 1886, 1887); and Senator Jean-Claude Gaudin (UMP) insisted that France, as a permanent member of the UNSC, should 'assume and discharge its responsibilities' (France, Sénat 2011: 2108).[29] These claims, however, were often framed in terms of a French duty to act commensurate with its standing as a great power; they lacked, in other words, the normative status found in British and Canadian debates.

The use of force is integral to French statecraft, but is not the instrument of first choice (Tardy 2007: 37; see also Irondelle and Besancenot 2010: 25). Senator François Zocchetto of the Alliance Centriste, for example, noted that the French public was 'disinclined to military engagement'. However, there was a fairly broad consensus in the National Assembly and Senate that the use of force in Libya was necessary. Some still questioned the risks attending military action, whereas others charged the government with hypocrisy for not taking similarly forceful action in Bahrain, Syria and Yemen.[30] Prime Minister Fillon responded to the charge by acknowledging the confluence of geopolitical realities and moral action: the French were concerned that if Qaddafi remained in power it could destabilise the Mediterranean basin and threaten French security (France, Assemblée nationale 2011b: 5219). Senator Josselin de Rohan (UMP), the president of the Senate Foreign Affairs Committee, enumerated three material components of the French *raison d'etat*: chaos in Libya would threaten the security of national energy supplies, increase illegal migration to France and create a weakened Libya that would seriously threaten 'peace in this part of Africa because of its strategic location' (France, Sénat 2011: 2100).

The French security culture is normally quite promiscuous in its preference ordering of unilateral, bilateral or multilateral action, but in this instance collective action was a key requirement for any French intervention. Prime Minister Fillon and Deputy Jean-Marc Ayrault of the Parti Socialiste insisted that any French intervention was contingent upon regional actors (notably the Arab League, Organisation of the Islamic Conference and the African Union) requesting action, the existence of a UN mandate and the participation of the UK and US, the two states other than France possessing the capabilities necessary to undertake the mission (France, Assemblée nationale 2011a: 1877–78, 1881). Both government and opposition, however, initially rejected NATO as the institutional vehicle for executing UNSCR 1973. This position reflected two concerns: first, a NATO role would unnecessarily inflame the Arab world; and second, transferring the operation to NATO would place France in the service of American rather than French interests. Once the operation became NATO led, however, Foreign Minister Juppé and Minister of Defence Gerard Longuet insisted that NATO command was essential if the operation were to succeed (France, Assemblée nationale 2011b: 5235; Longuet 2011: 6351). In this connection, Howorth (2013: 7) has suggested that France acquiesced in OUP for two reasons. The first diplomatic (a coalition of states participating in Operation Odyssey Dawn had insisted that it become a NATO operation) and the other pragmatic (only NATO 'had the operational planning facilities [Supreme Headquarters Allied Powers Europe, or SHAPE] to make it work').

On to Germany, finally; its security culture exhibits a reflexive multilateralism derived from the institutionalisation of German foreign policy in NATO and the EU, a self-imposed 'culture of restraint' in the exercise of German power, a profound scepticism towards the use of force in statecraft and a strict rhetorical (if not substantive) conformity with international norms and law (Harnisch 2006; Hellmann 2011; Maull 2012: 36; Oppermann 2012: 6–7). This security culture has undergone a subtle evolution since unification: multilateralism is no longer solely defined by *Westbindung* (Lau 2011; Sandschneider 2012), and the exercise of German power in the national interest has meant the country is prepared *not* to act with its allies or the broader international community. Its fidelity to international law, meanwhile, is narrowly defined as conformity with the law rather than a responsibility to enforce it.

These shifts of emphasis were manifest in the Bundestag debates over the Libyan crisis.[31] Rupert Polenz (CDU) suggested that intervention should be undertaken by a coalition of the willing outside of NATO (Germany, Deutscher Bundestag 2011b: 11144). Foreign Minister Westerwelle subsequently presented the German withdrawal of naval and air force personnel from NATO command as a constitutional requirement and insisted that it in no way impaired Germany's devotion to the Alliance (Germany, Deutscher Bundestag 2011c: 11179). Members of the CDU, Christian Social Union and FDP, similarly, considered the offer to redeploy German AWAC crews to Afghanistan as evidence of 'alliance solidarity'.[32]

Since the founding of the Federal Republic, German foreign policy has supported the primacy of international law in framing its foreign policy. Yet Germany in the Libya context felt no obligation to enforce UNSCR 1973,[33] and Responsibility to Protect was not viewed as a particularly compelling principle of action.[34] Stefan Lebich (Die Linke) went so far as to conclude that the legal requirements of Responsibility to Protect were not met and therefore the intervention was illegitimate. Peter Götz (CDU) claimed that Germany's non-participation in the no-fly zone would in fact protect Libyan civilians (Germany. Deutscher Bundestag 2011b: 11151; 11152).[35]

The high threshold for the commitment of armed forces to an allied operation and the instrumental preferences of civilian power in the conduct of foreign policy largely explains Germany's non-participation in OUP. The conditions justifying the use of force were detailed in May 2011: 'there must be a clear answer to the question of whether German interests require and justify an operation and what the consequences of non-action would be' (Germany, Ministry of Defence 2011: 4).[36] Foreign Minister Westerwelle remained convinced that a no-fly zone was of limited utility and could very well 'weaken rather than strengthen the democratic movements in North Africa' (Germany, Deutscher Bundestag 2011a: 10815).[37] These doubts were widely shared in the Bundestag,[38] and most agreed with the coalition government's assessment that enhanced economic sanctions alone would achieve the goals of UNSCR 1973 (Fras 2011; Merkel 2011).

Multilateralism had been the keystone of German foreign policy from the founding of the republic in 1949, and its meaning had been largely defined in terms of acting in concert with Germany's NATO allies or partners in the EU. The German abstention and subsequent withdrawal of personnel from NATO missions in the Mediterranean were justified against a four-fold reinterpretation of multilateralism. First, members of the coalition government (and opposition) delegated responsibility for enforcing UNSCR 1973 to a coalition of regional actors (notably Persian Gulf states) and questioned whether it was a Western responsibility to intervene. Second, some denied that Germany had departed from its reflexive multilateralism: Germany, after all, had joined approximately one-half of the NATO member states that refused to contribute to OUP, and its abstention on UNSCR 1973 was alongside that of four other regional powers – Brazil, China, India and Russia. Third, German politicians rightly noted that the resolution only required Germany to observe its proscriptions, not to enforce them. And finally, Germany's NATO membership no longer meant that wherever NATO leads, Germany should automatically follow (Germany, Deutscher Bundestag 2011b: 11145).

Conclusion

Does NCR explain the Canadian, British, French, German and Italian foreign policy responses to the Libyan crisis? Yes, if we accept that different intervening variables have varying degrees of saliency cross-nationally. Can those national policy responses be meaningfully aggregated to answer the four questions posed in the introduction? Yes, but with reservations. The empirical evidence generally confirms the four propositions derived from NCR (see Table 4.1); it also provides a partially affirmative answer to the question of whether NCR aids our under-standing of NATO more broadly.

In that light, we can now return to the questions raised in the introduction.

What is NATO?

The confirmation of Proposition 1 has three implications. First, the shift in the systemic and regional balances of power have compelled NATO's European allies to take a greater interest in and responsibility for their regional milieu, notably the Mediterranean basin. Second, the Qadaffi regime's brutal suppression of its

Table 4.1 Neo-classical realism and Alliance politics: summary findings

Proposition 1: NATO is the preferred mechanism for maintaining the European status quo or managing its change, particularly disturbances in the regional milieu.	*Confirmed*: Member states turn to NATO for the purposes of collective security in regional milieu.
Proposition 2: In a period of flux or crisis and the greater the divergence of national milieu goals or perceptions of threat, the more likely NATO will function as an institutional nexus for shifting coalitions of the willing.	*Confirmed*: Coalition of the willing emerged in the context of overlapping assessments of threat, but divergent assessments of the best means to mitigate it.
Proposition 3: The greater the alignment of intra-alliance domestic political processes and security cultures, the more likely will national preferences be successfully aggregated and the lower the risk of defection.	*Partially Confirmed*: Similar domestic political contexts produced dissimilar policies, whereas similar national security cultures produced similar policy responses.
Proposition 4: The greater the congruence of national threat assessments and preferred responses for meeting them, the greater will be NATO's durability and cohesion.	*Partially Confirmed*: Divergences in national threat assessments and instrumental preferences have reduced Alliance cohesion, but the tolerance of coalitions of the willing in non–Article Five contingencies provides, paradoxically, a foundation for NATO's durability.

citizens provided two milieu-derived impulses supporting a NATO intervention: all five of the NATO states considered here agreed that Libya posed a threat to regional stability and order, whereas the UK, France and Canada in particular viewed the events in Libya as posing a threat to the UN-sponsored system of global governance. Third, NATO remains the security institution of choice subject to qualification: Canadian and British fidelity to the Alliance is virtually automatic, Italy seeks to reconcile its Atlantic and European vocations, France is the most likely to champion coalitions of the willing outside NATO and Germany's dedication to NATO's role as a collective security organisation has been called into question. Although NATO remains the default security institution for non–Article Five contingencies, member-state responses to those contingencies reflect idiosyncratic calculations of domestic political advantage, perceived national interests and the relative diplomatic cost of passing the buck within the Alliance.

What is NATO for?

We should not assume that intervention in Libya presages a new era of intervention on NATO's periphery. A reluctance by NATO to engage *as an alliance* in both Iraq and Syria after the Libyan intervention is ample testimony to the fact that NATO is for the promotion of order, but only in circumstances of its members' choosing. The confirmation of Proposition 2 identifies the barriers to NATO's continuing evolution as an institution of collective security. In the Mediterranean basin, the NATO states are confronted by direct and indirect threats to national security posed by failed states, intra-state violence, the rise of hostile Islamist movements and uncertain transitions to democracy. These threats are ambiguous and asymmetrical in effect, the benefits of collective action diffuse and national calculations of interest are filtered through, and distorted by, the demands of democratic governance and national security cultures.

Member-state mobilisation and extraction capabilities also impinge on NATO's ability to execute its collective security function. The European members of the Alliance would appear (given the trajectory of defence spending as a share of GDP and the fiscal consequences of the Eurocrisis) to have reached the limits of their individual capabilities for the purposes of defence; budgetary constraints on operations emerged during OUP and parliamentary debates about the costs of conducting the operation have foreshadowed closer scrutiny of decisions to participate in expeditionary missions since (hence, the tentative involvement of France and the UK in the US-led coalition of the willing against Islamic State in Iraq and Syria, and the absence of a NATO operation in this case).

Who is NATO for (and what are the barriers to preference aggregation in NATO)?

The partial confirmation of Proposition 3 identifies national security culture as a significant barrier to preference aggregation, particularly with respect to the use of force and the securitisation of threats. The domestic political context provides limited insight into the future direction of preference aggregation, but it does contribute to our understanding of an ally's willingness to act at any given point in time. In the Libyan case, the constitutional and domestic political process demarcated the range of options available to a government (notably in Germany and Italy), but in other cases exerted little or no measurable affect (as in Canada, the UK and France).

Whither NATO, or why does NATO endure?

The partial confirmation of Proposition 4 reflects a decline in Alliance cohesion consequent upon the absence of an existential threat conjoined to divergent threat assessments and instrumental preferences.[39] Yet OUP also revealed the durability of the Alliance: NATO emerged as the first-choice security institution for North Americans *and* Europeans. Selective participation in OUP paradoxically represents the resilience of the Alliance rather than its imminent collapse. The operation was a coalition of the willing anticipated in ESDI: OUP was European led and conformed to the provisions of the original Western European Union–NATO Berlin agreement of 1996 (which permitted Europeans access to the collective assets and capabilities of NATO). Moreover, the European allies were able to sustain a testing military campaign, albeit with American assistance. OUP demonstrated that non–Article Five operations do not require a preponderance of American assets or leadership and that NATO can tolerate selective participation in milieu-shaping expeditionary operations.

The utility of NCR is clear, but it is offset by certain limitations. First, it is obvious from a consideration of OUP that each ally was affected by different intervening variables with differing force and consequence. NCR lacks a mechanism for identifying *ex ante* the ordering of the relevant intervening variables shaping a state's foreign policy (or, indeed, behaviour within an alliance) and therefore lends itself to ad hoc hypothesising.

Second, NCR lacks an explicit mechanism for understanding the aggregation of national policies for the purposes of collective action inside or outside an alliance; it can only identify with certainty those factors shaping national foreign policy choices at a given point in time. NCR thus provides a framework for identifying and understanding the vertices of conflict and interstices of cooperation between allies, but cannot claim to explain alliance behaviour as such. At best, it implies that the sum of national foreign policies explains NATO behaviour, but the manner by which aggregation occurs is left unexplored. NCR is therefore deficient, in theorising NATO qua NATO.

This also means an even more fundamental theoretical issue is left unresolved. If, as NCR claims, system-level factors are dominant (and domestic ones are treated as intervening variables), then examination of NATO remains a hard case for NCR. How do we square the analytical privileging of systemic pressures with an analysis which also claims to show that domestic factors shape (albeit in an admittedly underspecified manner) NATO action? What are the analytical limits, in other words, of analyzing domestic influences on Alliance behaviour? To simply assume as a general point that such influences are secondary is of little help when seeking to explain particular instances of alliance behaviour. It is in particular cases, after all, that such factors loom large. Why NATO did not intervene in Iraq in 2003 but did so in Libya in 2011 is inexplicable without recourse to domestic or state-level factors. But simply to assume these are secondary without being clear why is a cheat rather than a solution to the level-of-analysis problem. The theoretical quandary famously identified by David Singer (1961) many years ago remains a challenge for NCR.

Notes

1 This chapter benefited greatly from the close reading given it by Mark Webber and Adrian Hyde-Price. Thanks are also owed to Osvaldo Croce, Tom Dyson, Sonia Lucarelli, Alistar Miskimmon, and Lucas Moltof. The usual disclaimer applies.
2 The EU established its own enforcement mission, Operation EUFOR Libya, but this was never deployed.
3 Recent scholarship on NCR includes Kitchen (2010); Layne (2006); Legro and Moravcsik (1999); Lobell, Ripsmann and Taliaferro (2009); Quinn (2013); Rose (1998); Schweller (2004); Toje and Kunz (2012); and Zakaria (1999).
4 This formulation is adopted from Schweller (2004).
5 I have substituted national security culture for Rose's reference to ideational and cultural factors as the fourth intervening variable.
6 This dilemma is often treated as a binary choice of recent vintage, but it is not. Robert E. Osgood argued in 1960 that NATO had grappled with this question from the time of its founding.
7 This corollary is inferred from the discussion of mobilisation and extraction on national policy choice found in Zakaria (1999: 33–39) and Schweller (2009: 227–30).
8 Recent scholarship on role conceptions includes Bengstsson and Elgström (2012); Cantir and Kaarbo (2012); Harnisch (2012); and Krotz (2011).
9 On 10 March 2011, British Prime Minister Cameron and French President Sarkozy characterised the Qaddafi regime's actions as crimes against humanity and proposed what would become the essential elements of UNSCR 1973 (Cameron and Sarkozy 2011).
10 The monikers of the other major national operations were Operation Harmattan (France), Operation Ellamy (UK) and Operation Mobile (Canada).
11 Daalder and Stavridis (2011) write that the US was responsible for 25 per cent of the total sorties, and the UK and France were together responsible for 33 per cent. The figures cited in the text were extrapolated from disaggregated French Ministry of Defence statistics (total number and share), with fragmentary data for Canada, France, Italy and the UK. See Levitz and Blanchfeld (2011); France, Ministry of Defence (2012); Aeronautica Militare (2012); and United Kingdom, Ministry of Defence (2011).
12 In Afghanistan, which can be credibly defined as an Article Five operation (the mission had its origins in the 9/11 al Qaeda attack on the US), all member states of the Alliance made a contribution to the International Security and Assistance Force (ISAF), and the Europeans made a disproportionately large contribution to ISAF prior to the Obama surge in 2009. In the cases of KFOR (Kosovo) and SFOR (Bosnia-Herzgevonia), that pattern of disproportionately high European contribution was replayed, although there was significant free riding among eight NATO states in KFOR and six in SFOR. See Sperling and Webber (2009) for a full accounting.
13 In Germany, Development Minister Dirk Niebel stated on a number of occasions that the Libyan intervention was driven solely by the Western desire for oil (cited in Dierks 2011: 25; *Der Spiegel* 2011); in France, similar sentiments were expressed by Senators

Yves Pozzo di Borgo (Union pour un Mouvement Populaire) and Dominique Voynet (Europe Écologie le Verts) (France, Sénat 2011: 2108, 2110).

14 In 2010, Russia supplied Germany with up to a third of its oil and gas supplies. The equivalent figures for France were 17.23 per cent and 14.16 per cent, respectively, of its total oil and natural gas imports, whereas the same figures for Italy were 14.75 per cent and 19.86 per cent. Data drawn from Eurostat (2012b).

15 The German government also faced two potential legal challenges to policy. Hans-Christian Ströble (Bündnis 90/Die Grünen) threatened to mount a legal challenge to the continued role of eleven German soldiers under NATO command who were involved in target selection for OUP (Gebauer 2011). The German offer to resupply the NATO allies with precision-guided munitions may have also violated constitutional law because it constituted indirect support of a military mission not approved by the Bundestag. Ströble did not make good on his threat, and the resupply issue was moot once NATO declined to accept Germany's offer (Steinmann and Mertins 2011: 9; Steinmann 2011: 10).

16 Support for Responsibility to Protect as a principle of foreign policy was uniformly high in France (76 per cent), Germany (66 per cent), Italy (73 per cent) and the UK (69 per cent) (German Marshall Fund 2011: 39–40). No comparable data are available for Canada.

17 For detailed analyses of the Canadian, British, French, German and Italian security cultures, see, respectively, Croci (2010); Smith (2010) and Krahmann (2007); Irondelle and Besancenot (2010) and Tardy (2007); Harnisch and Wolf (2010); and Foradori and Rosa (2007, 2010).

18 Parliamentary debates focused on the content and implications of Responsibility to Protect for global governance and Canadian foreign policy. See the comments by Jean Dorion (Bloc Québécois), Borys Wrzesnewskyj (Liberal), Mario Silva (Liberal), Jack Harris (New Democratic Party) and Lois Brown (Conservative) (Canada, Parliament 2011a: 1615, 1740, 1825, 1850, 1925).

19 The centrality of the Canadian–American alliance is a core operating assumption of Canadian security policy. See Bland and Macdonald (2012) and Jockel and Sokolsky (2012).

20 On this issue, see the comments of Mark Eyking (Liberal), Lois Brown (Conservative), Bob Dechert (Conservative), James Lunney (Conservative) (Canada, Parliament 2011b: 1105, 1150, 1335, 1615) and the amendment to the legislation extending Canadian participation in OUP (Canada, Parliament 2011b: 1510).

21 Similarly, Ed Miliband (Labour), leader of the opposition, underscored the importance of responsibility to protect for framing the debate in the House, as did the spokespersons for Plaid Cymru, the Scottish National Party and Democratic Unionist Party (United Kingdom, House of Commons 2011b: 717, 739–40, 746–47).

22 On 21 March, Cameron expanded his observations about British national interests in Libya which ranged from fears of migration in the hundreds of thousands, Qaddafi's past and future support of terrorism in the UK and the destabilisation of North Africa (United Kingdom, House of Commons 2011b: 708).

23 Senators Luigi Ramponi (Popolo della Libertà) and Renato Farina (Popolo della Libertà) expressed this view in the Senate debate on UNSCR 197. It also figured prominently in public commentary as a rationale for the Italian willingness to intervene in the Libyan crisis (Italy, Senato della Repubblica. 2011: 20, 24; Polito 2011).

24 On Italy's colonial burden, see the comments of Margherita Boniver (Popolo della Libertà) during the 19 April 2011 Chamber of Deputies debate (Italy, Camera dei deputati. 2011: 9).

25 Deputies Massimo Bacci (Partido Democratico), Lapo Pistelli (Partido Democratico) and Gianni Vernetti (Misto-API) expressed this view (Italy, Camera dei deputati 2011: 10, 14, 15).

26 Those rejecting a 'coalition of the willing' in the Senate debate included Foreign Minister Frattini, Defence Minister Ignazio La Russa and Senators Massimo D'Alema (Partido Democratico) and Francesco Tempestini (Partido Democratico) (Italy, Senato della

Repubblica 2011: 7, 8, 10, 14, 21). Deputy Giorgio Tonini (Partido Democratico) made a similar point in the Chamber of Deputies (Italy, Camera dei deputati 2011: 13)

27   Senators Jean-Pierre Chevenèment (Mouvement Républicain et Citoyan) and François Zocchetto (Alliance Centriste) (France, Sénat 2011: 2104, 2100). Deputy Jean-Marc Ayrault (Parti Socialiste) referred to France as 'the country of freedom', and Foreign Minister Fillon referred to the Libyan operation as 'defending a certain idea of France and freedom'. Former Foreign Minister Dominque de Villepin claimed that 'France has lived up to its ideals' (France, Assemblée nationale 2011a: 1880, 1882; Hollinger, Politi and Parker 2011: 2).

28   Similarly, Senator Dominique Voynet (Europe Écologie le Verts) referenced the importance of French action to enhance global governance by protecting social change and the democratisation process in the Arab world (France, Sénat 2011: 2110).

29   Prime Minister Fillon claimed that the desire to defend human rights in Libya was equivalent to 'defending a certain idea of France and freedom' (France, Assemblée nationale 2011b: 1880); Senator Zocchetto characterised it as a decision 'inspired by the values of the Republic, respect for human rights, [and] the secular heritage of France' (France, Sénat 2011: 2100); and Deputy Guy Tessier (Union pour un Mouvement Populaire), president of the Committee on National Defence and Armed Forces, believed that the intervention preserved 'the image of France [as] actively defending human rights and engaging courageously in the fight against barbarism' (France, Assemblée nationale 2011a: 1889).

30   Foreign Minister Juppé and Senators de Rohan and Aymeri de Montesquiou (Radical) observed that the costs of inaction outweighed the risks attending a military intervention (Juppé 2011; France, Sénat 2011: 2100, 2111). Those expressing concern over the uncertain outcome of relying on force and the hypocrisy of selective action included Deputies Roland Muzeau (Parti Communiste Français) and François Bayrou (France, Assemblée nationale 2011a: 1885, 1888).

31   Reflecting the evolving nature of the German security outlook, the positions of politicians outlined here were heavily criticised by former occupants of government office. The domestic foreign policy elite was generally very critical of German foreign policy. Former Foreign Minister Joschka Fischer (2011) called it both a 'scandalous mistake' and the 'greatest debacle since the founding of the Federal Republic'. Former Chancellor Helmut Schmidt (2011: 52–53) referred to the German decision as 'the opposite of calculability' even though he agreed with the substance of the decision.

32   See the comments of Foreign Minister Westerwelle (Free Democratic Party), Defence Minister Thomas de Maizière (Christian Democratic Union), Andreas Schockenhoff (Christian Democratic Union) (Germany, Deutscher Bundestag 2011c: 11178, 11182–3, 1186–7) and Chancellor Angela Merkel (2011).

33   See the comments of Chancellor Angela Merkel (2011) and Foreign Minister Westerwelle, Rolf Mützenich (Social Democratic Party) and Silvia Schimdt (Social Democratic Party) (Germany, Deutscher Bundestag: 2011a: 10816, 10819, 10825).

34   Responsibility to Protect appeared in the 2011 Defence Guidelines, but it only referred to the German government's responsibility to protect German citizens outside Germany 'in case of imminent danger abroad' (Germany, Ministry of Defence 2011: 5.)

35   A motion put forward by Bündis90/Die Grünen explicitly supported Responsibility to Protect as a fundamental obligation of the international community. It did not advocate a commitment of German troops to OUP, but did ask the government to enforce the arms embargo. (Bündis90/Die Grünen 2011: 2, 4). Some outside observers concluded that Responsibility to Protect was little more than a fig leaf covering 'national egoism and national interests' (Schmidt 2011: 52; see also Pradetto 2011: 59).

36   Foreign Minister Westerwelle identified three additional criteria for the commitment of forces: Does Germany possess the requisite capabilities? Will the public accept German participation in a military operation? Does Germany want to participate? These criteria were not fulfilled in the Libyan case. In an interview in *Spiegel Online* (2011),

Westerwelle stated that he 'saw [himself] as part of a tradition of restraint' when asked to justify government policy.

37 Further, Andreas Schockenhoff and Phillip Mißfelder (Christian Democratic Union) insisted that not only must the Arab League declare itself in favour of a no-fly zone, but that they, along with the African Union, must be ready to implement it (Germany, Deutscher Bundestag 2011a: 10820, 10826).

38 See comments of Rupert Polenz, Jan van Aken (Die Linke), Rainer Stinner (Free Democratic Party) and Wolfgang Götzer (Christian Social Union) (Germany, Deutscher Bundestag 2011b: 11143, 11146, 11148, 11152). Rolf Mützenich, Heidemarie Wieczorek-Zeul (Social Democratic Party) and Renate Künast (Bündis90/Die Grünen) were critical of the government's abstention on UNSC Resolution 1973, but did not specifically endorse German participation in a military operation to enforce it (Germany, Deutscher Bundestag 2011b: 11140–42, 11145, 1149–50).

39 The reassertion of Russia evident over the Crimea/Ukraine crisis from 2014 has not yet provided such an existential threat to NATO, as the threat is felt very differently across the Alliance and in no way resembles the unifying function the Soviet Union/Warsaw Pact provided during the Cold War.

References

[All web sources listed were last accessed 12 June 2015.]

Abacus Data. (2011). *Abacus Data Poll: Canadians Split over Mission in Libya*, July, at: http://abacusdata.ca/.
Aeronautica Militare. (2012). *The Italian Airforce in Operations Odyssey Dawn and Unified Protector*, at: www.aeronautica.difesa.it/News/Documents/pdf/Cerimonia%20 chiusura%20Unified%20Protector_151211/Brochure%20Libya%20EN.pdf.
ARD. (2011a). *ARD DeutschlandTrend: Eine Umfrage zur politischen Stimmung im Auftrag der ARD-Tagesthemen und drei Tageszeitungen*, März, at: www.infratest-dimap.de/ umfragen-analysen/bundesweit/ard-deutschlandtrend/2011/maerz/.
ARD. (2011b). *ARD DeutschlandTrend*, September, at: www.tagesschau.de/inland/ deutschlandtrend1378.pdf.
Ash, T.G. (2011). 'France Plays Hawk, Germany Demurs', *The Guardian*, 3 March, at: www.theguardian.com/commentisfree/2011/mar/24/france-hawk-germany-demurs-libya-europe.
Baldwin, H. Rapporteur. (2013). 'Defence Spending, National Security and Alliance Solidarity', NATO Parliamentary Assembly, Economics and Security Committee at: www. nato-pa.int/shortcut.asp?FILE=3275.
Bellamy, A. J. and Williams, P. D. (2011). 'The New Politics of Protection? Côte d'Ivoire, Libya and the Responsibility to Protect', *International Affairs*, 87(4): 825–50.
Bengstsson, R. and Elgström, O. (2012). 'Conflicting Role Conceptions? The European Union in Global Politics', *Foreign Policy Analysis*, 8(1): 93–108.
Bertram, C. (2011). 'Deutschlands Aussenpolitik ist fahrlässig', *Zeit Online*, 17 June, at: www.zeit.de/politik/ausland/2011–06/bundesregierung-aussenpolitik-libyen.
Bland, D.L. and Macdonald, B. (2012). 'Canada's Defence and Security Politics after 2011: Missions, Means, and Money', in McDonough, D. S. (ed). *Canada's National Security in the Post-9/11 World: Strategy, Interests and Threats*, Toronto: University of Toronto Press.
Blitz, J. (2011). 'Cameron's Switch to More Active Role in Foreign Policy Alarms Defence Ministry', *Financial Times*, 10 March.
Bulmer, S. Jeffery, C. and Paterson, W. E. (2000). *Germany's European Diplomacy: Shaping the Regional Milieu*, Manchester: Manchester University Press.

Bündis90/Die Grünen. (2011). 'Antrag. Für eine neue Politik gegenüber den Länder Nordafrikas und des Nahen Ostens', *Drucksache 17/5192*, Deutscher Bundestag, 17. Wahlperiode, 23 March.

Cameron, D. (2011). 'Prime Minister's Statement on Libya', 28 February, at: www.gov.uk/government/speeches/prime-ministers-statement-on-libya.

Cameron, D. and Sarkozy, N. (2011). 'Letter from the PM and President Sarkozy to President Van Rompuy', 20 March, at: www.gov.uk/government/news/letter-from-the-pm-and-president-sarkozy-to-president-van-rompuy.

Canada, Parliament. (2011a). *House of Commons Debates, Official Report (Hansard)*, 145(145), Third Session, 40th Parliament, Monday, March 21.

Canada, Parliament. (2011b). *House of Commons Debates, Official Report (Hansard)*, 146(008), 1st Session, 41st Parliament, Tuesday, 14 June.

Cantir, C. and Kaarbo, J. (2012). 'Contested Roles and Domestic Politics: Reflections on Role Theory in Foreign Policy Analysis and IR Theory', *Foreign Policy Analysis*, 8(1): 5–24.

CBCnews. (2011). 'Government's Defeat Sets Up Election Call', 25 March, at: www.cbc.ca/news/politics/government-s-defeat-sets-up-election-call-1.1068749.

Cladi, L. and Webber, M. (2011). 'Italian Foreign Policy in the Post-cold War Period: A Neo-classical Realist Approach', *European Security*, 20(2): 205–19.

Croci, O. (2005). 'Much Ado about Little: The Foreign Policy of the Second Berlusconi Government', *Modern Italy*, 10(1): 59–74.

Croci, O. (2008). 'The Second Prodi Government and Italian Foreign Policy: New and Improved or the Same Wrapped up Differently?', *Modern Italy*, 13(3): 291–303.

Croci, O. (2010). 'Canada: Facing Up to Regional Security Challenges' in Kirchner, E. J. and Sperling, J. (eds). *National Security Cultures: Patterns of Global Governance*, London: Routledge.

Croci, O. and Valigi, M. (2012). 'L'Italia e l'intervento Internazionale in Libia', in Bosco, A. and McDonnell, D. (eds). *Politica in Italia. I Fatti Dell'anno e le Interpretazioni*, Bologna: Il Mulino.

Daalder, I. H. and Stavridis, J. G. (2011). 'NATO's Success in Libya', *New York Times*, 30 October, at: www.nytimes.com/2011/10/31/opinion/31iht-eddaalder31.html.

Daalder, I. H. and Stavridis, J. G. (2012). 'NATO's Triumph in Libya', *Foreign Affairs*, 91(2): 2–7.

Der Spiegel. (2011). 'Blood and Oil? German Minister Hints at Libya Mission Hypocrisy', *Spiegel Online*, 25 March, at: www.spiegel.de/international/germany/blood-and-oil-german-minister-hints-at-libya-mission-hypocrisy-a-753126.

Dierks, B. (2011). 'Die Moral der Duckmäuser', *Financial Times Deutschland*, 28 March.

Dueck, C. (2009). 'Neo-classical Realism and the National Interest: Presidents, Domestic Politics, and Major Military Interventions' in Lobell, S. E., Ripsman, N. M. and Taliaferro, J. W. (eds). *Neoclassical Realism, the State, and Foreign Policy*, Cambridge: Cambridge University Press.

Eurostat. (2012a). 'EU27 Trade Since 1988 By CN8 [DS-016890]', at: http://appsso.eurostat.ec.europa.eu.

Eurostat. (2012b). 'General Government Expenditure by Function (COFOG)', at: http://appsso.eurostat.ec.europa.eu/nui/show/do?dataset=gov_a_exp&lang=en.

Fitz-Gerald, A. (2012). 'Stabilisation Operations in Afghanistan and in the Future: The Need for a Strategic Canadian Approach', in McDonough, D.S. (ed). *Canada's National Security in the Post-9/11 World: Strategy, Interests and Threats*, Toronto: University of Toronto Press.

Fischer, J. (2011). 'Deutsche Aussenpolitik – eine Farce', *Süddeutsche.de*, at: www.sueddeutsche.de/politik/streitfall-libyen-ensatz-deutsche-aussenpolitik-eine-farce-1.1075362.

Foradori, P. and Rosa, P. (2010). 'Italy: Hard Tests and Soft Responses', in Kirchner, E.J. and Sperling, J. (eds). *National Security Cultures: Patterns of Global Governance*, London: Routledge.

France, Assemblée nationale. (2011a). *Déclaration du Gouvernement sur l'intervention des forces armées en Libye et débat sur cette declaration*, Assemblée nationale, XIIIᵉ législature, Session ordinaire de 2010–2011, 22 mars 2011, at: www.assemblee-nationale. fr/13/pdf/cri/2010–2011/cahiers/c20110144.pdf.

France, Assemblée nationale. (2011b). *Débat et vote sur l'autorisation de la prolongation de l'intervention des forces armées en Libye*, XIIIᵉ législature Session extraordinaire de 2010–2011, 12 juillet, sommaire électronique, at: www.assemblee-nationale.fr/13/pdf/ cri/2010–2011extra/20111012.pdf.

France. Ministry of Defence (2011) 'Opération Harmattan/Libye', at http://www.webcita tion.org/63rgPazcA.

France, Sénat. (2011). 'Séance de 22 mars 2011. Situation en Libye: Declaration du Government suivie', *Senát. Journal official de la Republique français*. Anneé 2011, No. 26 S. (C.R.). at: www.senat.fr/seances/s201103/s20110322/s20110322.pdf.

Frappi, C. and Varvelli, A. (2010). 'Le strategie di politica energetica dell-Italia. Criticità interne e opportunità internazionali', *Quaderni di Relazioni Internazzionali*, 13: 98–113.

Fras, D. (2011). 'Einen deutschen Sonderweg gibt es nicht' [Interview with Foreign Minister Guido Westerwelle], *Berliner Zeitung*, 14 April, at: http://www.berliner-zeitung. de/archiv/libyen—in-doha-fordert-die-kontaktgruppe-eine-politische-loesung–doch- nicht-einmal-ein-waffenstillstand-ist-in-sicht–vor-der-nato-tagung-heute-in-berlin- bekraeftigt-westerwelle-die-deutsche-haltung—einen-deutschen-sonderweg-gibt-es- nicht-,10810590,10782024.html.

Frattini, F. (2011). 'A European Plan for Mediterranean Stability', *Financial Times*, 18 February.

Frefel, A. Heckling, C. and Zepelin, J. (2011). 'Front gegen Gaddafi bröckelt', *Financial Times Deutschland*, 22 March.

German Marshall Fund. (2011). *Transatlantic Trends 2011 Partners. Key Findings*, at: http://trends.gmfus.org/archives/transatlantic-trends/transatlantic-trends-2011/.

Germany, Deutscher Bundestag. (2011a). *Stenografischer Bericht, Plenarprotokoll 17/95*, 95. Sitzung, 17. Wahlperiode, 16 März (Berlin: Deutscher Bundestag).

Germany, Deutscher Bundestag. (2011b). *Stenografischer Bericht. Plenarprotokoll 17/97*, 97. Sitzung, 17. Wahlperiode, 18 März (Berlin: Deutscher Bundestag).

Germany, Deutscher Bundestag. (2011c). *Stenografischer Bericht. Plenarprotokoll 17/98*, 98. Sitzung, 17. Wahlperiode, 23 März (Berlin: Deutscher Bundestag).

Germany, Ministry of Defence. (2011). *Defence Policy Guidelines. Safeguarding National Interests – Assuming International Responsibility – Shaping Security Together*, Berlin: Ministry of Defence, 18 May.

Global Security. (2011a). 'NATO Arms Embargo: Operation Unified Protector Naval Order of Battle', 1 August, at: www.globalsecurity.org/military/world/war/unified-protector- orbat.htm.

Global Security. (2011b). 'NATO No-Fly Zone: Operation Unified Protector Order of Battle, 1 August, at: www.globalsecurity.org/military/world/war/unified-protector-orbat-air.htm.

Global Security. (2012). 'Operation Unified Protector. NATO Arms Embargo. NATO No-Fly Zone' at: www.globalsecurity.org/military/world/war/unified-protector.htm.

Guérot, U. (2012). 'Eine deutsche Versuchung: ostliche Horizonte?', *Aus Politik und Zeit- geschichte*, 62(10): 9–16.

Hacke, C. (2011). 'Deutschland und der Libyen-Konflikt: Zivilmacht ohne Zivilcourage', *Aus Politik und Zeitgeschichte*, 61(39): 50–53.

Harding, T. (2011). 'Libya: Germany Replenishes NATO's Arsenal of Bombs and Missiles', *Daily Telegraph*, 28 June.

Harnisch, S. (2006). *Internationale Politik und Verfassung: Die Domestizierung der deutschen Sicherheits- und Aussenpolitik*, Baden-Baden: Nomos Verlag.

Harnisch, S. (2012). 'Conceptualising in the Minefield: Role Theory and Foreign Policy Learning', *Foreign Policy Analysis*, 8(1): 47–69.

Harnisch, S. and Wolf, R. (2010). 'Germany: The Continuity of Change', in Kirchner, E.J. and Sperling, J. (eds). *National Security Cultures: Patterns of Global Governance*, London: Routledge.

Heisbourg, F. (2012). 'The Defence of Europe: Towards a New Transatlantic Division of Responsibilities' in Valasek, T. (ed). *All Alone? What US Retrenchment Means for Europe and NATO*, London: Centre for European Reform.

Hellman, G. (2011). 'Normatively Disarmed, But Self-Confident', *IP Journal*, 31 January, at: https://ip-journal.dgap.org/en/article/18435/print.

Hollinger, P., Politi, J. and Parker, G. (2011). 'Sarkozy's Push for Action Wins Almost Universal Backing', *Financial Times*, 21 March.

Howorth, J. (2013). 'Libya, the EU and NATO: Paradigm Shift in European and Trans-Atlantic Security Arrangements?', available at: www.irworkshop.sites.yale.edu/sites/default/files/Libya%20Paper.doc.

IEA. (2011). *Facts on Libya Oil and Gas*, 21 February, at: www.iea.org/files/facts_libya.pdf.

Ifop. (2011). *L'approbation de l'intervention militaire en Libye. Regards croisés entre le Royaume-Uni et la France. Résultats dé taillés.* Juin 2011, at: www.ifop.com/media/poll/1558–1-study_file.pdf.

Irondelle, B. and Besancenot, S. (2010). 'France: A Departure from Exceptionalism?' in Kirchner, E. J. and Sperling, J. (eds). *National Security Cultures: Patterns of Global Governance*, London: Routledge.

Ischinger, W. (2012). 'Germany after Libya: Still a Responsible Power?' in Valasek, T. (ed). *All Alone? What US Retrenchment Means for Europe and NATO*, London: Centre for European Reform.

ISPI. (2011). *Italian Foreign Policy in 2010: Continuity, Reform and Challenges 150 Years after National Unity*, Milan and Rome: ISPI and IAI.

IPSOS MORI. (2011). *Libya Military Action Poll – Online GB*, 5–8 April.

IPSOS. (2011a). *Global @dvisor: Assessment of NATO's Military Intervention in Libya*, May.

IPSOS. (2011b). *Military Action in Libya: IPSOS Polling in Great Britain, USA, France, Italy. Topline Results*, 12 April.

Italy, Camera dei deputati. (2011). *Audizione del Ministro degli affari esteri, Franco Frattini, sui recenti sviluppi della situazione in Libia e nella regione mediterranea (ai sensi dell'articolo 143, comma 2, del Regolamento della Camera dei deputati)*, Commissioni Riunite III, (Affari Esteri E Comunitari) – IV (Difesa) della Camera dei Deputati, Resoconto stenografico (19 aprile 2011), at: http://leg16.camera.it/470?stenog=/_dati/leg16/lavori/stencomm/0304c0304/audiz2/2011/0419&pagina=s010.

Italy, Ministry of Foreign Affairs. (2011a). 'Libya. Frattini: The Situation Is Extremely Grave. Europe Must Shoulder Responsibility for the Flows of Migrants', 24 February, at: www.esteri.it%2Fmae%2Fen%2Fsala_stampa%2Farchivionotizie%2Fappro fondimenti%2F2011%2F02%2F20110224_libia_situazione_gravissima.html&ei=eY5 6VbXPDIrXyQO47ICAAw&usg=AFQjCNH_tYeQTE6WIwyjQ7g1GORZmojBWg& sig2=cdBk-yypfLcgZUJcNGyP9w&bvm= bv.95515949,d.bGQ.

Italy, Ministry of Foreign Affairs. (2011b). 'Minister Frattini's speech on "Security and Economy: the Geopolitics of a Changing Middle East" (The Aspen Institute)', Istanbul, 5 March, at: www.esteri.it/MAE/EN/Sala_Stampa/ArchivoNotizie/Interventi/2011/03/20110318_Aspen.htm?LNAG=ENG.

Italy, Ministry of Foreign Affairs. (2011c). 'Speech by Minister Frattini: Second Meeting of the Contact Group on Libya – Rome, 5 May 2011', 5 May, at: www.esteri.it/MAE/EN/Sala_Stampa/ArchivoNotizie/Approfondimenti/2011/04/20110428_GruppoContatto.htm.

Italy, Senato della Repubblica. (2011). *Comunicazioni del Governo sulle recenti determinazioni del Consiglio di sicurezza dell'ONU in mertio alla crisi in Libia'*, XVI Legislatura, Commiss. Riun. E Cong 3ᵃ⁻ 4ᵃ, Senato e III-IV Camera, 5° Res. Sten., n. 5 (18 marzo 2011), at: www.senato.it/service/PDF/PDFServer/DF/239509.pdf.

Jackson, M. (2011). 'Military Action Alone Will Not Save Libya', *Financial Times*, 4 April.

Jockel, J. T. and Sokolsky, J. J. (2012). 'Continental Defence: "Like Farmers Whose Lands Have a Common Concession Line"', in McDonough, D. S. (ed). *Canada's National Security in the Post-9/11 World: Strategy, Interests and Threats*, Toronto: University of Toronto Press.

Joffe, J. (2011). 'Sonderweg: Platz an der Sonne', *Zeit Online*, 20 April, at: www.zeit.de/2011/17/P-Atompolitik-Aussenpolitik.

Juppé, A. (2011). 'March 17, 2011—Libya – Press Conference of Mr. Alain Juppé, Minister of State, Minister of Foreign and European Affairs', at: https://pastel.diplomatie.gouv.fr/editorial/actual/ael2/print_bul.asp?liste=20110713.html.

Katzenstein, P. J. (ed). (1996). *The Culture of National Security: Norms and Identity in World Politics*, New York: Columbia University Press.

Kirchner, E. J. and Sperling, J. (eds). (2010). *National Security Cultures: Patterns of Global Governance*, London: Routledge.

Kitchen, N. (2010). 'Systemic Pressures and Domestic Ideas: A Neo-classical Realist Model of Grand Strategy Formation. *Review of International Studies* 36(1): 117–43.

Krahmann, E. (2007). 'United Kingdom: Punching Above Its Weight' in Kirchner, E. J. and Sperling, J. (eds). *Global Security Governance: Competing Perceptions of Security in the 21st Century*, London: Routledge.

Krotz, U. (2011). *Flying Tiger: International Relations Theory and the Politics of Advanced Weapons*, Oxford: Oxford University Press.

Krotz, U. and Sperling, J. (2011). 'The European Security Order between American Hegemony and French Independence', *European Security*, 20(3): 305–35.

Kuperman, A. J. (2013). 'A Model Humanitarian Intervention? Reassessing NATO's Libya Campaign', *International Security*, 38(1): 105–36.

Layne, C. (2006). *The Peace of Illusions: American Grand Strategy from 1940 to the Present*, Ithaca: Cornell University Press.

Lau, J. (2011). 'Macht mal – ohne uns!', *Zeit Online*, 24 März, at: www.zeit.de/2011/13/Deutschland-Aussenpolitik.

Legro, J. W. and Moravcsik, A. (1999). 'Is Anybody Still a Realist?', *International Security*, 24(2): 5–55.

Levitz, S. and Blanchfield, M. (2011). 'Harper Hails Dictator's Death in Libya, as Canadian Jets to End Mission Early', *The Canadian Press*', 2 October.

Liska, G. (1977). *Quest for Equilibrium: America and the Balance of Power on Land and Sea*, Baltimore: Johns Hopkins University Press.

Lobell, S.E. (2009). 'Threat Assessment, the State, and Foreign Policy: A Neoclassical Realist Model', in Lobell, S. E. Ripsman, N. M. and Taliaferro, J.W. (eds). *Neo-classical Realism, the State, and Foreign Policy*, Cambridge: Cambridge University Press.

Lobell, S. E., Ripsman, N. M. and Taliaferro, J. W. (2009). 'Conclusion: The State of Neo-classical Realism', in Lobell, S. E., Ripsman, N. M. and Taliaferro, J. W. (eds). *Neo-classical Realism, the State, and Foreign Policy*, Cambridge: Cambridge University Press.

Longuet, G. (2011). 'Demande d'autorisation de prolongation de l'intervention des forces armeés en Libye', *Sénat. Journal Official de la République française. Session extraordinaire de 2010–2011, Séance du Mardi 12 juillet 2011*, at: www.senat.fr/seances/s201107/s20110712/s20110712.pdf.

Macnamara, D. (2012). 'Canada's National and International Security Interests' in McDonough, D.S. (ed). *Canada's National Security in the Post-9/11 World: Strategy, Interests and Threats*, Toronto: University of Toronto Press.

Maull, H. W. (2012). 'Aussenpolitische Entscheidungsprozesse in Krisenzeiten', *Aus Politik und Zeitgeschichte*, 62(10): 34–40.

Merkel, A. (2011). 'Regierungserklärung von Bundeskanzlerin Angela Merkel zum Europäischen Rat am 24./25. März 2011 in Brüssel', 24 March, at: www.bundesregierung. de/Content/DE/Regierungersklaerung/2011/2011–03–24-merkel-europaescher-rat. html.

Miranda, V. V. (2011). 'Striking a Balance Between Norms and Interests in Italian Foreign Policy: The Balkans and Libya', *IAI Working Papers 11/11*, Rome: Istituto Affari Internazionali.

Moens, A. (2012). 'NATO and the EU: Canada's Security Interests in Europe and Beyond' in McDonough, D.S. (ed). *Canada's National Security in the Post-9/11 World: Strategy, Interests and Threats*, Toronto: University of Toronto Press.

OECD. (2012). *FDI Flows by Partner Country*, at: http://stats.oecd.org.

Olsen, J. (2012). 'The Spring 2011 Landtag Elections: Regional Specificities or National Electoral Dynamics', *German Politics*, 21(1): 116–28.

Oppermann, K. (2012). 'National Role Conceptions, Domestic Constraints, and the "New Normalcy" in German Foreign Policy', *German Politics*, 21(4): 502–19.

Osgood, R.E. (1960). 'NATO: Problems of Security and Collaboration', *American Political Science Review*, 54(1): 106–29.

Parker, G. and Blitz, J. (2011). 'Cameron's Lead on Libya Sows Confusion', *Financial Times*, 3 March.

Paul, T. V. (2005). 'Soft Balancing in the Age of U.S. Primacy', *International Security*, 30(1): 46–71.

Polito, A. (2011). 'The Italian Frontier', *Corriere della Sera*, 1 March, at: www.corriere. it/english/editoriali/Polito/01032011_3fe3737a-441e-11e0-b1c1-dd3fc08b55ae.shtml.

Posen, B. (2006). 'European Union Security and Defence Policy: Response to Unipolarity', *Security Studies*, 15(2): 149–86.

Pop, V. (2011). 'NATO to Enforce No-fly Zone on Libya', *EU Observer*, 25 March, at: http://euobserver.com.13/32060.

Pradetto, A. (2011). 'The Other Cost of Freedom', *Internationale Politik*, 5: 53–59.

Quinn, A. (2013). 'Kenneth Waltz, Adam Smith and the Limits of Science: Hard Choices for Neo-Classical Realism', *International Politics*, 50(2): 159–82.

Rasmussen, A. F. (2011). 'NATO After Libya', *Foreign Affairs*, 90(4): 2–11.

Ratti, L. (2006). 'Post-Cold War NATO and International Relations Theory: The Case for Neo-classical Realism', *Journal of Transatlantic Studies*, 4(1): 81–110.

Rose, G. (1998). 'Neo-classical Realism and Theories of Foreign Policy', *World Politics*, 51(1): 144–72.

Rynning, S. (1998). *Changing Military Doctrine: Presidents and Military Power in Fifth Republic France, 1958–2000*, London: Praeger.

Rynning, S. (2005). *NATO Renewed: The Power and Purpose of Transatlantic Coopera-tion*, Houndmills, Basingstoke: Palgrave Macmillan.

Sandschneider, E. (2012). 'Deutschland: Gestaltungsmacht in der Kontinuitätsfalle', *Aus Politik und Zeitgeschicht*, 62(10): 3–9.

Schmidt, H. (2011). 'The Opposite of Calculability: An Interview with Former German Chancellor Helmut Schmidt', *Internationale Politik* 4: 47–53.

Schweller, R. L. (2004). 'Unanswered Threats: A Neo-classical Realist Theory of Under-balancing', *International Security*, 29(2): 159–201.

Schweller, R. L. (2009). 'Neo-classical Realism and State Mobilisation: Expansionist Ide-ology in the Age of Mass Politics' in Lobell, S. E., Ripsman, N. M. and Taliaferro, J. W. (eds). *Neo-classical Realism, the State, and Foreign Policy*, Cambridge: Cambridge University Press.

Singer, J. D. (1961). 'The Level-of-Analysis Problem in International Relations', *World Politics*, 14(1): 77–92.

Smith, M. A. (2010), 'United Kingdom: How Much Continuity? How Much Change?', in Kirchner, E. J. and Sperling, J. (eds). (2010). *National Security Cultures: Patterns of Global Governance*, London: Routledge.

Sperling, J. and Webber, M. (2009). 'NATO: From Kosovo to Kabul', *International Affairs*, 85(3): 491–512.

Spiegel, P. and Hollinger, P. (2011). 'French Pave Way for Deal over Command', *Financial Times*, 24 March.

Spiegel Online (2011). 'Spiegel Interview with German Foreign Minister', 21 April, at: www. spiegel.de/international/germany/spiegel-interview-with-german-foreign-minister-gadhafi-must-go-there-s-no-question-a-752164.html.

Squires, N. (2011). 'Libya: Italy Fears 300,00 Refugees', *Daily Telegraph*, 23 February.

Steinmann, T. (2011). 'NATO verzichtet auf deutsche Bombenhilfe', *Financial Times Deutschland*, 30 June.

Steinmann, T. and Mertins, S. (2011). 'De Maizière überrumpelt Bundestag', *Financial Times Deutschland*, 29 June.

Stephens, P. (2011). 'Obama to Europe: Bon Courage', *Financial Times*, 25 March.

Straus, D. (2011). 'NATO Role Unsettles Ankara's Ambitions', *Financial Times*, 23 March.

Taliaferro, J. W. (2000–2001). 'Security Seeking under Anarchy: Defensive Realism Revisited', *International Security*, 25(3): 128–61.

Taliaferro, J. W. (2009). 'Neo-classical Realism and Resource Extraction: State Building for Future War' in Lobell, S. E., Ripsman, N. W. and Taliaferro, J. W. (eds). *Neo-classical Realism, the State, and Foreign Policy*, Cambridge: Cambridge University Press.

Tardy, T. (2007). 'France: Between Exceptionalism and Orthodoxy' in Kirchner, E. J. and Sperling, J. (2007). *Global Security Governance: Competing Perceptions of Security in the 21st Century*, London: Routledge.

The Economist. (2011a). 'Europe and Libya: Italy's Shame in Libya', 25 February.

The Economist. (2011b), 'NATO after Libya: A Troubling Victory', 3 September.

Toje, A. and Kunz, B. (eds). (2012). *Neo-classical Realism in European Politics: Bringing Power Back In*, Manchester: Manchester University Press.

United Kingdom. House of Commons. (2011a). 'UN Security Council Resolution', *Daily Hansard – Debate*, 18 March 2011, at: www.publications.parliament.uk/pa/cm201011/cmhansrd/cm110318/debtext/110318–0001.htm.

United Kingdom, House of Commons. (2011b). 'United Nations Security Council Resolution 1973', *Daily Hansard – Debate*, 21 March 2011, at: www.google.co.uk/search?q=www. publications.parliament.uk/pa/cm201011/cmhansrd/cm110321/debtext/110321–0001. htm&ie=utf-8&oe=utf-8&gws_rd=cr&ei=OpF6VdLxM5HB7 Aaa14DQCg.

United Kingdom, House of Commons. (2011c). 'North Africa and the Middle East', *Daily Hansard – Debate*, 24 March 2011, at: www.publications.parliament.uk/pa/cm201011/ cmhansrd/cm110324/debtext/110324–0001.htm.

United Kingdom, Ministry of Defence, (2011). '155/2011 — Defence Secretary Visits UK Forces in Italy as End of Libya Operations Is Announced', at: www.mod.uk/Defence Internet/DefenceNews/PressCentre/PressReleases/1552011DefenceSecretaryVisitsUk ForcesInItalyAsEndOfLibyaOperationsIsAnnounced.htm.

United Kingdom, Press Office (2011). 'Cameron and Obama Discuss Key Role of NATO in Libya', 23 March 2011, at: www.number10.gov.uk/news/cameron-and-obama-discusses-key-role-of-nato-in-libya.

United Nations. (2011). *Resolution 1973*, S/RES/1973 (2011), 17 March 2011, at: http://daccess-ddsny.un.org/doc/UNDOC/GEN/N11/268/39/PDF/N1126839.pdf? OpenElement

Walt, S. (1987). *The Origins of Alliances*, Ithaca: Cornell University Press.

Waltz, K. (1993). 'The Emerging Structure of International Politics', *International Security*, 18(2): 44–79.

Webber, M. (2015). 'The Perils of a NATO Rebalance to the Asia-Pacific' in Moens, A. and Smith-Windsor, B. (eds). *The Euro-Atlantic Meets Asia-Pacific: NATO, Partners and the US Rebalance*, Rome: NATO Defence College.

Webber, M., Sperling, J. and Smith, M. A. (2012). *NATO's Post-cold War Trajectory: Decline or Regeneration?*, Houndmills, Basingstoke: Palgrave Macmillan.

Westerwell, G. (2011). 'Rede des Bundesministers des Auswärtigen, Dr. Guido Wester-welle, zur Beteilung deutscher Streikraftäfte am Einsatz von NATO-AWACS in Rahmen der internationalen Sicherheitsunterstützungstruppe in Afghanistan vor dem Deutschen Bundestag am 23. März 2011 in Berlin'. *Deutscher Bundestag. Stenografischer Bericht, 98. Sitzung* (Berlin): 11178–79.

Wilson, D. M. (2011). 'Learning from Libya: The Right Lessons for NATO', Atlantic Council, *Issue Brief*, October, at: www.acus.org/publication/learning-libya-right-lessons-nato.

Wohlforth W. (1999). 'The Stability of a Unipolar World', *International Security*, 24(1): 5–41.

World Bank (2012). *General Government Final Consumption Expenditure (% of GDP)*, at: http://data.worldbank.org/indicator/NE.CON.GOVT.ZS.

YouGov. (2011a). *YouGov/The Sun Survey Results*, March, at: http://d25d2506sfb94s. cloudfront.net/today_uk_import/YG-Archives-Pol-Sun-Libya-140311.pdf.

YouGov. (2011b). *YouGov/The Sun Survey Results*, August, at: http://d25d2506sfb94s. cloudfront.net/today_uk_import/yg-archives-pol-sun-results-160811.pdf.

Zakaria, F. (1999) *From Wealth to Power: The Unusual Origins of America's World Role*. Princeton: Princeton University Press.

5 NATO and institutional theories of international relations

Frank Schimmelfennig

Few would question that NATO is an international institution. But is it more than the aggregate of its members' preferences and power? Institutionalist theories would answer this in the affirmative, given their claim that international institutions exert an independent effect on state behaviour and collective outcomes through an ability to shape, and in some instances change, international constellations of preferences and power. There is a great variety of institutional theories in International Relations (IR).This chapter analyzes NATO from the perspective of the two major families of theories that have been applied to explaining the post–Cold War persistence and development of the Western alliance: rational institutionalism, on the one hand, and sociological or constructivist institutionalism,[1] on the other. Both, meanwhile, have a historical-institutionalist variant emphasizing the 'inefficient histories' or 'stickiness' of institutions (March and Olsen 1998).[2]

From a rationalist perspective, NATO is a functional international institution with rules and procedures designed to facilitate and stabilise security cooperation between its members. The activities and design of NATO are, by this view, seen as dependent on responses to the underlying tasks of cooperation among allies. With the end of the Cold War, these tasks shifted from the enforcement problem of extended deterrence (by virtue of US nuclear protection of Western Europe) in the face of a clearly identified adversary, to coping with the proliferation of uncertain and heterogeneous threats. NATO transformed its activities and institutional setup accordingly – mainly in the direction of greater flexibility. In rationalist terms, NATO endures because of its possession of general institutional assets that help states coordinate and cooperate in an uncertain and volatile security environment.

By contrast, from a sociological or constructivist perspective, NATO is the military arm of an international community of (liberal democratic) states. NATO is designed to defend and expand this community and to uphold and disseminate its constitutive values and norms. NATO's institutional design, meanwhile, follows the community norms of liberal multilateralism. NATO persists because (and as long as) the Western international community persists, and it enlarges in concert with the expansion of that community.

Institutionalist analyses of NATO started to thrive in the 1990s for both real-world and academic reasons. The debate between neo-realism and neo-liberal institutionalism and the challenge of constructivist or sociological institutionalism to both these rationalist theories defined most of the theory-oriented work in the IR discipline at that time and subsequently. NATO's persistence, transformation, enlargement, and new missions provide interesting test cases for these theoretical debates.

This chapter starts by describing the basic assumptions of rational and socio-logical institutionalism and shows how these perspectives apply to alliances.[3] To illustrate the institutionalist analysis of NATO, the chapter then presents rational and sociological institutionalist accounts of four major developments of NATO in the post–Cold War period: persistence, flexibilisation, interventions, and enlarge-ment. These accounts also address the guiding questions of the volume: what is NATO, what and who is NATO for, and why does NATO endure? Rational institutionalism accounts for the persistence of NATO in terms of sunk costs and transferable assets and for its flexibilisation as a functional response to changing security problems. Interventions and enlargement are attributed to the security interests of the Alliance or its hegemonic leader, the US. By contrast, for socio-logical institutionalism, the persistence of NATO derives from the durability of the liberal international community at the heart of the Alliance. Flexibilisation, interventions, and enlargement are attributable to community identity and norms rather than to security interests. Finally, I note that strong versions of institutional theory – those, in other words, that regard international organisations as autono-mous and powerful bureaucratic actors – have not been prominent or supported in studies of NATO.

Institutionalisms

Following Robert Keohane (1988: 383), institutions can generally be defined as 'related complexes of rules and norms, identifiable in space and time'. In IR, two types of institutions have attracted most scholarly attention: international regimes and international organisations. Regimes are issue-specific complexes of rules and norms (such as the non-proliferation regime). Regimes regulate state behav-iour, but they do not act themselves. By contrast, international organisations are 'purposive institutions' with 'the capacity for action' (Keohane 1988: 384, fn. 2). Regimes and organisations are often linked with each other (international organi-sations develop and administer international regimes), but they are not necessarily co-extensive. Alliances are, at their core, international regimes of mutual military assistance. Not all alliances are international organisations, however, and NATO is arguably the most 'organised' alliance in history (Weitsman 2004: 17). NATO acts not only in the area of collective defence, but also in peacekeeping and peace enforcement (crisis management broadly defined), as well as through partnerships with a range of states and other international bodies ('cooperative security' in NATO parlance) (NATO 2010).

Categorising NATO as an international institution or organisation is a nec-essary but not sufficient condition for an analysis of the Alliance to qualify as 'institutionalist'. Institutionalists also subscribe to the claim that 'institutions mat-ter', and institutional theories attribute significant causal power to institutional characteristics. Once established, institutions shape actor behaviour in ways that cannot be fully explained by the constellations of power and preferences from which they may have originated. They may also redistribute power and change actor preferences in the course of time. Finally, in the form of organisations, institutions may become actors themselves, pursuing their own goals independently of their member states (Barnett and Finnemore 2004). In this respect, institutionalist theories of alliances depart from purely realist, liberal, and constructivist theories (see chapters by Hyde-Price, Sperling, Pohl, and Flockhart in this volume). The neo-realist balance-of-power theory (Waltz 1979) regards alliance formation, change, and decline as an epiphenomenon of shifts in the relative capabilities of great powers. Walt (1987) adds threat perceptions to the equation. Classical realism and its neo-classical variants leave additional room for state preferences such as revisionism or status quo orientation (Schweller 1994). Liberal theories start from the convergence or compatibility of domestic institutions and societal preferences (Risse-Kappen 1995; Siverson and Emmons 1991) to explain alliance formation and operation. In constructivist theorising, meanwhile, alliances reflect positive and negative collective identities such as cultures of friendship and enmity (Wendt 1999) or communities of values and norms (Risse-Kappen 1996).

To be sure, none of these theories is incompatible with an institutionalist perspective and, indeed, there are realist, liberal, and constructivist versions of institutionalism. In order to qualify as 'institutionalisms', however, they need to assume that, whatever the power-, preference-, or identity-based origins or determinants of alliances may have been, alliances assume an institutional quality of their own and produce significant institutional effects. Institutions in alliance politics are designed to promote some outcomes and prevent others. They remain stable against shifts in underlying power, preferences, and identities; they modify state behaviour; and they may even alter power relations, shape preferences, and change identities. It is NATO's purpose to stabilise and strengthen its members' preferences and behaviours in favour of cooperation with alliance goals.

Because institutions matter, institutionalists are not only interested in analyzing and showing how institutions affect actors and collective outcomes, but also how institutions come about, are designed, and are transformed. In other words, institutions are not only an independent but also a dependent variable of institutionalist research. Why do international organisations become more centralised, legalised, or bigger? And why do some international organisations have more authority, more democratic procedures, or a larger membership than others?

Institutional theories see NATO's institutional quality as a distinctive feature setting it apart from 'mere' alliances (McCalla 1996: 462; Webber 2013: 39–43.). This institutional quality makes NATO 'sticky'. The response to changes in NATO's international environment and at the domestic level of member states is likely to be characterised by inertia and a tendency towards preserving established rules and routines. Further, if NATO is not only regarded as a complex of rules inducing cooperative behaviour but also as an international organisation, institutionalist theories would expect NATO to establish a degree of autonomy vis-à-vis its members states and so to pursue its own bureaucratic goals. These are common assumptions and expectations of all institutional theories. In developing them (as noted earlier), we can distinguish between two main theories of international institutions and organisations: rational and sociological institutionalism.

Rational institutionalism

Rational institutionalism conceptualises the international environment as an anarchical and material one (Scott 1991: 167) characterised by an absence of hierarchical authority and the predominance of material structures such as the distribution of power and wealth. These material conditions are the most important explanatory factors for the processes and outcomes in international relations – including international institutions and alliances. In addition, rational institutionalism starts from the *homo oeconomicus* model of agency. It assumes that states act instrumentally and egoistically, choosing the behavioural option that promises to maximise their own welfare, or at least satisfy their selfish goals, under the circumstances.

From a rationalist perspective, international institutions are not constitutive of the international environment. Rather, they are created by international actors (most often states) as instruments that help them realise their self-interested goals. In a situation of international interdependence characterised by incentives to free-ride and exploit common resources, institutions induce and stabilise international cooperation by codifying and interpreting what counts as cooperative behaviour and by monitoring and sanctioning states' compliance with international rules (Keohane 1984). These insights apply specifically to international organisations. According to Abbott and Snidal (1998), formal international organisations are attractive to states because of two functional characteristics that reduce transaction costs: centralisation and independence. With regard to the former, international organisations render collective action more efficient by pooling activities and elaborating norms and by acting as a negotiating forum, neutral information provider, trustee, allocator, and arbiter. As for the latter, states delegate authority to international organisations in order to 'constrain and control one another' (Moravcsik 1998: 9). By thus removing the interpretation, implementation, and enforcement of agreements from the reach of domestic opposition and from the unilateral control of state governments, international organisations raise the visibility and the costs of non-compliance (Moravcsik 1998: 73–74). According to this functional view of international institutions, institutional design (membership, scope of activities, and decision-making and implementation rules) varies according to the type and seriousness of international cooperation problems they have been established to solve (Downs et al 1998; Koremenos et al 2001). Different cooperation problems, in other words, require different institutions.

Rationalist historical institutionalism partly deviates from this account. It, too, starts from the assumption of selfish and instrumentally rational states, which establish and design international institutions mirroring international constellations of preferences and power. It asserts, however, that international institutions may over time escape the control of states and create their own momentum.

International organisations thus develop their own bureaucratic interests and use the (initially limited) autonomy they have been given by states to expand their tasks and competences. In addition, cooperation in one policy area may create functional spillovers in others. States are often unable to fully anticipate the development of international problems and institutions or to rein in runaway international bureaucracies (Pierson 1996). Moreover, states often stick with existing institutions because they have made costly investments in building and adapting to them ('sunk costs') and because better alternatives are absent or uncertain (Keohane 1984: 100, 102).

Rational institutionalism can be easily applied to alliances and alliance organisations such as NATO. In this perspective, the design of alliance institutions varies with the nature of the threat and the problems of security cooperation that arise from countering it. Alliances are a response to the pervasive security dilemma in international politics, but, in turn, create their own problems of commitment and moral hazard (Snyder 1984). Alliance institutions potentially mitigate these by codifying assistance rules, facilitating alliance coordination, monitoring members' commitments, and sanctioning uncooperative behaviour.

Sociological institutionalism

In contrast to rational institutionalism, sociological institutionalism regards the environment of actors not as material in character, but rather cultural or social. As a consequence, this approach attributes *primary* causal status to non-material or ideational factors and, by extension, to the embodiment of these factors within institutions. Collective ideas embedded within institutions constitute and empower actors; these ideas shape actor identity (their perceptions of who they are, what they stand for, and how they differ from other actors) as well as their interests. Actors do not confront institutions as external constraints and incentives toward which they behave expediently. Rather, they are assumed to internalise or habitualise institutional rules and rule-following behaviour. In other words, sociological institutionalism starts from the *homo sociologicus* model according to which social actors act on the basis of roles, internalised cultural values, and social norms instead of their own individual utility. The most widely assumed logic of action is the 'logic of appropriateness' according to which 'political institutions are collections of interrelated rules and routines that define appropriate actions in terms of relations between roles and situations' (March and Olsen 1989: 160).

In line with sociological institutionalism, international organisations (as a form of international institution) are seen as 'community representatives' (Abbott and Snidal 1998: 24) as well as community-building agencies. The origins, goals, and procedures of international organisations are more strongly determined by the standards of legitimacy and appropriateness of the international community they represent (and which constitutes their cultural and institutional environment) than by the utilitarian demand for efficient problem solving. Accordingly, the design of institutions varies with the collective identities and norms of that community and with the requirements of community building and community representation. In addition, international organisations 'can become autonomous sites of authority [. . .] because of power flowing from at least two sources: (1) the legitimacy of the rational-legal authority they embody, and (2) control over technical expertise and information' (Barnett and Finnemore 1999: 707). Due to these sources of power, international organisations are able 'to impose definitions of member characteristics and purposes upon [. . .] governments' (McNeely 1995: 33). In this way, they not only regulate state behaviour but also shape state identities and interests. In other words, international organisations socialise states.

Although international organisations might stabilise international cooperation by creating and disseminating common identities and norms, they can also become dysfunctional in the long run. International organisations may be 'obsessed with their own rules at the expense of primary missions', adhere to community values and norms at the expense of functional exigencies, and become 'unresponsive to their environments', all of which may 'ultimately lead to inefficient, self-defeating behaviour' (Barnett and Finnemore 1999: 700). Moreover, organisations may seek to protect themselves against changes in their environment and against external scrutiny and reform by 'decoupling' their practical behaviour from explicit organizational rules and norms (Meyer and Rowan 1977).

A sociological-institutionalist analysis of alliances thus differs strongly from a rational-institutionalist one. First, alliances do not (only or primarily) serve the purpose of providing mutual military assistance to their members, but also pursue the purpose of strengthening and securing an international community based on common identities, values, and norms. Second, threats are not simply constituted by superior military capabilities, but also by rival international communities representing and promoting incompatible values and norms. Third, the core cooperation problems of alliances (commitment and moral hazard) are not solved by monitoring and sanctioning procedures that impose costs on defecting member states, but by strengthening the common identity of the member states and inducing them to internalise cooperative norms and habits. Finally, institutional designs are not functional but normative.

Both major institutional theories share basic assumptions about NATO as an institution that provides security to its member states, stabilises their cooperative behaviour, and adapts to changes in its environment in a self-preserving way. Beyond these common assumptions, however, they offer quite distinct answers to the guiding questions of this volume. In a rational-institutionalist perspective, NATO is a functional security organisation with mechanisms designed to overcome incentives for egoistic defection; it adapts its rules, procedures, and operations to changes in the nature and intensity of its members' security problems; and it endures due to sunk costs and the absence of better alternatives. By contrast, in a sociological perspective, NATO is the security organisation of the Western international community, designed according to the liberal norms of this community and in order to socialise states into these norms. Further, NATO follows these norms in the change and adaptation of its institutional design and operations, and it endures because the underlying international community endures.

In the following sections, these institutional theories are applied to four major post–Cold War developments in NATO: persistence, flexibilisation, enlargement, and intervention. In spite of neo-realist predictions to the contrary, NATO has survived the collapse of its enemy. At the same time, it has changed from a comparatively centralised and rigid military organisation to an alliance that allows for and encourages flexible commitments and engagements on the part of its members. Furthermore, it has created institutional arrangements that reach out to non-members and has expanded its membership from sixteen to twenty-eight states. Finally, in contrast to the Cold War period, NATO has actually fought wars.

Persistence

The endurance of institutions in the face of significant changes to their environment is a major issue for institutionalist theory (Clemens and Cook 1999). The persistence of NATO was a major puzzle in the immediate post–Cold War period and gave rise to a series of theory-driven analyses and disputes during the 1990s and 2000s (Duffield 1994; Hellmann and Wolf 1993; McCalla 1996; Thies 2009; Wallander 2000). According to neo-realism, alliances are a nuisance for autonomy-seeking states. States only form or join them if they are confronted with a superior power or a threat they cannot balance in their own right. If the external threat disappears or diminishes significantly, the alliance dissolves with it. For this reason, Kenneth Waltz and other neo-realists regarded NATO's years as 'numbered' once the Cold War ended (Mearsheimer 1990: 6–8; Waltz 1993: 76).

Institutionalists, by contrast, have developed arguments and explanations for the persistence of NATO in the face of the disappearing Soviet threat. On the basis of sunk costs, rational institutionalism has argued (as noted earlier) that institutions persist if states have invested heavily in them and if creating a new institution is more costly than maintaining and adapting an existing one. Clearly, in NATO's case, alternative institutions such as the Organisation for Cooperation and Security in Europe (OSCE), the EU, or the Western European Union (WEU) were also inferior in terms of military and/or decision-making capacity (Barany and Rauchhaus 2011: 291).

Wallander (2000), however, regards sunk costs as an insufficient condition for persistence. She claims that when their original purpose disappears, institutions will only persist if first, the participating states continue to possess common interests, and second, if the institution in question offers to its members assets that are not limited only to the institution's original purpose. In applying this argument to NATO, she shows that from its formation, the Alliance had always been based on a broader common interest than simply countering the Soviet threat; it was also geared toward managing conflicts and mistrust and to preserving the peace among its member states (see also Duffield 1994). In addition to specific institutional assets to deter the Warsaw Pact (flexible response, positional defence, and a collective defence commitment), NATO had developed other assets intended to achieve 'transparency, integration, and negotiation among its members' (Wallander 2000: 712). This latter category of political-military integration proved malleable and appropriate to dealing with alliance management after the Cold War concluded. Further, NATO was also possessed of general assets (its consensus-promoting decision-making procedures, its budget and infrastructure, its inter-operability policy, and its command structure) that could be transferred to new security problems (Wallander 2000: 717, 731). In sum, by pointing to the asset specificity and adaptability of institutions, Wallander develops a powerful argument that is able to explain variation in persistence (not all institutions survive) and why NATO as such has endured. It is also a genuinely institutional argument, going beyond simply asserting continuing common interests and preferences of the member states.

Turning to the sociological-institutionalist perspective, here persistence depends on the stability and legitimacy of the identities, values, and norms that provide the foundation and glue of institutions. Accordingly, NATO could be expected to persist as long as the underlying international community endures. At the most general level, then, NATO remains in existence because its member states have continued to be liberal democracies with shared political values and norms, and because these values and norms were reaffirmed and gained international legitimacy in the aftermath of the Cold War (involving as it did the demise of communism and a subsequent wave of democratisation). Although the Cold War ended over two decades ago, NATO's endurance reflects that fact that its liberal democratic identity has not been severely challenged in the post–Cold War period either from the inside (all NATO's states remain functioning democracies) or the outside (no alternative social system has led to defection).

NATO's identity as an alliance of democracies features prominently in many accounts of what makes NATO special and persistent, but not all of these accounts are institutionalist as such. Thies (2009), for instance, makes a domestic politics argument based on regular elections as a mechanism of solving crises and a constructivist argument that democracies perceive each other as partners and do not fear one another. The institutional qualities of NATO do not play a relevant role in Thies's arguments. By contrast, Risse-Kappen's (1995) contention that democratic countries establish specific norms of consultation and cooperation denotes an international institutional mechanism that contributes potentially to NATO's longevity.

Alternative institutionalist explanations have been based on organisational self-interest and decoupling. Such explanations shift the focus of the analysis from the interests or values of states to the NATO bureaucracy. In the account of McCalla (1996), for instance, the end of the Soviet threat led NATO officials to argue for the indispensability of the Alliance on the basis of expanded and redefined tasks. It is doubtful, however, whether these bureaucratic activities were either necessary or sufficient to secure NATO's survival. First, the organisation did not have to persuade its members of its usefulness; there were no relevant calls from member-state governments to dissolve or withdraw from NATO. Second, while surviving as an organisation, NATO has had to cope with budget cuts, reduction in personnel, and organisational restructuring and downsizing. These are not indications of successful bureaucratic politics.

In sum, both rational and sociological institutionalisms provide plausible explanations for the persistence of NATO in their focus upon NATO's broad common interests and values and institutional adaptability. By contrast, organisational power and self-interest do not seem to have played a relevant role in the persistence of the Alliance.

Flexibilisation

The development of flexibility

The flexibility of an international institution means the degree to which it allows member states to vary their level of participation and commitment. Whereas inflexible, rigid institutions and rules bind all member states all of the time to the same extent, highly flexible or fragmented ones allow for varying degrees of participation and commitment by member states across time. Flexibility can lead, for instance, to a system of graded or differentiated membership and to cooperation à la carte.

The development of high flexibility in the post–Cold War period constitutes a major change in NATO's design (Schimmelfennig 2007). The old Cold War NATO was designed to constrain and discourage flexibility. This was reflected in the uniform provision of NATO's core commitment. Article Five of the North Atlantic Treaty stipulates 'that an armed attack against one or more of them [. . .] shall be considered an attack *against them all* and consequently they agree that [. . .] *each of them* [. . .] will assist the Party or Parties so attacked' (NATO 1949; author's omissions and italics). Moreover, the integrated military command structure and the forward stationing of Allied forces (mainly in West Germany) in the 1950s were designed to reduce flexibility in responding to military attacks. The Allies would have been involved immediately in combat, as well as in executing defence plans; their room for manoeuvre, in other words, was severely curtailed. To be sure, even during the Cold War, France was able to formally withdraw from military integration (in 1966) while remaining a NATO member and cooperating à la carte with NATO's Supreme Command. And many other Allies had specific arrangements with NATO, for instance, with regard to the stationing of nuclear weapons on their territory. But the general thrust of institutional design was to include all member states in the deterrence of the Soviet threat and in the collective defence of NATO territory – and, consequently, to restrict the flexibility of their participation in that endeavour.

These general principles of institutional design have been fundamentally revised in the post–Cold War period. First, NATO has set up partnership arrangements with non-member states that allow for differing degrees of cooperation regulated in Individual Partnership Programmes. Partnership has varied from all but suspended activities (such as in the case of Belarus and, more recently, Russia) to intensive cooperation with the participants of the Membership Action Plan (MAP). Second, the main decisions of NATO's members on transformation have also been in favour of flexibility. As early as the Combined Joint Task Forces concept formalised in 1994, it was agreed that the military forces contributed by the allies to NATO operations would vary according to the circumstances and requirements of the mission; headquarters would be formed ad hoc, and NATO would cooperate with the (now defunct) WEU. Under the auspices of the European Security and Defence Identity (ESDI), NATO permitted the use of its capabilities for operations without US participation. Joint task forces created according to these concepts – such as the Combined Joint Chemical, Biological, Radiological and Nuclear Defence Task Force formed in 2003 – involved a selection of member states (and sometimes non-member states) on a voluntary and rotating basis. This concept followed the principle of 'separable but not separate' forces, allowing 'coalitions of the willing' to take advantage of NATO's organisational assets.

Another element of NATO's transformed force structure is the NATO Response Force (NRF) established in 2002. The flexibility of the NRF is apparent not only in its modular composition, its rotational system of participation, and its open design for all kinds of missions. It can also be seen in the principle that participating countries make 'contributions on their own terms, for durations of their choosing' (NATO 2015). At NATO's Wales summit in 2014, the NRF was enhanced by the creation of a Very High Readiness Joint Task Force – a 'spearhead' for the NRF which would call upon the resources of NATO's most militarily capable members. This force obtained interim operational capability in early 2015 with the participation of Germany, Norway, and the Netherlands.

In addition, just as NATO operations do not require the actual participation of all NATO members anymore, they are also open to participation by non-members, partners, and non-partners. For instance, twenty-two non-NATO countries participated in Stabilisation Force (SFOR) in Bosnia and nineteen non-NATO countries did so in Kosovo Force (KFOR) in Kosovo. Forty-three nations participated in the International Security Assistance Force (ISAF) in Afghanistan, with some partners such as Australia making a contribution more significant than that of many of NATO's own members. Non-members such as Finland, Sweden, and Ukraine, meanwhile, have become part of the NRF. Consistent with these trends, at the Wales summit a new Partnership Interoperability Initiative was unveiled which would allow those non-members (Georgia, Sweden, Jordan, Finland, and Australia) with a record of 'particularly significant contributions to NATO operations' 'enhanced opportunities' for cooperation (NATO 2014: paragraph 88).

Rational institutionalism and flexibilisation

Rational institutionalism explains changes in institutional design by reference to changes in the nature and intensity of the security problems that the member states confront (Schimmelfennig 2007; Wallander 2000). Institutional design, therefore, is functional, and flexibilisation is a functional response to the altered security environment of post–Cold War Europe and the security interests of NATO's members.

In the old NATO, the core threat was clearly identifiable (the Soviet Union and the Warsaw Pact) and common to all member states. Only the capabilities and vulnerabilities of NATO's members differed. The West European countries were immediately threatened by the massive conventional forces of the Warsaw Pact on their borders, against which they were incapable of defending themselves alone. Because of its geographical position, the US, by contrast, was not threatened in the same way. Throughout the Cold War it had a technological edge over the Soviet Union and a superior ability to project its military power globally. The common interests *cum* different capabilities and vulnerabilities created sufficient interdependence between the US and Western Europe to promote the building of a transatlantic alliance, but, as the functional theory of institutions would lead us to expect. these differences also created cooperation problems.

Enforcement problems of 'extended deterrence' (Huth 1988; Lebow and Stein 1990) were at the core of Cold War NATO. On the one hand, West European states had an incentive to free-ride under the US nuclear umbrella and to limit their investment in conventional forces to counter the conventional advantage of the Warsaw Pact (Thies 2003). On the other hand, the credibility of extended deterrence was always questionable. Whereas the US had a credible incentive to use nuclear weapons to retaliate against an attack on its own territory, it was doubtful whether it would really use nuclear weapons in the case of a conventional attack on Western Europe – because to do so would invite a catastrophic Soviet nuclear attack on US territory in response (Park 1986: 103). The US thus had an incentive to defect from the nuclear defence of Western Europe. Given these two enforcement problems of extended deterrence, the members of the Alliance had an interest in making each other's commitments as concrete and reliable as possible. International institutions designed to solve an enforcement problem require low flexibility because flexible rules allow countries to decide their level of commitment autonomously and thus further defection and free-riding. In this situation, it made sense for NATO to reduce flexibility through an integrated command and the forward stationing of allied troops.

The nature of the threat (and the ensuing problems of alliance cooperation) changed fundamentally with the demise of the Soviet Union and the Warsaw Pact. The dilemmas of extended deterrence and enforcement in effect disappeared. The nuclear umbrella ceased to be necessary to guarantee the security of Western Europe. The US did not have to fear any more that it might be drawn into a nuclear exchange because of the weak conventional forces of its allies, and European governments did not have to be concerned any more about the credibility of the US nuclear security guarantee. New cooperation problems emerged instead, however. Among NATO members, the absence of a common and clearly identifiable external threat brought the heterogeneity of strategic views and security interests among the allies to the fore. Prominent descriptions of these divergences (between the US, on the one hand, and many European countries, on the other) include global versus regional security interests and strategies, and a militarised foreign policy (attributed to the US) versus the emphasis on diplomatic, legal, and economic tools of foreign policy attributed to Europe (Kagan 2003). To be sure, these differences also existed during the Cold War and led to debates and conflicts among the allies. Yet the Soviet threat provided a strong focus, which urged them to cooperate despite their differences. The occurrence of diverging strategic views and security interests in the post–Cold War period has generated greater potential for *deadlock*, or decision-making blockages in NATO. Generally speaking, if an individual member state or a group of member states wants to act on a security issue that it considers relevant and wants to use NATO resources for that purpose, it is likely to be faced with other member states that do not share its concerns and so reject collective action. The archetypal case in this regard is the Iraq crisis of 2003 when NATO did not act due to unbridgeable differences among the allies. Others include the absence of consensus on membership for Georgia and Ukraine (an issue which gave rise to considerable debate in the late 2000s) and the absence of a NATO role against ISIS and Syria after 2014 (a mission pursued by some individual allies in a US-led coalition of the willing, but not within the NATO format).

In NATO's relations with its former enemies (the Central and East European countries [CEECs] and the successor states of the Soviet Union), the core problem immediately after the Cold War was *uncertainty* about the security preferences of the new and transformed states and about the emergence of new security threats in this region. Would the post-communist regimes consolidate democracy or develop into authoritarian states? Would they seek friendly relations with the West or follow new anti-Western ideologies rooted in nationalism or traditionalism? What would happen to the enormous armaments of the Soviet Union, including its nuclear weapons, now located in several independent states? Where would its military technology and knowledge spread? And finally, would the new states develop peaceful relations between one another, or would they become mired in new hegemonic struggles and ethnic strife? In other words, the cooperation problems for NATO resulted from both a lack of reliable information about the new security environment and a lack of trust in the newly emerging state actors of the region (Kydd 2001).

The flexibility of post–Cold War NATO is a plausible functional response to these problems of deadlock and uncertainty. On the first problem, flexibility has allowed allies to participate in NATO activities to differing degrees, reflecting their capabilities and their interests on particular security issues. The development of flexibility is likely if all the parties concerned need access to alliance resources and to the cooperation of their fellow allies but are aware that their specific security concerns may not generate general consensus and participation. Flexibility also makes sense if the security problem does not require all members to fully commit themselves in order to manage it effectively.

As for uncertainty, tackling this problem has required of NATO institutional features different from the binding commitments of the Cold War that were geared toward countering a clear and predictable security threat. Such arrangements have also been useful when NATO faced its emerging partners. Open and flexible arrangements with non-member countries have helped the allies learn about the preferences, the problems, and the trustworthiness of as many potential partners as possible. Such arrangements, consequently, have allowed NATO to vary the intensity of cooperation with partners based on the extent to which these states are relevant to NATO security concerns and share common interests (Koremenos et al 2001: 793).

The upshot of flexibility is that NATO has been able to pursue creative solutions to collective action problems. Among its membership, flexibility has had a clear operational impact. Operations in Bosnia, Kosovo, Afghanistan, and Libya allowed for varied rates of participation among the allies, thus ensuring that members who had reservations on the wisdom of a mission could be accommodated. Germany and Poland, for instance, stood aside from Operation Unified Protector in Libya in 2011, but that they were able to disassociate themselves from the mission in this way meant they had no incentive to block it politically. In Kosovo, similarly, Greece and new members, the Czech Republic and Hungary, did not elevate their reservations on NATO's Operation Allied Force to the point at which they withheld consensus. Hence, the controversial mission was able to go ahead with solidarity intact even if these states then took few practical measures to support it (Daalder and O'Hanlon 2000: 118, 129, 149, 163–164, 204).

Rational-institutionalist explanations of NATO's persistence and flexibilisation complement each other well. Both suggest that NATO's institutional assets have helped the Alliance make a successful transition after the Cold War. These assets have proven sufficiently robust in adjusting to new security challenges. That fact has convinced the allies that it is more useful to confront multiple security challenges with and through NATO than outside of it. Moreover, the rise of flexibility supports an institutionalist versus a purely preference-based explanation of NATO's persistence. If the latter mattered more, then NATO would have been unable to avoid deadlock when differences arose in the Balkans, Afghanistan, and Libya (see later in this chapter). Finally, the analysis of flexibility sheds further doubt on the explanatory power of organisational self-interest insofar as strong organisations can be assumed to prefer rigid and uniform commitments to ad hoc and à la carte cooperation.[4]

Sociological institutionalism and flexibilisation

In a sociological-institutionalist perspective, a move toward flexibility would be regarded as reflecting change and variation in member (and partner) identities and values in relation to the constitutive identity, norms, and rules of the institution. Graded membership accommodates differential compatibility with, and commitment to, the identity and normative standards of the institution, and flexible cooperation allows members to selectively participate in policies and missions according to their 'ideational fit'.

This logic applies well to partnership arrangements. The early activities of the North Atlantic Cooperation Council (now the Euro-Atlantic Partnership Council) and the Partnership for Peace focused on programmes of contact, consultation, and information dissemination and exchange. This included meetings and 'familiarisation courses' between officers and staff of the former Warsaw Pact; fellowships for the study of democratic institutions; and seminars, workshops, and open-ended ad hoc working groups on a wide variety of topics. These activities later formed the basis for more structured partnerships, which would result in the accession of aspirant members to NATO. This process can be understood as the international socialisation of new and or ex-communist countries to the values, norms, and habits of the Western international community that NATO represents (Gheciu 2005). To the extent that partners learn NATO norms and habits and share the values and identity of the community which NATO represents, then they have moved successfully through the stronger forms of partnership and denser cooperation, most importantly NATO's MAP. In parallel, countries have moved closer to NATO membership as they have become more democratic (Schimmelfennig 2002), and so the claim can be made that NATO has had a positive effect in encouraging democratisation and good governance (Schweickert et al 2011).

Can sociological institutionalism also explain flexibilisation among the members of NATO? At the basic level of identities and community values, such an explanation is unconvincing. The Western identity of the transatlantic community and its fundamental liberal democratic values have been reaffirmed rather than changed or contested since the end of the Cold War. Thus, there was no need for flexibilisation as a response to an identity crisis or value contestation. Moreover, if we assume that multilateralism is a constituent norm of a liberal international community (Deudney and Ikenberry 1999; Reus-Smit 1997; Risse-Kappen 1995), flexibilisation would be a step in the opposite direction.

Moving away from the shared fundamental identity and norms of liberal democracy, however, flexibility has made sense as an expression of diverging threat perceptions and different security cultures. In this regard, flexibility is able to accommodate differences between more globally and regionally oriented countries, more or less interventionist countries, and countries with either more multilateral or unilateral orientations. For instance, flexibility allows multilaterally oriented countries to refrain from (or limit their involvement in) NATO missions without UN backing (as was evident in Operation Allied Force over Kosovo) or less interventionist countries to stay away from missions of regime change (as was the case with Germany and the Libyan intervention). This explanation is structurally similar to the rational-institutionalist explanation of flexibility; it differs mainly on the motivation. Do states seek flexibility because of divergent geopolitical interests or material threats and interests, or do they seek flexibility because of divergent national security cultures and norms? This is an empirical question, which will be taken up in the section on interventions next.

In sum, both rational and sociological institutionalism can plausibly explain NATO's move towards flexibility in the post–Cold War period. But flexibilisation creates a theoretical problem for an institutional account of NATO. On the one hand, flexibility has been a choice of institutional design that shows that 'institutions matter'. On the other hand, the cooperation that occurs in a flexible international institution is likely to be institutionally underdetermined (at least by the formal rules of the institution), for flexible rules are specifically designed to give room to state preferences and capacities. To explore this issue, the next two sections consider two sets of substantive, cooperative decisions of NATO – those concerning intervention and enlargement.

Interventions

In contrast to the Cold War era, since the 1990s, NATO has not just deterred but has actually fought wars. In doing so, moreover, it has not acted out of self-defence, but has intervened in civil wars out-of-area. However, NATO's interventions have varied considerably in terms of levels of participation and resource commitment. Whereas the military interventions in Bosnia-Herzegovina (1995) and Kosovo (1999) were based on a consensual decision of NATO, conducted under NATO command, with the participation (albeit at varied levels) of almost all member states and a major commitment of (air) combat forces and peacekeeping troops, other operations have lacked the same spread of participation and commitment. NATO, as noted earlier, was unable to agree in 2003 on a mission in Iraq. In the case of Afghanistan, ISAF was a consensual operation under NATO command, but in its initial phases received 'the least financial and military assistance of any post-combat operation since the Second World War' (Williams 2013: 368). Whereas the SFOR and KFOR forces on the Balkans amounted to 17.5 and 19.5 troops per thousand inhabitants, the ratio in Afghanistan was, as of 2006, 1.9 – in a much more difficult terrain and inimical environment. Overall contributions increased markedly thereafter, but gave rise to disputes over burden and risk sharing as some members sought, in effect, to distance themselves from NATO's most costly and dangerous mission to date (Yost 2014: 139–145). In the case of Libya, NATO members eventually agreed on a NATO mandate, but roughly half of them did not participate in the operation (Yost 2014: 170–178). What, then, sets the interventions in the Balkans apart from these other military operations?

From a rational-institutionalist viewpoint, international security cooperation in a flexible institutional context is to be explained by the need to cooperate to counter a common threat and, if there is demand, by the higher efficiency of institutionalised cooperation compared with autonomous or ad hoc actions outside of an alliance framework. Yet neither Bosnia-Herzegovina nor Kosovo were of any major strategic interest to NATO as a whole or its most powerful members. After the Cold War, Yugoslavia lost its geopolitical relevance. Nor was there any need to intervene in order to prevent or stop negative security externalities of the civil wars for the NATO members. NATO countries were able to keep the refugee problem to manageable proportions, and they were neither threatened by nor drawn into the wars by any of the participants. In addition, why should cooperation have been weaker in the cases of Afghanistan and Libya? Islamist terrorism has presented a real and proven security threat to the member states of NATO, and the strategic relevance of the Middle East is far higher than that of the Balkans.

From a sociological-institutionalist perspective, the intensity of cooperation varies with the legitimacy of the mission. Military operations that are at the core of NATO's mission seek to protect the identity and values of the liberal international community and are in line with Alliance norms and so elicit high levels of participation and commitment. Thus, military cooperation in NATO is high if the Alliance's liberal–democratic and Euro-Atlantic identity is at stake, that is, if fundamental liberal norms are violated in the home region of the transatlantic community. In the 'ethnic cleansing' of Bosnia-Herzegovina and Kosovo, grave and systematic human rights violations were committed in the middle of Europe. Even in the absence of threats to their own security and geostrategic interest, NATO members felt compelled to intervene.

In Bosnia-Herzegovina, for a long time, the allies initially shied away from the risks and costs of an intervention and could not agree on a common strategy to help. By the summer of 1995, however, it had become clear that low-risk and low-commitment strategies such as humanitarian assistance, peacekeeping, diplomatic mediation efforts, and momentary threats or uses of force were not sufficient to stop human rights violations and end the plight of the Bosnian population. In particular, when Serbian forces overran the UN-protected areas of Srebrenica and Zepa and killed some 7,000 people – while Dutch peacekeeping forces stood by helplessly – Western governments came under strong public criticism and moral pressure to act decisively (Hasenclever 2001: 407–419).

By contrast, in Afghanistan and Libya, operations were targeted at countries outside NATO's transatlantic home region. This fact alone diminished the normative obligation of NATO's member states and the concomitant pull of cooperation. That said, NATO did act in these cases and, in Afghanistan at least, sustained a kinetic operation for over a decade. Normative legitimacy, therefore, did have some effect. The intervention in Afghanistan could be justified as a legitimate act of self-defence against a terrorist organisation that not only rejected the fundamental values and norms of the West, but also was determined to use violence against NATO member states. This explains the strong show of Alliance solidarity after 9/11 and the readiness of NATO members to join the US in fighting Al-Qaida and stabilising Afghanistan. The intervention in Libya, meanwhile, was legitimised by the responsibility to protect the Libyan population (see UN Security Council Resolution 1973). By contrast, the Iraq war of 2003 was not only outside the community region (as were Afghanistan and Libya), but was also not an act of self-defence and initially not motivated by the defence of community values (although it was later increasingly justified as a war to end tyranny and establish democracy in the Middle East). Accordingly, it produced not only weak participation and weak commitments, but also strong disagreement among the NATO allies.

Enlargement

NATO has not only survived the end of the Cold War; it has also expanded its membership from sixteen to twenty-eight states in three enlargement rounds in 1999, 2004, and 2009. In 1999, NATO admitted the Czech Republic, Hungary, and Poland. In 2004, the Baltic states, along with Bulgaria, Romania, Slovakia, and Slovenia, joined the Alliance. Albania and Croatia followed in 2009. Rational and sociological institutionalist theories stipulate different and potentially contradictory conditions for enlargement (Schimmelfennig 2003).

According to rational institutionalism, enlargement is a matter of cost–benefit calculation. Institutions expand their membership if a new member provides net benefits to the institution. The main benefits to an alliance are the contributions the new member makes to overall military and financial capabilities. There are good reasons to admit a new member state if its membership is useful to deter a rival, conduct successful operations, or enhance the alliance's geostrategic power in general. Costs exceed benefits if new members contribute little to alliance power, are likely to entangle the existing members in new conflicts, require high subsidies, and make alliance decisions and coordination more cumbersome.

This logic aside, rationalist institutionalism has severe problems in explaining NATO's post–Cold War enlargement (Schimmelfennig 2003: 40–50). First, there was no need for enlargement in order to balance superior power or external threats. The erstwhile enemy, the Soviet Union and the Warsaw Pact, had dissolved. Through the 1990s and much of the 2000s, the successor states (including Russia) were unable (and mostly unwilling) to match the military power of NATO. Rather, NATO enjoyed a higher degree of security and relative power than at any time before. What is more, given their military and economic weakness, the new CEEC members diluted rather than strengthened the military power and effectiveness of NATO. The new members were relatively poor, and their military forces lagged far behind NATO's. Bringing them up to NATO standards and ensuring interoperability would take a long time and/or require considerable subsidies. Further, NATO risked being entangled in post-Soviet territorial and ethnic minority conflicts. In sum, NATO members as a collective did not reap net benefits from enlargement. In addition to rising transaction and management costs, they incurred force-thinning costs and entrapment risks that were not balanced by the new members' contributions to NATO budgets and programmes and to NATO's military capabilities (Szyana 2001). From a rational-institutionalist point of view, NATO could have reaped the highest benefits from sticking to partnership rather than increasing its membership. As argued earlier, partnership allowed NATO to manage and overcome the uncertainty of the immediate post–Cold War period, exert a stabilising influence on the post-communist region, and cooperate with the countries of the region on an ad hoc basis without extending them a security guarantee, incurring the costs of enlargement, and risking tensions with Russia (Bernauer 1995: 186–187; Walt 1997: 179). This last point is not to be underestimated. It is precisely because NATO has offered Georgia and Ukraine the prospect of membership (via a declaration issued at the Bucharest summit in 2008) that Russia has sought to destabilise both countries (Sakwa 2014: 119).

Rational institutionalism thus fares poorly in accounting for enlargement. What of other institutionalist accounts? According to sociological institutionalism, enlargement decisions follow the membership norms and rules of an international organisation and are not determined by expedient interest-based calculations among the member states. The membership rules of a community organisation create an obligation to grant membership to all states which share or aspire to the collective identity of the community and are committed to their constitutive values and norms, even in the case of net costs to the existing members. If outsider states are recognised as legitimate members of the community on the basis of the values they uphold and the norms they follow, they are entitled to share the rights (but are also obliged to share the duties) of a community member, to participate in the community activities, and to benefit from community solidarity. Conversely, outsider states that do not share the community identity and culture are not admitted as members even if the members expect to reap the material benefits of accession.

NATO documents and statements (as well as those of leading politicians) emphasize the normative conditions and purposes of enlargement, which can be derived from NATO's origins in a liberal–democratic international community. For instance, in its 1995 Study on Enlargement, NATO (1995) declared that enlargement was 'important to protecting the further democratic development of new members'. As US President Clinton emphasized: '[c]ountries with repressive political systems, countries with designs on their neighbors, countries with militaries unchecked by civilian control, or with closed economic systems need not apply' (cited in Schimmelfennig 2003: 92). In the run-up to enlargement in 2004, the George W. Bush administration argued the case for further enlargement on the same identity-based grounds (Schimmelfennig 2003: 255–260). 'Every European nation', Bush declared in 2001, 'that struggles toward democracy and free markets and a strong civic culture must be welcomed into Europe's home'. On this basis, NATO membership, he suggested, was a possibility for 'all of Europe's democracies that seek it' (cited in Moore 2007: 76).

NATO's community values and norms not only provided a general rationale for eastern enlargement, but also help to explain the selection of countries for membership. According to these norms, NATO should only have admitted countries that were well advanced in the process of democratic consolidation and peaceful conflict management with their neighbours, and it should admit the forerunners of democratic consolidation ahead of the laggards. This is roughly what happened. The first three new members – the Czech Republic, Hungary, and Poland – were the forerunners and paragons of liberalisation and democratisation in the region in the 1990s. Moreover, none of them was engaged in major territorial and ethnic conflicts with their neighbours or in major domestic ethnic conflicts. The countries admitted in the second round in 2004 had a better democracy record and a longer period of peace and domestic stability than the remaining countries in the MAP (Albania, Croatia, Macedonia) (see Schimmelfennig 2003: 255–260).

As with persistence and flexibilisation, enlargement is not a case of organisational advocacy or routine. It has been driven by individual member states and accompanied by disagreements among them. When the CEEC governments first expressed an interest in joining NATO in the course of 1991, they were confronted with general reticence among the then allies. In 1993, a few policy entrepreneurs within allied governments – most notably US National Security Adviser Anthony Lake and German Defense Minister Volker Rühle – began to advocate the expansion of NATO against an overwhelming majority of member countries and even strong opposition within their own governments. It took until the end of 1994 to make enlargement official NATO policy (Goldgeier 1999). Enlargement was not a top-down policy of the NATO bureaucracy, but depended crucially on the entrepreneurship of government officials and, later, the advocacy of the Clinton administration.

Their case was helped by the community values and norms enshrined in NATO's treaty rules. The governments of aspirant members and the advocates of enlargement within NATO successfully portrayed the CEECs as traditional members of the Euro-Atlantic community now 'returning to Europe' and to liberal democracy. At the same time, they stressed the instability of democratic achievements in the region and framed NATO as a democratic community rather than a military alliance. Enlargement was thus an issue of democracy promotion and protection rather than one of military necessity or efficiency. On this basis, the advocates of enlargement could argue that NATO's liberal values and norms obliged the member states to stabilise democracy and, to that end, to grant the CEECs membership in the Alliance (Schimmelfennig 2003: 230–235). This type of argument has appeared less and less prominent as enlargement proceeds. Although a powerful narrative in 1999 and 2004, its significance has since diminished. That said, the case for Albanian and Croatian entry in 2009 was facilitated by a claim that both these states had made significant democratic progress in a particularly challenging corner of Europe (Pacukaj 2013; Vukadinovic 2010).

Conclusions

This chapter has introduced and applied institutionalist accounts of NATO. Whereas institutionalist theories agree that NATO is best analyzed as an international institution that stabilises cooperation among its member states, they offer different assumptions on what motivates states to establish institutions, how they generate and sustain international cooperation, how they are designed, how they adapt to changes in their environment, and how capable they are of pursuing their organisational self-interest and of decoupling themselves from external requirements.

We can draw a number of conclusions as to the empirical fit of institutionalist theories and what this tells us about NATO. First, institutionalist analyses focus on the allies as the major actors in NATO and as the masters of the organisation. Its members have decided to maintain NATO after the end of the Cold War and to transform the Alliance to make it fit for the new security environment. Both enlargement and NATO's interventions have been initiatives of the allies. There is no evidence that the NATO bureaucracy has had a major role in these developments or has pressed ahead with initiatives over and above what its members preferred. Institutionalist theories emphasizing organisational power and bureaucratic politics do not seem to be relevant for explaining the transformation of NATO (cf. Deni 2007).

NATO's role as an institution can, therefore, be usefully described as instrumental. It is an established set of informal and formal rules and procedures that encourages, facilitates, stabilises, and channels cooperation among the member states. According to rational institutionalism, NATO provides a variety of institutional assets that have continued to be useful for the member states and which have proven sufficiently adaptable to respond to an evolving security environment. According to sociological institutionalism, meanwhile, NATO continues to serve as the main security organisation of the Western liberal international community and has successfully inducted many former adversaries into the values and norms of that community (up to the point of admitting them as new members) through its instruments and procedures of socialisation, partnership, and enlargement.

NATO's environment has changed from one in which it confronts a direct, clearly identifiable, and common military and ideological threat (as in the Cold War) to one characterised by varied, diffuse, and out-of-area security challenges –giving rise to diverse member-state security concerns, threat perceptions, and policy preferences. This change, now of over two decades' duration, is reflected in the flexibilisation of NATO. By definition, flexibilisation weakens the formal institutional constraints on the member states. The most far-reaching and consensual post–Cold War commitments of NATO – enlargement and the large-scale intervention and peacekeeping operations in Bosnia-Herzegovina and Kosovo – have therefore relied on the informal power of the identity and norms of a liberal community. This community identity has proven to be the deep foundation of the Alliance.

Notes

1   For the sake of concision, 'sociological institutionalism' is the term preferred throughout this chapter.
2   Often, historical institutionalism is treated as a third variety of institutionalism (see Hall and Taylor 1996).
3   In so doing, the chapter draws on previous work published by Schimmelfennig (2003, 2007).
4   See also Deni's explanation of the restructuring of NATO's forces as an outcome of political bargaining among member states rather than organisational behavior (Deni 2007).

References

[All web sources listed were last accessed 12 June 2015.]

Abbott, K. W. and Snidal, D. (1998). 'Why States Act Through Formal International Organisations', *Journal of Conflict Resolution*, 42(1): 3–32.
Barany, Z. and Rauchhaus, R. (2011), 'Explaining NATO's Resilience: Is International Relations Theory Useful?', *Contemporary Security Policy*, 32(2): 286–307.
Barnett, M. N. and Finnemore, M. (1999). 'The Politics, Power, and Pathologies of International Organisations', *International Organisation*, 53(4): 699–732.
Barnett, M. N. and Finnemore, M. (2004). *Rules for the World: International Organisations in Global Politics*, Ithaca: Cornell University Press.
Bernauer, T. (1995). 'Full Membership or Full Club? Expansion of NATO and the Future Security Organisation of Europe', in Schneider, G. Weitsman, P.A. and Bernauer, T. (eds). *Towards a New Europe: Stops and Starts in Regional Integration*, Westport: Praeger.
Clemens, E. S. and Cook, J. M. (1999). 'Politics and Institutionalism: Explaining Durability and Change', *Annual Review of Sociology*, 25: 441–466.
Daalder, I. H. and O'Hanlon, M. E. (2000), *Winning Ugly: NATO's War to Save Kosovo*, Washington D.C.: The Brookings Institution.

Deni, J. R. (2007). *Alliance Management and Maintenance: Restructuring NATO for the 21st Century*. Aldershot: Ashgate.

Deudney, D. and Ikenberry, G. J. (1999). 'The Nature and Sources of Liberal International Order', *Review of International Studies*, 25(2): 179–196.

Duffield, J. S. (1994). 'NATO's Functions after the Cold War', *Political Science Quarterly*, 109(5): 763–787.

Downs, G. W., Rocke, D. M. and Barsoom, P. N. (1998). 'Managing the Evolution of Multilateralism', *International Organisation*, 52(2): 397–419.

Gheciu, A. (2005). *NATO in the "New Europe": The Politics of International Socialization after the Cold War*, Stanford: Stanford University Press.

Goldgeier, J. M. (1999). *Not Whether But When: The US Decision to Enlarge NATO*, Washington, D.C.: Brookings Institution Press.

Hall, P. A. and Taylor, R.C.R. (1996). 'Political Science and the Three New Institutionalisms', *Political Studies*, 44(5): 936–957.

Hasenclever, A. (2001) *Die Macht der Moral in der internationalen Politik. Militärische Interventionen westlicher Staaten in Somalia, Ruanda und Bosnien- Herzegowina*, Frankfurt: Campus 2001.

Hellmann, G. and Wolf, R. (1993). 'Neorealism, Neoliberal Institutionalism, and the Future of NATO', *Security Studies* 3(1), 3–43.

Huth, P. (1988). *Extended Deterrence and the Prevention of War*, New Haven: Yale University Press.

Kagan, R. (2003). *Of Paradise and Power: America and Europe in the New World Order*, New York: Knopf.

Keohane, R.O. (1984), *After Hegemony: Cooperation and Discord in the World Political Economy*, Princeton: Princeton University Press.

Keohane, R. O. (1988). 'International Institutions: Two Approaches', *International Studies Quarterly*, 32(4): 379–396.

Koremenos, B., Lipson, C. and Snidal, D. (2001). 'The Rational Design of International Institutions', *International Organisation*, 55(4): 761–799.

Kydd, A. (2001). 'Trust Building, Trust Breaking: The Dilemma of NATO Enlargement', *International Organisation*, 55(4): 801–828.

Lebow, R. N. and Stein, J. G. (1990). 'Deterrence: The Elusive Dependent Variable', *World Politics*, 42(3): 336–369.

March, J. G. and Olsen, J. P. (1989). *Rediscovering Institutions: The Organizational Basis of Politics*, New York: Free Press.

March, J. G. and Olsen, J. P. (1998). 'The Institutional Dynamics of International Political Orders', *International Organisation*, 52(4): 943–969.

McCalla, R. B. (1996). 'NATO's Persistence after the Cold War', *International Organisation*, 50(3): 445–475.

McNeely, C. L. (1995). *Constructing the Nation-State: International Organisation and Prescriptive Action*, Westport: Greenwood Press.

Mearsheimer, J. J. (1990). 'Back to the Future: Instability in Europe After the Cold War. *International Security*, 15(1): 5–56.

Meyer, J. W. and Rowan, B. (1977). 'Institutionalised Organisations Formal Structure as Myth and Ceremony', *American Journal of Sociology*, 83(2): 340–363.

Moore, R. (2007). *NATO's New Mission: Projecting Stability in a Post-Cold War World*, Westport: Praeger.

Moravcsik, A. (1998). *The Choice for Europe: Social Purpose and State Power from Messina to Maastricht*, Ithaca: Cornell University Press.

NATO. (1949). 'The North Atlantic Treaty', at: www.nato.int/docu/basictxt/treaty.htm.

NATO. (1995). 'Study on NATO Enlargement', 3 September, at: www.nato.int/cps/en/natolive/official_texts_24733.htm.

NATO. (2010). 'Active Engagement, Modern Defence. Strategic Concept for the Defence and Security of the North Atlantic Treaty Organisation' 19 November, at: www.nato.int/cps/en/natolive/official_texts_68580.htm.

NATO. (2014). 'Wales Summit Declaration', NATO Press Release (2014) 120, 5 September at: www.nato.int/cps/en/natohq/official_texts_112964.htm.

NATO. (2015). 'NATO Response Force', at: www.nato.int/cps/en/natolive/topics_49755.htm.

Pacukaj, S. (2013). 'NATO Enlargement and Albania's Path towards the Atlantic Alliance', *Academic Journal of Interdisciplinary Studies*, 2(2): 423–428.

Park, W. (1986). *Defending the West: A History of NATO*, Brighton: Wheatsheaf Books.

Pierson, P. (1996). 'The Path to European Integration: A Historical Institutionalist Analysis', *Comparative Political Studies*, 29(2): 123–163.

Reus-Smit, C. (1997). 'The Constitutional Structure of International Society and the Nature of Fundamental Institutions', *International Organisation*, 51(4): 555–589.

Risse-Kappen, T. (1995). *Cooperation among Democracies: The European Influence on US Foreign Policy*, Princeton: Princeton University Press.

Risse-Kappen, T. (1996). 'Collective Identity in a Democratic Community: The Case of NATO', in Katzenstein, P. J. (ed), *The Culture of National Security: Norms and Identity in World Politics*, New York: Columbia University Press.

Schimmelfennig, F. (2002). 'Liberal Community and Enlargement: An Event History Analysis, *Journal of European Public Policy*, 9(4): 598–626.

Schimmelfennig, F. (2003). *The EU, NATO and the Integration of Europe: Rules and Rhetoric*, Cambridge: Cambridge University Press.

Schimmelfennig, F. (2007). 'Functional Form, Identity-Driven Cooperation: Institutional Designs and Effects in Post-Cold War NATO', in Acharya, A. and Johnston, A. I. (eds). *Crafting Cooperation: Regional International Institutions in Comparative Perspective*, Cambridge: Cambridge University Press.

Schweickert, R., Melnykovska, I., Belke, A. and Bordon, I. (2011). 'Prospective NATO or EU Membership and Institutional Change in Transition Countries', *Economics of Transition*, 19(4): 667–692.

Schweller, R. L. (1994). 'Bandwagoning for Profit: Bringing the Revisionist State Back In', *International Security*, 19(1): 72–107.

Scott, W. R. (1991). 'Unpacking Institutional Arguments', in Powell, W. W. and DiMaggio, P. J. (eds). *The New Institutionalism in Organisational Analysis*, Chicago: University of Chicago Press.

Sakwa, R. (2014). *Frontline Ukraine: Crisis in the Borderlands*, London: I. B Tauris.

Siverson, R. M. and Emmons, J. (1991). 'Birds of a Feather: Democratic Politics and Alliance Choices in the Twentieth Century.' *Journal of Conflict Resolution*, 35(2): 285–306.

Snyder, G. H. (1984). 'The Security Dilemma in Alliance Politics', *World Politics*, 36(4): 461–495.

Szyana, T. (2001). *NATO Enlargement, 2000–2015: Determinants and Implications for Defence Planning and Shaping*, Santa Monica: RAND Corporation.

Thies, W. J. (2003). *Friendly Rivals: Bargaining and Burden-Shifting in NATO*, Armonk: M. E. Sharpe.

Thies, W. J. (2009). *Why NATO Endures*, Cambridge: Cambridge University Press.

Vukadinovic, L. C. (2010). 'Croatia', in Bebler, A. (ed). *NATO at 60*, Amsterdam: IOS Press.

Wallander, C.A. (2000). 'Institutional Assets and Adaptability: NATO after the Cold War', *International Organisation*, 54(4): 705–735.

Walt, S.M. (1987). *The Origins of Alliances*, Ithaca: Cornell University Press.

Walt, S.M. (1997). 'Why Alliances Endure or Collapse', *Survival*, 39(1): 156–179.

Waltz, K.N. (1979) *Theory of International Politics*, New York: Random House.

Waltz, K.N. (1993). 'The Emerging Structure of International Politics', *International Security*, 18(2): 44–79.

Webber, M. (2013). 'NATO after 9/11: Theoretical Perspectives', in Hallams, E., Ratti, L. and Zyla, B. (eds). *NATO beyond 9/11: The Transformation of the Atlantic Alliance*, Houndmills, Basingstoke: Palgrave.

Weitsman, P.A. (2004). *Dangerous Alliances: Proponents of Peace, Weapons of War*. Stanford: Stanford University Press.

Wendt, A. (1999). *Social Theory of International Politics*, Cambridge: Cambridge University Press.

Williams, M. J. (2013). 'Enduring, but Irrelevant? Britain, NATO and the Future of the Atlantic Alliance', *International Politics*, 50(3): 360–386.

Yost, D. (2014). *NATO's Balancing Act*, Washington D.C.: United States Institute of Peace Press.

6 NATO and liberal International Relations theory

Benjamin Pohl

Introduction

The end of the Cold War led many analysts to assume that NATO had become an anachronism. Absent an outside threat to provide for internal cohesion, some scholars even predicted that Europe might slip 'back to the future' with major power competition spreading instability across the continent (Mearsheimer 1990). Yet instead, the European security architecture has experienced further integration. NATO has proven able to reinvent itself, repeatedly acting as the institutional framework of choice for Western led crisis-management operations. Under the slogan of 'out of area or out of business' (Senator Richard Lugar, cited in Barry 1997: 204), the Alliance first intervened in the succession wars of Yugoslavia and later beyond the European continent, in Afghanistan and Libya. NATO has also pursued long-term maritime missions in the Mediterranean and off the Horn of Africa/Gulf of Aden (Yost 2014: 123–199). This transformation poses a puzzle. NATO's Cold War purpose of deterrence and collective defence had been rather straightforward and usually explained by reference to the need to balance against the Soviet Union and its Warsaw Pact allies. Thus, NATO served as a fine example of the neo-realist claim that considerations of balance of threat or power provided the primary driver behind international politics (Walt 1987; Waltz 1979). Given that the balancing logic evaporated with the removal of the Soviet threat, why then has NATO persisted?

To answer that question, this chapter puts forward a liberal framework for explaining NATO's recent development. It builds on Andrew Moravcsik's (2008) 'new liberalism' insofar as it focuses on the nexus between governments and the societies they represent. New liberalism shares realism's focus on 'national interests' as formulated by governments, but treats them not as a consequence of states' relative power position in the international system, but of their respective societies' preferences. At the same time, this liberalism is on the rationalist side of the debate in International Relations (IR) theory, and so assumes that governments primarily follow a consequentialist logic rather than one of (normative) appropriateness. The argument here is not that a liberal framework is more attuned than its theoretical alternatives in analyzing international relations as such, but rather that it has significant analytical leverage when it comes to contemporary Western foreign policy in general and the operation of NATO in particular. This chapter asserts that foreign policy is a function of governmental interests. Absent a direct existential threat, these interests will be strongly influenced by domestic political concerns as governments treat foreign policy as subordinate to the objective of staying in power.[1] NATO's member governments will, therefore, determine their positioning within the Alliance according to (perceived) domestic political exigencies. This has consequences for what NATO does and can do, and by extension, for what it is and can be.

The objective of this chapter is twofold: first, it seeks to provide a theory-driven explanation that links NATO's functions to governmental interests as defined by domestic politics. Although usually acknowledged to play some part in foreign policy making, domestic politics is arguably the most important omitted structural explanation in IR theory (Moravcsik 1997: 538–541).[2] Second, it addresses the questions of what and who NATO is for by making the case for re-evaluating the drivers behind the Alliance's interventions of the last twenty years. What I seek to show here is that NATO's operations can be plausibly portrayed as a response to varying domestic expectations about the objectives and limitations of foreign policy. This analytical framework can explain both the substantial cooperation within NATO and the substantial cleavages which divide it.

On this basis, the chapter proceeds as follows. The next section will summarise the main tenets of the 'new liberalism' in IR theory and distinguish it from competing approaches. It then applies these tenets to NATO (and specifically to the crisis management operations that have dominated the organisation's agenda) in order to demonstrate that the functions and actions of the Alliance are a consequence of the interaction of the preferences of its principals. The chapter then looks at the implications of this assumption for the future development of NATO. It concludes with some theoretical reflections.

New liberalism in IR theory

In explaining international politics, many IR theorists are reluctant to acknowledge the domestic level as being anything other than an intervening variable (Moravcsik 1997, 2000; Walt 1998: 34). Such a position is justified insofar as foreign policy behaviour is regarded, first and foremost, as a response to international crises and the interrelationships between various powers. Yet such crises, and the variety of policies they may trigger, are often (also) a function of domestic politics (Moravcsik 2008: 239–240). Strangely, the theoretical analysis of foreign policy to date still suffers from an 'omitted theory bias' in this respect (Moravcsik 1997: 538–541). This, in turn, is both a consequence of and a reason for the continuing conflation of national and governmental interests in much of the literature on international politics. However, if we assume that governments have an interest in securing the survival and welfare of their states, it would be logical to assume that they have a similar interest in securing their own survival and welfare, that is, in maintaining themselves in office (Bueno de Mesquita et al 2005). Consequently, we need to allow for the possibility that governments may attempt to use foreign policy not only for the first, but also for the second purpose. This does not imply that national and governmental interests necessarily conflict, but we cannot simply assume that a self-interested, rational government will pursue the national interest, unless, that is, we embrace some very idealistic assumptions.

For this reason, the present chapter puts governmental, not national, interests at the centre of its analysis and submits that these interests might be driven more by domestic than by international constraints and opportunities.[3] Support for governments will partly depend on the perceived legitimacy and competence with which they handle foreign affairs. Even if foreign policy is not particularly salient in citizens' electoral choices, the desire to please rather than irritate voters will inform policy making. This position is consistent with Moravcsik's 'new liberalism', according to which 'the foreign policy goals of national governments are viewed as varying in response to shifting pressure from domestic social groups, whose preferences are aggregated through political institutions' (Moravcsik 1993: 481; Moravcsik 2008). It implies that the fundamental purpose of foreign policy is not predetermined, but depends on the intensity of preferences of influential groups in society.

So what are the national preferences that direct foreign policy? According to liberal theory, these may be derived from both material and ideational interests. On the one hand, Western societies expect their governments to shape an international environment that is conducive to the values of domestic order, that is, liberal democracy (Owen 2002: 402; Schimmelfennig 2004: 4). On the other, these societies also expect that their own material interests in terms of security and welfare are taken into account, and that governments show competence in handling potential threats at the smallest possible price in blood or treasure. When it comes to military interventions, Lawrence Freedman (2000: 337–339) has described these two aspects as requiring government to weigh the 'CNN effect' against the 'bodybags effect'. Since both the necessity for particular foreign policy projects and their legitimacy relative to domestic norms varies cross-nationally, so, too, the national preferences that governments represent will likely differ.

This begs the question of how governments decide on their foreign policy positions. The mechanism which ensures that governments are taking societal preferences into account is two-pronged (Doyle 2008: 61). First, there is an incentive for governments to 'do something' in response to mediatised events (Robinson 2001). Direct public pressure will drive governments' foreign policy behaviour only in cases that capture headlines, although, as Lawrence Freedman pointed out, the 'CNN' and 'bodybags' effects 'may have come to grow in importance through anticipation' (Freedman 2000: 339). This anticipation effect is partly due to the fact that '[p]oliticians are motivated primarily by the desire to avoid blame' (Weaver 1986: 371). Moreover, even the absence of public pressure for action does not necessarily imply the absence of political opportunity. David Chandler (2003: 295) has pointedly argued that '[e]thical foreign policy is ideally suited to buttressing the moral authority of governments [. . .] because policy-makers are less accountable for matching ambitious policy aims with final policy outcomes in the international sphere'. In other words, because governments' self-interest relates to approval from domestic constituencies, it lies foremost in being seen to act ethically.

Critics may object that contemporary Western foreign policy is more than just a public relations exercise, which brings us to the second route by which foreign policy positions are derived. Overt foreign policy populism carries significant risks because government policy is, apart from the public at large, also monitored by foreign policy elites in political parties, the media, non-governmental organisations, bureaucracies and academia. Inasmuch as their opinion on the government's foreign policy record confers domestic legitimacy, these groups serve as transmission belts between governments and public opinion at large. Governments, therefore, have an incentive to ensure that their foreign policy is judged as competent and legitimate in the eyes of this 'expert' constituency.

This dual mechanism – broad public as well as elite support – however, does not mean that governments blindly follow public opinion. The relationship between governments and public opinion is both circular and deliberate (Power 2002: 509). It is circular insofar as governments follow popular sentiment, expecting publics to reciprocate in the form of positive feedback. It is deliberate in the sense that government is required on occasion to lead (not follow) opinion where there is uncertainty or controversy. Governments may thus act *against* public opinion, provided they expect such action to provide the best available pay-off in the longer run. As Richard Eichenberg (2005) argues with respect to US military interventions and Ebru Canan-Sokullu (2012) confirms for the major EU powers, 'victory has many friends'. The perceived risks of any foreign policy venture in terms of the likelihood of and price for visible success or failure will therefore shape governments' positioning on particular issues.

A focus on societal demands is not to suggest that governments are always able to achieve their foreign policy goals in accordance with idiosyncratic national preferences. Governments are, after all, significantly constrained in their behaviour by the interdependence of state preferences (Moravcsik 1997: 523). Interdependence first arises with respect to the object of foreign policy: as multiple attempts throughout history show, it is simply difficult to influence foreigners (Cooper 2004: 113–127). Yet nowhere is interdependence more palpable than in the case of multilateral foreign policy cooperation such as in NATO, where consensus between all members on whether and how to attempt to exert influence is a prerequisite to interaction with target countries. The foreign policy output of such an institution is usually not the average of governmental preferences. Liberalism instead assumes that the relative intensity of national preferences will be decisive in determining collective policy. '[T]he binding constraint' in this connection 'is generally "resolve" or "determination" – the *willingness* of governments to mobilize and expend social resources for foreign policy purposes' – rather than, that is, the availability of capabilities that realists emphasize (Moravcsik 1997: 524; emphasis original). This is not to say that availability does not matter – willingness is not of much use if social resources are insufficient for the purposes sought. However, many foreign policy decisions are not about the mobilisation of all resources: 'weaker' actors frequently carry the day because they care more intensely about the outcome. And even where the relative availability of capabilities does prove decisive, it is because there is a domestic political decision to comprehensively mobilise them.

By contrast, realist analysis would expect NATO to primarily serve the purpose of maximising member states' relative power and security, implying that the Alliance action serves to increase the relative power of its members. Constructivism, meanwhile, might expect NATO to be driven by a need to implement the international community's normative duties, for instance, the responsibility to protect vulnerable foreigners. Clearly, the treatment of these alternative explanations is somewhat stereotypical here. Given the lack of space, however, they cannot but serve as contrasting backdrops against which I explain the merits of the concept of governmental interests for understanding NATO's record.

Applying liberalism to NATO

To gauge the utility of liberalism in analyzing NATO, we need to consider first what precisely it is that we wish to explain. This chapter argues that 'what NATO is' can best be examined by looking at 'what NATO is for', the purpose that the organisation fulfils for its principals. That position is based on the assumption that international institutions are rationally designed, an assumption evidenced by the persistence with which states continue to invest resources in institutions in general, and in NATO specifically (Koremenos et al 2001: 767). Although NATO's purpose has been subject to considerable debate since the end of the Cold War, Richard Betts's (2009: 1) recent categorisation of the three 'faces' of the Alliance is a useful starting point. 'The first persona is the "enforcer", the pacifier of conflicts beyond the region's borders; the second is the gentlemen's club for liberal and liberalizing countries of the West; and the third is the residual function of an anti-Russia alliance'. How would a liberal framework explain these three functions?

Let us start with what is arguably the least consequential of these three faces: NATO's function as a club of liberal and liberalising countries. That function easily fits the liberal argument because one basic assumption of liberalism is that 'social actors provide support to the government in exchange for institutions that accord with their identity-based preferences; such institutions are thereby "legitimate"' (Moravcsik 1997: 525). To the extent that societies in both old and new NATO member states are committed to upholding liberal order, an institution that ensures that these values are locked into neighbouring countries is likely to add to each government's legitimacy.

Yet NATO's identity as a liberal club can also be brought into accordance with neo-realism and social constructivism. For realists, the West's extension of its domestic order (for instance, through NATO enlargement) can be interpreted as a means of control and power maximisation. Although such a strategy cannot be deduced from realist premises (which suggest that regime type is of secondary importance at most), the stabilisation of liberal regimes in Eastern Europe can be seen to increase overall US power. The foreign policy behaviour of the newly admitted NATO members, further, largely fits this conjecture. The reason for their support of US foreign policy priorities lies in the expectation that a resultant strengthening of ties to Washington will, in turn, be rewarded with a stronger US commitment to their protection from Russia (Ringsmose 2013). Yet the question why societies in Central and Eastern Europe should feel threatened by Russia rather than the much more powerful US (or Western Europe) brings us back to something neo-realism cannot explain – the Kantian peace between democracies, irrespective of their relative power (Levy and Thomson 2010: 104–117).

For constructivists, NATO's identity as a liberal club is much less of a problem to explain. It is a function of shared values and norms that have eventually resulted in a transatlantic 'security community' (Deutsch et al 1957; Risse-Kappen 1996). This constructivist argument draws on an older liberal tradition with respect to the way that shared norms contribute to community (Moravcsik 1997: 525), but constructivism has enriched that argument by investigating how this community and its institutions in turn affect members' preferences (Gheciu 2005; Schimmelfennig 2004). At the same time, such preference shifts were arguably only possible because societies identified with these liberal norms and appropriated them. This is an important caveat in that it explains why some, but by no means all, norms are shared. In fact, as will be discussed later, there are distinctively different brands of liberalism within the transatlantic alliance.

With liberal democracy largely consolidated across NATO members, the 'face' of NATO as a club of liberal or liberalising countries these days serves mainly as a stage for the other two identities: a platform for out-of-area operations and for deterrence against interference by Russia. Thus, although the 'liberal club' is reconcilable with all three theoretical frameworks, it constitutes a generic face of NATO that is relatively indeterminate. Its theoretical importance and further development depend on the drivers that underpin the Alliance's actions in both the defensive and offensive realms to which we now turn.

The most familiar face of NATO is the anti-Russian alliance – the ultimate guarantee against violent interference in the current European order. This function would appear to be a hard case for liberalism, suggesting as it does that 'balance of power' politics still drives at least one aspect of the Alliance. However, as Betts (2009: 3) points out, NATO's anti-Russian function has been an unintended side effect of NATO expansion, driven by the desire to pursue a liberal world order. The exclusion of Russia was arguably not premeditated but largely self-inflicted. A high-ranking member of the Clinton administration claimed that Russian membership in NATO was seriously considered (Webber et al 2004: 13). Moreover, the West repeatedly attempted to draw Russia into cooperative security endeavours through the NATO-Russia Council, as well as multiple offers to cooperate on crisis management operations. Realists might retort that intentions are less important than outcomes (Morgenthau 1973: 6). However, the resulting regional order in Europe is one of imbalance, where Russia faces a far stronger Western alliance. The lack of movement towards more balance, combined with the fact that all liberal democracies find themselves on one side, suggests again that regime type and trans-societal allegiances trump considerations of relative power.

This is not to imply that there is no balancing behaviour present in the relationship between NATO and Russia. Some of the new NATO members have at times treated the Alliance as an enabler for them to use anti-Russian rhetoric. Moreover, Russia's behaviour provides evidence (as is clear from the Crimean and Ukraine crises) that balancing against the US is not per se out of the question. Both cases, however, suggest that the sources and expected benefits of such behaviour are domestic. Some governments in Central and Eastern Europe, notably in Poland and Estonia, have used Russia bashing for domestic purposes. For the Russian government, great power grandstanding arguably serves as a substitute for all the other public goods it cannot (and does not feel inclined to) provide at home. Yet constructivists could also account for this behaviour by drawing on identity politics (Hopf 2002). So whereas a liberal approach again fares well, an explanation of NATO's Russia dimension is also possible through liberalism's theoretical alternatives.

This brings us to NATO's third identity: that of the out-of-area pacifier. Because this has been the most important persona of the Alliance, it is examined here in some detail. Liberalism suggests that external interventions can be traced to domestically derived governmental interests. As the next section will show, this is indeed visible across all three pivotal interventions that NATO has undertaken over the last twenty years: in the Balkans, in Afghanistan and in Libya. The following summary cannot do full justice to the full historical evidence on decision making in NATO capitals in these cases. In focusing on the domestic political dimension of decision making, it instead serves to illustrate how much domestic political calculations mattered, and thereby to underscore the plausibility of the liberal argument.[4]

Domestic politics and NATO interventions

Bosnia

Throughout the 1990s, the disintegration of Yugoslavia and the attendant ethnic cleansing presented formidable challenges to Western foreign policy makers. Despite their overwhelming power, seeming commitment to liberal values and professed interest in ending these wars, both Washington and European capitals repeatedly failed to achieve a coherent policy response. Instead, they manifested what one observer (Gow 1997) labelled a 'triumph of the lack of will'. NATO eventually intervened in Bosnia in 1995 and sought to impose a liberal peace based on democratic and multi-ethnic governance structures. Yet neither motives nor outcomes suggest a decisive role for geostrategic or normative drivers. Rather, Western governments were preoccupied with securing their own interests in balancing domestic demands for doing something about ethnic cleansing against their publics' ambivalent support for decisive military action.

Originally, most Western governments were concerned at becoming overly engaged in Bosnia. Anxious about the upcoming 1992 elections, the US administration of George H. W. Bush 'was content to accept the strangely possessive argument of EEC leaders who had claimed from the start of the Yugoslav war that this was "a European problem" ' (Malcolm 1996: 240). The Clinton administration which followed dithered on its Bosnia policy for a long time, torn between the moral impetus and domestic pressure to 'do something' and a wariness of becoming involved militarily (Power 2002: 293–327). Although 'Clinton had campaigned vociferously in support of greater US engagement in Bosnia', one adviser recalled, 'the Clinton administration failed to back its forceful campaign rhetoric with concrete action' once in power (Daalder 2000: 6–7; see also Rathbun 2004: 208). When Washington eventually decided to use force, it was with a view to the upcoming 1996 presidential election: the administration feared that if unresolved or worsening during the election year, the Bosnian crisis might be a liability that could destroy Clinton's foreign policy credibility (Daalder 2000: 93, 99, 109, 163; Power 2002: 436–437).

Concern over domestic politics was also reflected in the single-year mandate that was extended to Implementation Force (IFOR), the NATO force sent to guarantee the implementation of the Bosnian peace accords. As an administration official (Daalder 2000: 144) summed up, '[t]he debate about IFOR's role was driven to a considerable extent by political considerations of what the Congress and the public were likely to support a year before presidential elections'. Moral and strategic considerations were not entirely absent in America's Bosnia policy. However, the long vacillation, combined with the timing of the policy switch and the politics surrounding implementation, indicate that domestic political considerations were pivotal in determining Washington's shifting position.

A similar logic applied on the other side of the Atlantic. The European community, after an early and precocious declaration that 'the hour of Europe' had come, failed to get a grip on the crisis (Duke 2000: 213, 221–223). The perceived need for action led NATO's foremost European military powers, France and the UK, to participate in the weakly mandated UN force in Bosnia. United Nations Protection Force (UNPROFOR) visibly failed to stop the violence and was repeatedly humiliated by Serb militias. The Western powers' continued participation in a clearly failing operation does not make sense had they been fully committed to either maximising power or to protecting strangers. British and French commitment was instead conditioned by domestic sensitivities: the desire to live up to national self-conceptions as important powers and defenders of human rights, but coupled with an aversion to actually defend Bosnians lest this risky step backfire politically at home. In France, the centre-right government thus sought to use its engagement in Bosnia primarily as a means to demonstrate France's international standing and liberal vocation (Rathbun 2004: 136–137). The Conservative government in the UK, meanwhile, faced considerable intra-party opposition to enhanced engagement. This resulted in lack of resolve and, in turn, encouraged local militias to frustrate the purposes of British peacekeepers (Rathbun 2004: 47, 57–61). The irony here is that it was the supposedly national interest-oriented Tory party that had undermined Britain's armed forces by forcing them to accept multiple humiliations from an adversary it could easily have beaten back given the necessary political will. Germany, too, displayed vacillation. Although it was the Western power most affected by Bosnian refugees, the German government opted out of any military involvement because of domestic political constraints. James Gow (1997: 306) summed up the motivations in Western capitals regarding the war in Bosnia thus: '[t]he political worries of Western governments concerned popular opinion and the need to win votes at the next election'.

Kosovo

The intervention in Kosovo followed a similar logic, even if it played out differently in light of the Bosnian experience. Because their lack of decisiveness over Bosnia had exposed Western governments to the charge of moral weakness, the balance of political risk shifted such that avoiding blame for passivity partly outweighed the risk of becoming embroiled in some far-away conflict (Roberts 1999: 104; Freedman 2000). Yet this impetus was still insufficient to ensure a full commitment, and so Western governments' signalling of operational limitations once again undermined their foreign policy objectives even amidst a seemingly decisive air campaign (Operation Allied Force). As two close observers pointed out shortly after the conflict, 'the Clinton administration resorted to speaking loudly and carrying a small stick', and NATO similarly 'had a hope, but not a plan' (Daalder and O'Hanlon 2000: 17–18). In particular, 'due to Washington's preference to avoid casualties at nearly any cost', the use of ground troops was explicitly excluded until well into the air campaign. This policy, in turn, was the consequence of a Republican-dominated Congress that had threatened to cut off funding to the US-led air operation (Rathbun 2004: 211).

In Europe, domestic political considerations also played an important role. In the UK, the new Labour government had promised an 'ethical dimension' to its foreign policy. Whereas many analysts have credited Tony Blair's personal sense of mission for his hawkish position over Kosovo, this explanation is somewhat at odds with the fact that Blair had not been among the sizable group of Labour MPs who had earlier attempted to push the previous Conservative government into a more proactive stance regarding Bosnia (Daddow 2009: 550). Once in power, the Labour Party, however, had important reasons to overcome a perceived weakness on defence (Phythian 2010: 192–193). Moreover, as David Chandler (2003: 302) has pointed out, Blair's ' "moral mission" in the international sphere [was] crucial to enhancing his domestic standing'.

To take another example, if domestic political calculations shaped Western governments' decision making, why did Berlin decide to participate in the Kosovo war? After all, Germany's newly elected centre-left government risked a parliamentary vote of confidence on this intervention. Yet opposing the US and NATO would arguably have presented a bigger domestic liability. As one observer wrote, 'not to have participated in the NATO action would have fatally undermined the international position of the new government, precipitating a major political crisis' (Hyde-Price 2001: 21). In this respect, it is important to note that '[t]he first important domestic political consequence of the war was to improve the political reputation of the Chancellor' as well as other members of the government

(Hyde-Price 2001: 24). Similar to calculations in the UK, the Kosovo war also offered an opportunity to the incoming German government to claim the political centre, especially given that a majority of public opinion supported Germany's participation in the war (Baumann and Hellmann 2001: 77).

Domestic consequences in these different cases thus help explain the nature of support for intervention in both Bosnia and Kosovo. By contrast, realists might argue that policy in the former Yugoslavia is best accounted for by power politics. US behaviour, at least, could be explained by reference to offensive realism's claim that states always seek to maximise power. Yet the proposition that the Bosnian and Kosovan interventions were strategically driven is rather dubious. James Baker's (in)famous argument for dismissing American action at the outbreak of the Bosnian crisis because 'we got no dog in this fight' (cited in Danner 1997) suggests as much – as do the subsequent years of inaction. Why the US would later invest so heavily in a region of relatively limited geostrategic importance where European powers (if anyone) would be the major beneficiary of stability also seems to defy the logic of relative gains. The fact that Western governments repeatedly undermined their foreign policy objectives to pander to domestic sensibilities also suggests a preoccupation with governmental rather than national interest. At the same time, and with respect to alternative explanations based upon normative duties, the wavering policies of Western governments suggest that the duty to protect strangers was, at most, one consideration among others, and hardly decisive.

Afghanistan

If we accept that NATO's interventions in the Yugoslav secession wars were primarily driven by domestic politics, what of its subsequent intervention in Afghanistan? At face value, NATO's Afghan adventure falls more squarely into the realist framework, with American interest in uprooting global jihadists in the region receiving increasingly hesitant support from its NATO allies (Dempsey 2009). Yet it was domestic politics which made the Alliance's mission in Afghanistan one of societal transformation rather than counter-terrorism. To make the intervention palatable to his party, Tony Blair (2001) defined its purpose in terms of progressive objectives:

> [s]o I believe this is a fight for freedom. And I want to make it a fight for justice too. Justice not only to punish the guilty. But justice to bring those same values of democracy and freedom to people round the world [. . .] The starving, the wretched, the dispossessed, the ignorant, those living in want and squalor from the deserts of Northern Africa to the slums of Gaza, to the mountain ranges of Afghanistan: they too are our cause.

Afghanistan thus provided him with the moral high ground that is difficult to attain when talking about, say, reforming health care (Chandler 2003). The intention was likely sincere, but has to be contrasted with the actual investment into justice for Afghans that London has made (as opposed to empowering whichever warlord promised enough stability to facilitate withdrawal). The Labour Party (2010: 0:2) later went so far as to list 'bringing stability to Afghanistan' as among the country's top four challenges for the next decade – next to global competition, climate change and an ageing society. That the future of Afghanistan was declared an absolute policy priority is hard to rationalise in terms of British national interest; that it was used for canvassing voters illustrates the domestic political stakes.

The significance of Afghanistan for domestic politics has also been evident in Washington. Initially, resource commitments were very limited, especially when compared with Iraq (Bellamy and Wheeler 2008: 532). Yet expanding the war in Afghanistan represented the solution to a pivotal dilemma for presidential candidate Obama: How to exploit public sentiment against the war in Iraq without becoming vulnerable to the predictable Republican charge that a Democratic presidential hopeful was weak on national security? The successful solution lay in defining Iraq as a dumb war and Afghanistan as a necessary one. Pressured by a military that was adamant not to be seen to lose again, Obama went on to almost triple the number of US soldiers in Afghanistan while simultaneously indicating that their mission was a temporary one. In so doing, he walked the fine line between, on the one hand, declaring success and beginning a drawdown before the 2012 US elections, and on the other protecting his right flank against the charge that he had stymied an increasingly successful counter-insurgency campaign (Woodward 2010).

Domestic politics also played an important role for Europe's NATO members. First, Dutch party politics led to a unilateral withdrawal by one of the most Atlanticist of NATO members (*New York Times* 2010). A similar pattern informed the French rush for the exit around the time of the presidential elections of 2012 (Agence France Press 2011). The position of the German government also provides a good illustration of the impact of domestic calculations. On the one hand, Berlin needed to avoid blame for its relatively limited engagement in Afghanistan. With close transatlantic partnership a key aspect of Germany's security culture (Harnisch 2010: 62), and particularly valued by the centre-right (Busse 2003), the government constantly felt the need to justify to its more committed allies the caveats attached to German military engagement. On the other hand, the government also needed to contain widespread domestic criticism of an 'overly militarised' approach by NATO in Afghanistan (Kaim 2008). What better way out of this dilemma than to declare, as did Chancellor Angela Merkel upon visiting Afghanistan in November 2007, that military, police and civilian reconstruction were equally important and that 'if there is one area where Germany should do more, then it is for the time being in police-building' (Bundeskanzleramt 2007). This analysis was clearly based on the political risks in Germany rather than the situation in Afghanistan (Pohl 2014a: 99–125).

In short, both the Alliance's transformational agenda in Afghanistan and the subsequent efforts to wriggle out of earlier commitments demonstrate how domestic calculation has conditioned foreign policy positions. Whereas domestic politics first spurred Western governments to over-reach in their plans for transforming

Afghanistan, it later pushed them to settle for underachievement. This inconsistency shows that Western ideational commitment to help Afghans was qualified in that it was weighed against the attendant material costs. At the same time, the plan for the Alliance's retreat from Afghanistan was determined, not by benchmarks in terms of foreign policy objectives, as realists would have it, but by electoral politics in NATO member states.

Libya

NATO's intervention in Libya again demonstrated the primacy of domestic political considerations. Of twenty-eight NATO members, only fourteen committed military assets to the operation and only nine were willing to participate in attacks against Qaddafi's forces (*The Economist* 2011e). That diversity in itself poses puzzles for anyone asserting an overarching alliance logic. Further, both the strategic and normative arguments for intervention were less than clear-cut: the Qaddafi regime did not represent a threat to Western interests and had been cooperative in aborting its nuclear programme – a move earlier rewarded by high-profile visits of the Libyan leader to Paris and Rome. Although the emerging Libyan civil war was indeed a threat to regional stability and the 'Arab spring' in neighbouring Tunisia and Egypt, it was not clear that Western intervention would positively influence either regional stability or democratisation in neighbouring countries. And the answer, with the benefit of hindsight, is most probably not (Kuperman 2015). Many critics, from academia to the American military and the German government, feared being drawn into another long-term adventure of dubious benefit. The humanitarian case was similarly doubtful: the head of the International Crisis Group put the death toll at the moment of military intervention at about 250 people (Goris 2012; see also Roberts 2011). This presented a far lower threshold than in comparable cases. And whereas the death toll would likely have risen in the absence of Western intervention, the ensuing civil war probably entailed five-digit numbers of casualties within the first year only (Milne 2011). Libya's descent into chaos actually occurred after the NATO intervention, not before (Kirkpatrick, 2014).

Neither national interests nor humanitarian concern offers a plausible explanation for the intervention itself or for NATO governments' diverging reactions. Domestic politics does, however, provide a compelling account. The primary impetus for military action came from Paris where President Nicolas Sarkozy had somewhat immodestly declared that 'France had "decided to assume its role, its role before history"' (cited in Erlanger 2011). As *The Economist* (2010) had already noted of Sarkozy, 'the more he globe-trots, or is seen to be dealing with world affairs, the more his popularity rises'. The intervention, starting on 19 March 2011, offered Sarkozy a chance to flaunt his international leadership. Against the background of municipal elections the next day, and with the opposition demanding military action, domestic political incentives suggested he engage in this type of grandstanding (Bourmaud 2011). *The Economist* (2011b) assembled an impressive range of cooing commentary from the French media and rival politicians, noting that Sarkozy's 'personal interest in playing the unifying moral leader, doing the right thing in the name of timeless French values, is evident'.

Domestic political incentives also provide a plausible explanation for the behaviour of the British and American governments. In London, parliamentary support for the intervention was almost unanimous (*The Economist* 2011a). This likely provided a welcome respite for the Conservative–Liberal coalition from the divisive politics of austerity (Koydl 2011). The Obama administration wavered for some time before deciding to 'lead from behind' (Lizza 2011). The dilemma was obvious: the president 'presumably, would prefer to face re-election in 2012 without bearing sole responsibility for another war in the Arab world' (*The Economist* 2011d). Yet bearing the blame for a 'weak' foreign policy was also a risk. Thus, as the head of the International Crisis Group's North Africa project noted, '[i]t is reliably reported that Obama's fear of being accused of allowing another Srebrenica tipped the scales in Washington' (Roberts 2011).

Whereas domestic incentives shifted the balance in favour of intervention for France, the US and the UK, the opposite proved true for Germany. Anxious about the imminent elections in its heartland state, Baden-Württemberg, the Free Democrats, which had ministerial responsibility for foreign policy, sought to position themselves as the 'party of peace' (*The Economist* 2011c). For that purpose, the foreign minister not only excluded German participation in military 'adventures', but also insisted on German abstention in the mandating UN Security Council debate. This calculation backfired badly by rendering Germany isolated within NATO (Blechschmidt, Braun and Brössler 2011; Denkler 2011; Kohler 2011). Yet the result does not detract from the motives: the German position was formulated with an eye on expected domestic reactions, not its Western identity or geopolitical interests.

Domestic preferences and their consequences for NATO

The preceding section demonstrated how key national positions on pivotal NATO operations have corresponded to domestic political logic. The relationship between societal preferences and governmental interest constitutes the core of 'new liberalism'. But this insight poses an important question: Given that NATO is an arena in which member governments interact, and given also that government preferences often diverge, how then does NATO ever arrive at a policy or operation?

NATO's policy output is a compromise between the preferences of its member governments, arrived at in negotiations, yet it is usually not the average of their preferences. Instead, as noted earlier, preference intensity matters. If one or several governments are particularly committed to an operation, they can often determine policy. Unless, that is, the countervailing preferences are as strong – but they are often not, because in NATO governments can simply opt out of Alliance activities. Many operations have, therefore, resembled 'coalitions of the willing'. In Libya, as noted earlier, only half of the NATO members committed military assets to the operation, and fewer still engaged in military action. In Afghanistan, almost every member state contributed. Yet risk sharing was very uneven (see Ringsmose this volume) because the war was widely perceived as a US undertaking to which allies contributed according to expected domestic payoffs, especially in terms of the gain of being perceived as close to the US.

The fact that the US, as the most powerful NATO member, could not persuade allies to fully commit in Afghanistan (or Iraq for that matter) may only be a minor problem for realists who emphasize relative power over preference intensity in explaining policy outcomes. More problematic is that NATO's agenda in terms of crisis management operations does not square too well with US preferences themselves – as it should according to a power-based explanation. In Bosnia, Kosovo and Libya, it was French and/or British governments that pushed Washington into operations that it would rather have avoided. Once Chirac, Blair and Sarkozy had committed themselves to action (and thereby challenged Washington to come off the fence), however, the calculations in Washington changed. The risk of foregoing a leadership role in NATO and of being perceived as weak on national defence (the White House being occupied by a Democrat during all three crises) tempered an initial preference of avoiding foreign entanglement. More committed European governments thus managed to set the agenda, despite their relative lack of power.

Emphasising national differences should not give the impression that every NATO operation was hotly contested. In many ways, domestic expectations overlapped transnationally, driven by the societal demand that states and societies around the world adhere to liberal Western values (see later). One helpful way of conceptualising the path from societal preferences to multi-national policy outputs is that of preference congruence: Stephanie Hofmann (2013) has thus used the ideological congruence of political parties to explain why the member states eventually decided to equip the EU with a security and defence policy. The congruence in relation to NATO is, however, broader than this insofar as it is not limited to party ideology: domestic political incentives may overlap despite ideological differences. Jamie Gaskarth (2010) has thus shown how New Labour emphasized a value-based foreign policy bond with the US (but not its EU partners) while simultaneously promoting an ethical foreign policy that in some respects ran counter to US (but not EU partners') preferences. How united and purposeful NATO acts is thus determined by the congruence of the domestic political incentives of its member governments, whether based on party ideology or other domestic political calculations.

The question of preference congruence comes down to the purpose of the Alliance. Why do countries continue to cooperate in NATO? The previous analysis suggests that, collectively, they do so for two main reasons: to have an ultimate, credible security guarantee and to contribute to shaping a world order built on liberal values – wherever and whenever that fits into the domestic political struggle. What does such an analysis imply for NATO's future?

The security guarantee NATO provides is relatively non-controversial because it is of value to all members (Webber et al 2004: 9). Consider in this connection the utility of extended nuclear deterrence. Here, European societies benefit in that they do not have to invest considerable resources into acquiring a credible deterrent of their own.[5] The 'outsourcing' of the ultimate deterrent, moreover, facilitates the prevention of security competition between European states, all the more so as the political costs that this entails are limited. Why these costs remain so low can be explained by Washington's own interest in the guarantee's credibility: American society wants its government to preserve, if not expand, the global liberal order. This self-ascribed role has been apparent also in Washington's advocacy of enlargement, sometimes in the face of reluctance among its European allies. Equally, it has been apparent in the level of patience the US has demonstrated over defence burden sharing. The US would obviously prefer other democracies to commit greater resources to defence, but its commitment to European order and transatlantic cohesion has led it to tolerate a growing imbalance in the collective effort. If the US is committed to defending fellow liberal democracies, NATO offers a framework that enhances the effectiveness of this commitment because the Alliance deters potential challengers and (whatever the imbalance) thereby reduces the capabilities that the US has to commit to actual defence. NATO provides an efficient institution in this respect, not least because of the credibility its history imparts. NATO's European members (and Japan, which enjoys similar guarantees) have not suffered attack since World War Two. States which have not enjoyed explicit protection, by contrast, have been attacked, and this has then had to be corrected at much greater cost to the US (Betts 2009: 6). And because this role for NATO of security guarantor is anchored in overlapping respective societal preferences (it is a guarantee that is almost beyond question in domestic political discourse), it seems certain that NATO will continue to provide it.

NATO's role as a global crisis manager faces greater challenges. Not only has its intervention in Afghanistan been more prolonged and difficult than anticipated, but national interpretations of how best to work towards a more liberal global order diverge. Transatlantic partners do not differ greatly as to the order they would like to see come about, but the European brand of liberalism differs markedly from its American counterpart. Dividing NATO into the US and European or 'European' allies is, of course, a simplification, as it omits some allies and clusters together others whose preferences are internally further differentiated. Yet for the sake of brevity, here I focus on this most salient cleavage.

The European commitment to building a world order based on liberal values is more guarded than the American when it comes to the means and pace by which transformation is to take place. Rather than embracing a Wilsonian 'millennial' version of liberalism, as many US governments and especially the Bush administration have done (Rhodes 2003), Europeans aim to bolster such values mainly in a defensive way by seeking to strengthen and protect liberal tendencies in third countries. Thus, the EU's European Security Strategy proclaims that

> [t]he best protection for our security is a world of well-governed democratic states. Spreading good governance, supporting social and political reform, dealing with corruption and abuse of power, establishing the rule of law and protecting human rights are the best means of strengthening the international order.
>
> (European Council 2003: 10)

Consequently, most EU crisis-management operations have focused either on supporting transitions to domestic orders based on liberal values where there was some local process to this end or have sought to protect basic human rights (protecting refugees and food shipments, for instance) (Pohl 2014a). This evidently falls short in ambition when compared with American foreign policy objectives which include 'democratisation' (implying active measures to generate democracy, though US rhetoric often outshines policy) or even 'regime change' by forceful means (Krauthammer 2004; Rhodes 2003).

These differences in how to pursue a liberal global order have implications for NATO's function as a global crisis manager. On the one hand, US administrations hope to derive domestic legitimacy from using NATO as a tool for burden sharing in global policing and regard it as a friendlier alternative to the United Nations for providing international legitimacy (Daalder and Goldgeier 2006; Hunter 2004). Therefore, the US has shown a strong interest in NATO's role as an international crisis manager. On the other hand, many European governments, driven by domestic unease with global policing responsibilities and faced with societal pressure to limit defence spending, do not want NATO to take on ever more distant operations. The reactions of most European governments to US pressure for further intensification of the operation in Afghanistan prior to the drawdown after 2012 is a case in point (Dempsey 2009). Moreover, many European governments doubt NATO's legitimacy as a substitute for the UN. These differences are exacerbated by the asymmetry in preference intensity on the two sides of the Atlantic. US administrations, given domestic expectations of US leadership, often consider themselves to have much less of a choice in robustly addressing crises than their European counterparts. Because these differences are rooted in domestic preferences rather than merely strategic decisions of governments amenable to external influence, liberalism would suggest that NATO's role as a global crisis manager will likely remain limited.

Not all is lost for NATO in this respect, however. Although European NATO governments might benefit electorally from limiting their contributions to global policing, there are also costs attached to foregoing the NATO framework. When it comes to issues of international security that both Europeans and Americans are interested in addressing, NATO offers a precious institutional framework, quite simply because US involvement adds credibility and capability that is otherwise unavailable. The intervention in Libya, pushed for by Europeans but largely enabled by American capabilities, is a good example. Although there are alternative institutional frameworks such as the UN or the EU's Common Security and Defence Policy, their lower credibility in deterring potential challengers results in a comparatively greater need to demonstrate effectiveness (where that is possible), and thereby higher costs. Where transatlantic interests in crisis resolution are largely in parallel and where the potential difficulties of intervention are significant, then NATO remains the most attractive option.

In sum, we can see that most European governments value NATO above all as an alliance of last resort, whereas the US in particular has been interested in extending the organisation's reach to that of global crisis management in places such as Afghanistan. Whereas the focus on members' relative power would suggest that the US should get its way in extracting support for its global policy goals in return for continued provision of security on the European continent, a focus on preferences suggests otherwise. True, the US has been crucial to every operation that NATO has undertaken, but it has often failed to get other allies to join in meaningfully. In Afghanistan, its most engaged allies were the UK, Denmark and the Netherlands – countries that least needed US protection, but where societal approval of close ties with the US was strongest. Reflecting societal preferences (but not relative power), defence budgets in Europe remain much lower in terms of gross domestic product (GDP) percentage than in the US. Although the debate on NATO's role time and again produces debates on 'burden sharing', with the American side offering greater involvement in NATO decision making in return for greater European commitment, societal preferences suggest that neither side is truly willing to leave the current equilibrium. The Ukraine crisis has arguably demonstrated just how strongly such domestic preferences matter, even in comparison with palpable external threats. At the 2014 NATO summit, governments committed to 'reverse the trend of declining defence budgets', but over a time scale of a decade – hardly a reversal of the European predisposition toward defence austerity (NATO 2014, paragraph 14).

Conclusion

Some readers may wonder why this chapter has focused so much on national capitals rather than on NATO as such. The justification is that when it comes to understanding what NATO is for, the Alliance needs to be seen primarily as an arena, not as an actor. Its interventions have been a consequence of substantial but differentiated voluntarism on the part of its member governments and a shared but divergently interpreted notion that the West has some responsibility for defending and expanding liberal order. This chapter has illustrated how such a purpose has been rooted in societal expectations that governments do something about human rights abuses abroad, weighed against expectations that the resultant engagement should not be overly onerous. In this sense, Western foreign policies, and NATO's role therein, have been a function of the anticipated domestic political consequences of (in)action.

This chapter set out with the puzzle that NATO's continued existence posed for many neo-realists. It contended that liberalism could address that puzzle by underlining that societal expectations rather than systemic pressures drive contemporary foreign policy in the West. This argument does not refute balance of power theory so much as suggest that neo-realism's analytical leverage over the evolution of NATO and contemporary Western foreign policies is limited at best. Contrary to what John Mearsheimer (1990) predicted, balance among NATO members has not taken place after the Cold War. The reason for the false prediction lay in the assumption that anarchy is a constant rather than a variable (Wohlforth 2008). In reality, NATO governments do not face strong incentives to focus on the relative power of their fellow allies because the environment in which they operate does not resemble neo-realist assumptions of competition and self-help. Instead, they are incentivised to focus on domestic (rather than international) political struggles. As a senior British diplomat (Cooper 2004: 112–113) has argued, the days of a '*Primat der Außenpolitik*' (primacy of foreign policy) have now passed in Western democracies. Neo-realism might retort that NATO's longevity reflects the survival of its Cold War mission, but a balance of power attention to Russia (consequent upon the Ukraine crisis) has been a rather recent and belated exercise on NATO's part and still does not enjoin the domestic political passions of most of its members.

The passing of relative national power as the pivotal variable for NATO's purpose does not portend that the role of power is without significance. It is rather that the locus of the struggle for power has shifted from the international to the domestic and transnational stage. In this context, liberalism offers two distinct advantages over other IR theories. First, it presents the possibility of integrating the national and the international levels by grounding the latter in the social purposes selected at the former. Second, it combines ideational and material interests as sources of foreign policy behaviour in a single framework. The concept of 'governmental interests' assumes that governments pursue both, to the extent that this promises domestic political advantage. Some may argue that this is old wine in new bottles and that such a conceptualisation of liberalism brings it very close to neo-classical realism with its emphasis on national interests. However, the lack of a framework in which to combine systemic and domestic factors means that neo-classical realists end up with a stack of ad hoc variables lacking analytical purchase (Legro and Moravcsik 1999; Wivel 2005; see also Sperling this volume). By focusing on governmental interests, liberalism is more coherent in this regard.

Liberalism is also more consistent in its treatment of the diplomatic history of crisis management operations than a purely normative or ideational approach. For liberalism, the sources that account for NATO's most important engagements are material and ideational. NATO operations have involved strong ideational preferences insofar as Western societies (and governments acting on their behalf) have seen themselves as responsible for preventing events fundamentally at odds with their domestic values. Yet preferences have also reflected self-interest in that Western societies have expected protection from negative externalities, be that refugees and crime in the case of the Balkans or terrorist safe havens in the case of Afghanistan. Similar 'material' concerns are suggested by the recurring debates about risk and burden sharing. Consistent with liberal IR theory, weighing these issues has been a function of domestic politics rather than a question of moral appropriateness.

How useful, then, is liberalism as a theoretical framework? It is certainly not perfect. Its focus on domestic preferences provides a good account of the structural pressures constraining foreign policy making but does not really theorise agency. In this, it is a mirror image of neo-realism – though arguably a more satisfactory one. Much foreign policy in the security realm is directly formulated by governments in response to often unexpected and unwelcome external shocks.

Domestic interests loom large in the process of policy formulation because governments have to satisfy their domestic audience. But in so doing, governments are not mere recipients and aggregators of societal preferences; they exercise agency in interpreting and, ultimately, co-shaping these preferences. But what exactly are the causal paths that link the domestic level of analysis with policy outcomes (Rathbun 2010)? To answer that question suggests a research agenda that covers the relationship between governments' foreign policy motivations and a public that is largely reactive, if not indifferent, to foreign policy. Governments often act pre-emptively, with an eye to avoiding future blame and electoral sanctioning. How, then, can we better theorise the way such implicit constraints are translated into foreign policy? In formulating this challenge to liberal theory, we should be aware that liberalism's failure to truly explain agency is a weak spot that is familiar to other general and systemic theories of international relations; theories which identify constraints and pressures upon action but not whether governments will respond or resist them.

Linking these theoretical considerations back to NATO, what developments does liberalism forecast? As argued earlier, a liberal analysis suggests that the Alliance will likely continue to buttress its members' territorial security, whereas its forays into expeditionary missions will remain controversial and, therefore, limited. NATO's limited acceptance as a global crisis manager among European publics (as well as those of potential host countries) suggests that attempts to transform it into a non-inclusive yet global security organisation will continue to lack support. NATO will remain a credible alliance, but it will be just one among several crisis managers. NATO's original purpose was famously described by the first Secretary-General Lord Ismay (cited in Carpenter 2002: 78) as being 'to keep the Russians out, the Germans down, and the Americans in'. The need and urgency of these purposes have certainly declined with the passing of the Cold War, although the Alliance's anti-Russian function has recently gained in importance. Yet when it comes to NATO's most visible persona, the 'pacifier', the Alliance's most pressing challenge (but one which talks to its liberal origins) relates to a revised formulation – 'keeping the Europeans in'.

Notes

1   The Russian military intervention in Ukraine is changing NATO's threat environment, but to what extent this amounts to an existential threat to any but a handful of NATO states (the Baltics and perhaps Poland) remains to be seen. Domestic political factors, therefore, continue to be crucial in decision makers' calculations. As evidence, consider the fate of the most important outcome of the September 2014 NATO summit. At that event, the twenty-eight allies pledged to reverse cuts in defence expenditure. The large majority, however, driven by domestic fiscal pressures, promptly carried on cutting military spending. (See Raynova and Kearns 2015.)

2   Following Waltz, structural realists might retort that domestic politics is not structural but reductionist (Waltz 1979: 18–37). Waltz's argument is inconsistent, however (Moravcsik 1997: 523–524). The point is not that anyone can get whatever they want (which would, indeed, not be structural), but that, according to liberalism, the distribution and interdependence of preferences explains outcomes, much as the distribution and interdependence

of capabilities explain outcomes in structural realism. The difference with Waltz is that I argue that the ends of foreign policy making matter more than the means.
3   This strong dichotomy between the domestic and the international is primarily for the purpose of clarity. The boundaries between the two are increasingly blurring, for instance, where opinion makers such as *The Economist* have a direct impact on political choices outside of Britain. Yet such transnational mechanisms still follow a domestic political logic because the impact or otherwise of an opinion piece will be determined by the expected political outcomes for the respective government of heeding, rejecting or ignoring it.
4   For a more extensive application of the concept of governmental interests to specific operations, see Pohl (2014b).
5   This claim may appear counter-intuitive, given French and British determination to remain nuclear powers. However, any British and French government giving up on nuclear weapons would face huge domestic political risks in terms of being the one that 'lost' the country's great power status, so their continued use is perfectly consistent with an explanation focusing on domestic political incentives.

References

[All web sources listed were last accessed 12 June 2015.]

Agence France Press. (2011). 'Afgh: retrait en 2013 si Hollande élu ', 12 July.
Barry, C. (1997). 'Combined Joint Task Forces in Theory and Practice', in Gordon, P. H. (ed). *NATO's Transformation: the Changing Shape of the Atlantic Alliance*, Lanham: Rowman and Littlefield.
Baumann, R. and Hellmann, G. (2001). 'Germany and the Use of Military Force: "Total War", the "Culture of Restraint" and the Quest for Normality', *German Politics* 10(1):61–82.
Bellamy, A. J. and Wheeler, N. J. (2008). 'Humanitarian Intervention in World Politics', in Baylis, J. Smith, S. and Owens, P. (eds). *The Globalisation of World Politics. An Introduction to International Relations*, Oxford: Oxford University Press.
Betts, R. K. (2009). 'The Three Faces of NATO', *The National Interest*, March-April: 31–38.
Blair, T. (2001). 'Speech by the Prime Minister, Tony Blair, at the Labour Party Conference, October 2, 2001', at: www.theguardian.com/politics/2001/oct/02/labourconference.labour7.
Blechschmidt, P., Braun, S. and Brössler, D. (2011). 'Libyen: Deutsche Enthaltung "Wir wünschen viel Erfolg"', *Süddeutsche Zeitung*, 18 March at: www.sueddeutsche.de/politik/libyen-deutsche-enthaltung-wir-wuenschen-viel-erfolg-1.1074261.
Bourmaud, F-X. (2011). 'Consensus droite-gauche sur la résolution de l'ONU; À presque un an de l'élection présidentielle, les partis d'opposition tentent de relativiser le rôle du chef de l'État', *Le Figaro*, 19 March.
Bueno de Mesquita, B., Smith, A., Siverson, R. M. and Morrow, J. D. (2005). *The Logic of Political Survival*, Cambridge: MIT Press.
Bundeskanzleramt. (2007). 'Bundeskanzlerin Merkel in Afghanistan. 3 November, 2007', www.bundeskanzlerin.de/nn_700276/Content/DE/Reiseberichte/af-bk-in-afghanistan.html.
Busse, N. (2003). 'Die Entfremdung vom wichtigsten Verbuendeten. Rot-Gruen und Amerika', in Maull, H. W., Harnisch, S. and Grund, C. (eds), *Deutschland im Abseits? Rot-Gruene Aussenpolitik 1998–2003*, Baden-Baden: Nomos.
Canan-Sokullu, E. S. (2012). 'Domestic Support for Wars: A Cross-Case and Cross-Country Analysis', *Armed Forces and Society* 38(1):117–141.

Carpenter, T. G. (2002). *Peace and Freedom: Foreign Policy for a Constitutional Republic*. Washington D.C.: Cato Institute.

Chandler, D. (2003). 'Rhetoric without Responsibility: The Attraction of "Ethical" Foreign Policy', *The British Journal of Politics and International Relations* 5(3): 295–316.

Cooper, R. (2004). *The Breaking of Nations. Order and Chaos in the Twenty-First Century*, London: Atlantic Books.

Daalder, I. (2000). *Getting to Dayton. The Making of America's Bosnia Policy*, Washington, D.C.: The Brookings Institution.

Daalder, I. and Goldgeier, J. (2006). 'Global NATO', *Foreign Affairs* 85(5): 105–113.

Daalder, I. and O'Hanlon, M. (2000). *Winning Ugly: NATO's War to Save Kosovo*. Washington, D.C.: The Brookings Institution.

Daddow, O. (2009). ' "Tony's War" '? Blair, Kosovo and the Interventionist Impulse in British Foreign Policy', *International Affairs* 85(3): 547–60.

Danner, M. (1997). 'The US and the Yugoslav Catastrophe', *The New York Review of Books*, 20 November.

Dempsey, J. (2009). 'Letter from Europe: U.S. and NATO Allies Facing Hard Questions', *International Herald Tribune*, 18 March.

Denkler, T. (2011). 'Libyen, Westerwelle und Deutschlands Enthaltung. Der Krisen-Profileur', *Seuddeutsche Zeitung*, 18 March at: www.sueddeutsche.de/politik/libyen-westerwelle-und-deutschlands-enthaltung-der-krisen-profileur-1.1074028.

Deutsch, K. W., Burrell, S. A., Kann, R. A., Lee Jr., M., Lichterman, M., Lindgren, R. E. Lowenheim, F. L. and Van Read Wagenen, R. W. (1957). *Political Community and the North Atlantic Area: International Organisation in the Light of Historical Expericence*, Princeton: Princeton University Press.

Doyle, M. W. (2008). 'Liberalism and Foreign Policy', in Smith, S. Hadfield, A. and Dunne, T. (eds). *Foreign Policy. Theories, Actors, Cases*, Oxford: Oxford University Press.

Duke, S. (2000). *The Elusive Quest for European Security: From EDC to CFSP*, Houndsmills, Basingstoke: Macmillan Press.

Eichenberg, R. C. (2005). 'Victory Has Many Friends: US Public Opinion and the Use of Military Force, 1981–2005', *International Security* 30(1): 140–177.

Erlanger, S. (2011). 'Sarkozy Puts France at Vanguard of West's War Effort', *New York Times*, 21 March.

European Council. (2003). 'A Secure Europe in a Better World: European Security Strategy', Brussels, 12 December at: www.consilium.europa.eu/uedocs/cmsUpload/78367.pdf.

Freedman, L. (2000). 'Victims and Victors: Reflections on the Kosovo War', *Review of International Studies* 26(3): 335–358.

Gaskarth, J. (2010). 'Identity and New Labour's Strategic Foreign Policy Thinking', in Daddow, O. and Gaskarth, J. (eds). *British Foreign Policy. The New Labour Years*, Houndsmills, Basingstoke: Palgrave Macmillan.

Gheciu, A. (2005). 'Security Institutions as Agents of Socialisation? NATO and the "New Europe"', *International Organisation* 59(4): 973–1017.

Goris, G. (2012). 'Louise Arbour: "The West is Very Ambiguous about Human Rights". Interview', *Mondiaal nieuws*, at: www.mo.be/.

Gow, J. (1997). *Triumph of the Lack of Will: International Diplomacy and the Yugoslav War*, London: Hurst and Co.

Harnisch, S. (2010). 'Die Aussen- und Sicherheitspolitik der Regierung Merkel. Eine liberale Analyse der Grossen Koalition', *Zeitschrift fuer Aussen- und Sicherheitspolitik*, 3: 59–83.

Hofmann, S. C. (2013). *European Security in NATO's Shadow: Party Ideologies and Institution Building*. Cambridge: Cambridge University Press.

Hopf, T. (2002). *Social Construction of International Politics: Identities and Foreign Policies, Moscow, 1955 and 1999*. Ithaca: Cornell University Press.

Hunter, R. E. (2004). 'A Forward-Looking Partnership: NATO and the Future of Alliances', *Foreign Affairs* 83(5): 14–18.

Hyde-Price, A. (2001). 'Germany and the Kosovo War: Still a Civilian Power?', *German Politics* 10(1): 19–34.

Kaim, M. (2008). 'Germany, Afghanistan, and the Future of NATO', *International Journal*, 63 (3): 607–623.

Kirkpatrick, D. D. (2014), 'Chaos Spreads in Fractured Libya', *International New York Times*, 23–24 August.

Kohler, B. (2011). 'Deutschlands Libyen-Politik. Gebrannte Kinder', *Frankfurter Allgemeine Zeitung*, 19 March.

Koremenos, B., Lipson, C. and Snidal, D. (2001). 'The Rational Design of International Institutions.', *International Organisation* 55(4): 761–799.

Koydl, W. (2011). 'Libyen-Krieg: Großbritanniens Rolle Wie Cameron Obama zum Krieg trieb', *Sueddeutsche Zeitung*, 20 March at: www.sueddeutsche.de/politik/krieg-gegen-gaddafi-grossbritannien-wenn-der-gruenschnabel-pfeift-1.1074647.

Krauthammer, C. (2004). 'Democratic Realism. An American Foreign Policy for a Unipolar World', American Enterprise Institute, Irving Kristol Annual Lecture, 10 February, at: www.aei.org/publication/democratic-realism/.

Kuperman, A. J. (2015). 'Obama's Libya Debacle: How a Well-Meaning Intervention Ended in Failure', *Foreign Affairs*, 94(2): 66–77.

Labour Party. (2010). 'The Labour Party Manifesto 2010: A Future Fair for All'.

Legro, J. W. and Moravcsik, A. (1999). 'Is Anybody Still a Realist?, *International Security* 24 (2): 5–55.

Levy, J. S. and Thomson, W. R. (2010). *Causes of War*. Oxford: Wiley-Blackwell.

Lizza, R. (2011). 'Leading from Behind', www.newyorker.com/news/news-desk/leading-from-behind, 26 March.

Malcolm, N. (1996). *Bosnia. A Short History*, New York: New York University Press.

Mearsheimer, J. J. (1990). 'Back to the Future: Instability in Europe After the Cold War', *International Security* 15(1): 5–56.

Milne, S. (2011). 'If the Libyan War Was about Saving Lives, It Was a Catastrophic Failure', *The Guardian*, 26 October.

Moravcsik, A. (1993). 'Preferences and Power in the European Community: A Liberal Intergovernmentalist Approach', *Journal of Common Market Studies* 31(4): 473–524.

Moravcsik, A. (1997). 'Taking Preferences Seriously: A Liberal Theory of International Politics', *International Organisation* 51(4): 513–553.

Moravcsik, A. (2000). 'The Origins of Human Rights Regimes: Democratic Delegation in Postwar Europe', *International Organisation* 54(2): 217–252.

Moravcsik, A. (2008). 'The New Liberalism', in Reus-Smit, C. and Snidal, D. (eds). *The Oxford Handbook of International Relations*, Oxford: Oxford University Press.

Morgenthau, H. J. (1973). *Politics Among Nations: The Struggle for Power and Peace*, fifth edition. New York: Alfred A. Knopf.

NATO. (2014). 'Wales Summit Declaration' at: www.nato.int/cps/ic/natohq/official_texts_112964.htm.

New York Times. (2010). 'Editorial: Dutch Retreat', 25 February.

Owen, J.M. (2002). 'The Foreign Imposition of Domestic Institutions', *International Organisation* 56(2): 375–409.

Phythian, M. (2010). 'From Asset to Liability: Blair, Brown and the "Special Relationship"', in Daddow, O. and Gaskarth, J. (eds). *British Foreign Policy: The New Labour Years*, Houndmills, Basingstoke: Palgrave Macmillan.

Pohl, B. (2014a). *EU Foreign Policy and Crisis Management Operations: Power, Purpose and Domestic Politics*, London: Routledge.

Pohl, B. (2014b). 'To What Ends? Governmental Interests and EU (Non-)Intervention in Chad and DRC', *Cooperation and Conflict* 49(2): 191–211.

Power, S. (2002). *"A Problem from Hell": America and the Age of Genocide*, New York: Basic Books.

Rathbun, B. (2004). *Partisan Interventions: European Party Politics and Peace Enforcement in the Balkans*, Ithaca: Cornell University Press.

Rathbun, B. (2010). 'Is Anybody Not an (International Relations) Liberal?', *Security Studies* 19 (1): 2–25.

Raynova, D. and Kearns, I. (2015). 'The Wales Pledge Revisited: A Preliminary Analysis of 2015 Budget Decisions in NATO Member States', European Leadership Network, at: www.europeanleadershipnetwork.org/medialibrary/2015/02/20/04389e1d/ELN%20NATO%20Budgets%20Brief.pdf.

Rhodes, E. (2003). 'The Imperial Logic of Bush's Liberal Agenda." *Survival* 45(1): 131–154.

Ringsmose, J. (2013). 'Balancing or Bandwagoning? Europe's Many Relations with the United States', *Contemporary Security Policy* 34(2): 409–412.

Risse-Kappen, T. (1996). 'Collective Identity in a Democratic Community: the Case of NATO', in Katzenstein, P. (ed). *The Culture of National Security: Norms and Identity in World Politics*, New York: Columbia University Press.

Roberts, A. (1999). 'NATO's "Humanitarian War" over Kosovo', *Survival* 41(3): 102–123.

Roberts, H. (2011). 'Who Said Gaddafi Had to Go?', *London Review of Books*, 17 November.

Robinson, P. (2001). 'Theorising the Influence of Media on World Politics: Models of Media Influence on Foreign Policy', *European Journal of Communication* 16(4): 523–544.

Schimmelfennig, F. (2004). *The EU, NATO and the Integration of Europe Rules and Rhetoric*, Cambridge: Cambridge University Press.

The Economist. (2010). 'France's President. Super Nicolas, Saviour of the Universe', 27 May.

The Economist. (2011a). 'Bagehot. The Ghost of Tony. David Cameron Leads a Sceptical Nation to War', 24 March.

The Economist. (2011b). 'France's War President: Sarkozy Relaunched. Will a Popular Libyan Adventure Restore the President's Fortunes?' 24 March.

The Economist. (2011c). 'Germany's Embattled Chancellor. Angela at Bay. A Nervous Angela Merkel Contemplates Further Electoral Setbacks', 24 March.

The Economist. (2011d). 'Lexington. The Reluctant Warrior. Barack Obama's Risk-averse Handling of the War in Libya Holds Political Risks of its Own', 24 March.

The Economist. (2011e). 'NATO after Libya. A Troubling Victory', 3 September.

Walt, S. M. (1987). *The Origins of Alliances*, Ithaca: Cornell University Press.

Walt, S. M. (1998). 'International Relations: One World, Many Theories', *Foreign Policy* (110): 29–46.

Waltz, K. N. (1979). *Theory of International Politics*, Reading: Addison-Wesley.

Weaver, R. K. (1986). 'The Politics of Blame Avoidance', *Journal of Public Policy* 6(4): 371–398.

Webber, M., Croft, S., Howorth, J., Terriff, T. and Krahmann, E. (2004). 'The Governance of European Security', *Review of International Studies* 30(1): 3–26.

Wivel, A. (2005). 'Explaining Why State X Made a Certain Move Last Tuesday: The Promise and Limitations of Realist Foreign Policy Analysis', *Journal of International Relations and Development* 8(4): 355–380.

Wohlforth, W. C. (2008). 'Realism and Foreign Policy', in Smith, S. Hadfield, A. and Dunne, T (eds). *Foreign Policy. Theories, Actors, Cases*, Oxford: Oxford University Press.

Woodward, B. (2010). *Obama's Wars*, New York: Simon and Schuster.

Yost, D. S. (2014). *NATO's Balancing Act*, Washington D.C.: United States Institute of Peace Press.

7 Understanding NATO through constructivist theorising

Trine Flockhart

Why constructivism has not developed into a more influential theoretical perspective is an interesting question for NATO research. Constructivism seems eminently suited to rectifying the shortcomings of other International Relations (IR) theories: namely, realism's inability to explain the endurance of NATO after the Cold War and liberalism's difficulty in accounting for the organisation's uneven adherence to its own liberal principles (evident in the toleration extended to non-democratic members – Greece, Portugal and Turkey during the Cold War). It is odd, therefore, that the two mainstream theories of realism and liberalism continue to be the theories of choice among most NATO scholars.

Constructivism challenges assumptions about how the world works inherent in both theories. The constructivist conviction that 'the world is of our making' (Onuf 1989) upends the realist view that the fundamentals of the international system are pervasive and enduring (Harrison 2002: 148–149), and its assumption that shared knowledge is mutually constituted (and continuously reconstituted) challenges the liberal conviction of a specific route to progress. Yet for all this, constructivism is said to lack theoretical purchase for, unlike both realism and liberalism, it does not provide a clear vision of a specific world order. This is a view grounded in a widespread understanding that constructivism has nothing substantial to say about who the main actors are in IR or what problems or issues should be addressed by them (Slaughter 2011: paragraph 19). However, although this criticism may have had some relevance to early constructivist thinking, constructivist scholars have for a number of years been busy applying their insights to substantive problems, including those relating to NATO (Adler 2008; Flockhart 2005; Gheciu 2005a). Constructivism, in fact, offers a concrete means of changing dysfunctional practices even if, as constructivists acknowledge, this is far from easy (Hopf 2010).

In this spirit of practical application, constructivism is used here to address the four questions posed in the introductory chapter. In so doing, it is mindful that the Alliance itself has presented answers to the first two questions (what is NATO and what is NATO for?) on several occasions during its long existence. NATO's utility to its members and, by extension, its power of persistence is, in part, explained by this continuous constitutive process. Hence, one must look closely at how the Alliance has constructed, maintained and occasionally changed its identity/identities and associated narrative(s). The ambivalence about what NATO is is grounded in the plurality of identities the Alliance is able to accommodate and the changing relationship between them. To address the remaining two questions – why NATO endures and who it is for? – it is pertinent to consider how these identities and narrative constructions, as well as associated its patterns of performance (routinised practices and purposive actions), in NATO have developed – and, by extension, how changes to any one of these factors have, on occasion, launched the Alliance into crisis.

Before engaging with these issues, the chapter first provides an outline of what might be regarded as the 'essence of constructivism'. It then directly considers the questions posed earlier before proceeding to consider the importance of identity for an understanding of NATO as an agent, one that has been able to adapt in response to a changing security environment and thus confound predictions of its imminent demise. The chapter concludes with a discussion of constructivism's usefulness for theorising NATO.

The essence of constructivism

To pinpoint the exact nature of constructivism is not an easy task. Constructivists maintain that just as the essence of liberalism is difficult to identify and hard to separate from the essence of realism, so constructivism means different things to different people. However, all constructivisms share a number of key concerns and propositions without which it would not be a coherent body of thought (Pettman 2000: 11). In the same way that it would be difficult to imagine a form of liberalism that rejected the possibility of progress or a realism that was impervious to power, so, too, certain ideas are the core to constructivist thinking. The essence of constructivism can be summarized in three key propositions, which arguably distinguish it from other theoretical perspectives (Flockhart 2012).

The first is that the reality, which we mostly take as given, is in fact a project under continuous construction. Constructivists understand the world as coming into being rather than existing as a pre-given entity. It is 'constructed', in other words, through a mutually constitutive relationship between structure and agent. On the one hand, this offers up the prospect of agent-led change. Yet, on the other, constructivists recognise the limitations of agent practice. Practice is often habitual and deeply embedded within paths that constrain the ability of agents to undertake new action (Hopf 1998:180).

Second, and related, constructivists maintain that structure cannot be understood by reference purely to material forces such as resources and power. Structure consists also, even primarily, of ideational factors. In this view, our understanding of reality is derived from inter-subjective knowledge and the interpreted nature of social reality. Portions of reality, in other words, are regarded as 'facts' (i.e., *as if* they were real) through shared knowledge demonstrated and made observable through human practice (Pouliot 2004: 320). Constructivists emphasise, therefore, ideational structures such as rules and norms. These act as socialising influences by specifying the appropriate behavior for an agent with a given identity

(Wendt 1992: 399). For this reason, constructivists argue that looking at NATO simply from a material perspective allows one to say little of substance. Only by comprehending NATO's ideational dimension and the practices associated with it does a fuller picture of the Alliance come into view.

Third, constructivists focus on identity, although they do not agree on precisely what this means or, indeed, how identity is constituted. Alexander Wendt (1999), widely recognised as having brought attention to identity as the main constitutive influence on interests and preferences, distinguishes between four categories in this regard: personal/corporate identity, type identity, role identity and collective identity (Wendt 1999: 224). Broadly speaking, the first two of these are related to 'what the agent is', whereas the latter two focus in addition on 'what the agent does'. In Wendt's conception personal/corporate identity and type identity are essentialist qualities (Epstein 2011: 329) said to be intrinsic to specific bodily (or territorial or organisational) characteristics of the agent in question. Role and collective identities, meanwhile, are relational, constituted through interaction with others. All four sorts of identity are in play in the case of NATO, but the question of how each is constituted is the subject of considerable controversy within the constructivist camp (Epstein 2011). That said, all identities are assumed to be constitutive of interests and preferences, and so condition action in particular domains (Hopf 1998: 175). A particular identity implies that actors will be subject to certain sets of norms, which, in turn, specify appropriate forms of behavior.

Constructivism certainly entails a different focus than either realism or liberalism; realism emphasises material rather than social and ideational factors, whereas liberalism operates with a relatively fixed (as opposed to changing) set of ideas. Yet it can be difficult to glimpse how some of these admittedly abstract points apply to real problems and real policy making, not least the continued evolution and endurance of NATO. This chapter shows that constructivism is perhaps closer to being a substantive theory than its critics suggest. Constructivists *are* concerned with specific questions – especially how identities and interests can give rise to dysfunctional practices such as rivalry and war making, and how through socialisation and institutionalisation, identity change can be effected and so, by extension, how such practices can be ameliorated (Flockhart 2006; Gheciu 2005b). In this sense, constructivism offers alternative understandings to some of the most central themes of international politics, including the four questions posed about NATO in this volume.

Constructivism when applied in this way builds upon the work of, among others, Karl Deutsch et al (1957), who theorised that changed interactions across borders might lead to new social relationships and eventually the establishment of a 'security community'.[1] The work of Deutsch and his colleagues did not for many years receive due recognition, but since the publication of Adler and Barnett's (1998) influential volume, the concept of security community has enjoyed a growing influence. In this connection, a burgeoning constructivist literature has produced convincing empirical evidence that the processes taking place in, for example, NATO, can produce new relationships based on friendship and cooperation rather than rivalry or enmity, and that prior identities and interests have been fundamentally changed, giving rise to practices of cooperation rather than previously dysfunctional practices of conflict (Bellamy 2004; Kavalski 2008).

The clearest constructivist statement of such processes can be found in the work of Alexander Wendt (see also earlier). Wendt asked if it really is the case that, in the absence of political authority in the international system, states are compelled (as realists would have it) toward self-help behavior. His answer was a clear and resounding 'no'. Self-help and power politics do not follow logically from anarchy because self-help is not a structural feature as suggested by Waltz (1979: 111), but an institution based on particular inter-subjective understandings about Self and Other that are reinforced through the practice of agents. This argument stresses, above all, the importance of shared knowledge: people act towards objects (including other people) on the basis of the meanings the object (or person) has for them. This means that states act differently towards enemies than they do towards friends because enemies are threatening and friends are not (Wendt 1992: 396). The behavior of 'purposive actors' is thus a consequence of obtained knowledge or shared ideas rather than being structurally determined (Wendt 1999: 1).

Wendt suggested the existence of three different 'cultures of anarchy': a conflictual (Hobbesian) culture based on self-help as suggested by realists, a competitive (Lockean) culture based on competition and rivalry as suggested by many liberals and a cooperative (Kantian) culture based on friendship as suggested by, for example, Deutsch. The implication here is not only that anarchy is 'what states make of it', but that cultures of anarchy can be changed. This is, indeed, the substantive crux of constructivist theorising because if, as maintained by Wendt, the reason we find ourselves in a self-help system is because practice made it that way (Wendt 1992: 407), then by implication practice can also 'un-make' a dysfunctional conflictual culture. Constructivists argue that it is precisely in such 'un-makings' of past conflictual practices that NATO plays an important role.

What is NATO and what is NATO for?

To understand what NATO is and what it is for, constructivists would suggest looking closely at how the identity of the Alliance has been constructed, maintained and occasionally changed, as well as how identity has been articulated through narrative and demonstrated through performance in embedded practices and purposive action.[2] In the following sections these two questions are addressed by drawing upon NATO's own strategic documents and performance. These sections consider both the security environment of the Cold War and the post–Cold War periods with an emphasis placed on how NATO's identity, narrative and performance, as well as its practice and action, have changed.

NATO during the Cold War: success despite dysfunctional practices

During the first forty years of its existence, the answer to the question 'what is NATO?' was seemingly straightforward. NATO was simply considered to be a defence alliance. This was its type identity; its role identity, meanwhile, was expressed in the North Atlantic Treaty, in particular the collective defence pro-visions of Article Five, fleshed out, in turn, in a number of Strategic Concepts, which aimed at providing the Alliance with strategic direction and which codi-fied decisions on its day-to-day management (Ringsmose and Rynning 2011). All Cold War Strategic Concepts clearly defined NATO as a defence alliance with the role of defending its members in the face of the evident danger posed by the Soviet-led Warsaw Pact.[3]

However, NATO also had a second type-identity as a forum for dialogue and cooperation among allies, which suggested very different answers to the two questions posed here. For example, Article Two of the Treaty specifies that NATO would contribute toward peaceful and friendly international relations by strength-ening a rule-based international order and by bringing about a better understand-ing of the principles upon which that order is based (NATO 1949: Article 2). Although the secondary 'partner (type) identity' was less clearly articulated than the primary 'defence alliance (type) identity', both were in line with American grand strategy which emphasized both *power* and *partnership* (Kupchan and Trubowitz 2007).

During NATO's early history, its partner identity was mainly visible internally insofar as the Alliance was a forum for dialogue and cooperation among its mem-bers. This was manifest with the accession of Greece and Turkey in 1952, West Germany in 1955 and Spain in 1982. With the stabilisation of East–West relations in the late 1960s, NATO also started to define its partner identity along an exter-nal dimension as a commitment to a more cooperative approach in its relations with the Warsaw Pact. This was expressed in the Harmel Report (NATO 1967: paragraph 5), which stated that 'the way to peace and stability in Europe rests in particular on the use of the Alliance constructively in the interest of détente'. However, it must be acknowledged that throughout the Cold War, the external dimension of the 'partner identity' was secondary to its internal dimension. More-over, overall primacy was always given to the 'defence alliance identity' of NATO given the exigencies of the Cold War.

The ambiguities surrounding NATO's type and role identities arose not through an inability on NATO's part to express what it was for. It arose, rather, because NATO sustained in parallel two type identities (defence alongside partner) with two related role identities (involving relations among allies as well as with adversaries). Over the years, the dual character of the Alliance has undoubtedly given rise to some perplexity, especially as realism and liberalism seemed una-ble to account for the apparent contradictions contained in NATO's two-pronged approach to security, and because different allies would emphasise one or other role identity over another.

So far the chapter has only touched on NATO's type and role identities. How-ever, as mentioned earlier, Wendt's four types of identity are all in play in the case of NATO. The North Atlantic Treaty does not directly mention a specific enemy merely that the Alliance would defend its members against any threat to their territory, NATO's corporate and collective identities were clearly constructed on the basis of a concrete and menacing Other in the form of the Soviet Union and the Warsaw Pact. Consequently, throughout the Cold War the official answer to the question 'what is NATO' was straightforward. It was a cohesive Alliance held together by common values, shared risks and shared burdens, serving the interests of its members by providing them with defence against an overwhelming military threat.[4] That narrative was reinforced through practices of consensus-based decision making, even if consensus was often difficult to achieve. Unity was seen as paramount to ensure the promise of solidarity contained in Article Five, whereas capability was essential for the credibility of extended deterrence. As a result, NATO developed several deeply embedded practices designed to demonstrate Alliance cohesion and capability. In the face of a clearly uneven distribution of capabilities on either side of the Atlantic, however, the actual performance of the Alliance was characterised by a long string of controversies occasioned, first, by questions over the reliability of the American nuclear guarantee with the Europeans fearing a lack of US commitment to their defence (Schwartz 1983), and, second, by European 'burden shifting' with the Americans resentful that the Europeans were not pulling their weight in conventional defence (Thies 2003).

Paradoxically, therefore, practices that developed in NATO to support the narrative of an Alliance founded on shared values, shared risks and shared burdens, in effect, ended up being seemingly dysfunctional because these virtues were difficult to realise. This dysfunction was, however, absorbed by the Alliance. In this connection, NATO's response to its 'nuclear dilemmas' (Schwartz 1983) is perhaps best known, something which entailed a shift from massive retaliation to 'flexible response' in the strategy of nuclear deterrence but which brought with it a constant internal debate over the appropriate mix of conventional and nuclear forces and the utility of theatre (i.e., a European) nuclear war. As Beatrice Hauser (1994: 58) has suggested 'the Alliance was in some danger of breaking apart over [the] diversity of interests' that these debates generated. However, ultimately it held together through a series of complex compromises on strategy (between Europe's leading powers – West Germany and the UK most notably – and the US), which worked well enough, in large part, because they never had to be tested in the heat of war (Hauser 1994: 64–65).

Burden sharing, meanwhile, was intended to buttress NATO's identity as a defence alliance, while also reinforcing the internal dimension of the 'partner identity' through practical cooperation in defence planning. Despite the early establishment of practices such as annual (later biennial) defence reviews, the Alliance constantly fell short of its own capability targets. But instead of fixing the problem either through increases in defence spending to bring capabilities into line with the stated goals or, alternatively, to adjust capability goals sufficiently downwards, the European allies seemed willing to accept the inevitability of a capability gap and the continued existence of a crisis narrative about burden sharing. Although dysfunctional at one level, this narrative served a more positive purpose, underscoring the status of the US as *primus inter pares* and the Europeans as the grateful allies who had tried (but ultimately failed) to live up to agreed defence commitments.[5] Moreover, because agreed conventional force goals went unmet, NATO's nuclear practices could be justified, especially in a context of the entrenched conventional force superiority enjoyed by the Warsaw Pact.

The persistence of a crisis narrative in relation to two of the most important practices of the Alliance would logically suggest that NATO during the Cold War was a weak construct. Yet apart from the French withdrawal from NATO's integrated military structure (but not from membership as such), no member state withheld its support throughout the Cold War. Moreover, although different allies clearly had different interests (especially on the planned use of nuclear weapons) NATO was able to develop a practice of 'constructive ambiguity', such that the Alliance as a whole was able to express its preferences in a manner that effectively papered over deep and enduring differences. But the main strength of the Alliance during the Cold War was, undoubtedly, its clearly defined corporate and collective identity when faced by a very visible menacing Other. In that sense, it is possible to say that NATO endured because all members valued their membership enough to tacitly accept first, the ambiguity inherent in almost all of NATO's substantive decisions, and, second, the dominant narrative of a cohesive Alliance founded on shared values *and* interests.

For allies in NATO, being a member of such a 'club' (or social group) (Tajfel 1982; Turner 1987) provided a sense of belonging in a world that was clearly divided into different spheres and where defection from the social group would have detrimental effects, not only on individual states' identity, but also on their practical defence arrangements. Although its practices may have appeared at times illogical, and despite the recurrence of crises about burden sharing, NATO nevertheless maintained a sufficient level of unity throughout the Cold War and was able, albeit sometimes with difficulty, to undertake the necessary purposive action as and when required.

NATO after the Cold War: success despite a weakened identity

It is well known that the end of the Cold War catapulted the Alliance into a deep identity crisis and that many scholars, realists especially, assumed the years of the Alliance to be numbered (Waltz 1993: 76). Yet, more than two decades on, the Alliance is still here. To understand why, the questions 'what is NATO?' and 'what is NATO for?' have an ongoing relevance.

The end of the Cold War clearly represented a change in the power structure of the international system. A neo-realist would point to that structure as consisting primarily of material factors (including, most importantly, the distribution of capabilities up to and including nuclear weapons) and so, the Soviet Union's collapse required some rebalancing of power. For a constructivist, however, such a rebalancing was not only about capabilities. In an ideational understanding of structure, the Soviet Union/Russia could no longer be constructed as the menacing Other, and the formerly communist states of Central and Eastern Europe were being re-constituted as friends rather than foes. The end of the Cold War meant, therefore, that NATO's corporate and collective identities had altered fundamentally. In constructivist theorising, this constituted a 'critical juncture' (Finnemore and Sikkink 1998) which dislodged the existing ideational structure, launched the Alliance into a period of cognitive inconsistency and gave rise to an existential fear that NATO's underlying foundations were unraveling.

Yet constructivists agree that even in situations of such major upheaval, identity structures and embedded practices can prove resilient. The question of 'what is NATO?' was brought up in Alliance circles as soon as the Cold War appeared to be at an end. At the London Summit in June 1990, NATO leaders performed a 'straight swap' between the two established type identities. NATO's secondary identity (the partner identity) became its primary identity, whereas the previous primary identity (the defence identity) was placed in the background. This was particularly clear in the London Declaration, which stated that:

> our Alliance must be even more an agent of change. It can help build the structures of a more united continent, supporting security and stability with the strength of our shared faith in democracy, the rights of the individual, and the peaceful resolution of disputes. We reaffirm that security and stability do not lie solely in the military dimension, and we intend to enhance the political component of our Alliance as provided for by Article 2 of our Treaty.
>
> (NATO 1990: Article 2)

In addition, NATO reformulated its threat perception to one that was multi-faceted and multi-directional (NATO 1991: Article 8); and it made a move to construct a new role identity by broadening the range of security challenges to include instabilities that might arise from economic, social and political difficulties, including ethnic rivalries and territorial disputes (NATO 1991: Article 9). Thus, whereas its defence alliance identity receded, NATO still maintained an important military role – to be able to meet new challenges in a new security environment and to counter a possible, if unlikely, threat from a diminished Soviet Union/Russia.

But perhaps the most profound change in post–Cold War NATO has been the shift toward new forms of purposive action. NATO fired no shots in anger during the Cold War, and its purposive action was confined to undertaking military exercises and the occasional decision to ensure the credibility of extended nuclear deterrence. Most of NATO's action during the Cold War consisted of rhetorical affirmation of unity, shared values and American verbal reassurances of its commitment to Europe's defence. The situation in the post–Cold War environment has been completely different. The Alliance has been extraordinarily busy along two paths of purposive action: first, by engaging with an ever-increasing circle of partners and a process of enlargement; and second, by undertaking a wide range of crisis management and peace support operations.

Along the first of these paths, and in response to the changes in central and eastern Europe, the Alliance followed up the promise of the London Declaration to 'extend [. . .] the hand of friendship' (NATO 1990; Article 4) through the establishment of the North Atlantic Cooperation Council (NACC) and from 1994 the Partnership for Peace (PfP) programme. Moreover, by the mid-1990s, NATO had indicated a firm commitment to an enlargement of its membership (NATO

1995). Although the question of what NATO is for had not been settled, the issue of enlargement had: by this point it was no longer a question of *if* the policy would occur, but of *when* (Goldgeier 1999).

Along the second path, and in response to the Balkan crises, NATO followed up its stated intentions in the 1991 Strategic Concept by taking the important decision to go out-of-area. NATO's involvement in the Balkans initially developed rather haphazardly, from the monitoring and enforcement of a UN-imposed arms embargo up to decisive intervention in Bosnia (Operation Deliberate Force in 1995) that paved the way for the Dayton peace accords and the installation of an operation unprecedented in scope and scale – the IFOR-SFOR NATO peacekeeping mission. Although the process of becoming involved in crisis management was ad hoc, it meant NATO had crossed an important threshold, and (given political agreement) seemed able to do so again.

Since then the Alliance has continued a high level of activity along both paths of purposive action. It has nearly doubled its membership, moving from sixteen to twenty-eight members and in 2011 expressed a commitment to 'a partnership policy with any nation across the globe' that shared NATO's 'interest in peaceful international relations' (NATO 2011: paragraph.7). Along the path of operations, meanwhile, the Alliance has engaged in conflict prevention and crisis management in Kosovo, Afghanistan and the Gulf of Aden. In 2011 it also undertook a humanitarian intervention under a UN-sanctioned mandate in Libya. NATO in the post–Cold War period has mounted over thirty-five operations and until the uncertain outcome of the ISAF/Operation Resolute Support in Afghanistan, it has been largely successful in those it has mounted.

NATO thus appears a very different organisation from the NATO of 1990 or the NATO of the Cold War. It has effectively developed a new 'identity structure' consisting of a corporate and type identity (what NATO is) that embraces identities of defence alliance, forum for partnership and cooperation and institution of crisis management. In parallel, the Alliance has constructed a narrative about its role and collective identity (what NATO does) that sees it as a provider of collective defence, a socialising agent of democratic norms and an agent of multilateral operations.

This is precisely the combination that is codified in NATO's 2010 Strategic Concept, where three core tasks are identified: collective defence, cooperative security and crisis management (NATO 2010).

In official NATO parlance, it is common to hear that NATO is no longer 'just' a defence alliance. But then again, NATO never was 'just' a defence alliance. What is clear is that the multiple identities of NATO are much more explicit. Such clarity is, however, not without its problems. The answer to the questions 'what is NATO?' and 'what is NATO for?' has come to include all identities and roles identified earlier. Yet, in practice, few allies align themselves with all of these, and the question of which should take precedence is far from settled. The answer to that question depends, to a large extent, on who is asked – NATO's new members being more likely to emphasise the defence alliance identity (particularly in view of the deterioration in relations with Russia following the Crimea and Ukraine crises), whereas older members might emphasise the partner identity, and a few may prefer the crisis management identity. Given these different answers, it is clear that NATO's transformation has not been an easy process, and, as has been customary in all of NATO's history, the position expressed in official documents still covers a wide range of views well camouflaged through the use of 'constructive ambiguity'.

Who is NATO for and why does it endure?

Answers to the questions 'who is NATO for?' and 'why does NATO endure?' ought to be straightforward as these relate to NATO's corporate and collective identities, which are/ought to be less contested than the type and role identities outlined earlier.

From a constructivist perspective, NATO can be conceptualised as a 'social group'. Such a conceptualisation draws on work in social psychology (Turner 1987) where shared norms and values are seen to provide group members with a sense of belonging or 'we-feeling' (Deutsch et al 1957: 129). Social psychology suggests that individuals will go to great lengths to join a social group that can provide them with a collective identity, especially one that carries prestige and thus the benefits of status and self-esteem (Lebow 2008; Rubin and Hewstone 1998). When read across to the behavior of states as actors, NATO is attractive in this regard because it is associated with a clear collective identity derived from a long history as a Euro-Atlantic security community with attendant identity markers of democracy, human rights and political stability. Some states (Turkey and France, for instance) may have registered a periodic scepticism toward the Alliance because it contradicts other identity politics but, by and large, this is a collective identity that has become embedded within the strategic culture of NATO's longer-established members. It is also especially appealing to prospective and new members where identity politics have developed amid the turbulence of post-Soviet/communist transition. That attraction, in turn, serves NATO's own normative purposes; NATO has tended to extend its membership to states which have demonstrated a purposeful commitment to alliance values (Gheciu 2005a).

As long as NATO is seen as a status-giving social group, members, prospective members and partners who share NATO's values and norms are likely to perceive the Alliance as 'useful'. However, these social benefits do not 'float freely' of strategic calculation.[6] Collective identity formation is now well understood to occur in juxtaposition to an Other, something whose disruptive character and/or behavior contrasts with the order that follows from the Self (Neumann 1999: 30–31). As intimated earlier, NATO's collective identity, by this view, was consolidated by reference to the Other of Soviet communism during the Cold War, but has been weakened since by the absence of an unambiguous replacement (Behnke 2013: 180–191). This is not to say that NATO (or Western) norms have gone unchallenged (the atrocities in the Balkans in the 1990s or of ISIS in Syria and Iraq more recently are both an affront in this regard); it is rather to point out that the violation of norms does not always pose a threat to NATO's members as such. This can have a damaging effect on collective identity in the sense that the benefits of self-esteem, status and we-feeling are likely to erode in the absence of a direct threat. Yet the reverse will also apply. The norms associated with NATO are cast into relief and so appear more attractive when directly challenged. In this sense, the actions of Russia vis-à-vis Ukraine and the pledge by President Putin that Russia would come to the aid of ethnic Russians living outside Russia's borders serve to add to the perceived value of NATO. This applies both to states who construe such behavior as a threat (notably the Baltic states and Poland) but equally other NATO states whose sense of social solidarity (institutionalised in collective defence provisions) prompts support for their more beleaguered members. Here, the Alliance provides for the collective defence in the face of what might be construed as Russian destabilisation, but equally, stands as a normative bulwark to Russia's anti-democratic tendencies. In this understanding of the Alliance, membership provides both a concrete security guarantee and the reassurance and sense of belonging that comes from being part of a social group of high standing. Russia has not (yet) replaced the Soviet Union as NATO's unambiguous Other (it does not pose a sufficient sense of imminent and purposeful threat to all allies to do so), but its recent behavior has become a cause of NATO's collective identity.

Constructivism and the problem of change

The possibility of change offered by constructivism's core assumption of a mutually constitutive relationship between structure and agency sets the theory apart from both realism and liberalism. Yet NATO's continuous transformation – a process that has persisted long after the initial critical juncture occasioned by the end of the Cold War – still poses a problem for constructivism. Specifically, constructivism cannot account fully for why patterns of action and practice changed more fundamentally than anticipated and then seemed to carry on for so long. Nor can the conventional Wendtian form of constructivism explain why the dynamism of the 1990s seemed to falter during the first decade of the twenty-first century only to accelerate again in its second decade.

Paradoxically, the problem for a constructivist explanation is not a lack of agent-led change, but a plethora of it, even in the face of an absence of further events that have been perceived as critical junctures relevant to NATO.[7] Neither the material nor the identity changes that took place as a result of the end of the Cold War can fully explain why NATO has developed into an alliance that is busy doing things once unimaginable and doing them in a particular way. Yet, if constructivism is to have a claim to policy relevance, it must be able to explain why NATO has responded positively in some instances (mounting testing operations in the Balkans, Afghanistan and Libya, for instance) but not in others (Iraq and Syria). In order to better understand NATO's development, it is necessary to complement the structural bias of conventional constructivism with a number of self-constitutive agent-level processes while also incorporating the occurrence of events into our understanding of what influences identity and narrative constructions.[8] Doing so necessitates revisiting some of the core tenets of constructivism

– especially the mutually constitutive relationship between structure and agency, the essentialist assumption about agents' identity and the notion that practice tends to reinforce the status quo rather than bring about change.

As already noted, constructivists assume that structure and agency are mutually constitutive (Dessler 1989; Giddens 1984; Wendt 1999), but they generally do not ask how structural input is processed by the agent to constitute identity and influence behavior. Moreover, by focusing on the dialectic between structure and agency, we have no way of theoretically accounting for the influence of past actions and the haphazard occurrence of events on the constitution of identity. For example, when NATO took the important decision to go out-of-area in the Balkans – to be sure, this was a decision that was made possible by the recently changed structural environment (i.e., a context of post–Cold War politics); however, that change was not a sufficient cause for the decision, nor does it explain why the Alliance then continued its out-of-area activity such that it developed new type and role identities.

This example implies a greater independent role for the agent than is suggested by the agent–structure dialectic. It also problematises Wendt's essentialist 'self' in which corporate and type identity are seen as intrinsic to the body and, therefore, highly resistant to change. In Wendt's conception of type identity, NATO *is* a defence alliance and a forum for dialogue and cooperation. Yet clearly the events in the Balkans caused the Alliance to add another type identity, becoming additionally a crisis management institution – a move that was codified in the Strategic Concepts of 1999 and 2010. The problem here is flagged by Charlotte Epstein (2011) who, by utilising insights from Jacques Lacan, presents a convincing case that there is nothing intrinsic or essentialist about identity. Identity (type and corporate) cannot be solely intrinsic because agents – being composed of people and so subject to general psychological principles – are able to reflect on their environment and on their actions. Therefore, in order to understand why NATO (as an agent composed of many people acting on its behalf) has been able to change 'what it is', 'what it is for', 'who it is for' and, in the process of so doing, 'to endure', constructivists need to take account of psychological processes. This necessitates more specific agent-level theorizing than has hitherto been the case in conventional constructivism.

Drawing on the work of Giddens (1991), it can be assumed that in the absence of a critical juncture, agents undertake purposive action in relation to considerations of 'ontological security'. A sufficient level of ontological security is only likely to be present when an agent has a stable and comforting view of self and a sense of order and continuity in regard to the future, to relationships and experiences (Giddens 1991: 38). Anxiety derived from ontological insecurity occurs when a person's self-identity and biographical continuity are challenged, when a stable cognitive environment cannot be sustained (Steele 2005: 526) or when agents' purposive actions fail causing them to feel shame and lowered self-esteem. Actions to redress this condition result in pride, increased self-esteem and so an enhancement of ontological security. In this connection it seems that NATO's initial (and successful) actions in out-of-area crisis management in the Balkans produced the positive emotions that are necessary for ontological security and so meant the Alliance was positively inclined to undertake such actions again.

Further, ontological security is established, maintained or increased through continuous self-constitutive agent-level processes. As explained by Giddens, identity is found in the capacity to keep a particular narrative going (Giddens 1991: 54); it is through such narratives that individuals maintain biographical continuity and so maintain a stable identity. Moreover, because human beings are hardwired to prefer stability and predictability, they value routines which stabilise their cognitive environment (Mitzen 2006: 342). Everyday life often calls for the breaking of routines and an ability to cope with change (Craib 1998), and it is ontologically secure individuals who are best able to adapt to such circumstances; they have the ability to reflect on the utility of their routinised practices and to undertake purposive (corrective) action when needed. They are also able to cope with the change their action induces and to incorporate that change into their narrative and identity constructions.

It seems that for much of the 1990s when NATO undertook new purposive action and changed certain embedded practices, it was able to do so initially because of existential fear caused by the changes in the structural environment following the end of the Cold War, which brought NATO's continued utility (and existence) into question. This was a situation which propelled the Alliance into taking urgent action in areas that could not previously have been anticipated. However, conventional constructivism cannot explain why NATO subsequently was able to maintain that high level of activity. By adding a more agent-centered approach and focusing on ontological security, NATO's adaptation through the re-constitution of its type and role identity during much of the 1990s takes on a new meaning. Its interventions in the Balkans, along with vigorous enlargement and partnership processes, all had a positive effect on NATO's self-esteem and allowed for the construction of a new identity supported by a coherent narrative that cast the Alliance as the premier security organisation in Europe, one that had prevailed where the EU and the UN had come unstuck. Being able to adapt and to take on new tasks became part of NATO's identity and of the narrative about 'what NATO is'. Ontological security is, however, a fragile condition particularly vulnerable to unsuccessful action and to events or other externally generated changes that cannot be accounted for in the narrative of the time. During the 1990s NATO had undertaken a major re-evaluation and so had become characterised by gradually increasing levels of ontological security, the subject of a narrative as Europe's premier security organisation and the agent of successful purposive action along the paths of crisis management, partnership and enlargement. Events during the first decade of the twenty-first century would force it again to face up to the problem of change.

NATO's ontological security and self-esteem had already been dented by the 1999 campaign in Kosovo which, although publicly presented as a success, was characterised internally by disagreements and recriminations between the European Allies and the Americans, as the long-standing gap in capabilities became readily apparent. Moreover, when after 9/11 the Bush administration rejected

NATO's offer of help in Afghanistan (even after the US agreed to the North Atlantic Council's invocation of Article Five for the first time in NATO's history), it undermined NATO's identity as a unified defence alliance. As it became clear that the Bush administration had no intention of continuing the well-established practice of negotiation and persuasion, one of NATO's most lasting and cherished practices was dislodged with severe consequences for the allies' cognitive stability and hence for the ontological security of the Alliance. The preparations for the Iraq war in 2003 brought these divisions to a head, leaving the narrative about a cohesive Alliance and a negotiated order in tatters (Cox 2005; Peterson 2004).

As the first decade of the 2000s moved on, the negative dynamics in the Alliance became worse as the purposive action related to NATO's partner identity and crisis management identity started to go seriously wrong. NATO, following the 'big bang' accession of seven states in 2004, started to experience enlargement fatigue (it also suffered a serious split over the merits of membership for Georgia). The potential for further norm promotion through partnership also seemed to be exhausted as the relevant formats in the Mediterranean, the Middle East, the former Soviet Union and Central Asia appeared increasingly ineffectual. It was, however, along the crisis management path that things started to get seriously out of hand. Not only did the ISAF operation entail a level of combat that most of the participating nations had not been prepared for,[9] but the mission was increasingly characterised by a very uneven distribution of risks and burdens, and the application by many European allies of restrictive national caveats on their contributing personnel. Unable to demonstrate progress in Afghanistan, and with the mission more and more costly of both lives and treasure, NATO found itself caught in a negative and undermining form of purposive action. The difficulties confronting ISAF meant a crisis narrative of possible failure in Afghanistan started to take hold (Rynning 2012: 112–144) and with it a downturn in ontological security.

By the end of the Bush years, the Alliance was in a sorry state with an all-but-collapsed ontological security, a severely shaken identity, deep divisions, a negative narrative and established practices of negotiation and persuasion apparently a thing of the past. These processes reinforced by a seemingly failing mission in Afghanistan meant that by 2008 NATO had, according to a constructivist account, probably reached the low point of its post–Cold War existence. Had the situation persisted, this might well have spelled its end.

The situation has, however, altered fundamentally since. One of the first priorities of the new Obama administration was to restore the transatlantic relationship. Obama's first visit to Europe was the occasion of the NATO fiftieth anniversary summit in Strasbourg/Kehl in April 2009. Here, the Alliance returned to the two paths of purposive action by pledging to get the ISAF mission back on track and by admitting Albania and Croatia as new members. Moreover, NATO took the long-awaited decision to begin the process of formulating a new Strategic Concept, described as a document that would 'define NATO's longer-term role in the new security environment of the twenty-first century' (NATO 2009). At the following summit held in Lisbon in November 2010, the North Atlantic Council adopted the document and NATO agreed an 'enduring partnership' agreement with Afghanistan, which more clearly set out a roadmap for the continued role of the Alliance in the country accompanied by an agreement that the ISAF mission as such would terminate by the end of 2014.

The 2010 Strategic Concept was widely perceived as launching NATO in a new direction 'making it fit for purpose in addressing 21st century challenges' (NATO 2010: paragraph 36) It is certainly true that the document was innovative. It clearly spelled out all three type identities introduced in this chapter, listing them as NATO's three core tasks: collective defence (defence alliance identity), cooperative security (partner identity) and crisis management (security institution identity). It thus provided precisely the kind of direction that the Alliance seemed to lack during the previous decade. However, in the period since, the record of implementing the intentions of the Strategic Concept has been mixed in relation to all three core tasks.

Partnership and cooperation

After 2010, the Alliance set out energetically to rationalise the rather messy partnership portfolio which had developed over the previous two decades. The process started with some success as NATO was able to agree a new, more flexible partnership policy in 2011. This defined a clearer role for those partners that contributed to NATO's missions (such as Sweden, Finland and Australia), but which (as non-NATO members) lacked official influence on operational planning (Flockhart 2014). On other counts, however, the record has been less than impressive, especially regarding the ambition to 're-set' the partnership with Russia to a new and more cooperative footing (*The Economist* 2012). The relationship with Russia, rather, has continued on a downward trend (one it had been on since at least the Kosovo crisis of 1999) evidenced by Moscow's long-time refusal to cooperate on missile defense and the steep deterioration in relations that followed Russia's annexation of Crimea in March 2014. As a result, the relationship can no longer be described as a partnership as such, and NATO has suspended all practical cooperation with Moscow. The record is also not impressive in relation to the ambitions expressed in the Strategic Concept to improve partnerships in the Middle East and elsewhere, and to establish a more constructive relationship with the EU. Equally, NATO's partnerships with Ukraine, Iraq and Pakistan, meanwhile, have seemed more a cause of trouble and anxiety for NATO than of reinvigorated purpose. Nevertheless, partnership continues to hold a prominent (though declining) place in NATO's narrative. At the Wales summit, NATO launched the Interoperability Platform with twenty-four partners supplemented by the Partnership Interoperability Initiative with the five partners 'that make particularly significant contributions to NATO operations' (NATO 2014: paragraph 88).

The recent record on enlargement has also been less than exciting. The Alliance reiterated at the 2014 Wales summit that 'NATO's door [would] remain open to all European democracies' which fulfill the criteria for membership (NATO 2014, paragraph 92). Three states – Bosnia, Montenegro and Macedonia – at that point enjoyed access to Membership Action Plans, but there appeared to be no urgency in facilitating their entry into NATO. The lack of a consensus on membership for Georgia and Ukraine also persisted. Indeed, in light of Russia's active destabilisation of both countries, the geo-political limitations of the enlargement project had become clear. Debate continued as to the merits of membership for both states, but the support this course had enjoyed under the Bush administration evaporated under Obama. Thus, following Albania and Croatian entry in 2009, it was not at all clear where the future of enlargement lay (Simakovsky 2013).

Crisis management

Following the 'surge' agreed to in December 2009, the much more concerted effort at training Afghan security forces and the end of the ISAF mission, the NATO narrative about the mission in Afghanistan noticeably improved (Rynning 2012: 144–206). Nevertheless, it seems unlikely that NATO will ever be able to define its long mission in Afghanistan as a success. Success seems now to constitute 'exiting with honour' (Fergusson 2010: 367) rather than the previous very noble, but probably unattainable, goal of establishing a form of Afghan democracy. The upside is that the Alliance is no longer caught in a cycle of negative purposive action in a far-away country with seemingly endless problems.

Along the crisis management path, NATO also undertook the first-ever UN-mandated mission under the principle of Responsibility to Protect in Libya in the spring of 2011. Again, the record is mixed because although the Alliance was able to conduct Operation Unified Protector with limited direct American involvement, only eight allies took part. Moreover, the operation was seen by Russia and China as having gone beyond the UN mandate to protect the civilian population, with the consequence that once intervention in Syria came on to the international agenda, it was blocked in the Security Council. Even though crisis management, rhetorically speaking, remains one of NATO's core tasks and an integral element of NATO's identity, it seems likely that this task will hold a less prominent role for the foreseeable future, as those members who have always preferred NATO to be primarily a defence alliance have gained strength following the Russian aggression towards Ukraine, whereas those who have traditionally favored NATO's expeditionary role (the UK and the US most obviously) have lost the political will to sustain such missions given their heavy human and financial cost.

Collective defence

Following the London summit in 1990, NATO's collective defence identity came to occupy a less prominent position in NATO's narrative and purposive action. However, with the entry of new Central and East European members, the Alliance's centre of gravity has shifted eastwards and so questions of collective and territorial defence have become more prominent (Rynning and Ringsmose 2009). In his much-publicised farewell speech of June 2011, the out-going US Secretary of Defence Robert Gates (cited in Shanker 2011) placed the issue at the centre of attention as he predicted a 'dim if not dismal future' for NATO if the European allies did not improve their contributions to collective defence. That speech led to action in NATO with the launch at the Chicago summit in 2012 of Smart Defence and the Connected Forces Initiative. Both initiatives represented an attempt to improve capabilities under conditions of (rapidly) contracting defence budgets, and both can be seen as examples of purposive action designed to strengthen NATO's defence alliance identity. With the dramatic deterioration in the relationship with Russia, that identity and purposive action to support it has acquired a degree of urgency. At the Wales summit in September 2014 the Alliance was able to agree new measures to strengthen NATO territorial defence – most notably agreement on a Readiness Action Plan, a Spearhead Force which would be able to launch in a matter of days, as well as a continuous presence on NATO's eastern flank, including the pre-positioning of armaments and equipment (NATO 2014). The (re)-introduction of purposive action related to collective defence may well be the biggest change in NATO's recent history.

Conclusion: NATO's prospects and the utility of constructivism

The analysis of this chapter has shown that NATO endures because, with the exception of the 'dark decade' of the 2000s, the Alliance has maintained a stable corporate and collective identity based on shared values. This provides its members with the esteem associated with belonging to a status-giving social group. Moreover, the existence of three parallel type and role identities has enabled different members to each emphasise their preferred identity, whereas the tacit agreement not to openly disagree about such fundamental questions as 'what NATO is' has enabled the Alliance to continue as though these identities are entirely complementary.

NATO has also been able (to varying degrees) to maintain a supporting narrative of cohesion and solidarity based on shared values and a practice of negotiation reinforced through consensus decision making. During the 1990s this was reinforced by purposive action facilitated by a beneficial (for NATO) constellation of factors in the external environment, such as EU and UN impotence in the Balkans, which endowed the Alliance with a high level of self-esteem.

The Alliance was, however, launched into crisis at the beginning of the new millennium because of a highly damaging convergence of both practice and action, and because the Bush administration undermined long-established (and highly cherished) practices. NATO's efforts have since been concentrated on re-establishing its ontological security. The prospects for doing so look promising, though much will depend on the continued adherence to the principles established in the 2010 Strategic Concept and on the expeditious implementation of the decisions taken at the Wales summit to bolster NATO's capabilities. Without these, NATO will not be able to maintain its revived emphasis on the defence alliance identity. Meeting capability goals has, in that sense, become more important than at any time during the last quarter of a century because NATO's defence alliance identity is, following the deterioration of relations with Russia, no longer in the background.

NATO's strength lies in its three-pronged identity – as a defence alliance, a forum for cooperation and dialogue and as a crisis management institution. This gives it an adaptability that is very unusual among international institutions. As long as NATO can maintain flexibility in how it ranks these three identities in light of its external circumstances, and as long as it can construct a convincing narrative to support them, reinforced in turn by action and practices, then the prospects for NATO's continued endurance are good.

As for more theoretical matters, the benefit of constructivism lies in its ability to get at aspects of NATO's development that are not visible to the more traditional perspectives of realism and liberalism. By focusing on identity, constructivism is able to differentiate between NATO's performance as a defence alliance, a forum for partnership and cooperation and a crisis management organisation. Without an understanding of multiple identities, these would appear contradictory. By utilising the constructivist approach outlined here, policy makers are, in fact, furnished with an identity-based 'roadmap' on how to proceed as the challenges of new ongoing change in the international environment once again makes it imperative for NATO to react. From this perspective NATO's days – or, indeed, years – are not numbered as many realists once assumed, because NATO is much more flexible and adaptive than a traditional defence alliance with a fixed identity could ever be. Even so, it remains to be seen if the constructivist approach can move from the abstract 'world of theory' to the pragmatic 'world of policy'.

Notes

1 Karl Deutsch and his associates were arguing in the 1950s that increased trans-border interactions would gradually lead to 'mutual sympathy and loyalties [. . .] trust and mutual consideration' (Deutsch et al 1957: 36), which in turn would produce new identities (a 'we-feeling'). Deutsch argued that a so-called 'security community' might result, which would be characterised by 'dependable expectations of peaceful change'. (See also Adler and Barnett, 1998: 34).

2 'Practice' is understood here as mainly concerned with competent routinised performance. 'Action', following Charles Taylor (1964) is conceptualised as behavior directed towards a specific goal and linked with desires, intentions and purposes – attributes that are not necessarily present in the more habitual nature of practice.

3 Strategic Concepts were adopted in 1949, 1952, 1957 and 1968. As Ringsmose and Rynning (2011: 9) have written, these documents 'were explicit' in addressing 'an easily identifiable adversary, the Soviet Union, and set out to define guidelines for the Alliance's military defence.' The Cold War Strategic Concepts are available at: www.nato.int/archives/strategy.htm

4 As well as in the Strategic Concepts, this clarity of purpose is evident in a series of other keynote NATO documents: 'The Report of the Committee of Three' of 1956, the 'Ottawa Declaration' of 1974 and the 'Washington Statement on East-West Relations' of 1984. See Webber, Sperling and Smith (2012: 23–24).

5 As suggested by Hay (1999), crisis narratives can be political constructs invoked by the agent to give the appearance that a specific problem is recognised and that action to fix the problem will be taken. As seemed to be the case with burden sharing in NATO, the crisis narrative became permanent and actually supported an identity that expressed the problem. I have raised this issue in a number of interviews with NATO officials, who have all (off the record) supported the view presented here – that the

crisis narrative on burden sharing served (and continues to serve) a useful function in justifying American leadership of the Alliance.

6   The phrase here is adapted from Risse-Kappen (1994).

7   Although it might be argued that 9/11 constitutes a critical juncture, this is not the case from a NATO identity perspective. The Alliance was quick to invoke Article Five in support of the attack on the United States. Because the decision was made unanimously, it was actually seen as a major achievement, which supported NATO's identity as a defence alliance.

8   Events are undertheorised in constructivism, as they belong neither at the agent or structural level. Moreover, policy is frequently dismissed as reactive, that is not indicative of an agent's (i.e., NATO's) inherent character. The view taken here is that policy is, by necessity, 'reactive' and that the often-haphazard occurrence of events ought to be included in theorizing as a 'stochastic' element of the social and material world. See Suganami (1999).

9   Confidential interviews with NATO official, April 2010.

References

[All web sources listed were last accessed 12 June 2015.]

Adler, E. (2008). 'The Spread of Security Communities: Communities of Practice, Self-Restraint and NATO's Post Cold War Transformation', *European Journal of International Relations* 14(2): 195–230.

Adler, E. and Barnett, M. (eds). (1998). *Security Communities*, Cambridge: Cambridge University Press.

Behnke, A. (2013). *NATO's Security Discourse after the Cold War*, London: Routledge.

Bellamy, A. (2004). *Security Communities and their Neighbours: Regional Fortresses or Global Integrators?* Houndsmills, Basingstoke: Palgrave.

Cox, M. (2005). 'Beyond the West: Terrors in Transatlatia', *European Journal of International Relations* 11(2): 203–233.

Craib, I. (1998). *Experiencing Identity*. London: Sage.

Dessler, D. (1989). 'What's at Stake in the Agent-Structure Debate?' *International Organisation* 43(3): 441–473.

Deutsch, K. W., Burrell, S. A., Kann, R. A., Lee Jr., M., Lichterman, M., Lindgren, R. E., Lowenheim, F. L. and Van Read Wagenen, R. W. (1957). *Political Community and the North Atlantic Area: International Organization in the Light of Historical Expericence*, Princeton: Princeton University Press.

Epstein, C. (2011). 'Who Speaks? Discourse, the Subject and the Study of Identity in International Politics', *European Journal of International Relations* 17(2): 327–350

Fergusson, J. (2010). *Taliban: The Unknown Enemy*, Boston: De Capo Press.

Finnemore, M. and Sikkink, K. (1998). 'International Norms Dynamics and Political Change', *International Organisation* 52(4): 887–917.

Flockhart, T. (ed). (2005). *Socializing Democratic Norms*, Houndsmills, Basingstoke: Palgrave.

Flockhart, T. (2006). '"Complex Socialisation": A Framework for the Study of State Socialisation', *European Journal of International Relations* 12(1): 89–118.

Flockhart, T. (2012). 'Constructivism and Foreign Policy', in Smith, S. Hadfield, A. and Dunne, T. (eds). *Foreign Policy. Theories, Actors, Cases*, Oxford: Oxford University Pres

Flockhart, T. (ed). (2014). *Cooperative Security: NATO's Partnership Policy in a Changing World*, Copenhagen: Danish Institute for International Studies.

Gheciu, A. (2005a). *NATO in the "New Europe": The Politics of International Socialisation after the Cold War*, Stanford: Stanford University Press.

Gheciu, A. (2005b). 'Security Institutions as Agents of Socialisation? NATO and the "New Europe"', *International Organization* 59(4): 973–1012.

Giddens, A. (1984). *The Constitution of Society: Outline of the Theory of Structuration*, Cambridge: Polity Press.

Giddens, A. (1991). *Modernity and Self-Identity: Self and Society in the Late Modern Age*, Cambridge: Polity Press.

Goldgeier, J. M. (1999). *Not Whether but When: The US Decision to Enlarge NATO*, Washington D.C.: The Brookings Institution.

Harrison, E. (2002), 'Waltz, Kant and Systemic Approaches to International Relations', *Review of International Studies* 28(1): 143–162.

Hauser, B. (1994). 'The Development of NATO's Nuclear Strategy', *Contemporary European History* 4(1): 37–66.

Hay, C. (1999). 'Crisis and the Structural Transformation of the State: Interrogating the Process of Change', *British Journal of Politics and International Relations*, 1(3): 317–344.

Hopf, T. (1998). 'The Promise of Constructivism in International Relations Theory', *International Security* 23(1): 171–200.

Hopf, T. (2010). 'The Logic of Habit in International Relations', *European Journal of International Relations* 16(4): 539–561.

Kavalski, E. (2008). *Extending the European Security Community: Constructing Peace in the Balkans*, London: IB Tauris.

Kupchan, C. and Trubowitz, P. (2007). 'Grand Strategy for A Divided America', *Foreign Affairs* 86(4): 71–83.

Lebow, R. N. (2008). *A Cultural Theory of International Relations*, Cambridge: Cambridge University Press.

Mitzen, J. (2006). 'Ontological Security in World Politics: State, Identity and the Security Dilemma', *European Journal of International Relations* 12(3): 341–370.

NATO. (1949). 'The North Atlantic Treaty', at: www.nato.int/docu/basictxt/treaty.htm.

NATO. (1967). 'The Future Tasks of the Alliance: Report of the Council (The Harmel Report)', at: www.nato.int/archives/harmel/harmel.htm.

NATO. (1990). 'Declaration: On A Transformed North Atlantic Alliance', 5–6 July 1990 at: www.nato.int/cps/en/natolive/official_texts_23693.htm.

NATO. (1991). 'The Alliance's New Strategic Concept', 7–8 November at: www.nato.int/cps/en/natolive/official_texts_23847.htm.

NATO. (1995). 'Study on NATO Enlargement', 3 September at: www.nato.int/cps/en/natolive/official_texts_24733.htm.

NATO. (2009). 'Strasbourg/Kehl Summit Declaration', NATO Press Release (2009) 044, 4 April at: www.nato.int/cps/en/natolive/news_52837.htm?mode=pressrelease.

NATO. (2010). 'Active Engagement, Modern Defence. Strategic Concept for the Defence and Security of the North Atlantic Treaty Organization'. 19 November, at: www.nato.int/cps/en/natolive/official_texts_68580.htm.

NATO. 2011. 'Active Engagement in Cooperative Security: A More Efficient and Flexible Partnership Policy', at: www.nato.int/nato_static/assets/pdf/pdf_2011_04/20110415_110415-Partnership-Policy.pdf.

NATO. (2014). 'Wales Summit Declaration', NATO Press Release (2014) 120, 5 September at: www.nato.int/cps/en/natohq/official_texts_112964.htm.

Neumann, I. B. (1999). *Uses of the Other: 'The East' in European Identity Formation*, Manchester: Manchester University Press.

Onuf, N. G. (1989). *World of Our Making: Rules and Rule in Social Theory and International Relations*, Columbia: University of South Carolina Press.

Peterson, J. (2004). 'America as a European Power: the End of Empire by Integration?' *International Affairs* 80(4): 613–629.

Pettman, R. (2000). *Commonsense Constructivism: Or the Making of World Affairs*, Armonk: M. E.Sharpe.

Pouliot, V. (2004). 'The Essence of Constructivism', *Journal of International Relations and Development* 7(3): 319–336.

Ringsmose, J. and Rynning S. (2011). 'Introduction: Taking Stock of NATO's New Strategic Concept', in Ringsmose, J. and Rynning, S. (eds). NATO's New Strategic Concept: A Comprehensive Assessment. *DIIS Report*. Copenhagen, Danish Institute for International Studies

Risse-Kappen, T. (1994). 'Ideas Do Not Float Freely: Transnational Coalitions, Domestic Structures and the End of the Cold War', *International Organisation*, 48(2): 185–214.

Rubin, M. and Hewstone, M. (1998). 'Social Identity Theory's Self-Esteem Hypothesis: A Review and Some Suggestions for Clarification', *Personality and Social Psychology Review*, 2(1): 40–62.

Rynning, S. (2012). *NATO in Afghanistan: the Liberal Disconnect*, Stanford: Stanford University Press.

Rynning, S. and Ringsmose. J. (2009). 'Come Home, NATO?: The Atlantic Alliance's New Strategic Concept', *DIIS Report*, Copenhagen: Danish Institute for International Studies.

Schwartz, D. (1983). *NATO's Nuclear Dilemma*. Washington, D.C.: Brookings Institution.

Shanker, T. (2011). 'Defence Secretary Warns NATO of "Dim" Future', *New York Times*, 10 June, at: www.nytimes.com/2011/06/11/world/europe/11gates.html?_r= 0.

Simakovsky, M. (2013). 'Flexible Expansion: NATO Enlargement in an Era of Austerity and Uncertainty', *Foreign Policy Papers*, Washington, D.C.: German Marshall Fund.

Slaughter, A. M. (2011). 'International Relations, Principal Theories' in Wolfrum, R (ed). *Max Planck Encyclopedia of Public International Law*, Oxford: Oxford University Press.

Steele, B. J. (2005). 'Ontological Security and the Power of Self-identity: British Neutrality and the American Civil War', *Review of International Studies* 31(3): 519–540.

Suganami, H. (1999). 'Agents, Structures, Narratives', *European Journal of International Relations* 5(3): 365–386.

Tajfel, H. (1982). *Social Identity and Intergroup Relations*, Cambridge:, Cambridge University Press.

Taylor, C. A. (1964). *The Explanation of Behaviour*, London: Routledge and Kegan Paul.

The Economist. (2012). 'Russia and NATO: Rethink the Reset', 19 May, at: www.economist.com/node/21555580.

Thies, W. J. (2003). *Friendly Rivals: Bargaining and Burden-Shifting in NATO*, New York: M. E. Sharpe.

Turner, J. (1987). *Rediscovering the Social Group: A Self-categorization Theory*, London: Blackwell-Wiley.

Waltz, K. N. (1979). *Theory of International Politics*, Reading: Addison-Wesley.

Waltz, K. (1993). 'The Emerging Structure of International Politics', *International Security* 18(2): 44–79.

Webber, M., Sperling, J., and Smith, M. A. (2012). *NATO's Post-Cold War Trajectory: Decline or Regeneration?* Houndmills, Basingstoke: Palgrave Macmillan.

Wendt, A. (1992). 'Anarchy Is What States Make of It: The Social Construction of Power Politics', *International Organization* 46(2): 395–421.

Wendt, A. (1999). *Social Theory of International Politics*, Cambridge: Cambridge University Press.

8 Securitisation theory and the evolution of NATO

Gabi Schlag

It is often stated that NATO remains the cornerstone of transatlantic security cooperation, symbolising the special bonds between North America and Europe.[1] Since its foundation in 1949, the Alliance has undergone a remarkable transformation in its mission and membership and has survived many internal crises. Having reacted creatively to a changed security environment after the dissolution of the Warsaw Pact, NATO in the wake of Russian assertiveness over Ukraine has seemingly been placed back in the business of territorial defence. Stephen Walt (2014) has even stated that 'NATO owes Putin a big thank you' for showing that the Alliance 'still matters'.

NATO's mission has, however, always been ambitious and complex: ensuring peaceful relation between Western states, integrating a re-armed West Germany, modernising national military capacities, providing effective territorial defence of Western Europe during the heyday of the Cold War and securing member states against diffuse risks and dangers in the years that have followed. In this light, NATO needs to be regarded as more than simply a *military* alliance based on the collective defence pledge contained in Article Five of the North Atlantic Treaty. Security politics, broadly conceived, are its *raison d'état*, including nuclear deterrence and collective defence, but also border control and training missions, expeditionary out-of-area operations and the less obvious military policies of enlargement and partnership.

That 'security' and security policy refer to more than just military defence has been an issue of academic and political dispute since the 1980s when questions of environmental security, human security, 'societal' security and so on scored high on the political agenda of Western societies (Buzan and Hansen 2009: 156–255). Bearing in mind these debates between advocates of a narrow and of a widened concept of security, members of the so-called Copenhagen School have argued that 'security' is not fixed but is essentially a 'speech act'. Here, security implies a specific grammar based on the invocation of a threat to a valued referent object. That object (be it a state, a nation, a social or ethnic group, or an individual) is, following a logic of securitisation, afforded protection when threatened, including through extraordinary measures which might not conform to the normal procedures of political, hence democratic, decision making (Buzan, de Wilde and Wæver 1998; Wæver 1995). The labeling of political challenges as security issues can consequently be explained by reference to the manifold articulations of politicians and experts, which have stretched the very meaning of security, often giving rise to ambivalent consequences for security politics itself.

It is rather surprising that this 'linguistic turn' in security studies, exemplified by the Copenhagen School, has only occasionally addressed NATO's existence, politics and continuous transformation (Behnke 2013). There is an extensive literature which theorises the transatlantic Alliance in relation to a wide range of traditional approaches such as realism, institutionalism, alliance theory and constructivism (Duffield 1994; Gheciu 2005; Glaser 1993; Hellmann and Wolf 1993; McCalla 1996; Risse-Kappen 1995, 1996; Schimmelfennig 2003;Snyder 1990; Wallander 2000; Walt 1997). With the end of the Cold War, these debates converged on the question of whether NATO would dissolve or survive. Hellmann (2008: 30), however, has argued that by emphasising large-scale causal processes of transformation 'the *structure* of the most prominent explanations is often quite similar irrespective of paradigmatic ancestry'. A handful of so-called 'critical' approaches, including discourse theory, post-structuralism and practice theory, have been applied to NATO since the early 1990s, although the interest in alliances as such has been rather limited (Adler 2008; Behnke 2013; Bially Mattern 2005; Hellmann 2006; Jackson 2003; Klein 1990; Neumann and Williams 2000; Pouliot 2010).

In what follows, I focus on one particular body of work that has emerged from the field of critical security studies since the mid-1990s, namely Securitisation Theory (ST) most prominently associated with the Copenhagen School. Specifically, I argue that ST provides a sophisticated toolbox for analyzing the origin, evolution and transformation of NATO. The main conceptual and methodological advantage of ST is twofold. First, ST directs our attention to discourses and practices at work which continuously *re*-constitute NATO as a collective security actor. Here, the Alliance is not taken for granted, but is valued for its changing nature and ongoing processes of community formation (Hellmann et al 2014; Tilly 1998). The existence (and persistence) of NATO thus largely depends on the symbolic discourses mobilised by its members in the light of changing strategic challenges, be it the danger of Soviet expansion in the early 1950s, mass human rights violations in Kosovo in 1999 or the annexation of Crimea by Russia in 2014. Second, this focus on community formation rather than a fixed common identity bears the added value of not overstating NATO's political and normative foundation, one in which a serious crisis and the break-up of the institution is often perceived as a worst-case (but conceivable) scenario. Rather, conflicts and disputes over NATO's mission indicate how any community of states is based on changing discourses of (in-)security – that is, on structures of meaning (in use) which potentially change over time.

The following section provides a brief introduction to ST based on its three key pillars: de-/securitisation, security sectors and regional security complexes. The chapter's second part focuses on three periods of NATO's evolution: (1) the foundational years of NATO in the early 1950s, (2) détente as expressed by the Harmel Report in 1967 and (3) NATO's transformation after the end of the Cold

War in the early 1990s. These three periods serve as spotlights for showing how ST sheds light on how to analyze and theorize NATO.

What is securitisation theory (for)?

ST can claim to be one of the most prominent and successful research programmes on security of the post–Cold War period. Since its first publications on societal security and migration in the late 1980s and early 1990s, the Copenhagen School, centered on the Copenhagen Peace Research Institute (COPRI), has advanced the academic debate on the very meaning of security and security politics. This literature on securitisation has steadily grown since Ole Wæver's conceptual outline of a speech-act approach to security in 1995.

ST has been widely used, refined but also criticised for its narrow focus on speech acts.[2] Compared with the many paradigmatic approaches presented in this volume, ST is a conceptual toolbox rather than an axiomatic theory with ontological assumptions. As for theory, Ole Wæver partly follows Waltz (1979: 8) in describing it 'as a picture, mentally formed, of a bounded realm or domain of activity'. He significantly adds that a 'theory is political primarily through the way it conditions analyses, because a theory is a construct that enables particular observations about cases' (Wæver 2011: 466).[3] Wæver also states that a theory is not found but creatively made, emphasising that the core of a theory refers to 'some *idea* for how to conceive of a field' (Wæver 2003: 1, note 3; italics in the original) – 'securitization as an act', he suggests, is such an idea (Wæver 2011: 468).[4]

Security as a speech act: securitization and the state of emergency

Although the Latin noun *securus* means freedom from pain, security includes a variety of meanings which have evolved over time (Daase 2010). From the mid-seventeenth century, providing internal and external security became a main task of the nation-state and was necessary to legitimise its government (Conze 1984: 843). The political triumph of the term security then occurred in the twentieth century most symbolically expressed in the concepts of collective security understood as a way to secure peace (Conze 1984: 861). Security always implied different political and social connotations, but it was not until the mid-1980s that non-military issues scored high on the international security agenda, including questions of environmental degradation, natural disasters and human trafficking. Declaring these issues as relevant for security politics often implied giving them more attention and priority in domestic politics. Whereas critics (mostly from the political left) were concerned with the militarisation of development politics, academic scholars feared the dissolution of security as a coherent research field (Walt 1991: 223).

Bearing this debate between a narrow and a wide concept of security in mind, ST emphasizes the *inter*-subjective and *performative* quality of security. ST takes side with neither the wide or narrow position on the meaning of security; its aim is to understand the social processes by which insecurities and referent objects of security are constituted, that is, through a process of *securitisation*. ST has a conceptually narrow focus on a specific form of speech act ('existential threat', 'survival of a valued referent object', 'call for immediate action')[5] but an empirically wide focus on different actors, objects and sectors (Wæver 2011: 469).

Thus, ST does not give an answer to the contested question of whether migration (for instance) is 'really' a security problem, but directs attention to the discourses whereby 'migration' might become an issue of security politics when actors refer to it in a security-related manner. In other words, ST 'insists on securityness being a quality not of threats but of their handling, that is, the theory places power not with "things" external to a community but internal to it' (Wæver 2011: 468).

Further, this focus on the inter-subjectivity of security does not mean that security is simply a construction, something people have in their mind that does not really exist and thus does not really matter. Rather, security is the performative effect of an inter-subjective communication process understood as 'the move that takes politics beyond the established rules of the game' (Buzan, de Wilde and Wæver, 1998: 23). Security, in short, is a speech act performed by powerful political actors which means that something is *done* by uttering 'security' (Wæver, 1995: 55, 79–80 note 23).

Conceptualized as a speech act, ST assumes that 'security' follows a specific discursive form: it is about the invocation of a threat to a referent object which is seen as a danger to survival; it is the call for an immediate response and of protection measures (Buzan, de Wilde and Wæver, 1998: 21). Because the survival of the referent object is considered a just cause, securitisation legitimises the use of extraordinary measures, including the use of force, to protect it. By this act, defining something as a security issue takes it beyond the established rules and procedures of political contestation and frames it as an existential problem. This move is 'similar to raising a bet – staking more on the specific issue, giving it principled importance and thereby investing it with basic order questions' (Wæver 1995: 80 fn. 24).

The concept of a speech act – that something is done by naming threats and dangers – directs our attention to the sayings and doings that *constitute* security as a social and political field. Taking this performative conception of security means seriously acknowledging the illocutionary and perlocutionary power of speech acts, and recognising 'that it indicates realms where political action could have been different' (Guzzini 2005: 508). It is not just a word one utters; it is a social practice with tremendous political consequences and normative implications.

Understanding de-securitisation: politics as public contestation

Understanding securitisation as a social practice relies on a political theory which is mostly implicit in the formulations of ST. Some critics have argued that ST rests on the doctrine of decisionism associated with Carl Schmitt, the notion that the validity of a decision (or act) is a function, not of its content, but the fact that it was taken by a particular, authoritative actor. The Schmittian legacy in ST, Williams (2003: 515) stresses, should not be conflated with Schmitt's political advocacy of a 'Führer-ideology' in the Third Reich but 'by an understanding of the politics of enmity, decision, and emergency'. Speaking security is commonly based on enemy constructions and so raises public attention and enables actors to break free from constraining decision-making rules. Guzzini (2011: 332), in this light, notes that 'whereas exceptionalism is the fundament of the "political" in Schmitt, it is the end of the political in securitisation studies'.

Wæver's conception of securitisation and politics differs markedly from Schmitt's notion of exceptionalism and the friend–enemy dichotomy. With reference to Hannah Arendt, he writes that 'politics is productive, irreducible and happens *among* people as an unpredictable chain of actions' (Wæver 2011: 468; italics in the original). Politics thus implies public contestation among people over political questions, including those debates where political issues are framed, opinions are formed and arguments are exchanged in the first place. Politics, though, always implies that decisions *could* have been different but are driven by specific forces that encompass a decision.

Bearing such a conception of politics in mind, securitisation then directs our attention precisely to the practices and discourses that move issues out of public contestation, where actions are taken among people, and into a sphere of emergency, where mostly elites are in charge. Emergency implies that the time for deliberation has passed and that a decision whether to act (creating security) or not to act (remaining insecure) has to be made (Wæver 1998).

The notion of the political in ST has also generated a debate on the concept of de-securitisation and the dissolution of friend–enemy constructions. As Buzan, de Wilde and Wæver (1998: 4) write:

> security should not be thought of too easily as always a good thing. It is better [. . .] to aim for de-securitisation: the shifting of issues out of the emergency mode and into the normal bargaining process of the political sphere.

Claudia Aradau (2004: 390) has argued that choosing between securitisation and de-securitisation is 'a choice about the politics we want'. For Aradau, the formulation of securitisation as a move towards a state of exception, including strong friend–enemy dichotomies, is measured against the background of democratic procedures (Aradau 2004: 392). Whereas democratic institutions slow down decision-making processes, the successful invocation of 'security' regularly hastens these processes. Consequently, democratic control exercised by publics or courts is often marginalised or even suspended. De-securitisation, Aradau (2004: 400) then claims, requires 'a process of re-thinking the relation between subjects of security, and of imagining localised, less exclusionary and violent forms of interaction'. She concludes, that

> [i]f securitisation orders social relations according to the logic of political realism and institutionalizes an exceptionalism of speed, extraordinary measures and friend/enemy, de-securitisation is a normative project which reclaims a notion of democratic politics where the struggle for emancipation is possible.
>
> (Aradau 2004: 406)

Huysmans (2006: 125, italics added) leads us in a similar direction by suggesting that de-securitisation 'refers to the process of *unmaking* the fabrication of domains of insecurity'; 'de-securitisation unmakes politics that identify the political community on the basis of exceptions of hostility' (Huysmans 2006: 130). De-securitisation is thus a critical strategy which relocates political questions in a public sphere where they are not articulated in terms of an existential threat. Schou Tjalve (2011: 442) claims, similarly, that the endeavor of de-securitisation is 'not a matter of constructing forms of political order in which securitizing moves are less likely to *occur*. It is a matter of constructing forms of political order in which securitising moves are less likely to *succeed* (italics in original)'.

Wæver has added that 'de-securitisation is preferable in the abstract, but concrete situations might call for securitisation', though de-securitisation 'fosters critical attention to the costs of securitisation' (Wæver 2011: 469), in particular to the production of a state of emergency, an acceleration of decision-making processes and the empowerment of governments. Studies of de-securitisation in this light might be helpful in mapping how issues move on and off the security agenda, whereas understanding de-securitisation as a constitutive logic of community plays an important role directing our attention to community formations where existential threats and hostility have ceased to exist (Adler 2008; Tilly 1998; Wæver 1998).

Security sectors and regional patterns of security practices

Whereas speech-act theory leads to a rather specific analytical focus on securitising moves by politically powerful agents, the concept of 'security sectors' allows for a broader empirical consideration of how different referent objects interact within different arenas of security (Buzan, Wæver and de Wilde 1998: 27). The military and political sectors traditionally relate to the security of the state and of sovereignty; societal security articulates threats in terms of an endangered collective identity. The referent objects in the economic and ecological sector, meanwhile, often remain unspecified, but have been of central interest in recent years due to the debate on climate change and global economic crisis (Boy, Burgess, Leander 2011; Floyd 2010). Sectors and referent object are not fixed, but subject to historical changes as the enlargement of security politics (and studies) exemplifies (Albert and Buzan 2011).

Beyond sectors, Buzan and Wæver's (2003) approach to regional security complexes is based on a combination of realist and constructivist thinking. 'On the material side', they write, 'it uses ideas of bounded territoriality and distribution of power. [. . .]. On the constructivist side, [it] builds on securitisation theory [. . .] which focus on the political process by which security issues get constituted' (Buzan and Wæver 2003: 4). Advocating a regionalist approach to security, the authors map out 'actual patterns of security practices', that is processes of securitisation and de-securitisation that are regionally clustered (Buzan and Wæver 2003: 41). Thus, regional security complexes are 'defined by durable patterns of amity and enmity' (Buzan and Wæver 2003: 45). Buzan and Wæver (2003: 73) go on to suggest that

> one needs to look at [. . .] pattern of security connectedness in three steps: (1) is the issue securitised successfully by any actors?; (2) if yes, track the links and interactions from this instance [. . .] ; (3) these chains can then be collected as a cluster of interconnected security concerns.

It is surprising that NATO does not play a major role in their analysis. Europe and the US are divided by Buzan and Wæver into two regional security complexes, and the authors casually state that '[s]ecurity politics during the Cold War mostly consisted of struggles over how intensely to securitise superpower rivalry versus [how] to de-securitise it through détente or deterrence' (Buzan and Wæver 2003: 352). NATO after the Cold War, meanwhile, is posited as part of the institutionalisation of Europe's military sector (Buzan and Wæver 2003: 370).

Before turning to NATO's transformation, let me briefly summarise how ST provides a useful framework for theorising and analyzing the Alliance. Focusing on practices of securitisation (and de-securitisation) helps to understand how cooperation 'took a unique form as the North Atlantic alliance developed into an *organisation* (NATO) uncharacteristic for alliances' (Buzan and Wæver 2003: 354). Using ST for theorising NATO, however, is not an attempt to isolate cases of securitising speech act comparable to 'smoking guns'[6] or 'a kind of single bombshell event' (Guzzini 2011: 335). A broader historical perspective rather, focusing on the evolution and transformation of the Alliance, shows how NATO's political organisation and symbolic power has been the product of a security discourse oriented around securitising, de-securitising and re-securitising practices.

The evolution of an alliance: practices of securitisation and de-securitisation

Since its foundation in 1949, NATO and its member states have witnessed many ups and downs. Periodising NATO's history, however, remains a contested endeavor. According to its major Strategic Concepts, I distinguish three periods: first, the formative years between 1949 and 1966 with massive retaliation as NATO's key security strategy; second, the intra-Alliance crisis, the evolution of flexible response and détente between 1967 and the end of the 1980s; and third, the beginning of the post–Cold War period in the early 1990s. These periods are rather broad and loose constructions but seem helpful in order to address processes of securitisation and de-securitisation in relation to NATO's security discourse.[7] The decisions on new or revised and restated Strategic Concepts in 1949, 1968 and 1991 serve as spotlights here. The most recent Strategic Concepts of 1999 and 2010, as well as NATO's engagement in Afghanistan, are not included in this study for reasons of space. However, the transformations covered in this chapter more than suffice to highlight the applicability of ST when studying the Alliance.

Founding a transatlantic alliance: securitising 'the East' and de-securitising 'the West'

When tensions between the Western powers and the Soviet Union intensified after World War Two the formalisation of a transatlantic alliance was perceived as a means to counter and deter an apparent eastern threat.[8] Whereas France and the UK, the driving forces behind the initiative to form a military alliance, called for a lasting American presence in European affairs, the Truman administration, driven by isolationist sentiments in Congress, was more reserved in pursuing such a project (Kaplan 1999: 7–28; Osgood 1962).[9] Most controversial here was the issue of military assistance. Whereas the US government preferred a non-binding and declaratory formulation, French diplomat Armand Bérard and British diplomat Sir Frederic Hoyer-Millar, both delegates to the so-called 'exploratory talks', insisted on a reliable and forceful assurance of US military assistance (Kaplan 1999: 16–17). When the Truman government drafted a compromise formula, US objections to a formalised alliance were overcome. In a memo to President Truman in 1948, his advisor Clark Clifford remarked that the preamble of a transatlantic declaration should make clear that 'the main object of the instrument would be to preserve Western civilization in the geographical area covered by the agreement'.[10]

The North Atlantic Treaty, signed on 4 April 1949 by representatives of ten West European states plus the US and Canada, outlined the principles of the new alliance – consultation (Article Four) and collective defence (Article Five) – and called for the development of an organisational structure (Article Nine). The preamble of the treaty states:

> The parties to this Treaty reaffirm their faith in the purpose and principles of the Charter of the United Nations and their desire to live in peace with all peoples and governments. They are determined to safeguard the freedom, common heritage and civilization of their peoples, founded on the principles of democracy, individual liberty and the rule of law. They seek to promote stability and well-being in the North Atlantic area.
>
> (NATO, 1949a)

The contractual language ('parties', 'Treaty') of the preamble postulated a community based on shared principles as laid out in the Charter of the United Nations closely linked to democracy, liberty, and the rule of law. In the late 1940s, such an equivalence between these principles and Western democracies was not surprising, given the overall perception of a clash between a 'free world' on the one side and 'communist' totalitarian systems on the other. However, the preamble uses an interesting formulation: it assumes that a community of like-mined states is already in existence due to the act of '*re*-affirming' a common faith expressed in another legal document, the Charter of the United Nations, as well as '*re*-affirming' a shared desire to live in peace. Such a community is then defined by referring to freedom, common heritage and civilization, as well as the principles of democracy, individual liberty and the rule of law.

Invoking NATO as an assumed value community symbolised a willingness to dissociate its foundation from the specific political circumstances of 1948–1949. It united the geographical, historical and political project of a 'Western' alliance between North America and (Western) Europe. That said, although the term 'area' evoked associations of space and territory, the boundaries of this entity remained rather vague due to the geographical fuzziness of the term 'North Atlantic' (Franke 2010).[11] As the preamble suggests, NATO members do not defend each other against a specific, identifiable threat, but share a political space with various social and cultural relations worthy of being secured at any time.

NATO at the time was generally described as a system of collective defence; yet as an expression of an already existing geopolitical community this was of a particular type. For most West European states, Article Five formalised the (military) assistance of its transatlantic partner and the commitment of the US to rebuild western Europe. Military assistance, though, was not simply a higher act of inter-state diplomacy; rather it was invoked with a strong notion of solidarity. As Article Five states:

> The Parties agree that an armed attack against one or more of them in Europe or North America shall be considered an attack against them all and consequently they agree that, if such an armed attack occurs, each of them, in exercise of the right of individual or collective self-defence recognised by Article 51 of the Charter of the United Nations, will assist the Party or Parties so attacked by taking forthwith, individually and in concert with the other Parties, such action as it deems necessary, including the use of armed force, to restore and maintain the security of the North Atlantic area.
>
> (NATO 1949a)

Article Five was perceived as a 'pledge' made by the US to defend its West European allies alarmed by the superior strength of Soviet conventional forces.[12] Framing this pledge in terms of mutual assistance and the indivisibility of transatlantic security was strongly symbolic even if the commitment contained in Article Five was not intended to be automatic (the parties would assist with such measures as deemed necessary). This compromise made possible the co-existence of different interpretations of the Treaty's core clause. For the US Congress, opposed to the 'entanglement' of the US in a European alliance, it expressed a certain freedom of choice in how American support to allies could be exercised. For West European states, meanwhile, Article Five confirmed the solidarity and military assistance of US conventional and in particular nuclear forces if such assistance should become necessary.

Article Five is usually described as the cornerstone of collective defence. Its institutional consequences, though, were somewhat ambivalent: on the one hand, it expressed the defensive purpose of the Alliance (to '*restore* [. . .] security'); on the other, it made possible a policy of internal planning, preparation and precaution in order to '*maintain* the security of the North Atlantic area' (emphasis added). In relation to the geopolitical imagination of a community, regional defence planning was one central institutional consequence which constituted NATO as a political as well as military organisation in the early 1950s. Although Article Five is mostly seen as the 'heart' of NATO, it was only in combination with Article Four (consultation) and Article Nine (the creation of the North Atlantic Council) that an integrated military command structure, the standardisation and modernisation of forces and even a common nuclear policy could develop so quickly.

NATO's first Strategic Concept was drafted in October 1949 and intended to 'ensure unity of thought and purpose' (NATO 1949b; Pedlow 1997; Wheeler 2001: 123). The kind of community imagined by the signatories placed a strong emphasis on unity. The Strategic Concept thus envisaged that NATO might take any measure to provide for the defence of the North Atlantic area with the integration of 'political, economic, and psychological as well as purely military means' (NATO 1949b: paragraph.1) seen as a central requirement of efficient defence. Deterrence and, if necessary, collective defence was set up as a core strategy of prevention *and* preparation, a position expressed succinctly in the inscription on the insignia of the Allied Command Europe: 'vigilance is the price of liberty'.

Key to NATO strategy was an 'ability to deliver the atomic bomb promptly' and this was seen as a 'primarily [. . .] US responsibility' (NATO 1949b: paragraph 7a). Alongside this, the main purpose of NATO was to effectively coordinate and integrate collective defence planning in order to 'unite the strength of the North Atlantic Treaty nations' (NATO 1949b: paragraph 6). This policy included the standardisation of national military doctrines, combined training exercises, the exchange of intelligence information and 'cooperation in the construction, maintenance and operation of military installations of mutual concern' (NATO 1949b: paragraph 8d). Anticipating a potential war with the Soviet Union, NATO's military planning was legitimised as an act of defence which was based on several 'assumptions' about Soviet intentions, for example '[t]hat the USSR will *initiate* air attacks on the North Atlantic Treaty nations in Europe and the Western Hemisphere' (NATO 1950: paragraph 5b, italics added). The Soviet Union was invoked as an expansionist and aggressive adversary with stronger conventional forces than those of the Western allies. Hence, a common nuclear policy was justified as the primary means of preventing war, something which, in turn, guaranteed the influence of the European allies on US security policy (Risse-Kappen 1995; Tuschhoff 1999).

The evolution of NATO's integrated military command structure, including a common nuclear policy, was made possible, then, by a security discourse which invoked a geopolitical community of solidarity based on unity and common values. This discourse, however, does not express straightforward securitising speech acts – the 'smoking guns' – as some readers might expect. The performance of security works in more subtle ways. Despite the clear focus on the Soviet Union as an ideological competitor, NATO's foundation was not articulated simply in terms of rivalry and enmity. It was also done by reference to solidarity (Article 5), consultation (Article 4) and integration (Article 9). Although securitising the Soviets triggered institutional cooperation and integration, inner-alliance relations in parallel became de-securitised. A major war between the member states was not perceived as possible any longer and, together with the European Community, NATO succeeded in fostering a 'Western non-war community' (Wæver 1998), which, crucially, following NATO membership of West Germany in 1955, embedded Europe's centre of political and military gravity.

The strong emphasis on unity and common values pulled NATO member states towards a common goal, hence securitising the Soviet Union and de-securitising intra-Alliance relations were two sides of the same coin. But unity stalled when NATO's security discourse was interrupted by debates on non-military aspects of security and the (mostly) French criticism of US dominance in the 1960s.

Détente and the construction of non-military security: re-securitising 'Europe' and de-securitising 'East–West relations'

When President Charles de Gaulle refused to subordinate French (nuclear) forces to the control of NATO's Supreme Allied Commander Europe (SACEUR) in 1966, the allies witnessed a serious interruption of Western unity. De Gaulle argued that an independent nuclear capacity for France, the *force de frappe*, was means sufficient for the defence of Europe. This was incompatible with the actual power structure of the Alliance involving as it did American control of nuclear forces. De Gaulle's decision to remove French military capabilities from NATO's integrated command structure also played to French concerns at US influence in global affairs. But whatever its cause, the French action was perceived as indicative of a growing intra-Alliance crisis (Haftendorn 1996: 5; Locher 2007).

Interesting in this connection is how de Gaulle invoked an image of an endangered Europe facing altered risks of a nuclear attack by the Soviets. Pictured from the perspective of ST, de Gaulle intended to securitise two rather contrary referent objects – 'Europe' on the one hand and 'national sovereignty' on the other – by problematising intra-alliance power-relations. This period of NATO's transformation and France's re-nationalisation of nuclear forces benefited from at least three circumstances: perceptions of a 'Soviet threat' were diminishing in Europe, public resistance to defence spending and military modernisation in west European societies was rising, and the growing military entanglement of the US in Vietnam shifted attention and resources to Asia. Taken together, these events undermined the credibility of massive retaliation and made a strategic revision likely (Haftendorn 1996: 5). In response, US Secretary of Defence Robert McNamara proposed the new concept of 'flexible response' which remained NATO's official nuclear strategy until the end of the Cold War (NATO 1968). Further, in a public address given before the society of newspaper editors, he criticised 'the tendency to think of our security problem as being exclusively a military problem' (McNamara 1966) and initiated a discussion on non-military aspects of security (and Alliance) policies.

The Harmel Report, published in December 1967, took forward this debate on non-military aspects of security. Despite de Gaulle's pessimistic depiction of a change-resistant Alliance, the report characterised NATO as a 'dynamic and vigorous organisation which is constantly adapting itself to changing conditions' (NATO 1967: paragraph 3). The new doctrine of 'peaceful co-existence has changed the nature of confrontation' between the East and West, but not the 'basic problem', the report argued (NATO 1967: paragraph 4). It went on to ascribe two main functions to NATO. The first – deterrence of aggression and, if necessary, the collective defence of the territories of the allies was consistent with NATO's traditional mission. The second, a 'search for progress towards a more stable relationship [with the Soviet bloc] in which the underlying political issues can be solved' (NATO 1967: paragraph 6), marked a seeming historic shift toward détente. 'The ultimate political purpose of the Alliance', the Harmel report stated, 'is to achieve a just and lasting peaceful order in Europe accompanied by appropriate security guarantees' (NATO 1967: paragraph 9). But although this formulation might appear to be a factor of de-securitisation, military defence remained constitutive of the Alliance.

Thus, although the Harmel report embraced détente and East–West cooperation as a future task of the Alliance, the new Strategic Concept of 1968 (which embraced 'flexible response') belied a highly sceptical view of the intentions of the Warsaw Pact and the Soviet Union. Having just witnessed the withdrawal of France from NATO's integrated military command, one central aim of the revised Strategic Concept was to restore unity and strategic consensus between the European allies and the US. The document not only stated that 'credible deterrence' preserved peace and provided for the 'security of the North Atlantic Treaty area' but, in light of a perceived fragmentation of NATO, emphasised the 'close, positive and continuing collaboration' of the allies in the face of a clear threat:

> Soviet leaders have not renounced as an ultimate aim the extension of Soviet Communist influence throughout the world. [. . .] the fundamental issues underlying the tension between East and West have not been resolved. In this context the Soviets will try to exploit any weaknesses to their own advantage.
>
> (NATO 1968, paragraph .3)

On the one hand, 'flexible response' represented a still-contested strategic approach allowing for different interpretations of deterrence and the role of nuclear weapons (Daalder 1991: 17, 41; Risse-Kappen 1995: 184–187). Yet, on the other, the Strategic Concept restored unity by re-securitising 'the Soviets', in the process shifting détente and arms limitation talks either to the Conference for Security and Cooperation in Europe (CSCE) or to bilateral negotiations between the US and the Soviet Union (giving rise *inter alia* to the Strategic Arms Limitation Treaty in 1971). Although Adler (2008) has argued that NATO was a main driver of cooperative security practices which spread to other European institutions, the Alliance's strategic discourse in the late 1960s directs as much, if not more, attention to the maintenance of its key military role. NATO and the CSCE were two sides of the same coin (détente) but linked to quite different discourses and practices.

The CSCE (and later on the Organisation for Security and Cooperation in Europe [OSCE]) slowly transformed East–West relations and fostered a process of community building based on political consultation and mutual trust, liberal standards, conflict prevention and peaceful settlement of disputes and assistance (Adler 2008: 132). Although NATO (1971: paragraph 12) appraised the CSCE as an initiative aimed at 'reducing the barriers that still exist [in Europe]', the Alliance's ongoing efforts to obtain sufficient defence capabilities indicated a continuing scepticism toward the Soviet Union and its allies. NATO (1971: paragraph 26) argued 'that sufficient and credible defence is a necessary corollary to realistic negotiations on security and co-operation in Europe', and accused the Soviet Union of accelerating the arms race. This representation of ambivalent Soviet intentions and actions justified, in turn, a 'need for [a] continued and systematic improvement of NATO's conventional forces and for the maintenance of adequate and modern tactical and strategic nuclear forces' (NATO 1971: paragraph 28). Yet it is worth mentioning that the re-securitisation of the Soviet Union at this point was ambivalent and variable. With the beginning of talks on mutual and balanced force reductions (MBFR) between NATO member states and the Warsaw Pact in 1973, practices of détente were still in place.

In a nutshell, one could say that representations of détente and deterrence as mutually dependent secured the power basis of the Alliance in the face of an 'Eastern' counterpart which was perceived as an intransigent antagonist. Thus, although intra-alliance de-securitisation was applied to 'Europe' more broadly (through support for détente), this was paralleled by a re-securitisation of the Soviet Union and its rearmament policy. With the disputes over a modernisation of allied Pershing missiles and NATO's twin-track decision in 1979, 'East–West relations' would go on once again to experience common patterns of securitisation, although negotiations between NATO and the Warsaw Pact continued within the MBFR framework and the CSCE.

Re-securitising NATO after the end of the Cold War?

In 1991 NATO adopted a 'new' Strategic Concept. The first years of the 1990s were widely perceived as a period of uncertainty regarding the future direction of security relations between the East and West, yet NATO clung to some familiar tropes. The very title of NATO's keynote statement introduced the subject as a well-known entity; it was *new* but the Strategic Concept retained the identical title to that of its 1968 predecessor. There was thus a taken-for-grantedness in its assumption that NATO, despite the shifts occasioned by the end of the Cold War, would continue to exist.

That said, the central question the Strategic Concept was intended to answer was a profound one: What purpose should NATO serve when a direct territorial threat to the allies had diminished, even vanished? In a world without the Soviet threat, 'Europe' and its (future) transformation was presented as the main referent object of security, including a vision of 'moving beyond past divisions towards one Europe whole and free' (NATO 1991: paragraph 29). Clear distinctions of military and ideological alignment as articulated in the early 1950s had disappeared as well; new, but still uncertain, political relations were developing.

The new Strategic Concept, equally, reactivated geopolitical connotations of the past by focusing primarily on Europe's territorial and political transformation in 'the East', or to be more precise in Central and Eastern Europe (CEE). The Strategic Concept, written while the Soviet Union was still extant, distinguished between the Soviet Union, on the one hand, and the CEE countries, on the other – the 'USSR's former satellites' which 'have fully recovered their sovereignty' (NATO 1991: paragraph 1). Due to political changes in 'the East', the allies also detected 'significant changes' in the West: German unification and the development of a 'European identity in security and defence' aligned to the European Community and the Western European Union (NATO 1991: paragraph 2). Within the document, Western order significantly was presented as an expanding project already anticipating the incorporation of CEE:

> All the countries that were formerly adversaries of NATO have dismantled the Warsaw Pact and rejected ideological hostility to the West. They have, in varying degrees, embraced and begun to implement policies aimed at achieving pluralistic democracy, the rule of law, respect for human rights and a market economy. The political division of Europe that was the source of the military confrontation of the Cold War period has thus been overcome.
>
> (NATO 1991: paragraph 1)

These references to 'pluralistic democracy', 'the rule of law', 'human rights' and 'market economy' occur like a renaissance of the preamble of NATO's founding treaty and symbolically marked the victory of 'the West' over its ideological rivals. As Neumann (2001: 145) has argued, the invention of the category CEE was quite important in opening up the possibility for NATO as well as EU eastern enlargement (see also Schimmelfennig 2003). Such language made it possible to conceive of the CEE countries as being liberated from communist rule and as *returning* to a democratic and free Europe.

The perception of a vanishing Eastern threat and of the re-making of Europe, however, required a revision of NATO's flexible response strategy, including a rationalisation of why NATO should persist at a time when major war was highly unlikely. The integrative appeal of NATO for CEE states was thus accompanied by a new threat assessment. 'In contrast with the predominant threat of the past', the Strategic Concept declared, 'the risks to allied security that remain are multi-faceted in nature and multi-directional which makes them hard to predict and assess' (NATO 1991: paragraph 8). This presentation of diffuse risks relied on a concept of uncertainty and precaution. Some scholars have argued that '[r]isk is becoming the operative concept of Western security' (Rasmussen 2001: 285). Indeed, it was against the background of NATO's existing planning capacities that risk management was constructed as a plausible response to new insecurities and instabilities. This reconfiguration is an example of how a wide concept of security, advocated since the mid-1980s, was captured by the allies in order to justify NATO's continuation.

With the end of the Cold War antagonism, NATO's security discourse also placed a new emphasis on political coordination and cooperation as outlined in Article Four of the North Atlantic Treaty:

> Alliance security interests can be affected by other risks of a wider nature, including proliferation of weapons of mass destruction, disruption of the flow of vital resources and actions of terrorism and sabotage. Arrangements exist within the Alliance for consultation among the Allies under Article 4 of the Washington Treaty and, where appropriate, coordination of their efforts including their responses to such risks.
>
> (NATO 1991: paragraph 12)

Bearing this discursive shift from Article Five to Article Four in mind, out-of-area missions were the most visible institutional consequences of a (re)securitisation process. NATO's military engagement was put into practice when the Allied Mobile Force, a small multinational force established in 1960, was deployed in southeast Turkey during the Gulf War in 1991. The violent fragmentation of Yugoslavia in the following years was perceived as a test case for NATO's self-proclaimed mission of providing regional stability and security. Hence, the Partnership for Peace programme originated initially as a Partnership for Peacekeeping (Wallander 2000: 721). Similarly, the North Atlantic Cooperation Council, composed of NATO member states, representatives from CEE and the former Soviet Union, established an ad hoc group on cooperation in peacekeeping in December 1992

> with the aim of developing a common understanding on the political principles of and the tools for peacekeeping, and to share experience and thereby develop common practical approaches and co-operation in support of peacekeeping under the responsibility of the UN or the CSCE
>
> (NATO 1993: preamble)

Such an initiative to develop common rules and procedures for the conduct of peacekeeping operations strengthened relations between NATO members and non-members, as well as between NATO, the CSCE and the UN, in order to react to precisely the new challenges expressed in the 1991 Strategic Concept. Peace should be 'protected', war should be 'prevented' and in the event of a crisis, NATO forces should 'contribute to the management of such crises and their peaceful resolution' (NATO 1991: paragraph 42). Combined with the identification of new uncertainties and risks, this notion of crisis played an important role. It legitimised the development of rapid reaction forces and multinational forces in order to prevent (or at least contain) critical situations below the level of an inter-state militarised dispute.

Despite this new emphasis on NATO's ability to conduct crisis management, the fear of war still loomed at the back of risk assessment. In the light of various uncertainties – whether a regional crisis, unpredictable risks or inter-state war – the Alliance had to be prepared for nearly anything. Nuclear forces thus were still seen as playing a significant political role 'to preserve peace and prevent coercion and any kind of war' (NATO 1991: paragraph 54). After all, US nuclear forces stationed in Europe symbolised the strong political bond of transatlantic solidarity between the allies. This practical connection, in turn, reinforced NATO's foundational narrative of a geopolitical community of solidarity – now poised to geographically expand to the east.

Since NATO's first out-of-area missions in the mid-1990s in the Balkans, the public perception of the Alliance has shifted from a system of collective defence to an international security actor, even a 'global NATO' (Daalder and Goldgeier 2006). Through the invocation of multifaceted risks and challenges (a rather imprecise kind of securitisation), the allies have secured the existence of NATO as the manifestation of Western security cooperation while extending its institutional membership to the east via continuous enlargement. NATO's first decade after the end of the Cold War shows how allies were able to re-shape the strategic discourse of the Alliance by including an unspecific, yet ambitious security agenda.

Conclusion: what is NATO (for)?

Many scholars would probably state that much has changed since the early 1990s. Eastern enlargement has made NATO's membership and strategic discourse more diverse, disputes over the Iraq war in 2003 were regarded as the most serious crisis in NATO's history and the conflict in Ukraine and the progress of ISIS in Syria and Iraq symbolise the sorts of challenge the Alliance will have to face in years to come. Statements that NATO is in crisis, the 'alliance crisis syndrome' as Thies (2009: 2) has aptly named it, are nothing new but do direct our attention to more substantial questions: what is NATO (for) – and why has it endured for so long despite its history of crisis? ST's examination of NATO's past provides some helpful insights in these regards.

In a strictly positivist sense, ST does not explain the foundation, transformation and/or continuity of the Alliance where norms, interests or common threat assessments might be described as the major causes of cooperation. What ST does, however, is provide a conceptual toolbox for describing causal mechanisms (Guzzini 2011) – what happens, in other words, when actors speak security and move political questions on (re-securitisation) and off (de-securitisation) the security agenda. It shows the specific regional patterns of de-/securitization in the transatlantic regional security complex with its unique and overlapping institutions (NATO, EU, OSCE). Thus, ST might be a critical resource for (neo)realist accounts of NATO. Alliance formation, as Walt (1985: 4) has prominently argued, can be regarded 'as a response to threats', either in terms of balancing the source of danger or allying with the most powerful state. As simple as this argument may sound, it leaves open the question of who poses a danger to whom, and how and why insecurities might change over time. ST is able to give an empirically grounded answer to these questions.

Accordingly, a comparative study on patterns of securitisation/de-securitisation across time and institutions would be highly valuable in order to understand how different NATO is. Threats and insecurities have not ceased to exist even if North

America and Europe are zones of peace(ful change) among states. The main puzzle, then, is not the continuity of the Alliance after the dissolution of the Warsaw Pact, but rather its ability to invoke and often hegemonise what security means while consolidating non-violent relations internally.

Addressing NATO's future, ST also suggests some conclusions. Although reliable predictions are always difficult and risky (as neo-realist claims of NATO survival show),[13] it is possible to argue that the Alliance will endure as long as actors (member states as well as NATO officials) succeed in articulating insecurities of different kinds and thus legitimise NATO as the central institution where these problems are negotiated and dealt with. The example of NATO's post–Cold War re-orientation through its 1991 Strategic Concept and subsequent strategic discourse illustrates how the Alliance has navigated this challenge. At the Cold War's end, the Alliance seemingly confronted a situation of de-securitisation as its erstwhile Soviet adversary disappeared from the stage. Indeed, de-securitisation was the premise of policy as NATO embraced former Warsaw Pact states through enlargement and embarked upon a structured partnership with Russia. But in parallel, NATO securitised other issues by widening its remit of responsibility, an act given authoritative expression in the Strategic Concept and then extended in successor documents in 1999 and 2010. These strategic articulations were manifest in a wholesale shift of mission evidenced most obviously in interventions in the Balkans in the 1990s, as well as later in Afghanistan and Libya. The culmination of this process is the re-securitisation of Russia which has occurred as a consequence of the crisis in Ukraine.

As for the question what is NATO (for), an answer here is more complicated and might contradict assumptions that the Alliance has retained its relevance through securitising (or, indeed, de-securitising and re-securitising) specific threats. NATO has been more than a military alliance from its very beginning, symbolising a special bond between Europe and North America. Continuous articulations of threat assessments make NATO members work and even fight together but they are not the foundation of the Alliance as such: it is, rather, the invocation of a community of like-minded states (and societies) which share something important (democracy, human rights and a market economy) in common and deemed worthy of protection. Thus, Thomas Risse-Kappen (1996: 4) has argued that the Alliance is not based primarily on common interests and threat perceptions, but on a collective democratic identity symbolising an 'alliance of democracies'. His claim is persuasive but it needs qualifying (Sjursen 2004). Since the foundation of NATO, its members have invoked the Alliance as the cornerstone of Western security cooperation based on common symbolic values. Whenever these values have been endangered, the allies have been able to mobilise and legitimise new policies in order to (re-) affirm NATO's unity, including a lasting institutional structure of political and military cooperation, coordination and even integration. It is the capacity of the members to articulate the values they stand for as universal and the alliance they form as legitimised to defend them at home and, if necessary, to realise them abroad, which attaches true value to NATO. In other words, the presumed 'democratic identity' of each member and of NATO itself cannot be taken for granted but is the performative effect of a shared security discourse which changes its content over time. As Behnke (2013: 1) has argued 'the continued existence and political relevance of the Alliance rests on its ability to reproduce "the West" as a geo-cultural space that serves as its security referent object'. Processes of securitisation and de-securitisation are the symbolic, yet powerful expression of this community.

Notes

1 This chapter is part of a larger research project at the Goethe University Frankfurt entitled 'Securitising the West: The Transformation of Western Order', funded by the Cluster of Excellence 'The Formation of Normative Orders' (Hellmann, Herborth, Schlag and Weber 2014). I would like to thank the editors, in particular Mark Webber, and the participants of the ECPR workshop in 2009, especially Ulrich Franke, for their many insights and helpful comments. All remaining inconsistencies remain my own responsibility.

2 Hits for 'securitisation' in full text search (October 2014): *Security Dialogue* 176; *European Journal of International Relations* 49; *Review of International Studies* 59; *International Studies Quarterly* 17; *International Organisation* 29; *International Security* 6. A similar statistic can be found in Gad and Petersen (2011: 316). For an assessment of different aspects of the theory, see Balzaq (2011); for a non-Western view, see Bilgin (2011); for the evolution of security studies as a research field, see Buzan and Hansen (2009).

3 For some readers it might sound peculiar that Wæver, a self-proclaimed 'pessimistic constructivist' (Wæver 2000), cites and appreciates a neo-realist like Kenneth Waltz. Wæver (2009), however, argues that Waltz's notion of theory is consistently misinterpreted in the discipline and argues that Waltz developed his theory exactly *against* the common definitions of empiricism and positivism.

4 For a critical discussion of Wæver's notion of speech-act theory see McDonald (2008), Huysmans (2011), Stritzel (2011) and (2007).

5 Wæver (2011: 469) adds that this fixation on a specific form is a weakness of ST ('a contemporary security theory should be able to explore changes to the security form itself'). Some scholars argue that the concept of risk (and risk society) delineates such a change of form, even a conceptual transformation.

6 Thanks to Benjamin Herborth for introducing me to this apt metaphor.

7 For a more detailed periodisation of NATO's evolution, see Kaplan (2004).

8 For historical accounts of the formative years of the Alliance, consult Heller and Gillingham (1992) and Kaplan (1999).

9 Such an isolationistic position was most explicit in the Vandenberg resolution, drafted by Senator Arthur Vandenberg, which passed the Senate in June 1948.

10 *Memo by Clark Clifford to Harry S. Truman*, ca. 1948; available at: www.trumanlibrary. org/whistlestop/study_collections/nato/large/documents/pdfs/16–10.pdf#zoom=100.

11 The Truman archive has a copy of a revised draft of the North Atlantic Treaty from 14 January 1949. In this document, alternative descriptions of the area are indicated, ranging from 'Europe or America" to 'the sea and air space of the western Mediterranean, West of longitude 12' East". See www.trumanlibrary.org/ whistlestop/study_collections/ nato/large/documents/pdfs/4–1.pdf#zoom=100.

12 Kaplan (2004: 3) writes that the notion of a pledge was used by the Canadian diplomat Escott Reid. The adjective 'military' used in former drafts of Article Five was substituted in the final version by the more circumspect formulation of 'including the use of armed forces' (Kaplan 2004: 4).

13 Relevant here is the much-cited opinion of Kenneth Waltz (1993: 76) that 'NATO's days might not be numbered, but its years are'.

References

[All web sources listed were last accessed 12 June 2015.]

Adler, E. (2008). 'The Spread of Security Communities: Communities of Practice, Restraint, and NATO's Post-Cold War Transformation', *European Journal of International Relations*, 14(2) 195–230.

Albert, M. and Buzan, B. (2011). 'Securitisation, Sectors and Functional Differentiation', *Security Dialogue*, 42(4–5): 413–425.

Aradau, C. (2004). 'Security and the Democratic Scene: De-securitisation and Emancipation', *Journal of International Relations and Development* 7(4): 388–413.

Bailly Mattern, J. (2005). *Ordering International Politics: Identity, Crisis and Representational Force*, London: Routledge.

Balzaq, T. (ed). (2011). *Securitisation Theory: How Security Problems Emerge and Dissolve*, London: Routledge.

Behnke, A. (2013). *NATO's Security Discourse after the Cold War*, London: Routledge.

Bilgin, P. (2011). 'The Politics of Studying Securitisation? The Copenhagen School in Turkey, *Security Dialogue* 42(4–5): 399–412.

Boy, N. Burgess, J. P. and Leander, A. (2011). 'The Global Governance of Security and Finance', *Security Dialogue*, 42(2): 115–122.

Buzan, B. and Hansen, L. (2009). *The Evolution of International Security Studies*. Cambridge: Cambridge University Press.

Buzan B., De Wilde, J. and Wæver, O. (1998). *Security: A New Framework for Analysis*. Boulder: Lynne Rienner.

Buzan, B. and Wæver, O. (2003). *Regions and Powers: The Structure of International Society*, Cambridge: Cambridge University Press.

Conze, W. (1984). 'Sicherheit, Schutz', in Brunner, O., Conze, W. and Koselleck, R. (eds). *Geschichtliche Grundbegriffe. Historisches Lexikon zur politischen-sozialen Sprache in Deutschland*, Bd. 5, Klett-Cotta: Stuttgart.

Daalder, I. H. (1991). *The Nature and Practice of Flexible Response. NATO Strategy and Theater Nuclear Forces since 1967*, New York: Columbia University Press.

Daalder, I. H. and Goldgeier, J. (2006). 'Global NATO', *Foreign Affairs*, 85(5): 105–113.

Daase, C. (2010). 'National, Societal, and Human Security: on the Transformation of Political Language', *Historical Social Research*, 35(4): 22–40.

Duffield, J. S. (1994). 'NATO's Functions after the Cold War', *Political Science Quarterly*, 109(5): 763–787.

Floyd, R. (2010). *Security and the Environment: Securitisation Theory and US Environmental Security Policy*, Cambridge: Cambridge University Press.

Franke, U. (2010). *Die NATO nach 1989: Das Rätsel ihres Fortbestandes*, Wiesbaden: VS Verlag.

Gad, U. P. and Petersen, K. L. (2011). 'Concepts of Politics in Securitisation Studies', *Security Dialogue* 42(4–5): 315–328.

Gheciu, A. (2005). 'Security Institutions as Agents of Socialization? NATO and the "New Europe"', *International Organization*, 59(4): 973–1012.

Glaser, C. L. (1993). 'Why NATO Is Still Best: Future Security Arrangements for Europe', *International Security*, 18(1): 5–50.

Guzzini, S. (2005). 'The Concept of Power: A Constructivist Analysis', *Millennium: Journal of International Studies*, 33(3): 495–521.

Guzzini, S. (2011). 'Securitisation as a Causal Mechanism, *Security Dialogue* 42(4–5): 329–341.

Haftendorn, H. (1996). *NATO and the Nuclear Revolution: A Crisis of Credibility*, Oxford: Oxford University Press.

Heller, F. H and Gillingham, J. (eds). (1992). *NATO: The Founding of the Atlantic Alliance and the Integration of Europe*, New York: St. Martin's Press.

Hellmann, G. (2006). 'A Brief Look at the Recent History of NATO's Future', in Peters, I. (ed). *Transatlantic Tug-of-War: Prospects for US-European Cooperation*, Münster: Lit. Verlag.

Hellmann, G. (2008). 'Inevitable Decline Versus Predestined Stability: Disciplinary Explanations of the Evolving Transatlantic Order', in Anderson, J. Ikenberry, G. J. and Risse, T. (eds). *The End of the West: Crisis and Change in the Atlantic Order*, Ithaca and London: Cornell University Press.

Hellmann, G. and Wolf, R. (1993). 'Neorealism, Neoliberal Institutionalism and the Future of NATO', *Security Studies*, 3(1): 3–43.

Hellmann, G., Herborth, B., Schlag, B. and Weber, C. (2014). The West: A Securitising Community?' *Journal of International Relations and Development*, 17(3): 367–396.

Huysmans, J. (2006). *The Politics of Insecurity*. London: Routledge.

Huysmans, J. (2011). 'What's in An Act? On Security Speech Acts and Little Security Nothings', *Security Dialogue*, 42(4–5): 371–383.

Jackson, P. T. (2003). 'Defending the West: Occidentalism and the Formation of NATO', *The Journal of Political Philosophy*, 11(3): 223–252.

Kaplan, L. S. (1999). *The Long Entanglement: NATO's First Fifty Years*, Westport: Praeger.

Kaplan, L. S. (2004). *NATO Divided, NATO United: The Evolution of an Alliance*, Westport: Praeger.

Klein, B. (1990). 'How the West Was One: Representational Politics of NATO', *International Studies Quarterly*, 34(3): 311–325.

Locher, A. (2007). 'A Crisis Foretold: NATO and France, 1963–66', in Wenger, A., Nuenlist, C. and Locher, A. (eds). *Transforming NATO in the Cold War*, London: Routledge.

Mattern, J. B. (2005). *Ordering International Politics: Identity, Crisis and Representational Force*, Abingdon: Routledge.

McCalla, R. B. (1996). 'NATO's Persistence after the Cold War', *International Organisation*, 50(3): 445–475.

McDonald, M. (2008). 'Securitization and the Construction of Security', *European Journal of International Relations* 14(4): 563–587.

McNamara, R. S. (1966/1999). 'Address given to the convention of the American Society of Newspaper Editors, 18 May 1966 Montreal', in: Copeland, L., Lamm, L. W. and McKenna, S. J. (eds). *The World's Great Speeches*, fourth edition, Mineola: Dover Publications.

NATO. (1949a). 'The North Atlantic Treaty', at: www.nato.int/docu/basictxt/treaty.htm.

NATO. (1949b). 'Memorandum by the Standing Group to the North Atlantic Military Committee Transmitting the Strategic Concept for the Defence of the North Atlantic Area', 19 October, at: www.nato.int/docu/stratdoc/eng/a491019a.pdf.

NATO. (1950). 'North Atlantic Military Commitee Decision on MC 14 Strategic Guidance for North Atlantic Regional Planning. Note by the Secretary', 28 March, at: www.nato.int/docu/stratdoc/eng/a500328c.pdf.

NATO. (1967). 'The Future Tasks of the Alliance: Report of the Council (The Harmel Report)', at: www.nato.int/archives/harmel/harmel.htm.

NATO. (1968). 'Report by the Military Committee to the Defence Planning Committee on Overall Strategic Concept for the Defense of the North Atlantic Treaty Organisation Area', 16 January, at: www.nato.int/docu/stratdoc/eng/a680116a.pdf.

NATO. (1971). 'North Atlantic Council, Final Communiqué', 9–10 December, at: www.nato.int/docu/comm/49–95/c711209a.htm.

NATO. (1991). 'The Alliance's New Strategic Concept', 7–8 November, at: www.nato.int/cps/en/natolive/official_texts_23847.htm.

NATO. (1993). 'Report to the Ministers by the Ad Hoc Group on Cooperation in Peace-keeping', 11 June 1993, at: www.nato.int/docu/comm/49–95/c930611b.htm.

Neumann, I. (2001). 'European Identity, EU Expansion and the Integration/Exclusion Nexus', in Cederman, L-E. (ed). *Constructing Europe's Identities: The External Dimension*, Boulder: Lynne Rienner.

Neumann, I. and Williams, M. (2000). 'From Alliance to Security Community: NATO, Russia, and the Power of Identity', *Millennium: Journal of International* Studies, 29(2): 357–387.

Osgood, R. E. (1962). *NATO: The Entangling Alliance*, Chicago: University of Chicago Press.

Pedlow, G. (1997). *The Evolution of NATO Strategy, 1949–1969* (Brussels), available at: www.nato.int/archives/strategy.htm.

Pouliot, V. (2010). *International Security in Practice: The Politics of NATO-Russia Diplomacy*, Cambridge: Cambridge University Press.

Rasmussen, M. V. (2001). 'Reflexive Security: NATO and International Risk Society', *Millennium: Journal of International Studies*, 30:2, 285–309.

Risse-Kappen, T. (1995). *Cooperation Among Democracies: The European Influence on U.S. Foreign Policy*, Princeton: Princeton University Press.

Risse-Kappen, T. (1996). 'Collective Identity in a Democratic Community: The Case of NATO', in Katzenstein, P. (ed). *The Culture of National Security: Norms and Identity in World Politics*, New York: Columbia University Press.

Schimmelfennig, F. (2003). *The EU, NATO and the Integration of Europe: Rules and Rhetoric*, Cambridge: Cambridge University Press.

Sjursen, H. (2004). 'On the Identity of NATO', *International Affairs*, 80(4): 687–703.

Snyder, G. H. (1990). 'Alliance Theory: a Neo-realist First Cut', *Journal of International Affairs*, 44(1): 103–123.

Stritzel, H. (2007). 'Towards a Theory of Securitisation: Copenhagen and Beyond', *European Journal of International Relations* 13(3): 357–383.

Stritzel, H. (2011). 'Security, the Translation', *Security Dialogue*, 42(4–5): 343–355.

Thies, W. (2009), *Why NATO Endures*, Cambridge: Cambridge University Press.

Tjalve, V. S. (2011). 'Designing (De)security: European Exceptionalism, Atlantic Republicanism and the "Public Sphere"', *Security Dialogue* 42(4–5): 441–452.

Tilly, C. (1998). 'International Communities, Secure or Otherwise', in Adler, E. and Barnett, M. (eds). *Security Communities*, Cambridge: Cambridge University Press.

Tuschhoff, C. (1999). 'Alliance Cohesion and Peaceful Change in NATO' in Haftendorn, H., Keohane, R. O. and Wallander, C. (eds). *Imperfect Unions: Security Institutions over Time and Space*, New York: Oxford University Press.

Wæver, O. (1995). 'Securitisation and De-securitisation' in Lipschutz R. D. (ed). *On Security*, New York: Columbia University Press.

Wæver, O. (1998). 'Insecurity, Security, and Asecurity in the West European Non-war Community' in Adler, E. and Barnett, M. (eds). *Security Communities*, Cambridge: Cambridge University Press.

Wæver, O. (2000). 'The EU as a Security Actor: Reflections from a Pessimistic Constructivist on Post-Sovereign Security Orders', in Kelstrup, M. and Williams, M. C. (eds), *International Theory and the Politics of European Integration*, London: Routledge.

Wæver, O. (2003). 'Securitisation: Taking Stock of a Research Programme', unpublished draft.

Wæver, O. (2009). 'Waltz's Theory of Theory', *International Relations*, 23(2): 201–222.

Wæver, O. (2011). 'Politics, Security, Theory', *Security Dialogue*, 42(4–5): 465–480.

Wallander, C. (2000). 'Institutional Assets and Adaptability: NATO after the Cold War', *International Organisation* 54(4): 705–735.

Walt, S. M. (1985).'Alliance Formation and the Balance of World Power', *International Organisation*, 9(4): 3–43.

Walt, S. M. (1991). 'The Renaissance of Security Studies', *International Studies Quarterly*, 35(2): 211–239.

Walt, S. M. (1997). 'Why Alliances Endure or Collapse', *Survival*, 39(1): 156–179.

Walt, S. M. (2014). 'NATO Owes Putin a Big Thank You', *Foreign Policy*, 4 September, at: http://foreignpolicy.com/2014/09/04/nato-owes-putin-a-big-thank-you/.

Waltz, K. N. (1979). *Theory of International Politics*, Reading: Addison-Wesley.

Waltz, K. N (1993). 'The Emerging Structure of International Politics', *International Security*, 18(2): 44–79.

Wheeler, M. O. (2001). 'NATO Nuclear Strategy: 1949–1990' in Schmidt, G. (ed). *A History of NATO: The First Fifty Years Volume.3*, Basingstoke: Palgrave Macmillan.

Williams, M. C. (2003). 'Words, Images, Enemies: Securitisation and International Politics', *International Studies Quarterly* 47(4): 511–531.

9 NATO and the risk society

Modes of alliance representation since 1991

Michael John Williams

With the fall of the Berlin Wall in 1989 and the subsequent dissolution of the Soviet Union, many observers argued that NATO would follow its Cold War contemporary the Warsaw Pact into the history books (Mearsheimer 1990: 52). But instead of being relegated to history, NATO soldiered on through the 1990s and 2000s, becoming in the process more active than ever in the management of international security. For some, this was a paradoxical development. Why did NATO endure given that the enemy that prompted its creation ceased to exist in 1991? That the question was framed in this way owed much to the influence of neo-realism. In the early 1990s, neo-realism viewed NATO as a simply a traditional military alliance, a collection of states that banded together to balance a threatening opponent state or group of states. For realists, an alliance is 'a formal or informal relationship of security cooperation between two or more sovereign states' (Walt 1987: 1, note 1). Cooperation amongst these states hinges on the presence of an external threat that forces states together. Once that threat is gone, an alliance, by this logic, should dissolve. It was the threat posed by the Soviet Union that brought NATO together in 1949; its collapse consequently led some to the conclusion that NATO would also inevitably shut up shop (Waltz 1993: 76).

The problem with neo-realism is that its preference for parsimony has given rise to a narrow set of assumptions on how system structure (the ordering principle of anarchy most importantly) determines the behaviour of states. Although it is true that there is much repetition in the behaviour of states, this may be less to do with the influence of structure and more a consequence of the fact that the options of states are genuinely limited. Structure for Waltz (1990: 34) 'shapes and shoves' the behaviour of states, but beyond this the discretion of states is limited also by domestic political, economic and even cultural factors. Consequently, as Hans Morgenthau (1948: 4) put it, at best, the academic field of International Relations (IR) is about probabilities rather than absolute laws 'the first lesson the student of international politics must learn and never forget is that the complexities of international affairs make simple solutions and trustworthy prophecies impossible'. A fundamental assumption of this chapter, therefore, is one that rejects an 'epistemic realism whereby the world comprises material objects whose existence is independent of ideas of beliefs about them' (Campbell 1993: 7). Instead, following Campbell (1993: 8), the chapter utilises a 'logic of interpretation that acknowledges the improbability of cataloguing, calculating and specifying "real" cause, concerning itself instead with considering the manifest political consequences of adopting one mode of representation over another'.

More specifically, it focuses on how a discourse of risk within NATO created a path for the organisation's endurance in the 1990s, and on into the 2000s. This discourse-driven study is rooted in a constructivist approach that argues that shared ideas, norms, and values constitute an independent causal force in IR that is distinct from material structures (Wendt 1992). Such an approach does not discount material interests, but rather follows Max Weber's (1920: 252) argument that 'images of the world' tend to serve as 'switches determining the tracks on which the dynamism of interests keeps actions moving'. Attention to the role of ideas is long-standing in certain of the social sciences (sociology, for instance) but placing ideas centre stage in IR was rather novel when constructivism set about that task from the early 1990s. Today, however, IR approaches that view the world as socially constructed and thus contingent on norms and values have become mainstream (Adler 2013: 112).

The constructivist view that values and norms take on a certain explanatory power is strengthened when coupled with institutionalist writing on NATO. This literature argues that, once established, organisations tend to endure. This is the case for a number of reasons, all of which apply to the Alliance. First, well-developed organisations take on a bureaucratic form, and the bureaucracy (and the epistemic community which surrounds it) possesses a vested interest in functional adaptation in order to ensure its survival (McCalla 1996: 456–457). Adaptation, further, is likely to be successful when those bureaucratic interests are nested within organisations whose assets are 'portable' – capable, in other words, of being moulded to new purposes (Wallander 2000: 709). The possession of assets such as this adds another utilitarian calculation. Organisations created for one purpose need not disappear once that purpose has been exhausted; it is 'less costly' to maintain and adapt an organisation than it is to create a new one because of the 'sunk costs' in the existing organization (McCalla 1996: 462). It is a waste of resources, in other words, to disband an organisation when it could be adapted to confront new challenges. The importance of ideas and the functionality of organisations are thus the two basic assumptions of the analysis that follows. Institutional analysis explains why organisations can endure, but it does little to explain why NATO evolved to take on the tasks and operations it did. Accepting the institutional premise of organisational endurance, which has been written about extensively elsewhere (see Schimmelfennig this volume), and coupling it with a study of the risk society allows one to more fully appreciate the ontological drivers behind NATO's evolution.

The risk society is a sociological concept utilised to describe the state of late or post-modernity in the Western world (see Bauman 2005; Beck 1999; Beck and Williams 2004; Giddens 1990, 2002; Giddens and Pierson 1998). Sociologists argue that the essence of modernity was control and boundaries. Modernity was centred upon the concept of the nation-state and premised on the evolutionary principle that humanity was moving forward towards some better and achievable future. In modernity, industrialised societies were organised around the distribution of 'goods' such as health, education and welfare. Modernity was underpinned by a specific linear way of thinking, described by Max Weber as 'means-ends' rationality. In the current phase of modernity (what might be termed 'late modernity'), society, by contrast, is about the distribution of the 'bads'. These flow across territories and are not confined within the borders of a single state. The risk society is about seeking to minimise and channel the 'bads' resulting from globalisation, thereby creating a new space for the social and political. Modernity was about the establishment of 'ontological security', essentially a narrative of change that helped people develop expectations of the future and understand how to best proceed in any given situation. Late modernity does not have this element of predictability and is characterised by the unexpected (Giddens 1991: 36). Ontological security is a rare commodity these days. Unlike the Cold War when the US and Soviet Union played a gruesome game of international politics based upon mutually agreed rules and diplomatic norms, all overshadowed by the possibility of nuclear war, today it is hard to determine who the enemy is, what capabilities it possesses and what logic motivates its actions. Although governments in NATO might point to Iran, Iraq, Syria or North Korea as candidates for state-based threats, the wider context of risk looms large. Increasingly states and order are being challenged, not just by other states, but by transnational and globalised entities, be they communities, events or organisations. These challenges do not fit neatly into the conceptual framework of threats that has been dominant in international relations since the peace of Westphalia of 1648. Instead, policy makers have conceived of them as security risks. Recent evidence of such risks relate to the al Qaeda terrorist network responsible for the 9/11 attacks, social movements across the Middle East that toppled dictators and the non-state organisation Islamic State (ISIS) that overran large swathes of Iraq and Syria in late 2014. Equally, a phenomenon such as climate change also constitutes a risk – one without an actor or agency; a risk, moreover, whose consequences are difficult to predict with accuracy and even more difficult to counter.

The understanding of risk in this chapter is informed by the writings of Charles Manning (1962), Barry Buzan and Richard Little (2000) and Hedley Bull (1977). Here, risk is both an idea and an analytical concept: an idea that is incorporated into the thinking of states and their policy makers, and an analytical concept that is designed to capture the social structures of the international system. Further and following Buzan (2014: 19), I do not conceptualise risk as an 'analyst's idea, invented externally to the practice' but rather, assume that 'the analyst reconstructs the idea of international society already contained in the collective discourse and reproduced in practice'.

Studying the discourse of NATO in the 1990s and early 2000s allows us to examine how 'textual and social processes are intrinsically connected and to describe, in specific contexts, the implications of this connection for the way we think and act in the contemporary world' (George 1994: 191). To this end, I will first outline the concept of the risk society, before looking at the development of a discourse of risk within NATO during the 1990s. A study of NATO's narrative in its Strategic Concepts of 1991 and 1999 illustrates that the Alliance came to a consensus position, interpreting the strategic environment not as one defined by quantifiable threats, but rather one filled with myriad and often opaque security risks. This new security framework led it to move from a reactive to a proactive posture. No longer was NATO acting against aggressive action targeted at allies; instead, it was proactively seeking to manage security risks that *might*, at some point, come to pose a danger to the Alliance, but that were not yet a direct danger. Understanding NATO in this way has implications for the present as well as the recent past. In conclusion, therefore, I consider NATO's position in relation to contemporary risk management.

Conceptualising the risk society

The attacks on US targets on 11 September 2001 changed the way many people in the Western world viewed international relations. In particular, it had a traumatic impact on Americans and their perception of the world beyond the Atlantic and Pacific oceans. People's behaviour changed as a result of 9/11. The collapse of the World Trade Centre in a conflagration of fire and smoke after two passenger planes were flown directly into the buildings prompted many people to stop flying. The retreat from commercial airlines meant that, particularly in the US, the number of people travelling on the nation's highways increased significantly. These individuals sought to avoid the risk of flying for fear of a terrorist act, preferring the supposed safety of their automobiles. But the problem with this logic is that air travel, even in an age of radical Islamic terrorism, is exponentially safer than travelling by road.

German psychologist Gerd Gingrenzer (as reported by Gardner 2008: 3) documented the impact of the shift from air to automobile travel following 9/11. He concluded that even if terrorists hijacked and crashed one plane a week, a person flying once a month had only a one in 135,000 chance of being killed, compared with the annual one in 6,000 odds of being killed in an automobile accident. Therefore, as Americans took to their cars after 9/11, road fatalities shot up dramatically. Gingrenzer (as reported by Bower 2004) created a computer model to study automobile travel in the US before and after the 9/11 attacks. He found that when compared with automotive fatalities for the same months from 1996 to 2000, an additional 353 people died in car crashes in October through December 2001. Just in those three months alone, surplus road fatalities exceeded the 266 fatalities on the airplanes used in the 9/11 attacks. According to Gingrenzer, the shift from planes to cars in the US lasted about one year. He calculated that during this twelve-month period a total of 1,595 people died as a result of the post-9/11 plane-to-car shift (Gardner 2008: 3). This figure is more than half the total number killed in the terrorist attacks, and six times higher than the number of individuals on-board the planes that crashed into the World Trade Centre. Why then did people abandon the relative safety of air travel for the rather more dangerous method of automobile travel?

An economically determined rational actor would logically not make this switch. But the problem with such models and assumptions is that people are not strictly rational-choice oriented. We are social beings that construct the world around us from a number of stimuli that we interpret within a specific cultural context developed through our life experiences. The increase in road fatalities after 9/11 did not generate the same sort of impression that 9/11 did. This is not surprising. Individuals tend to overestimate the risk associated with a memorable event (such as a plane being hijacked and used as a guided missile) as opposed to the risk from more mundane (yet far deadlier) activities such as driving or riding in a car (Slovic, Fishchoff and Lichtenstein 1981). This happens because some social problems are accorded more importance than others. People tend to focus less on the actual probability of a catastrophic event occurring than its scale – the horrific manifestation of the risk in other words. Hence the dramatic shift following 9/11 from air travel to the roads, despite the fact that road travel remained quantifiably more dangerous than flying.

Following 9/11, concerns over terrorism also grew in Europe. The 2003 *Transatlantic Trends* survey conducted by the German Marshall Fund, noted that 70 per cent of Europeans thought international terrorism was an 'extremely important' threat facing the world (26 per cent thought it 'important'). These numbers exactly mirrored survey findings in the US (German Marshall Fund 2003: 12). Three years later, populations on both sides of the Atlantic continued to fear terrorism, with 79 per cent of Americans and 66 per cent of Europeans citing it as 'extremely important' (German Marshall Fund 2003: 7). Thus, throughout the early 2000s terrorism served to underpin the security phraseology of risk, but a host of other challenges ranging from the possibility of cyber attacks to the instability caused by refugees fleeing North Africa and the Middle East also fed this mindset. Such concerns have continued to preoccupy policy makers and publics in the US and especially in Europe following the advent of ISIS in Iraq and Syria. Western intelligence experts estimated in 2014 that some 12,000 foreign fighters were working with ISIS in the Middle East, 3,000 of whom were from Europe. There was a concern that some European fighters could pose serious security challenges at home once they returned. 'While not every one of them poses a threat, clearly there is potential for a large number of them to be of concern', a senior British intelligence source said. 'It's simply not possible to monitor so many people for 24 hours a day for an unlimited amount of time. There just aren't the resources' (cited in Neubert, Jamieson and Burke 2014).

Risk, however, is not new to the age of terrorism in which we now live. How we think and write about risk, however, has changed a great deal over the centuries. The word 'risk' first entered the English language about 400 years ago. Today it is often used colloquially as a synonym for danger or peril. Threat and risk are also used interchangeably, despite the differences between the two concepts. Philologically, risk has two possible origins. It may stem from the Latin word '*risico*', first used by sailors pushing the boundaries of seventeenth-century cartographers. Alternatively, it may derive from the Arabic word '*risq*' (transliterated), referring to the acquisition of wealth and good fortune. Risk in the modern world is basically a combination of the two. The dominant definition of risk in modernity was born in the maritime insurance industry where it came to represent the balance between potential positive acquisitions through exploration (*risq* in the Arabic sense) and the inherent danger of that undertaking (*risico* in the Latin). The development of economic and financial systems led, over time, to the increased quantification of risk to represent possible losses and gains. The quantification of risk that developed in economics was predicated on the removal of uncertainty. Kathleen Tierney (1999: 219) notes 'risk analyses outside the social sciences generally consider the probabilities associated with the occurrence of particular events as objective, knowable, and quantifiable; risk analysis is seen as a method for developing estimates that approximate reality'. This understanding of risk, however, is increasingly seen as inappropriate when applied to situations that are fluid and uncertain. As Yaacov Vertzberger (1995: 349) has argued:

> Risk must be approached in a non-technical manner, and hence the common distinction between risk and uncertainty is neither realistic nor practical when applied to the analysis of non-quantifiable and ill-defined problems, such as those posed by important politico-military issues.

According to mainstream definitions, risk exists when a decision maker has 'perfect knowledge of all possible outcomes associated with an event and the probable distribution of their occurrence'. However, a decision maker may lack knowledge of the probable distribution of the 'outcomes associated with an event', and so uncertainty is present (Vertzberger 1995: 349). Risk is essentially uncertainty; to cite Vertzberger (1995: 350) once more, risk exists in

> [s]ituations where probabilities of outcomes are not only uncertain but the situation is ambiguous and adverse; that is, [the situation] poses a plausible possibility that at least some outcomes are unknown and will have adverse consequences for the decision-maker's interests and goals.

The marriage of risk and uncertainty stems from a need to control the future. As Beck (1999: 3) puts it '[r]isk is the modern attempt to foresee and control the future consequences of human action [. . . I]t is an [institutionalised] attempt, a cognitive map, to colonise the future.' Risk becomes a medium between security and destruction, what Beck (1999: 135) refers to as a 'no-longer-but-not-yet' scenario. No longer do we possess a feeling of security, but we have not yet plunged into disaster and destruction.

Danger is not synonymous with risk. Whether it was pre-modern man being eaten by a bear or modern man being blown away by The Bomb, danger has always existed even if human beings have rationalised it differently over time. Danger is objective; risk is not. In the pre-modern era, it was commonly held that an earthquake or flood was the wrath of the gods. Today, most people understand and accept the science behind these dangers. But we are not more secure. The objective danger of the earthquake still exists, even if how we think about it has changed. Throughout our evolution the primary security concerns of one era have given way to those of the next. Once early man overcame natural hazards such as the possibility of starvation or falling prey to wild animals, she or he focused on new problems such as how to establish control over land and provide defence against others who might covet his or her possessions. It was at this point that the concept of danger was translated into threat or risk. Danger is a neutral term that denotes a negative outcome. Risk is an equation or estimation of the odds that danger will be realised or that a given course of action may have an adverse effect.

Threat also is not synonymous with risk. To treat it as such is analytically sloppy and an abuse of the English language. Threat relies on three components: an actor (to pose/be interpreted as the threat), a capability (to follow through on the threat) and a hostile intention. Central to the concept of threat is power, classically defined by realists as involving military force (Berenskoetter 2007: 6). Without power, it is impossible to pose, and difficult to be perceived, as a threat. It is not uncommon today to hear that 'terrorism is the greatest threat facing the US' or that 'global climate change is a major threat'. These are grave misuses of the word, as threat is determined by intention. The *Oxford English Dictionary* (Fowler and Fowler 1969: 888) defines threat as the 'intimidatory announcement of the action the speaker will take if his (sic) wishes are not complied with'. Threat thus requires an actor who expresses *intention* and has the *ability* to do harm (power, in other words). Without power (the ability to inflict intentional damage), there can be no real threat. Most of the security issues facing the NATO allies today are not threats. Terrorism, weapons proliferation, climate change, disease, migration and inequality are all amorphous and ambiguous issues that do not pose a 'threat' in the conventional sense, but they are most certainly not benign. They are, therefore, best conceptualised as risks and, unlike threats they are not bound in time or space. Threats of course are subject to perception; one can perceive a threat where there is none, but perception is based on an interpretation of the opponent's intention. A threat is, nonetheless, based on a quantitative ability to do actual harm. The same cannot be said of risk, since risk is not based on capability at all. Risk is a social construct, an attempt to control the future – once a risk is realised, it stops being a risk and is a catastrophic event. Risk is about the possibility, not the occurrence, of the event. Thus, although perception can be an important part of both the construction of a risk and the construction of a threat, the two are very different modes of thinking about security.

Threats are bound to their actor and its capabilities in a given context. A threat demands a response, but things are not so clear-cut with risks. As Francois Ewald (1991: 207) writes, 'to calculate a risk is to master time, to discipline the future'. The conceptualisation of something as a security risk places it beyond the immediate into a more distant world that ultimately justifies the need to act today (we seek to control the future, in other words, by acting in the present). With its reach into the future, risk is an incredibly powerful concept. The risks we perceive and the way we proscribe action is dictated by the knowledge that we possess, knowledge defined as beliefs an actor takes to be true. Elevated to the political level, it is socially shared knowledge, what Wendt (1999: 140–141), drawing on D'Andrade (1984), labels as the culture that helps 'determine how states frame international situations and [how they] define their national interest'.

To help sum up the differences and relations between danger, threat and risk let us take the pressing topic of nuclear weapons. A missile armed with a nuclear device is an objective danger. If detonated simply by accident, it will do great harm. This nuclear missile can also be, or could evolve into, a threat. The possession of this weapon by an actor (let's assume state A) that has publicly stated that if its opponent Z does action X, it will fire a nuclear missile at its opponent makes this a threat: there is potency (the possession of a nuclear weapon), the weapon is possessed by someone (the state) and that actor has a clear intention to use it in a specific case. Naturally, in these circumstances state Z will perceive state A as a threat based on its capability and the bellicosity of its language even if that language is open to interpretation. Threat, either rendered or perceived, is still based on a quantifiable capability and a distinct, identifiable actor. But we can also see this nuclear weapon as a risk. By this line of logic, the existence of the nuclear weapon in one state gives rise to a wider set of considerations. What if state A decides to share its nuclear capability with a non-state actor who might use it against the national interest of state Z? What if the government of state A is unstable and is overrun by 'terrorists' who then use the nuclear weapon outside the rationality of individuals responsible for the security of their own population? And what if the development of a nuclear weapon by state A precipitates a run on weapons, leading to an arms race with other states in the region? These 'what if' scenarios are not threats, in that they lack intention and direction, but they do pose a possible security risk.

Nuclear proliferation is a good example of risk logic, one that demonstrates how the risk society co-exists in late modernity with a more traditional threat-based security preference. The same logic could be applied to terrorism. Take one terrorist group al Qaeda. Who or what is Al Qaeda? Where are its headquarters located? What sort of military capabilities does it possess? Are these limited to small arms and improvised explosive devices? Or has Al Qaeda procured larger conventional or unconventional weapons somewhere? Was Al Qaeda in Iraq directly linked to bin Laden's organisation, or was it inspired by it, like some sort of terrorist franchise?

As these two examples illustrate, in the risk society proliferation is a problem that goes beyond states, making it even more difficult to calculate the second-order effects of action in international relations. 'A risk society' writes Giddens (1999: 3) 'is not intrinsically more dangerous or hazardous than pre-existing forms of social order [. . .] Rather, it is a society increasingly preoccupied with the future (and also with safety), which generates the notion of risk'.

Risk, although not entirely new, has taken on new dimensions. As Giddens (2002: 26) writes:

> Risk has always been involved in modernity, but [. . .] in the current period risk assumes a new and peculiar importance. Risk was supposed to be a way of regulating the future, or normalising it and bringing it under our dominion. Things haven't turned out that way. Our very attempts to control the future tend to rebound upon us, forcing us to look for different ways of relating to uncertainty.

The tendency for risk to 'rebound' on us is labelled by Beck the 'boomerang effect'. This phenomenon manifests itself in two ways. First, attempts to tame uncertainty often have the paradoxical effect of increasing anxiety about risk through an intensity of focus and concern. Second, acting to manage a risk often entails in itself risky behaviour, what John Adams refers to as 'risk compensation'. Adams (1995: 41) illustrates this argument with the example of the seatbelt. The seatbelt, intended to save the lives of drivers, also perversely encourages people to drive faster and more recklessly, thereby resulting in a higher frequency of accidents. For Adams (1995: 139), '[t]he more we attempt to "colonise" the future, with the aid of the category of risk, the more it slips out of our control'.

This is perhaps the best way to sum up NATO's attempts to 'control' security risks since 1989. In understanding how NATO and its members have conceptualised the security environment since the end of the Cold War, we can understand how the concept of risk has come to permeate transatlantic security discourse and policy, offering a strong rationale for NATO's continued existence, but also sowing seeds of discord.

Changing security perceptions in the North Atlantic area during the 1990s

Risk became a central feature of NATO politics in the 1990s. One of NATO's core tasks has historically been defence planning. During the Cold War, planning was premised on quantifying, with a rather large degree of empirical certainty, the strengths of the Soviet and Warsaw Pact militaries. Planning was based on a discourse of threat and oriented around a strategy of deterrence. But with the Cold War's end, defence, and especially deterrence, became untenable concepts. In the absence of a clearly defined threat, risk therefore emerged as a compelling concept to order NATO security policy.

The best sources for analysis in this regard are NATO's authoritative Strategic Concepts written in 1991 and 1999. Risk, as an ordering concept for Western security policy, made its first appearance in the 1991 NATO Strategic Concept (NATO 1991: paragraph 7):

> The security challenges and risks which NATO faces are different in nature from what they were in the past. The threat of a simultaneous, full-scale attack on all of NATO's European fronts has been effectively removed and thus no longer provides the focus for Allied strategy.

Instead, NATO had to manage risks that were 'multi-faceted in nature and multi-directional' making them harder to 'predict and [to] assess'. As a result, the Alliance needed to 'be capable of responding to such risks if stability and the security of alliance members are to be preserved' (NATO 1991: paragraph 8).

Risk was attractive for at least two reasons. First, by highlighting the growing and increasingly random possibility of harm, it encapsulated the uncertainty of the era in a readily understandable manner. Second, risk allowed for a considerable flexibility of interpretation and so lent itself to a wide variety of situations. This was important because unanimity among the allies about what specific challenges they were to address was near impossible to achieve. Risk, in one sense, offered the possibility of a modern interpretation of 'flexible response'. This very flexibility meant NATO policy makers could accord priority to the organisation's tasks dependent on circumstance and mindful of a broad menu of issues. As the 1991 Strategic Concept (NATO 1991: paragraph 9) noted:

> Risks to allied security are less likely to result from calculated aggression against the territory of the Allies, but rather from the *adverse consequences of instabilities* that may arise from serious economic, social and political difficulties, including ethnic rivalries and territorial disputes (emphasis added).

In this way, risk management became all-encompassing and seemingly all-powerful as a legitimising concept for policy. The Strategic Concept went so far as to specifically state that such issues, if they remained limited to Central and Eastern Europe (CEE), would 'not directly threaten the security and territorial integrity of members of the Alliance'. Importantly, however,

> '[t]hey *could* [. . .] *lead* to crises inimical to European stability and even to armed conflicts, which *could* involve outside powers or spill over into NATO countries, having a direct effect on the security of the Alliance'
> (NATO 1991: paragraph 9, emphasis added)

It is impossible to ignore the cognitive construction here as one of risk, not threat. European and American policy makers in NATO were not so much worried about what was happening, rather, they were worried about what *could* happen. By conceptualising the European (and, indeed, later global) security environment in this way, leaders were trying to discipline the future so as to bring it, seemingly, under their control, in the process adapting existing tools, such as NATO, to this new task.

Despite conceptualising the emerging security environment as one defined by numerous security risks, the Alliance did not take to this analysis like a duck to water. Indeed, in the years following the writing of the 1991 Strategic Concept, NATO faltered. The collapse and disintegration of Yugoslavia created a series of conflicts that challenged Euro-American leadership. The first of the Balkan wars in the early 1990s spurred NATO to the forefront of Euro-Atlantic security, but not without difficulty. The Clinton administration was wary of getting involved in the outbreak of ethnic hostilities in Bosnia and hoped that Europeans would assume more responsibility for security in what was essentially Europe's back yard in the post–Cold War era. In the early 1990s, it was not apparent that NATO would be a critical vehicle of European stability. In the former Yugoslavia, the initial preference on both sides of the Atlantic was for the Organisation for Security and Cooperation in Europe (OSCE) and the newly formed European Union (EU) to act. But as Ronald Asmus (2002: 12) put it 'the OSCE was too weak; the EU was too slow'. As the conflict worsened and Europe continued to stall, there was, according to *Washington Post* journalist Daniel Williams (1993), 'a growing sense in the Clinton administration that its Bosnia policy, widely criticised as vacillating and inept, was about to be partner to the starkest pageant of mass suffering in Europe since World War II'. Although the Bosnian conflict posed no direct conventional threat to NATO allies, it was seen as a possible source of regional destabilisation, affecting NATO indirectly through cross-border migration flows, the need for humanitarian assistance and competition with Russia. Jakub Grygiel (2009) would subsequently coin the term 'vacuum wars' to describe the phenomenon of weak states creating a space for conflict between great powers.

In this challenging context, Washington needed to remain involved in European security politics. It gave preference to NATO, which was logical, given that the US had a seat at the table (which it lacked in the EU) and that NATO offered the military capability necessary to enforce peace in the Balkans. Clinton dispatched veteran US diplomat Richard Holbrooke to negotiate an end to the conflict, whilst simultaneously working politics through NATO to develop a semi-cogent Euro-American response to the crisis (Holbrooke 1999), one that culminated in Operation Deliberate Force and the deployment of I-FOR/S-FOR to police the Dayton peace accords.

Slowly, then, NATO evolved from an organisation predicated on deterrence to one concerned with reactive risk management. And as well as operating in a crisis setting, NATO adapted through a policy of enlarging its membership. The possibility of post-communist instability, coupled with very real pressure from the new democracies of CEE to join NATO meant that soon after the Cold War's end some allies began pushing for NATO to adapt and enlarge (Asmus 2002: 29–40). The American and German governments largely led this argument. According to Hyde-Price (2000: 152), enlargement was a 'clear triumph [for] US-German trans-governmental cooperation'. Although there was not always agreement on the size of enlargement (the German government, for example, was itself internally split over which countries should join with the Ministry of Defence, favouring limited enlargement and the Foreign Office preferring a wider undertaking), there was a consensus within the Alliance that growth was good for NATO. And this impetus to secure CEE states went well with the desire of the NATO bureaucracy to stay in business. With the end of the Warsaw Pact removing the main rationale for NATO's existence, a new narrative of security was required if the organisation was to remain relevant. But there can be no doubt that NATO enlargement was also driven by grave concerns over stability and uncertainty. If the Cold War was anything, it was regular and predictable – policy makers generally knew what to expect from each other – but with the sudden implosion of the Soviet Union the rules of the game dissolved.

NATO as an alliance began to see inaction in the wake of Soviet collapse as dangerous, and a narrative around the idea of 'insecurity and risk' in Europe was made increasingly robust as the decade wore on so much so that as NATO Secretary General Lord Roberston (2001) argued '[t]he new strategic environment offers us a unique luxury; the opportunity to set the agenda ourselves. And setting the agenda is what the NATO of the twenty-first century is all about'. The implication here was clear: the new democracies of Europe might fail or Russia might become resurgent should NATO prove unable to act. The result was a re-visioning of the organisation's role.

Concerns over a power vacuum in CEE saw NATO expand to take in new democracies of the region (three new members, the Czech Republic, Hungary and Poland, acceded in 1999 – the first enlargement of NATO since Spain's entry in 1982). The Alliance had already made explicit the security benefits of such a policy. The 1995 Study on Enlargement (NATO 1995: paragraph 2) noted:

> NATO enlargement will extend to new members the benefits of common defence and integration into European and Euro-Atlantic institutions. The benefits of common defence and such integration are important to protecting the further democratic development of new members. By integrating more countries into the existing community of values and institutions, consistent with the objectives of the Washington Treaty and the London Declaration, NATO enlargement will safeguard the freedom and security of all its members in accordance with the principles of the UN Charter. Meeting NATO's fundamental security goals and supporting the integration of new members into European and Euro-Atlantic institutions are thus complementary goals of the enlargement process, consistent with the Alliance's strategic concept.

As part of a tandem effort alongside the EU (and, to lesser extent, the OSCE), NATO would provide a framework for these states to foster structures of governance supported by militaries that bought into NATO's values of civilian control. NATO was, after all, a 'political-military' alliance, and in the 1990s it recognised that the opportunities to achieve Alliance objectives through political means were greater than ever before. The 'growth of freedom and democracy' in Europe, the 1991 Strategic Concept suggested, would increase predictability and stability in security affairs (NATO 1991: paragraph 28). Selling NATO as a civilisational structure provided a discourse for policy makers such as Clinton, Robertson and others (UK Prime Minister Tony Blair, for instance) who wanted the Alliance to take on new roles that the transatlantic community of states would support. This normative exercise was intrinsically linked in the liberal mind with stability and security, as countless essays on the 'democratic peace' would attest (Doyle 1986; 2005; Russett 1994; Williams 2001). Indeed, as US diplomat Ronald Asmus (2002: 25) argued '[u]sing NATO to help consolidate democracy and a new peace in Central and Eastern Europe was one of these [goals]. Stopping ethnic cleansing beyond the Alliance's borders was another'.

This sentiment was clear also in then British Prime Minister Tony Blair's (1999) speech to the Economic Club of Chicago in which he unequivocally linked the promotion of democratic values to increased security and stability:

> If we can establish and spread the values of liberty, the rule of law, human rights and an open society then that is in our national interests too. The spread

of our values makes us safer. As John Kennedy put it 'Freedom is indivisible and when one man is enslaved who is free'?

And it was not just NATO that sought to devise policy based on the idea of the democratic peace and the expansion of Western civilisational structures. The EU was equally moved to use what Ian Manners (2002) has called the organisation's 'normative power' to spread Western values so as to stabilise neighbouring countries in the hope of one day integrating them into a wider Europe. Whether or not this normative exercise does actually expand democracy while promoting peace and stability is not the issue here (Reiter 2001); it is sufficient for our purposes to illustrate that within the mindset of Euro-American policy makers the two were seen as mutually connected. And accompanying this was a strengthening of the role concept of the Alliance as a community of values, one whose existence was not predicated primarily on an enemy foil (i.e., the erstwhile Soviet Union), but on defending liberal values.

Alliance policy makers believed that if NATO did not act to incorporate the fledgling democracies into Europe, they might fail and that, in turn, may have an adverse effect on the security of the established liberal democracies of the Alliance. Risk was emerging as the new dominant narrative for the Alliance. NATO enlargement eastward was both a response to and a perpetuation of a new security narrative as, indeed, was stabilising areas of turmoil close to the heart of Europe.

With the war in Kosovo bringing the 1990s to a close in Europe, NATO's interventions and continuing discourse about the security environment prompted a further rewriting of its role. The 1999 Strategic Concept – adopted in the midst of NATO's Operation Allied Force against Serbia – referred numerous times to new opportunities and risk, with the latter covering a wide gamut of issues such as 'oppression, ethnic conflict, economic distress, the collapse of political order, and the proliferation of weapons of mass destruction'. With so many risks to be managed, the Alliance, it was argued, 'must safeguard common security interests in an environment of often unpredictable change' (NATO 1999: paragraphs 3–4). These shifts in NATO's self-definition, suggested that the Alliance was transitioning from a 'security community' into a 'risk community' where 'cultural definitions of appropriate types or degrees of risk define the community, in effect, as those who share the relevant assumptions' (Beck 1999: 16). A security community is an entity where there are 'real assurances that the members of the community will not fight each other physically, but will settle their disputes in some other way' (Deutsch et al 1957: 6). A 'risk community', meanwhile, is group with shared expectations of peaceful change among their own number reinforced by a shared concern with external security risks that transcend their national borders. The notion of NATO as a community of risk is implicit in the 1999 Strategic Concept; NATO; the document asserts aims to 'shape its security environment and enhance the peace and stability of the Euro-Atlantic area' (NATO 1999: paragraph12).

To summarise, the decade of the 1990s saw within NATO the disappearance of the Cold War security paradigm and the adoption of a paradigm based on the management of risk. Evidence for this is found in the language of the 1991 and 1999

Strategic Concepts. National documents in the US and Europe also offer supplementary evidence that policy makers were looking to risk as an ordering concept for policy. The American Quadrennial Defence Review of 1997, for instance, outlined three 'alternative paths' to respond to the 'threats, risks, and opportunities' presented by an unpredictable global environment. These involved differing assumptions about how to configure American military posture, but all three, to differing degrees, entailed an acceptance of risk (US Department of Defence 1997: 1–3). In the UK, similarly, the 1998 Strategic Defence Review noted that 'the confrontation of the Cold War [had] been replaced by a complex mixture of uncertainty and unpredictability'. In the face of 'a newer style of security risk', the British government and armed forces would be required 'to move from stability based on fear to stability based on the active management of these risks' (Secretary of State for Defence 1998: 4, 9). Indeed, the idea of risk become so captivating that by 2005, the NATO Parliamentary Assembly issued report *171 ESC 05 E – Policy Implications of the Risk Society*, detailing the complex nature of the international environment and the 'highly problematic' challenges posed for NATO allies by the risk society (Gennip 2005: paragraph 4).

Conclusion: the risk society and a revanchist Russia

The use of risk within the North Atlantic area is one that has evolved as both an idea and analytical concept. The idea of risk has generated a security paradigm that has allowed NATO to legitimate its continued existence in a world without the Soviet Union. Risk is not an idea that exists externally to practice (Buzan 2014: 19). NATO texts and the social processes around them, as well as the policies derived from those texts, have actively described and also shaped the world in which NATO exists.

If the Alliance had chosen to more narrowly define its mission; if it had, for example, hewn to a threat-based paradigm of security, centred on post–Soviet Russia, it is highly unlikely that NATO would have found itself performing out-of-area missions. But because the policy elites in NATO saw the world as one of myriad and amorphous dangers and chose to conceptualise this in terms of risk, NATO took on a broad set of tasks, putting it on the path to operations first in the former Yugoslavia and subsequently in places such as Afghanistan and Libya. Risk management, by its very nature, necessitated a proactive approach rather than the defensive one favoured by the Alliance in the Cold War.

The incorporation of risk into NATO thinking provided the Alliance with a new lease of life, but it also opened up a window of controversy in that risk required NATO to engage in tasks for which it is not ideally suited. First, risks cannot be quantified in the same way as military threats. We already know that allies can differ on threat perception, even when there is a quantifiable measurement (e.g., military capability) of the threat being posed. Finding consensus on risk is even more difficult, because there is often no quantifiable basis for judging the urgency of a particular risk or the means to address it. Second, the missions that NATO has undertaken in the name of risk management, from the Balkans to Afghanistan and Libya, have been the result of local instabilities. NATO has acted to prevent something terrible from happening (ethnic cleansing, refugee flows, narcotic and weapons trafficking, terrorist attack). This has required state building, but military force, NATO's specialty, is only one (rather small) part of this enterprise. NATO has assumed responsibility as a security provider in environments disturbed by a wide assortment of issues (political, economic, developmental) over which it has wielded little capability or control. That NATO has often looked like an alliance in crisis is largely because it has been one. Risk may have given NATO a continued reason for existence, but it does not guarantee it a smooth ride.

In the risk society NATO is more than just a military alliance as conceived by structural approaches to international relations. NATO as an organisation does not simply respond to the world around it; it actively shapes it. And this shaping, in turn, creates new realities, prompting another cycle of change and innovation. The strategic situation with regard to Russia is emblematic of this cycle. NATO's view that risks in CEE could be managed by enlargement and the promotion of democracy might have managed the risk of instability amongst weak, post-communist states, but it also led to a Russian counter-reaction. For the Kremlin, NATO's eastward enlargement has been seen not as stabilising, but rather as an encroachment onto its traditional sphere of influence. This logic reached it apotheosis in Russia's annexation of the Crimea in 2014, an act President Putin (Reuters 2014) claimed was partly a response to enlargement and the need to prevent NATO from 'drag[ging] Ukraine' into the Alliance.

It is now the task of scholars to study NATO during this renewed period of East–West tension to see if the risk paradigm holds, or if the Alliance will reconfigure itself more narrowly. The conceptualisation of NATO as a risk community, however, does not preclude the inclusion of a threat-based security paradigm in relation to how the Alliance configures its policies and structures. Given the still-extant Article Five commitment, NATO military planners have maintained plans for the defence of allies in Europe against a hostile, state-based threat. At its 2014 summit in Wales, NATO was tasked with developing up-to-date plans to deal with crisis response, including addressing the challenge from Russia (Hale 2014). But problematically for NATO, this new challenge does not fit neatly into any Cold War parallel. A Warsaw Pact invasion during the Cold War would have been a classic ground war. It would have involved tanks, planes and infantry. Combatants would have been in uniform and, theoretically, they would have abided by the laws of war. The recent conflict in Ukraine, however, has not unfolded in such a manner. Russia has adopted the language of R2P – Responsibility to Protect – to justify intervention in Crimea and eastern Ukraine. And this intervention has been assisted militarily by, but without ascription to, Russia. As such, this new way of war if extended to vulnerable NATO states could conceivably avoid setting off the tripwire of Article Five. The attendant intra-Alliance debate this would occasion, further, suggests that enough discord would be present among the allies to prevent the emergence of a consensus position on how to deal with the crisis. Such a scenario is particularly worrying for new NATO members like Estonia or Latvia, countries whose large Russian populations might be a useful pretext for Russian destabilisation. Thus, despite the seeming return of nineteenth-century geopolitics to Europe (Rynning 2015), Russia's behaviour has stoked a sense of uncertainty within NATO more likely to facilitate risk-oriented thinking than a return to a threat-based security paradigm.

References

[All web sources listed were last accessed 12 June 2015.]

Adams, J. (1995). *Risk*, London: Routledge.
Adler, E. (2013). 'Constructivism in International Relations: Sources, Contributions and Debates', in Carlsnaes, W., Risse, T. and Simmons, B. A. (eds). *Handbook of International Relations*, London: Sage Publications.
Asmus, R. (2002). *Opening NATO's Door: How the Alliance Remade Itself for a New Era*, New York: Columbia University Press.
Bauman, Z. (2005). *Liquid Life*, Cambridge: Polity Press.
Beck, U. (1999). *World Risk Society*, Cambridge: Polity Press.
Beck, U. and Williams, J. (2004). *Conversations with Ulrich Beck*, Cambridge: Polity Press.
Berenskoetter, F. (2007). 'Thinking about Power', in Berenskoetter, F. and Williams, M. J. (eds). *Power in World Politics*, London: Routledge.
Blair, T. (1999). 'Doctrine of the International Community', speech to the Economic Club of Chicago, 22 April, at: www.pbs.org/newshour/bb/international-jan-june99-blair_doctrine4–23/.
Bower, B. (2004). '9/11's Fatal Road Toll: Terror Attacks Presaged Rise in US Car Deaths', *Science News*, 17 January.
Bull, H. (1977). *The Anarchical Society: A Study of Order in World Politics*, London: Macmillan.
Buzan, B. (2014). *An Introduction to the English School of International Relations*, Cambridge: Polity Press.
Buzan, B. and Little, R. (2000). *International Systems in World History: Remaking the Study of International Relations*, Oxford: Oxford University Press.
Campbell, D. (1993). *Politics without Principles: Sovereignty, Ethics and the Narratives of the Gulf War*, Boulder: Lynne Rienner.
D'Andrade, R. (1984). 'Cultural Meaning Systems', in Schweder, R. and LeVine, R. (eds). *Culture Theory: Essays on Mind, Self and Emotion*, Cambridge: Cambridge University Press.
Deutsch, K. W., Burrell, S. A., Kann, R.A., Lee Jr., M., Lichterman, M., Lindgren, R. E., Lowenheim, F. L. and Van Read Wagenen, R. W. (1957). *Political Community and the North Atlantic Area: International Organization in the Light of Historical Expericence*, Princeton: Princeton University Press.
Doyle, M. W. (1986). 'Liberalism and World Politics', *American Political Science Review* 80(4): 1151–1169.
Doyle, M. W. (2005). 'Three Pillars of the Liberal Peace', *American Political Science Review*, 99(3): 463–466.
Ewald, F. (1991): 'Insurance and Risks', in Burchell, G., Gordon, C. and Miller, P. (eds). *The Foucault Effect: Studies in Governmentality*, Chicago: University of Chicago Press.
Fowler, F. G. and Fowler, H. W. (1969). *The Pocket Oxford Dictionary of Current English*, Oxford: The Clarendon Press.

Gardner, D. (2008). *Risk: The Science and Politics of Fear*, London: Virgin Books.

George, J. (1994). *Discourses of Global Politics: A Critical (Re)Introduction to International Relations*, Boulder: Lynne Rienner.

Gennip, J. V. (Rapporteur). (2005). 'Policy Implications of the Risk Society', NATO Parliamentary Assembly, 2005 Annual Session, at: www.nato-pa.int/Default.asp?SHORTCUT=672.

German Marshall Fund (2003), *Transatlantic Trends*, at: http://trends.gmfus.org/files/archived/doc/2003_english_key.pdf.

Giddens, A. (1990). *The Consequences of Modernity*, Cambridge: Polity Press.

Giddens, A. (1991). *Modernity and Self-Identity: Self and Society in the Late Modern Age*, Cambridge: Polity Press.

Giddens, A. (1999). 'Risk and Responsibility', *Modern Law Review* 62(1): 1–10.

Giddens, A. (2002). *Runaway World: How Globalisation Is Reshaping Our Lives*, London, Profile Books.

Giddens, A. and Pierson, C. (1998). *Conversations with Anthony Giddens: Making Sense of Modernity*, Cambridge: Polity Press.

Grygiel, J. (2009). 'Vacuum Wars', *The American Interest* 4(6): 40–45.

Hale, J. (2014). 'Alliance's Ability to Swiftly Tackle Crises a Top Focus of NATO Wales Summit', *Defence News*, 3 September, at: www.defensenews.com/article/20140903/DEFREG01/309030030/Alliance-s-Ability-Swiftly-Tackle-Crises-Top-Focus-Wales-Summit.

Holbrooke, R. (1999). *To End a War*: New York: Random House.

Hyde-Price, A. (2000). *Germany and European Order: Enlarging NATO and the EU*, Manchester: Manchester University Press.

Manners, I. (2002). 'Normative Power Europe: A Contradiction in Terms?', *Journal of Common Market Studies*, 40(2): 235–258.

Manning, C. (1962). *The Nature of International Society*, London: Macmillian.

McCalla, R. B. (1996). 'NATO's Persistence after the Cold War', *International Organisation* 50(3): 445–475.

Mearsheimer, J. J. (1990). 'Back to the Future: Instability in Europe after the Cold War', *International Security*, 15(1): 5–56.

Morgenthau, H.J. (1948). *Politics Among Nations: The Struggle for Power and Peace*, New York: Alfred A. Knopf.

NATO. (1991). 'The Alliance's New Strategic Concept', 7–8 November, at: www.nato.int/cps/en/natolive/official_texts_23847.htm.

NATO. (1995). 'Study on NATO Enlargement', 3 September, at: www.nato.int/cps/en/natolive/official_texts_24733.htm.

NATO. (1999). 'The Alliance's Strategic Concept', 24 April, at: www.nato.int/cps/en/natolive/official_texts_27433.htm.

Neubert, M., Jamieson, A. and Burke, S. (2014). 'Rise of ISIS Heightens Threat of Terrorism to West, Experts Warn' *NBC News*, 29 June, at: www.nbcnews.com/storyline/iraq-turmoil/rise-isis-heightens-threat-terrorism-west-experts-warn-n141661.

Reiter, D. (2001). 'Why NATO Enlargement Does Not Spread Democracy', *International Security* 25(4): 41–67.

Reuters. (2014). 'Putin Says Annexation of Crimea Partly a Response to NATO Enlargement', 17 April, at: www.reuters.com/article/2014/04/17/us-russia-putin-nato-idUSBREA3G22A20140417.

Robertson, Lord. (2001). 'NATO in the New Millennium', Mountbatten Lecture, University of Edinburgh, 15 February, at: http://nato.int/docu/speech/2001/s010215a.htm.

Russett, B. (1994). *Grasping the Democratic Peace: Principles for a Post-Cold War World*, Princeton: Princeton University Press.

Rynning, S. (2015). 'The False Promise of Continental Concert: Russia, the West and the Necessary Balance of Power', *International Affairs*, 91(3): 539–552.

Secretary of State for Defence. (1998). *Strategic Defence Review: Modern Forces for the Modern World*, at: http://fissilematerials.org/library/mod98.pdf.

Slovic, B., Fishchoff, B. and Lichtenstein, S. (1981). 'Perceived Risk: Psychological Factors and Social Implications', *Proceedings of the Royal Society*, 376(1764): 17–34.

Tierney, K. J. (1999). 'Toward a Critical Sociology of Risk', *Sociological Forum* 14(2): 215–242.

US Department of Defence. (1997). *Report of the Quadrennial Defence Review*, at: www.bits.de/NRANEU/others/strategy/qdr97.pdf.

Vertzberger, Y.Y.I. (1995). 'Rethinking and Reconceptualising Risk in Foreign Policy Decision-Making: A Sociocognitive Approach', *Political Psychology* 16(2): 347–380.

Wallander, C.A. (2000). 'Institutional Assets and Adaptability: NATO after the Cold War', *International Organisation* 54(4): 705–735.

Walt, S. M. (1987). *The Origins of Alliances*, Ithaca and London: Cornell University Press.

Waltz, K. N. (1990). 'Realist Thought and Neo-realist Theory', *Journal of International Affairs*, 44(1): 21–37.

Waltz, K. N. (1993). 'The Emerging Structure of International Politics', *International Security*, 18(2): 44–79.

Weber, M. (1920). *Gesammelte Aufsätze zur Religionsociology*, Tübingen: J.C.B. Mohr.

Wendt, A. (1992). 'Anarchy Is What States Make of It: The Social Construction of Power Politics', *International Organisation* 46(2): 391–425.

Wendt, A. (1999). *Social Theory of International Politics*, Cambridge: Cambridge University Press.

Williams, D. (1993). 'Steps and Missteps in Search of a Workable Policy on Bosnia. As the Situation Worsened, the US Strategy Was Driven by Emotion, Not Broad Principle', *The Washington Post*, 22 August.

Williams, M. C. (2001). 'The Discipline of the Democratic Peace: Kant, Liberalism and the Social Construction of Security Communities', *European Journal of International Relations* 7(4): 525–553.

10 NATO

A public goods provider

Jens Ringsmose

When former US Secretary of Defence Robert Gates attended his last NATO ministerial meeting in Brussels in June 2011, he publicly warned that the Alliance could face a 'dim if not dismal future'. According to Gates (2011), unfair burden sharing was the main reason behind NATO's predicaments. 'The blunt reality', he cautioned, 'is that there will be dwindling appetite and patience in the US Congress [. . .] to expend increasingly precious funds on behalf of nations that are apparently unwilling to devote the necessary resources [. . .] to be serious and capable partners in their own defence'. Gates successor, Chuck Hagel (2014), repeated the complaint three years later, urging America's allies to 'invest more strategically to protect [their] military capability and readiness.' And if that were not sufficient to make the point clear, Vice-President Joe Biden in February 2015 declared that 'NATO is not a self-sustaining organisation'. It is, he continued, an organisation whose strength reflects the defence commitment of its members, a commitment still borne disproportionately by the US, to the increasing frustration of American voters and politicians (Biden 2015).

The Europeans (and Canadians), such was the pointed message of these comments, ran the risk of becoming irrelevant to the US, if they failed to rectify their defence deficiencies. This, of course, was seen to undermine the main multilateral setting, that of NATO, in which America's defence cooperation with allies has occurred. American concerns with burden sharing are a proxy for the health of the Alliance. As its concerns mount, so commentary points to the possibility of the US running out of patience with its allies and thus NATO being set upon a process of inexorable decline (Schmitt 2014).

In fact, Washington has never been satisfied with the European allies' military capabilities and Western Europe's reliance on American security guarantees. Even before the signing of the North Atlantic Treaty in April 1949, US policymakers worried about the Europeans 'making a sucker out of uncle Sam' (President Eisenhower cited in Trachtenberg 1999: 153). And during the Cold War, this sense of being exploited by the smaller allies only increased as it became clear that the Europeans were unwilling to raise defence spending (measured as a percentage of gross domestic product [GDP]) to the levels of the United States.

This seemingly chronic variance in military spending levels and the accompanying debate over burden sharing has been a major factor in the development of a public goods or economic theory of alliances, one which has a very particular applicability to NATO. Whereas other theories presented in this volume help to explain and understand the origins, endurance, transformation or some other fundamental aspect of NATO affairs, public goods theory (PGT) has been used almost exclusively to investigate one specific dimension – the political economy of the Alliance. It is, in other words, a middle-range theory concerned with questions such as: How are the economic, political and human burdens shared within the Alliance? How does the nature and overall composition of what NATO produces (defence, deterrence, stability, humanitarian relief and so on) affect the severity of collective action problems? What mission types are most likely to give rise to free-rider behaviour? And in what ways does the deployment of military forces of an individual ally impinge upon other member states' incentives to purchase arms and use armed force? Hence, from a PGT perspective, NATO is first and foremost a cost-sharing arrangement, a provider of public goods set up by rational states with overlapping strategic interests. NATO's endurance and effectiveness is thus primarily seen as a product of the incentives created by different types of task and mission.

This chapter sets out to explore NATO from a PGT perspective. It is divided into three main sections. The first is devoted to a brief overview of how PGT has been applied to NATO in different ways since Mancur Olson and Richard Zeckhauser first utilised the approach in 1966. The chapter's second section examines how the burden-sharing debate within NATO changed as a result of the Alliance taking on new missions in the 1990s. New roles meant new burden-sharing metrics and so a shift occurred from the input to the output side of the national defence equation. The Alliance's embrace of a new set of tasks also confronted most European allies with the need to send military forces into harm's way. Consequently, and in particular since NATO assumed responsibility for stabilisation in Afghanistan, *risk sharing* became a key item on the Alliance's burden-sharing agenda. As the discussion will make clear, the benefits spawned by NATO's new mission portfolio are closer to being pure public goods than those produced by the Alliance's traditional activities. Most importantly, out-of-area operations tend to produce security goods that are non-excludable. In theory, NATO should not, therefore, have been able to deploy a substantial number of forces to Afghanistan. This paradox is one that requires an explanation. The chapter's third section, therefore, presents a novel PGT-based explanation for NATO's apparent ability to overcome incentives to free-ride in out-of-area operations. I argue that as long as NATO produces traditional benefits (in the shape of collective defence) and is led by a member state (the US) favouring global engagement, then it is likely to be able to provide forces for out-of-area operations. Hitherto, public goods theorists have tended to ignore this nexus (one instinctively made by many NATO allies) between the traditional (and excludable) benefits of Alliance membership and the new, more purely public, products spawned by out-of-area operations.

In outlining this argument, I am aware that the focus of the burden-sharing debate has shifted as NATO's ISAF mission has come to an end and NATO's attention has moved to the priority of reassuring its eastern members in light of the Ukraine crisis. This return to collective defence concerns brings with it more traditional burden-sharing demands. However, the lessons of the out-of-area phase of NATO's post–Cold War history are important for they are indicative of what happens when the Alliance undertakes a major, demanding and sustained mission. These are lessons of lasting significance.

NATO: the Cold War collective actor

It was Mancur Olson and Richard Zeckhauser (1966) who first utilised PGT to study alliances (see Oma 2012 for a review of the relevant literature). In a seminal article the two political economists presented and tested a theoretical framework based on Mancur Olson's (1965) pioneering (and more general) work on 'collective action problems'. Centre stage in Olson and Zeckhauser's economic theory of alliances is the assumption that security provided through alliances entails a distinct type of benefit or public good – a 'pure public good', that is, a good distinguished by *non-rivalness* and *non-exclusiveness*. Security provided by an alliance is *non-rival* in the sense that adding new members will not detract from the security already available to existing members; it is *non-exclusive*, meanwhile, as no member state can be excluded (at an affordable cost) from consumption once security is supplied and membership is granted.[1]

From this basic assumption, Olson and Zeckhauser posited a key hypothesis about the sharing of burdens within alliances: that the larger and wealthier member states (measured in terms of GDP) will devote a greater share of their national income to the provision of security than their smaller allies. The main logic here is that all members of an alliance that provides pure public goods will have strong incentives to free-ride and to profit from the defence investments made by their brothers-in-arms, but some more so than others. Due to the varying abilities of member states' to produce genuine security, an alliance will be characterised by an asymmetry of incentives favouring the weaker member states. This has first of all to do with the absolute amount of security resulting from different nations' equal (relatively speaking) defence investments. When a small state increases its spending on defence to, for instance, 2 per cent of GDP, it will affect only marginally the alliance's overall ability to deter or defend against an attack. This is, of course, well understood by policy makers in small states. As stated by a realist scholar (Handel 1990: 150; see also Ringsmose 2009) of minor powers: 'they [the small alliance members] know that whatever they do they cannot hold out against the onslaught of an attacking super power. Hence any investment in their own defence is a waste of resources'. If, on the other hand, a larger member of an alliance increases its defence expenditures by a similar percentage of GDP, then the alliance is strengthened considerably. The implication here is clear: the utility of an alliance is dependent upon the efforts of its stronger members and because the stronger members favour these benefits too, they will put the effort in to maintain it. The upshot (sometimes referred to as the exploitation hypothesis) is that 'defence spending burdens are [. . .] shared unevenly; large, wealthy allies will shoulder the defence burden for smaller, poorer allies' (Sandler and Hartley 1999: 30–31).

When Olson and Zeckhauser tested these propositions against the empirical evidence provided by the history of NATO, they found their main hypothesis largely corroborated. In relative terms, the larger allies (the US, the UK and France) spent a great deal more on defence and deterrence than did the smaller allies in the period from 1949–1966 (see Table 10.1). Olson and Zeckhauser (1966: 134–135) thus concluded that 'the largest members of NATO bear a disproportionate share of the burden of common defence'.

However, when the sharing of burdens in NATO began to appear less lopsided in the 1970s and 1980s, a second generation of PGT scholars began to question Olson and Zeckhauser's framework, as well the original classification of the benefits produced by NATO as pure public goods (see the discussion in Boyer 1993: 20–27). If alliance output was indeed characterised by non-rivalness and non-exclusiveness, why, then, were the smaller member states less inclined to free-ride than during the 1950s and 1960s? How could the shrinking differences in military expenditures be explained from a PGT perspective?

Todd Sandler and his colleagues proposed the most compelling answer to this conundrum. In a series of articles, they (Sandler and Cauley 1975; Sandler, Cauley and Forbes 1980; Sandler and Forbes 1980; Sandler and Hartley 1999: 34–51) demonstrated how the Olson and Zeckhauser model was in fact a (very) special case, as alliances (according to their revisionist conceptualisation) usually produce a mix of pure and impure public goods as well as purely private goods. The depiction of alliance output (i.e., security) as an exclusively pure public good was, in other words, deemed too simplifying an assumption. Accordingly, Sandler and his colleagues set out to elaborate on some of Olson and Zeckhauser's key premises.

First, Sandler et al made a distinction between the different ways in which security can be provided. Whereas Olson and Zeckhauser had implicitly assumed that security is a somewhat monolithic phenomenon, second-generation PGT scholars acknowledged that security can come in the shape of both defence and deterrence. Defensive forces can block or roll back an armed attack, whereas deterrent forces should make an enemy abstain from attacking in the first place through threats of retaliation. Moreover, military expenditures also often produce purely private (that is, ally-specific) goods as in, for instance, domestic security, technological spin-offs or fiscal stimulation of the national economy.

Second, Sandler argued that the different outputs resulting from military expenditures vary greatly in terms of 'publicness' (the degree of non-rivalness and/or non-exclusiveness). In general, however, defensive forces are less likely to satisfy the criteria of non-rivalness and non-exclusiveness than are deterrent forces. Although security guarantees based on nuclear deterrent forces can be relatively easily extended to new members of an alliance with little or no marginal costs, the security stemming from conventional (defensive) forces are more likely to be subject to consumption rivalry and exclusion. Or to put it differently: once a strategic deterrent force is created, it can (theoretically) be used to secure an infinite

Table 10.1 NATO members' defence budgets as a percentage of GDP, 1949–1989

Country	1949–54	1955–59	1960–64	1965–69	1970–74	1975–79	1980–84	1985–89
Belgium	4.0	3.6	3.4	3.1	2.9	3.2	3.2	2.8
Canada	5.3	5.3	3.9	2.7	2.1	2.0	2.0	2.1
Denmark	2.5	3.0	2.8	2.7	2.2	2.3	2.4	2.0
France	7.2	7.0	6.0	5.0	3.9	3.8	4.0	3.8
Greece	5.7	5.1	4.1	4.2	4.7	6.8	6.6	5.8
Italy	4.0	3.5	3.0	2.9	2.5	2.1	2.1	2.3
Luxembourg	2.1	2.2	1.21	1.1	0.8	1.0	1.2	1.0
Netherlands	5.1	5.1	4.4	3.8	3.1	3.1	3.0	2.8
Norway	3.7	3.5	3.3	3.6	2.9	2.8	2.7	2.9
Portugal	3.8	4.1	6.0	6.7	6.9	4.0	3.4	2.8
Spain							2.3	2.2
Turkey	4.3	3.8	3.9	3.6	3.3	4.3	3.8	3.4
UK	8.2	7.3	6.2	5.5	5.2	5.0	5.0	4.7
United States	8.9	8.9	8.0	8.0	6.5	4.9	5.6	6.0
W. Germany	3.8	3.8	4.4	4.0	3.5	3.4	3.4	3.0
Average	4.9	4.7	4.3	4.0	3.6	3.4	3.4	3.2

Source: Author's calculations using data provided by the Stockholm International Peace Research Institute (2015), 'Military Expenditure Database'.

number of states against potential aggressors; a defensive conventional force must be shared among alliance members, and prioritising some members will come at the expense of others.

Sandler and his colleagues incorporated this more nuanced conceptualisation into a 'joint product model of alliances'. Underlining the 'impure' nature of most public goods provided by an alliance as well as the multiple types of alliance outputs, the model paid explicit attention 'to *the ratio of excludable benefits* (private and impure public outputs) *to total benefits* (Sandler and Hartley 1999: 35, italics in original). Depicting the Olson and Zeckhauser framework as an extreme situation, Sandler et al thus hypothesised the disproportionate sharing of burdens as the result of this ratio: the higher the ratio of excludable benefits, the less free-riding. In the words of Wallace J. Thies (1987: 305):

> Sandler and his colleagues were led by the logic of their analysis to stress the incentives that alliance member would feel to supplement the protection that they derived from their partners with their own efforts. In their view, as the 'impurities' in the collective good become more pronounced and the private benefits of military spending increase in importance, the willingness of all allies, regardless of size or wealth, to allocate resources to military spending should increase, with a consequent decline in the importance of tendencies such as disproportionality in burden sharing.

Utilising the joint product model to explain the more proportionate sharing of burdens in the years after 1966, Sandler et al highlighted the effects of NATO changing its main strategic concept from 'massive retaliation' in the early Cold War period to one of 'flexible response' after 1966. In line with the model's predictions, the shift from a high degree of reliance on nuclear weapons to a strategy emphasising the importance of conventional forces coincided with decreasing differences in national spending levels. Evidently, the changing ratio of impure public goods to total benefits had a significant impact on NATO burden sharing.

Whereas Sandler and his colleagues had taken their point of departure as the varying outputs produced by alliances, other scholars (Ivanov 2011) making use of PGT have conceptualised the security provided by NATO as a 'club good' – that is, a good or benefit that is, first and foremost, distinguished by *exclusiveness*. The basic assumption underpinning this line of research is that the security produced by individual alliance members can be withheld from those allies unwilling to contribute adequately to the common good. The implication here is that the larger member states can arm-twist their smaller partners (by threatening not to guarantee their security) into investing more in defence and security than they would otherwise have done. Accordingly, free-riding tendencies are alleviated.

From this perspective, even deterrence (conceptualised as a pure public good by Sandler et al) has some of the characteristics of a club good, as the main provider (the US in the case of NATO) can choose to withhold it.[2] In the words of Bruce M. Russett (1970: 94) '[n]onexcludability is not necessarily met, because of a nation's will or ability to regulate the credibility of deterrence'. Or, according to Wallace J. Thies (1987: 304): 'credibility can also be controlled to some extent by the country that might be called on to make good its threats, thus violating the non-exclusiveness condition'. Seen in this light, military expenditure becomes the 'price of admission into the collective effort' for smaller allies (Thies 2003: 11); for the larger member states it means that they are less a prisoner of their own size than originally suggested by Olson and Zeckhauser. The largest member states can in fact pressurise smaller allies into increasing their military expenditures and thereby make burden sharing less disproportionate.

In sum, PGT scholars of alliances in general (and of NATO in particular) have mainly focused on how to explain variations in military expenditures. The starting point of their analyses has been the classification of alliance output as private, pure and/or impure public goods. As NATO has transformed itself from a traditional alliance concerned with collective defence to a more outward-looking organisation, a number of PGT scholars predicted that the internal burden-sharing debate would intensify since the Alliance was likely to produce more pure public goods. This argument is taken up in the remainder of the chapter.

NATO transformed

How did the burden-sharing politics of NATO evolve as the Alliance entered the post–Cold War era, and what are the theoretical implications? These questions are addressed in this section, with a particular emphasis to two issues: the measures (or indicators) that NATO has employed to assess individual member states' contribution to the common good, and the rise of risk sharing as a key item on the Alliance's burden-sharing agenda. The section concludes by arguing that the collective benefits produced by NATO's new operational priorities are mainly non-excludable. In comparison with the Alliance's Cold War functions, NATO's new 'products' are, in fact, characterised by a higher degree of 'publicness'.

Measuring the burden: from input to output

In parallel with its transformation from a provider of defence and deterrence to an exporter of stability, NATO has adopted a range of new measures of allied contributions. Traditional input indicators (first and foremost, defence spending as a share of GDP) are still important points of reference, but alternative measures also gained traction from the 1990s. In general, during the 1990s and 2000s, the output side was given greater precedence over pecuniary input measures. As we shall see later, inputs still matter, but the legacy of the shift to qualitative indicators is likely to be a lasting one. NATO states (and NATO planners) are well aware that crude spending measures are often difficult to achieve and, moreover, are not always an accurate measure of allied contributions (Deni 2015). Burden-sharing discussions have thus grown much more complex and multifaceted; more indicators are now being employed when individual allies' contributions to the collective efforts are being evaluated. But this is not always straightforward. Former NATO Secretary General Jaap de Hoop Scheffer (2008) has observed how NATO has adopted burden-sharing mechanisms that focus on contributions to 'critical operational activities'. Such measures, he suggests, raise important questions:

> How does one decide what is a fair contribution from a country of 50 million people against a contribution from a country with a population of only 4 million? How can you evaluate a contribution of light infantry against the provision of critical enablers such as helicopters or air-to-air refuelling tankers?

Accordingly, perceptions of the value and costs of individual contributions vary. One significant effect of this multi-dimensional comparison of burdens is that member states can perform impeccably in some realms while failing miserably in others. Another is that nations will persistently promote the indicators that portray them as contributing more than might have been expected. Agreeing on the appropriate metrics is thus at the heart of NATO's post–Cold War burden-sharing politics. The net result is that it has become more challenging to identify the model ally and the 'burden shifters' of NATO.

Perhaps the most significant effect of the Alliance's more active role in world affairs has been an increased focus on the ability and political will to project military power at distance and for long periods. Deployability and sustainability are, of course, nothing new to the militaries of the US, Canada, France and the UK as they prepared to send their armed forces to the European theatre and elsewhere throughout the Cold War. In the first half of the 1990s, however, projecting military power was something quite novel and exceptional to most European allies. Spearheaded by the US, NATO, therefore, adopted various schemes to convert territorial defence forces into expeditionary ones. The Defence Capabilities Initiative from 1999, the Prague Capabilities Commitment agreed at NATO's summit in Prague in November 2002 and the NATO Response Force (NRF) launched that same year were but three examples of initiatives aimed at transforming NATO and Europe's armed forces to meet new security threats beyond the transatlantic area (Rynning 2005: 102–140).

Concomitantly, defence investments in and of themselves were no longer deemed an adequate burden-sharing indicator; in the new security environment money had to be spent wisely with an eye on the ability to deploy forces far away from European capitals. In the words of a senior US NATO diplomat: 'with the end of the Cold War a brigade ceased to be just a brigade – to be recognized, a brigade needs to be relevant'.[3] In 1998, the US Ambassador to NATO (as paraphrased in Lepgold 1998: 98) even warned 'that unless European governments expand their force-projection capabilities to relieve some of the pressure on US forces outside Europe, Americans would view the allies as free riders, and support for the [A]lliance would erode'. At the Istanbul summit in June 2004, NATO leaders endorsed the then most ambitious set of formal output measures – the so-called 'usability targets'. The agreed aim for national land forces was that 40 per cent must be structured, prepared and equipped for deployed operations and 8 per cent must be undertaking or planned for sustained operations. The 40/8 target was adopted in the Comprehensive Political Guidance (CPG) at the Riga summit in 2006, and was subsequently revised upwards to 50/10 (Ringsmose and Rynning 2009: 23–24). Although some allies embraced the usability targets rather reluctantly, the deployability and sustainability ambitions have come to be a significant component of NATO's burden-sharing metrics. Unsurprisingly, this development has been warmly welcomed by some of the low-spending allies that are now able to reconcile small defence budgets with an improved reputation (based on transformed military forces) inside the Alliance.[4]

Although output measures have thus become central to NATO's post–Cold War burden-sharing debate, traditional input measures (military expenditures as a share of GDP) have been revived in recent years. Prompted by the demand for additional forces in Afghanistan and Iraq, the US especially, but also the UK and France, stepped up the pressure on other European allies to enhance their military spending (House of Commons Defence Committee 2008: 53–57). Moreover, the economic crisis affecting most NATO allies made it more tempting for member states to cut their military expenditures; beating swords into ploughshares has seemed the natural thing to do in times of austerity. This is a process that has affected all allies, even the US (which since 2012 has made significant reductions of its own). However, the effects have been deleterious to NATO's combined military capabilities – hence the insistent calls for a reversal of defence cuts by a succession of NATO secretaries general (see, for instance, Rasmussen 2013). Further, as the largest spenders have been forced to make cuts in an age of defence austerity so their own reductions have made them more sensitive to the poor performance of others. The US, for instance, has redoubled its demand that the Europeans do more even as it seeks to do less – aware that cuts to its own defence require of its fellow NATO allies greater self-reliance. These processes culminated in the Wales summit declaration of September 2014 (NATO 2014: paragraph 14). Spurred on by the British and the US (and in the face of opposition from defence cutters such as Germany and Canada), NATO reaffirmed a commitment that all allies spend 2 per cent of GDP on defence, albeit with the rider that this might take up to a decade to achieve.

The increased importance of risk sharing

To appreciate the significance of risk sharing, consider first an example from outside NATO: Japan and Germany and their contributions to the 1991 Gulf War. Although the world's two leading 'civilian powers' provided considerable financial support to the US-led coalition fighting the war, their efforts did not earn them much applause internationally. On the contrary, so-called 'chequebook diplomacy' came to be associated with free-riding and an unwillingness to share the risks of military action. Such behaviour prompted an officer of one of the war-waging nations to comment acidly, 'they buy – we die' (cited in Forster and Cimbala 2005: 21).

In NATO, such issues have been recurrent since the 1990s as the Alliance has moved to mount challenging missions out-of-area. The very nature of these missions (kinetic in effect with Allied personnel being put in harm's way) has meant profound collective action problems have arisen shaped by risk-sharing contro-versies (Kay and Khan 2007). Attention in this regard has focused on how the human and political hazards associated with operations have been distributed: Who should provide how many troops for what areas and what mission? The most telling illustration of the resulting risk-sharing quarrels has, without doubt, been the dispute over the national caveats and restrictions applied by some NATO members contributing to ISAF, particularly following the extension of the mis-sion to the perilous south and east of the country after 2006. The issue here was not simply the number of troops that individual allies had deployed to the mis-sion area, but also about where and how the deployed forces were authorised to operate. Whereas one group of countries (most notably the UK, the US, Canada, Poland, the Netherlands and Denmark) committed relatively high numbers of troops to fight the Taleban-dominated insurgency in the most dangerous parts of the country, another group (including Germany, Italy and Spain) put strict limita-tions on, in the words of columnist Roger Cohen (2008), 'when, why and where soldiers will fight and die', preferring to 'do the soft-power, school-building, Euro thing'. According to the German government, until 2010 German soldiers were not even fighting a war, but taking part in 'eine risikobehaftete Einzats' (literally a 'risky operation') (Graw 2008). Former US Defence Secretary Robert Gates was thus moved to warn of a 'two-tiered alliance', characterised by 'some allies willing to fight and die to protect people's security and others who are not' (cited in *The Economist* 2008).

Afghanistan aside, a new and as yet unexplored risk-sharing issue is that linked to NATO's promotion of the pooling and sharing of military capabilities – the so-called Smart Defence initiative. The economic crisis afflicting the majority of allies has led NATO to launch a number of policies within this framework aimed at rationalising and enhancing military capabilities, thereby reducing the 'transat-lantic capability gap'. This scheme, if successful, would provide NATO-Europe with more and better capabilities for the same investment (Pintat 2013). Because a number of Smart Defence initiatives are based on the idea that the smaller allies in particular should focus their defence investments (thereby avoiding costly dupli-cation) so the implication follows that some allies will have to give up capabilities and rely on those of their brothers-in-arms. This is, for instance, what the Baltic states have done in the realm of air defence, leaving it to other allies to police their airspace. Although such arrangements are undoubtedly cost effective, they also increase the dependency of those states giving up distinct capabilities. From a risk-sharing perspective, Smart Defence is, therefore, associated with the loss of sovereignty, higher dependency and a greater risk of being unable to respond to a particular security challenge.

It should be recalled in this connection that NATO has 'a long history of obtain-ing and maintaining capabilities on a multinational basis' going all the way back to the early 1950s (Yost 2014: 81). Further, small allies within NATO have a very real interest in such initiatives because they have very limited defence budgets and face disproportionately larger costs in defence production and in mounting complex national missions (Urbelis 2013: 18). It is for this reason, that the three

Baltic states as well as Albania, Slovenia and Iceland have (as noted earlier) been more than willing to rely on fellow allies to police their air space. This, David Yost (2014: 170) suggests is Smart Defence in action, for it allows these small states to 'dedicate their scarce defence resources to other tasks.' Air policing is a task that has become that much more significant following the deterioration of NATO–Russia relations in the wake of the 2014 Ukraine crisis. It illustrates well the risk some allies are prepared to take in defence of others. Yet Smart Defence has its limits – whereas small states benefit, the larger regard it as entailing both political and economic costs. This problem is described well in a report of the NATO Parliamentary Assembly (Pintat 2013: 7):

> [Smart Defence] faces the obstacle of national sovereignty. Put starkly, it means depending upon another country for a possibly essential military capability and – the other side of the coin – providing capabilities for another country's operations and [being] at the service of their interests

The risk-sharing issue here is not about unequal contributions in operations (as NATO troops experienced in theatre in Afghanistan), but rather the fact that some states risk a greater loss than others should Smart Defence eat into their dearly held sovereign prerogatives. This state of affairs has two stubborn characteristics. The first is of long standing – the reluctance of states such as Germany, France, the UK and the US – to cede the advantages enjoyed by their national defence manufacturers for the sake of common projects. The second is more recent (although it has echoes of intra-NATO practices in the Cold War) and pertains to the mistrust some states may feel toward their fellow allies in the face of danger. As the Ukraine crisis has made clear, dangers are felt unevenly in NATO and states react accordingly. Why should Poland, a state which has increased its defence expenditure in the face of Russian destabilisation in Ukraine, wish to share its resources with other more thrifty allies? And why, one observer has noted, 'should Poland share its resources when NATO is not prepared to deploy troops on a permanent basis in the country?' (Dempsey 2014: 22).

From club goods to pure public goods

Since the 1970s, PGT scholars have generally been of the view that much of what NATO produced during the Cold War is best conceived of as impure public goods characterised by exclusiveness; club goods in other words. As described earlier, this state of affairs helped mitigate free-riding tendencies as the US, the main producer of security, was able to compel smaller allies to contribute to the defence of Western Europe by linking security guarantees to national military investments. Thus, to some extent, national defence spending became the price of American protection.

As NATO moved to out-of-area peace support operations (PSOs) after the Cold War, PGT regarded such activities as likely to produce pure public goods and, as a consequence, generate significant individual incentives to free-ride (Sandler and

Hartley 1999: 102; Shimizu and Sandler 2002). The benefits achieved through PSO activities (peace, stability and the remedying of human rights violations) are non-excludable and non-rival, and so more 'public' than the mix of security goods generated by NATO's traditional tasks of collective defence. All nations, and not only troop-contributing countries, might profit from a successful out-of-area operation. States which participate in PSOs cannot control who consumes the goods which result or the circumstances under which such goods might be enjoyed. Individual Alliance members have, therefore, few incentives to contribute economically or militarily to out-of-area operations. Why provide forces if stronger and more capable allies will do the job? And why run the risk that others will free-ride on one's own efforts? As a result, most out-of-area operations, it has been argued, are likely to suffer from a lack of involvement by the allies and hence be underprovided. In the words of Joseph Lepgold (1998: 90):

> Peace operations are of course discretionary. But if NATO members carry them out, they cannot feasibly exclude those who do not contribute from consuming the good(s) that these operations produce. For this reason it can be very difficult to force non-contributors to share the burden.

Compounding this collective action problem is the fact that nations only rarely contribute to PSOs or overseas counterinsurgency missions in order to defend vital national interests. The problems that these missions aim to alleviate are seldom perceived as posing a direct and clearly defined threat to the well-being of the troop-contributing countries, even if national policy makers try to portray them as such with the aim of mobilising domestic support. Thus, for most participating countries, out-of-area military activities are 'wars of choice'. For most members of NATO, not even the mission to Afghanistan was seen as a 'war of necessity'. Some governments (the British and American most notably) did refer to ISAF as geared toward the danger of Islamic fundamentalism and the risk of terrorist attacks, but that message was never uniform across all NATO governments and even in London and Washington it was articulated with diminishing conviction. Political reluctance to support a perilous military mission, therefore, often sharpens the collective action problems associated with PSOs.

At first glance, therefore, PGT scholars' scepticism about NATO's ability to perform beyond the European theatre seems to be well founded. Different types of out-of-area operation do indeed appear to pose 'all the wrong kind[s] of incentives for the Alliance to succeed' (Lepgold 1998: 79). Should NATO leaders consequently redefine the Alliance's raison d'être once again and 'go back to basics'? Will it be a mistake to ignore the advice of the so-called 'neo-traditionalists' and their call for a 'rebalancing' of the Alliance's strategic vision (Ringsmose and Rynning 2009). Such questions may have been answered by NATO's re-orientation eastward consequent upon the crisis in Ukraine. However, we still need to understand the dynamic within the Alliance before this rebalance became compelling. If the reasons for involvement out-of-area were weak, as PGT suggests, then the several thousand European troops deployed to Afghanistan and Kosovo over a period of two decades begs the question of how the allies managed to negate free-rider incentives and to overcome collective action problems. This question is tackled in the following section, through the articulation of alternative PGT interpretation of NATO action beyond the European theatre.

'Regional NATO' as a *sine qua non* for a 'global NATO'

In the mid-1950s, NATO's first secretary general, Lord Ismay, famously remarked that the true purpose of the transatlantic Alliance was 'to keep the Americans in, the Russians out and the Germans down' (cited in Yost 1998: 52). Deterrence and the formation of a European security community were the objectives, American engagement in Europe the means. Although the post–Cold War Alliance has sometimes been portrayed as a vehicle primarily for out-of-area operations, it remains the case that NATO is still perceived by several allies as a vital provider of the regionally anchored security products succinctly identified by Lord Ismay. Indeed, tasks centred on Europe and its periphery (whether looking east to Russia or south to the arc of crisis that abuts NATO member Turkey) have since 2014 become NATO's priority consequent upon the crisis in Ukraine and the civil wars in Syria and Iraq (Breedlove 2015). NATO's 2014 summit initiated a number of measures such as the Readiness Action Plan and an enhancement of the NRF, which reflected this shift of emphasis, notwithstanding the fact that the Alliance was still in the thick of a major engagement in Afghanistan (as the summit was held, ISAF was due to give way to the smaller but still important follow-on mission, Resolute Support).

Little scholarly attention has been paid to the inter-relatedness of NATO's multiple security outputs. Specifically, public goods theorists have tended to ignore the important link made by many NATO allies between the provision of the traditional, and excludable, benefits and the more public products spawned by out-of-area operations. Taking this link into account, it is possible to reach the conclusion that NATO can, in fact, overcome some of the collective action problems associated with missions to countries and regions beyond the Euro-Atlantic area.

The essence of the argument here is that the detrimental effects of non-excludability and a high degree of publicness in one area can sometimes be offset by the possibility of exclusion in others. In other words, collective action problems associated with various types of out-of-area operations can be mitigated when an alliance is simultaneously engaged in, for instance, territorial protection. Although individual allies have little incentive to contribute to a perilous and costly military operation generating a pure public good, it might nonetheless decide to take part if the country's leading policy makers believe that some other and more coveted benefit produced by the Alliance or a major ally would otherwise be withheld. When members of an alliance, rightly or wrongly, assume that the excludable goods provided by their more powerful partners are dependent on (or at least positively related to) the fair sharing of burdens in out-of-area operations, they will tend to contribute to the mission, regardless of the lack of direct incentives presented to them. Somewhat paradoxically, second and third tier allies that are primarily concerned with territorial defence, regional security and strong bilateral links to their senior partner might even make out-of-area operations their major military priority. The *quid pro quo* logic that characterises a traditional defensive alliance is thus reoriented and tied to operations aimed at providing stability, peace and humanitarian relief.

If such reasoning applies to NATO, we would expect most European allies to have contributed to ISAF partly because they want to acquire some of the traditional and excludable benefits provided by the Alliance – that is, territorial protection and a close relationship with Washington. During the Cold War, adequate defence investment was perceived by many junior allies to be the price of admission to a reliable American security guarantee. In the post–Cold War period, we would expect the European allies to calculate that the best way to strengthen (or avoid the weakening of) their bonds with the US would be to contribute to American-led operations such as, in the case considered here, ISAF. According to this line of reasoning, the allies who put the highest premium on NATO's traditional products should be the ones, together with the US, who would have shouldered the heaviest burdens in Afghanistan. Ironically, the continued political and strategic relevance of NATO's Cold War purposes thus becomes a partial prerequisite for the ability of the Alliance to act globally in a collective manner. In short, 'regional NATO' is what made 'global NATO' possible. Such logic was well put by Norway's Foreign Minister Espen Barth Eide (cited in *The Economist*, 2009: 69–70). 'Focussing on home missions', he suggested in 2009, 'make[s] NATO relevant to Europeans and ultimately boosts support for away mission[s]'.

So, what allies would we have expected to contribute disproportionately to the mission in Afghanistan if the aforementioned interpretation applies? First, are those countries bordering or located close to Russia. These are the same countries that have called for a rebalancing of NATO's strategic priorities as well as a resurrection of 'regional NATO' and of Article Five collective defence. Many of the so-called 'Article 5ers' (including most East European countries and, to some extent, Norway), realise that their security comes in the shape of American security guarantees, and so their contribution to ISAF was viewed as an 'insurance premium' aimed at preserving US protection (via NATO) for their own territorial defence. Second, we would expect allies who perceive of themselves as strong Atlanticists to have also shouldered a disproportionate burden in Afghanistan. Because these nations identify their 'special relationship' with Washington as important to their security and international influence, they, too, would have been willing to contribute significantly to ISAF, both in terms of troops and risk sharing. These, by and large, are the same countries that have supported the US in its efforts to reform NATO (Noetzel and Schreer 2009). 'The Atlanticists' include, most prominently, the UK, Canada, the Netherlands and Denmark. This group has perceived its contributions to ISAF as the price of political influence, as an effort to curry favour with Washington and as a means of retaining a crucial link to the senior partner.

To assess the validity of this PGT argument, it is helpful to look at ISAF burden sharing in 2010 when NATO-Europe troop numbers in Afghanistan were at their highest. And, indeed, the general picture is very much in line with the theoretical expectations spelled out earlier. As assumed, the Atlanticists and the Article 5ers were clearly providing a disproportionately greater share of military assets to the operation (see Table 10.2). Regardless of the burden-sharing indicator employed, it is the allies in these two categories that were among the top-ten contributors when measured in relative terms. Whether calculated as a percentage of the individual member state's number of inhabitants, number of deployable land forces or as a percentage of the allies' total military personnel, it was, in broad terms, the nations closest to Russia and the allies with a self-perception as close to the US that took on the most significant burdens.

The asymmetry becomes even more evident when comparing the relative ISAF contributions with the individual member states' share of the Alliance's total population and total GDP. Only three nations – the US, the UK and Estonia – provided more forces to ISAF than the relative size of their economies and their populaces would lead us to expect; Latvia, Bulgaria, Denmark, Canada, Poland and the Netherlands came close. In accordance with the theoretical expectations, the greatest discrepancy between the share of ISAF contribution and the relative size of the economy and number of inhabitants were to be found in Germany, France, Spain, Italy, Turkey, Belgium and Greece.

Another way to examine the sharing of burdens in Afghanistan is to assess the differences in exposure to risk – in other words 'risk sharing'. Following Sperling and Webber (2009: 507), risk has three distinct dimensions: 'the stationing of troops in "safe" as opposed to "dangerous" regional commands within Afghanistan; the number of combat deaths; and the numerous caveats which keep national forces out of harm's way'.

Looking at the geographical dispersion of the allies' troop commitments in 2010 it is clear that the Atlanticists and the Article 5ers were significantly overrepresented in the most unruly parts of Afghanistan – that is, the south and east of the country (see Table 10.3). Although some allies belonging to these two categories (including Norway and Latvia) declined to deploy their forces to the provinces along the Afghan–Pakistani border, the more kinetic operations conducted in these areas were almost completely dominated by forces from countries with a (perceived) strong interest in a close relationship to Washington.[5] Tellingly, Germany, Spain, Italy, Greece and Belgium all opted for the more stable areas in and around Kabul and the northern and western provinces.

Also, the sharing of human sacrifices in Afghanistan has been highly asymmetric. Clearly, the US and the UK have taken the greatest toll (about 84 per cent of all fatalities), but Canada, Germany, France, Denmark, Spain and the Netherlands also have paid a high cost for their engagement in Afghanistan. However, calculated as a share of number of inhabitants, it is clearly the Atlanticists and the Article 5ers that have suffered the highest level of casualties Danish, American, British, Estonian, Canadian, Norwegian, Dutch and Latvian forces in particular have been exposed to significantly greater risk than most other allies. This, of course, reflects the fact that these nations have been willing to deploy their forces to the must unstable parts of the country. But it also mirrors the absence of formal

Table 10.2 NATO troop commitments to ISAF, April 2010

	ISAF (April 2010)	ISAF / per 100,000 inhabitants	ISAF /% military personnel (national total)	ISAF / % of national deployable land forces	Troop commitment (share of ISAF')	GDP (share)	Population (share)
US	62,415	20.32	4.05	6.43	62.89	45.23	34.38
UK	9,500	15.54	4.89	12.08	9.57	6.97	6.84
Denmark	750	13.64	2.90	12.30	0.76	0.98	0.62
Estonia	155	11.93	5.15	30.82	0.16	0.06	0.15
Netherlands	1,885	11.21	4.09	10.64	1.90	2.50	1.88
Norway	470	10.08	2.46	4.99	0.47	1.17	0.52
Canada	2,830	8.45	4.40	6.47	2.85	4.18	3.75
Bulgaria	525	7.29	1.55	10.23	0.53	0.14	0.81
Poland	2,515	6.54	1.93	10.35	2.53	1.34	4.31
France	3,750	5.85	1.08	4.12	3.78	8.35	7.17
Italy	3,150	5.68	2.11	6.02	3.32	6.63	6.50
Germany	4,665	5.67	1.85	7.40	4.70	10.26	9.21
Belgium	590	5.67	1.59	8.45	0.59	1.46	1.17
Latvia	115	5.15	2.11	12.14	0.12	0.08	0.25
Romania	1,010	4.55	1.34	21.24	1.02	0.51	2.49
Lithuania	145	4.08	1.68	12.72	0.15	0.11	0.40
Slovenia	75	3.74	1.15	4.75	0.08	0.16	0.22
Spain	1,270	3.13	0.92	3.02	1.28	4.56	4.53
Turkey	1,795	2.34	0.35	0.76	1.81	1.88	8.59
Greece	70	0.65	0.05	0.32	0.07	1.07	1.20
Total	**99,249**						

Sources: NATO (2015), 'ISAF Placemat Archives'; IMF (2015), 'World Economic Outlook Databases'; the European Defence Agency (2015), 'Defence Data Portal'; CIA (2015), 'World Factbook'; author's own calculations.

Table 10.3 NATO risk sharing in Afghanistan (ISAF and OEF), June 2013

	Fatalities	*Fatalities (share)*	*Fatalities per mil. inhabitants*	*Area of deployment*
Denmark	43	1.33	7.82	South
US	2,235	69.11	7.28	East / South / Kabul
UK	444	13.73	7.27	South
Estonia	9	0.28	6.93	South
Canada	158	4.89	4.72	South
Norway	10	0.31	2.15	North / Kabul
Netherlands	25	0.77	1.49	South
Latvia	3	0.09	1.34	North
France	86	2.66	1.34	East / South / Kabul
Poland	36	1.11	0.94	East
Romania	19	0.59	0.86	South / Kabul
Spain	34	1.05	0.84	West / Kabul
Italy	47	1.45	0.81	West / Kabul
Germany	54	1.67	0.66	North / Kabul
Lithuania	1	0.03	0.28	West
Portugal	2	0.06	0.19	South
Turkey	14	0.43	0.18	East / Kabul
Greece	0	0.00	0.00	Kabul
Total	**3,234**			

Sources: *iCasualties.org (2015)*, 'Operation Enduring Freedom'; NATO (2015), 'ISAF Placemat Archives'; CIA (2015), 'World Factbook'; author's own calculations.

restrictions put on the use of their contingents – which brings us to the third and final dimension of risk sharing: national caveats.

According to senior NATO officials, it was only fourteen out of the forty nations participating in the ISAF mission in late 2008 that had no written restrictions on the use of their forces. The remaining twenty-six troop contributors had applied a total of some seventy caveats outlining when, where and how to employ their troops. These formal restrictions (ranging from limitations on geographical mobility to the banning of night-time operations and the exclusion of certain types of offensive engagements) were, however, only the tip of the iceberg. In reality, many (perhaps all) ISAF nations employ different kinds of unwritten or informal caveats that would only be observable when certain kinds of actions were asked of the individual ally. These limitations were just as damaging to the operational effectiveness as formal caveats, which, after all, the ISAF commanders could take into account in the operational planning process (Ringsmose and Thruelsen 2009).

A number of European allies were long criticised for being too risk-averse and for placing too many caveats on their forces. For operational reasons the Alliance has no publicly available inventory or catalogue listing the various restrictions applied by different member states. Yet, according to NATO officials, it has been the allies putting the highest premium on NATO's traditional security benefits that have generally put the lowest numbers of caveats on the use of their troops. Most of the armed forces provided by a number of NATO's East European members and by the Atlanticists have thus been relatively flexible and unrestricted.[6] This observation once more supports the argument presented earlier: apparently, it is the allies that put the highest premium on a close relationship with the US that are also the allies willing the carry the greatest risk.

In sum, the evidence presented here corroborates the alternative PGT hypothesis put forward earlier. Many of the NATO allies who most covet the traditional club goods still produced by the Alliance are indeed also among those that contributed most to the ISAF mission in Afghanistan. NATO's relative success in deploying troops beyond the Euro-Atlantic area on the one hand, is thus explained by its continued tasks, on the other, as a provider of security in Europe and a route to strong relations with the US. The latter, for many allies, provides the motive for the former.

Conclusion

Seen through the lens of PGT, NATO is, first and foremost, a burden-sharing arrangement set up by rational state actors with overlapping security interests. At its heart, the Alliance is designed to let each member state take advantage of the security initiatives taken by other allies. The analytical starting point of PGT analyses of NATO is invariably the nature of the benefits and goods provided by the Alliance. Based on the overall composition of the goods produced, PGT scholars thus deduce hypotheses about the collective action problems likely to beset the Alliance when sharing common burdens. As is the case with all theories, PGT highlights particular features of reality and ignores others. Rooted in political economy and a highly parsimonious model of alliances, PGT leaves many aspects of NATO unaccounted for, yet, at the same time the theory tells us something fundamental about how the Alliance works and, in particular, about the collective action problems facing its members.

PGT scholars have generally identified the benefits produced by NATO's post–Cold War mission portfolio as 'more public' than most of the Alliance's traditional outputs. On the face of it, NATO should, therefore, have been unable to deploy substantial numbers of troops for extended periods to (for instance) Afghanistan. However, based on PGT logic, the argument of this chapter is that the collective action problems posed by NATO's new roles can, in fact, be mitigated. To many smaller European allies, NATO membership is still, first and foremost, an entry ticket to American security guarantees and the provision of regionally anchored (European) security. And as long as the allies continue to perceive of NATO as a provider of such excludable club goods, then many of them have ample incentives to contribute to missions elsewhere. That linkage has facilitated NATO's ability to provide necessary forces for US-led out-of-area operations, in Afghanistan most notably.

This linkage was compelling when out-of-area missions were of paramount importance to the US (and, therefore, NATO). What is interesting for future analyses is how that linkage has diminished in importance now that NATO (and, therefore, the US) has turned greater attention to the traditional task of collective defence in the European theatre. As we have seen, this has brought collective action problems of their own as East Europeans particularly have become ever aware of their exposure to danger and the burden of commitment to national defence even within an alliance setting.

The analysis presented in this chapter, one underpinned by the role of the Alliance as a provider of public goods, is not, therefore, definitive insofar as its analysis has been premised on one particular (albeit important) sphere of activity (allied contributions to out-of-area missions in general and that of ISAF in particular). A public goods perspective on NATO needs to be taken forward by asking a series of pertinent research questions.

First, the previous analysis calls for more country-specific case studies of exactly how individual allies make the linkage between their contributions to NATO's out-of-area mission and the more excludable goods expected to flow from participation in these operations. Are they explicit about the anticipated returns from their investments in out-of-area operations? And to what extent is such *quid pro quo* logic openly employed in the argumentation of contributing forces? Second, if, indeed, the analysis presented in this chapter captures some of the main elements of the burden-sharing considerations made by smaller allies, we would expect these states to take part in out-of-area missions for the sake of *different types* of excludable goods. Following this logic, allies that have security concerns about their neighbours or feel threatened will participate to obtain strong security guarantees, whereas states that feel generally secure will contribute to get other less essential private goods, such as prestige, access, influence and political capital. Third, and connected, if states such as the UK (by no means a small state in NATO terms) participated in out-of-area partly to consolidate its relationship with the US – what then happens if the calculation appears misplaced? There is a strong line of argument that the UK, although demonstrating its political mettle in Afghanistan, performed poorly in operational terms. Its efforts thus damaged (rather than enhanced) the 'special relationship'.[7] Finally, PGT does not exclude an assessment of how factors other than the nature of the goods produced by the Alliance can potentially counter incentives to free-ride. More scholarly attention should thus be paid to the ways in which NATO's burden-sharing regime (including its norms, decision rules and procedures for the fair sharing of costs) mitigates collective action problems. In other words, how do NATO's defence planning processes and the institutionalisation of distinct burden-sharing indicators affect tendencies to free-ride?

Studies aiming at addressing questions such as these would have to be rooted in a qualitative research design and consequently differ from most existing PGT studies. Yet, a change of methodology might very well be the recipe needed to take PGT examinations of NATO one step further.

Notes

1 Classic examples of pure public goods include firework displays and lighthouses. For more on public goods, non-rivalness and non-exclusiveness, see Sandler and Hartley (1999), and Chalmers (2000).

2 In fact, NATO's collective security guarantee (Article Five of the North Atlantic Treaty) does not entail any automatic and armed answer to an aggression against a

member state – only a commitment by its members to 'take such action as [is] deem[ed] necessary'.

3 Interview at NATO headquarters, October 2009.

4 Denmark is a good example in this respect. In the words of the former Danish Minister of Defence Søren Gade (2005): '[b]y transforming our armed forces we get better value for money. We will thereby be able to deploy more troops to international operations. Today, Denmark has deployed more than 1,000 troops to international operations in primarily Kosovo, Afghanistan, Iraq and Sudan. That should be compared to the size of the Danish population – which is just above 5 millions. So already today we carry a fair share of the burden. But we intend to do more! [. . .] By transforming our armed forces, we will be able to double our capacity to participate in international operations from 1,000 to 2,000 troops [. . .] And this will all be done within the existing level of the defence budget'.

5 Lithuania was not present in either the south or in the east, but the small Baltic country did run a Provincial Reconstruction Team (PRT) by itself in the Western province of Ghor bordering the war-torn province of Helmand.

6 Email correspondence with former senior NATO official, March 2009; Interview with NATO officials, December 2009 and June 2013.

7 On the general point see Meyer (2015); on British–American tensions in theatre in Afghanistan see Fairweather (2014): 381–383.

References

[All web sources listed were last accessed 12 June 2015.]

Biden, J. (2015). 'Remarks by the Vice-President at the Munich Security Conference', 7 February, at: www.whitehouse.gov/the-press-office/2015/02/07/remarks-vice-president-munich-security-conference.

Boyer, M. (1993). *International Cooperation and Public Goods*, Baltimore: The Johns Hopkins University Press.

Breedlove, General P. (2015). 'Statement of General Philip Breedlove, Commander US Forces Europe', House Armed Services Committee, February 25, at: www.eucom.mil/mission/background/posture-statement.

Chalmers, M. (2000). *Sharing Security: the Political Economy of Burdensharing*, Houndmills, Basingstoke: MacMillan Press.

CIA (2015). 'The World Factbook', 1 June, at: www.cia.gov/library/publications/the-world-factbook/.

Cohen, R. (2008). 'The Long Haul in Afghanistan', *New York Times*, February 28.

Dempsey, J. (2014). *Why Defence Matters: A New Narrative for NATO*, Washington D.C.: Carnegie Europe.

Deni, J. (2015). 'Burden Sharing and NATO's 2 Per Cent Goal', *Strategic Europe*, April 14, at: http://carnegieeurope.eu/strategiceurope/?fa=59767.

European Defence Agency (2015). 'Defence Data Portal', June 1, at: www.eda.europa.eu/info-hub/defence-data-portal.

Fairweather, J. (2014). *The Good War: Why We Couldn't Win the War or the Peace in Afghanistan*, London, Jonathan Cape.

Forster, P. J. and Cimbala, S. J. (2005). *The US, NATO and Military Burden-Sharing*, London: Frank Cass.

Gade, S. (2005). 'The Danish Response to the Transformation Challenge', Speech by Mr. Søren Gade, Minister of Defence, at: www.nato.int/docu/speech/2005/s050414c.htm.

Gates, R. (2011). 'The Security and Defence Agenda (Future of NATO)', speech in Brussels, 10 June, at: www.defense.gov/speeches/speech.aspx?speechid=1581.

Graw, A. (2008). 'Jung will von einem Kriegszustand nicht wissen', *Welt-online*, 4 September, at: www.welt.de/politik/article2391658/Jung-will-von-einem-Kriegszustand-nichts-wissen.html.

Hagel, C. (2014). Speech to the Munich Security Conference, 1 February, at: www.defense.gov/Speeches/Speech.aspx?SpeechID=1828.

Handel, M. (1990). *Weak States in the International System*, London: Frank Cass.

House of Commons Defence Committee. (2008). 'The Future of NATO and European Defence', *Ninth Report of Session 2007–08*, London: House of Commons.

iCasualties.org (2015). 'Operation Enduring Freedom', June 1, at: http://icasualties.org/OEF/index.aspx.

IMF (2015). 'World Economic Outlook Databases', June 1 at: www.imf.org/external/pubs/ft/weo/2015/01/weodata/index.aspx.

Ivanov, I. D. (2011). *Transforming NATO: New Allies, Missions, and Capabilities*, Lanham: Lexington Books.

Kay, S. and Khan, S. (2007). 'NATO and Counter-insurgency: Strategic Liability or Tactical Asset?', *Contemporary Security Policy*, 28(1): 163–181.

Lepgold, J. (1998). 'NATO's Post-Cold War Collective Action Problem', *International Security*, 23(1): 78–106.

Meyer, C. (2015). 'Our Special Relationship Hangs by A Thread', *Daily Telegraph*, 15 January.

NATO. (2015). 'ISAF Placemat Archives', June 1, at: www.rs.nato.int/isaf-placemat-archives.html.

NATO. (2014). 'Wales Summit Declaration', NATO Press Release (2014) 120, 5 September, at: www.nato.int/cps/en/natohq/official_texts_112964.htm.

Noetzel, T. and Schreer, B. (2009). 'Does a Multi-tier NATO Matter? The Atlantic Alliance and the Process of Strategic Change', *International Affairs*, 85(2): 211–226.

Olson, M. (1965). *The Logic of Collective Action*, Cambridge: Harvard University Press.

Olson, M, and Zeckhauser, R. (1966). 'An Economic Theory of Alliances', *Review of Economics and Statistics*, 48(3): 266–279.

Oma, I. (2012). 'Explaining States' Burden-Sharing Behaviour within NATO', *Cooperation and Conflict*, 47(4): 562–573.

Pintat, X rapporteur. (2013). 'From Smart Defence to Strategic Defence: Pooling and Sharing from the Start', NATO Parliamentary Assembly, Defence and Security Committee, Report 146 DSCFC 13 E rev.1

Rasmussen, A.F. (2013). 'Defence Matters', speech to the NATO Parliamentary Assembly, 11 October, at: http://www.nato.int/cps/en/natohq/opinions_104038.htm

Ringsmose, J. (2009). 'Paying for Protection: Denmark's Military Expenditures during the Cold War', *Cooperation and Conflict* 44(1): 73–97.

Ringsmose, J. and Thruelsen, P. D. (2009). 'NATO's Counterinsurgency Campaign in Afghanistan: Are the Classical Doctrines Suitable for Alliances?', *UNISCI Discussion Papers*, No. 22.

Ringsmose, J. and Rynning, S. (2009). 'Come Home NATO? The Atlantic Alliance's New Strategic Concept', *DIIS Report* 4, Copenhagen: Danish Institute for International Studies.

Russett, B. M. (1970). *What Price Vigilance? The Burdens of National Defence*, New Haven: Yale University Press.

Rynning, S. (2005). *NATO Renewed: The Power and Purpose of Transatlantic Cooperation*, New York: Palgrave Macmillan.

Sandler, T. and Cauley, J. (1975). 'On the Economic Theory of Alliances', *Journal of Conflict Resolution*, 19(2): 330–48.

Sandler, T., Cauley, J. and Forbes, J. (1980). 'In Defence of a Collective Goods Theory of Alliances', *Journal of Conflict Resolution*, 24(3): 537–547.

Sandler, T. and Forbes, J. (1980). 'Burden Sharing, Strategy, and the Design of NATO', *Economic Inquiry*, 18(3): 425–44.

Sandler, T. and Hartley, K. (1999). *The Political Economy of NATO: Past, Present, and into the 21st Century*, Cambridge: Cambridge University Press.

Scheffer, J. de Hoop. (2008). 'Towards Fairer Burden-Sharing in NATO', *Europe's World*, June 1, at: http://europesworld.org/2008/06/01/towards-fairer-burden-sharing-in-nato/#.VWhzTZOwRn8.

Schmitt, G. J. (2014). 'Scrimping on NATO', *International New York Times*, 3 September.

Shimizu, H. and Sandler, T. (2002). 'Peacekeeping and Burden Sharing: 1999–2000', *Journal of Peace Research*, 39(6): 651–668.

Stockholm International Peace Research Institute (2015). 'Military Expenditure Database', June 1, at: www.sipri.org/research/armaments/milex/milex_database.

Sperling, J. and Webber, M. (2009). 'NATO: from Kosovo to Kabul', *International Affairs*, 85(3): 491–511.

The Economist (2008). 'A Ray of Light in the Dark Defile: The State of NATO', 28 March.

The Economist (2009). 'Have Combat Experience, Will Travel; NATO and Its Future', 28 March

Thies, W. J. (1987). 'Alliances and Collective Goods: A Reappraisal', *Journal of Conflict Resolution* 31(2): 298–332.

Thies, W. J. (2003). *Friendly Rivals: Bargaining and Burden-Shifting in NATO*, New York: M. E. Sharpe, Inc.

Trachtenberg, M. (1999). *A Constructed Peace: The Making of the European Settlement, 1945–1963*, Princeton: Princeton University Press.

Urbelis, V. (2013). 'Implications of Smart Defence Initiative for Small Members of NATO', *Lithuanian Annual Strategic Review 2012–2013*.

Yost, D. (1998). *NATO Transformed: the Alliance's New Roles in International Security*, Washington D.C.: United States Institute of Peace Press.

Yost, D. (2014). *NATO's Balancing Act*, Washington D.C.: United States Institute of Peace Press.

11 Learning the hard way

NATO's civil–military cooperation[1]

Jörg Noll and Sebastiaan Rietjens

NATO operations, such as KFOR in Kosovo and ISAF in Afghanistan, have been combined missions that are multifaceted, demanding, and subject to the vagaries of complex environments. The variety of challenges NATO has faced in the post–Cold War period has meant an ongoing process of adaptation and change (Rynning 2013). This chapter shows, by utilising organisational learning (OL) theory, how the complexity of an organisation and the political and societal demands from its environment complicate the institutionalisation of new concepts. The central question we address is: Why has it been so difficult for NATO to learn and institutionalise new concepts after the Cold War? In considering this question, we use NATO's concept of civil–military cooperation (CIMIC)[2] as an illustrative case study.

New concepts, embedded in doctrines and strategies, are landmarks in an organisation's survival. They reflect how the organisation has managed to adapt to new security environments and political challenges. However, as empirical research shows, military organisations are difficult to change and to analyse. Since the end of the Cold War, change, or the lack of it, within military organisations has fired the curiosity of the scientific and practitioner communities. Within military sociology (Avant and Lebovic 2002) or history (Black 2002), analysts have provided at least partial answers to questions of change and adaptation. Those answers have often focused on technical innovation (Rosen 1991), the role of political and military leaders (Noll 2005), and the consequences of change for the individual soldier (Amersfoort, Moelker, Soeters and Verweij 2013) or the national military organisations of which they are part. Practitioners, meanwhile, have focused on the subject of change less through structural comparison and more through a description of personal experiences (Pappalardo 2004).

Two important concepts that appear in these approaches are 'best practice(s)' and 'lessons learned'. Often researchers and critical soldiers have identified problems within a particular military organisation or operation and so have advocated paths toward improving efficiency and effectiveness through focused recommendations. Or, they have identified differences between two apparently similar empirical phenomena and drawn from such analyses observations about the nature of change and the lessons learned (Nagl 2002, 2010; Tettweiler 2011). Although the concept of lessons learned in its broadest sense has been applied previously to military organisations and missions, it has often been done with no theoretical focus (Farrell 2008) or with a rudimentary theoretical treatment (Terriff, Osinga and Farrell 2010) that does not allow for (structured focused) comparison. Without theory, however, it is difficult to arrive at 'valid descriptive or causal inference' (King, Keohane and Verba 1994: 18). Our starting point is that the concept of (organisational) learning has to be theoretically elaborate and applied to military and international organisations in a more rigorous fashion than hitherto. In this chapter, we conceive of OL as an instance of middle-range theory, which as George and Bennett (2005: 8) suggest, 'provide[s] [. . .] contingent and specific generalisations for policymakers and allow[s] researchers to contribute to more nuanced theories' by identifying 'recurring conjunctions of mechanisms.'

OL theories are alert to the distinction between institutions and organisations. In International Relations (IR) theory, institutions are often associated with rules and norms that (might) change states'/actors' behaviour (Krasner 1984). Organisational studies drawn from, *inter alia* sociology, political science, public administration, and economics, meanwhile, focus on processes within organisations, whether or not in relation to their environment. It is about 'patterned interactions among individuals or groups of individuals; [the] stability of such patterns over time; formal and informal constraints to individual conduct; and the shared values and perception of meaning by the members of the [organisation]' (Kuipers 2004: 12). IR scholars will note that the debate about actors versus structures is also an important part of institutional studies. An organisation tends to be viewed as amenable to the demands of politicians and policy makers that the body in question perform certain preferred policy functions. An institution more broadly understood takes on a somewhat different quality, being less subservient to the functional demands of its members and thus more able to influence their behaviour (Boin 2001: 4).

We begin this chapter with an overview of OL theory and do so on the assumption that OL has had little application so far in IR (Reiter 1994). We then develop an OL model that allows us to analyse the development of CIMIC within NATO. Using three missions (those in Bosnia, Kosovo, and Afghanistan) we show the difficulties NATO has faced when developing CIMIC. National political and military considerations have sometimes frustrated the evolution and implementation of the approach. Further, NATO's institutional design and internal processes appear not well suited to quick adaptation in response to a volatile environment and to new strategic challenges.

Organisational learning theory

Thinking about OL dates back many decades, even back to the Industrial Revolution (Easterby-Smith and Lyle 2003). It was Herbert Simon who first coined the term 'organisational learning' in his studies of decision making, that concerned with the idea of 'bounded rationality' being perhaps the best known (Morgan 1997). Organisational learning can be distinguished from a learning organisation. We do not pay attention to the latter, which is dominated by practitioners and consultants giving prescriptive advice (Argyris 1999: 1). Instead, our contribution focuses on the more academic-dominated and theory-infused OL approach.

Although it has now come of age, there is no single definition of OL.Table 11.1 gives an overview of definitions by leading OL scholars published in a survey of the field.

Although somewhat dated (but see also Table 11. 2.), these definitions show a diversity of concepts as well as dichotomies: the individual–organisation distinction, for instance. Here, debate exists as to whether it is an organisation as such which is capable of learning (based on anthropomorphic assumptions of organisational characteristics) or whether it is more appropriate to think of the individuals within the organisation that are learning. Another important debate within the field concentrates on the normative aspects of organisational learning: as soon an organisation's performance improves, analysts tend to infer from that fact that successful learning has occurred. Yet, because many factors contribute to any given outcome (some of which cannot be easily grasped), it is not necessarily the case that the organisation is itself (through learning) responsible for such a positive outcome. Further, the issue of timespan also needs to be borne in mind. Across what period of time is performance to be measured, and how are we to gauge the performance of organisations that work in a volatile environment with frequently changing demands from both the inside and outside? We agree,

Table 11.1 Definitions of organisational learning

Year	Researchers	Definition of Organisational learning
1963	Cyrert and March	Adaptive behaviour of organisations over time
1965	Cangelosi and Dill	A series of interactions between adaptation at the individual, or subgroup levels and adaptation at the organisational level
1978	Argyris and Schön	The process by which organisational members detect errors or anomalies and correct them by restructuring the organisational theory in use
1979	Duncan and Weiss	The process within an organisation by which knowledge about action-outcome relationships and the effect of the environment on these relationships is developed.
1985	Fiol and Lyles	The process of improving actions through better knowledge and understanding
1988	Levitt and March	Organisations are seen as learning by encoding inferences from history into routine behaviour
1991	Huber	An entity learns if, through the process of information, the range of its potential behaviours is changed. Organisations learn as any of its units acquires knowledge that it recognises as potentially useful to the organisation.
1993	Weick and Roberts	Organisational learning consists of the interrelated actions of individuals, that is their 'heedful interrelation' which results in a 'collective mind'.

Source: Derived from Prange (1999: 28–30).

Table 11.2 Types of learning

Phenomenon	Comparison to Organisational Learning
Individual Learning	OL differs from individual learning in that the translation of learning into changed behaviour has organisation-wide consequences.
Knowledge Transfer	OL is distinct from knowledge transfer (which is principally a one-off interaction with the organisation's environment) in that it is applicable, remembered, and used by organisational members in an enduring manner.
Individual Memory	OL is created through the shared experiences and collective past of the members of an organisation.
Organisational Change	Organisational change is suggestive of a series of (perhaps unrelated) distinct actions over time. Organisational learning, rather, is an ongoing dynamic process.

Source: Derived from Wiseman (2007: 1114)

therefore, with Huysman (1999: 61–63) that OL is a process with either a positive or a negative outcome, or, indeed, one that even contributes to an upholding of the status quo. In other words, change itself is not an indicator of organisational learning. Table 11.2 summarises the distinctions between OL and similar phenomena to clarify related concepts.

From individual to organisational learning

The link between individual and organisational learning seems to be crucial in the learning process. Taken literally, individual learning is restricted to disconnected members of an organisation with no organisation-wide effects. However, in aggregate, individual learning does affect the organisation of which those individuals are part. Organisations are composed of individuals, and they can learn independently of any specific individual but not independently of all individuals (Kim 1993: 37). Defining learning as 'the acquiring of knowledge or skill' incorporates the connection between thought (the 'acquisition of skill or know-how') and action (the 'acquisition of know-why' (Kim 1993: 38). Learning only takes place when new knowledge is translated into different, replicable behaviour. And since learning is a process whereby knowledge is created through the transformation of experience (Kolb 1984: 38), it is important to find out what people learn and how they understand and apply that in subsequent behaviour.

Repetition, or implementation of knowledge in cycles, appears to be relevant for learning (Kim 1993: 38–39; Kolb 1984) as well as cognitive style, which is a person's preferred way of gathering, processing, and evaluating information (Hayes and Allinson 1998: 847–850). Learning influences how people organise and interpret information and how they understand change. That, in turn, influences how they integrate their interpretations into a mental model and constitutive theories that guide their actions. Mental models represent a person's worldview and provide the context to view and interpret new material (Kim 1993).

The distinction between individual and organisational learning is accepted across the whole field of organisational learning, even if that distinction is a blurred one. Some scholars have broadened the debate by introducing an additional element: group learning. According to Back (in Burnes 2004: 981), groups link the individual to the organisation, but they also influence individual behaviour. Crossan, Lane, and White (1999) show that it is necessary to analyse the learning processes at all three of these levels, for although the learning modes are different at each, they are nonetheless supplementary to one another. We will elaborate on this theme in the next section, but before doing so it would be useful to consider in more detail the learning of the organisation itself.

As mentioned earlier, there is little agreement on the nature of learning within organisations. One of the basic concerns here is whether learning at the organisational level is the sum of individual learning or an integral part of organisational functioning, regardless of whether the individuals who occupy it learn or not (Antonacopoulou 1999: 10). It could well be argued that an understanding of learning within organisations at the individual level helps provide valuable insights into the factors that promote or impede learning within organisations as such. Yet here we confront a seeming conundrum: organisations consist of individuals, but they are more than simply collections of these individuals; and the same is true of organisational learning (Simon 1991: 125). Although organisations do not have brains, they do have cognitive systems and memories. They 'preserve certain behaviours, mental maps, norms and values over time' (Hedberg 1981, 6). According to Dekker and Hansén (2004: 217), organisations can collect information systematically by experimenting, benchmarking, carrying out research and development, and evaluating their 'normal' performances. Thus, organisational learning is not just the accumulation of individual learning (March and Olsen: 1975), but a cyclical process that links individual belief to individual action to organisational action to environmental response and back to individual belief again (Friedman 2001: 398). Such a process involves developing, sharing, and making explicit mental models (Kim 1993) and the encoding of conclusions drawn from individual experiences into routines (standard operating procedures, rules, structures, policies) that guide organisational behaviour. In this way, a relation between the cognitive and behavioural dimensions is established (March and Olson 1975, Dekker and Hansén 2004).

Notwithstanding the complexity of the link between individual, group and organisational learning, it becomes clear that organisations learn through their individual members and that they are affected directly or indirectly by individual and group learning. It is, therefore, necessary to incorporate all three levels – individual, group, and organisation – when analysing OL. Such a model has been developed by Crossan, Lane, and White (1999): the '4 I framework' of organisational learning to explain strategic renewal. Although developed to explain corporate renewal and learning, it is in our view fruitful to draw from this model a perspective that helps to understand NATO's strategic renewal and specifically the development and implementation of new concepts such as CIMIC.

These four I's represent the social and psychological processes of intuiting, interpreting, integrating, and institutionalising. Here, learning is multileveled and takes place from individual to group to the organisation through two mechanisms: 'feed-forward learning' (that is, through experiencing change and learning by innovation), and 'feedback learning', which values knowledge that already exists within the organisation based on familiar practices (Vera and Crossan 2004: 224–226). Feedback tends to be top-down (from organisation to individual), whereas feedforward tends to be bottom-up (from individual to organisation) (see Figure 11.1).

Crossan, Lane, and White's (1999) model is focused essentially on internal processes. Huysman (2000) similarly sees internal organisational learning as an institutionalising process through which individual knowledge becomes organisational knowledge communicated by a dominant coalition within the organisation. But members of an organisation are also influenced by external knowledge. According to March and Olson (1975: 150–168), an organisation can be considered a behavioural system that interacts with its external environment and changes its behaviour as a result of stimuli coming from that environment. Here, individuals within an organisation adapt cognitively to external stimuli and that, in turn, gives rise to organisational action. That action, then, may generate an environmental response. Huysman (1996: 91–106) sees such external learning as an extension of the internal learning process. External learning proceeds in two ways: first of all by reacting to (feedback) information and second by learning

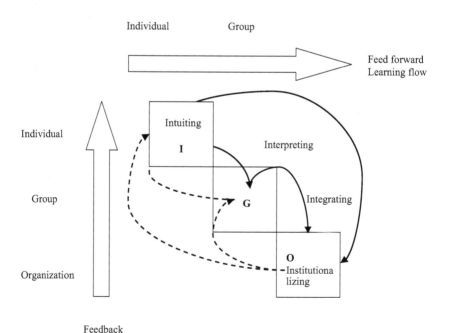

Figure 11.1 Framework of organisational learning

from experiences of other organisations. The main difference between learning from others and feedback learning (see also earlier) is that feedback learning is the transfer of knowledge that originates from experience of existing processes, and learning from others is the introduction of new knowledge that originates from external innovations. Learning from others is about the capacity of an organisation to recognise, incorporate, adjust, and communicate back new information to its environment.

Huysman (1996) argues that there is no superior way of learning. Different forms of learning must be combined to achieve a beneficial outcome. We believe that the same applies to the theory of OL. Different models provide different tools and perspectives for analysing OL. Crossan, Lane, and White (1999) combine the theory of learning with strategic innovation and emphasise mechanisms of learning across different levels; March and Olson (1975) include cognitive and behavioural aspects; and Huysman (1996) focuses on the construction and institutionalisation of knowledge deriving from inside and outside the organisation.

A combination of these several elements is shown in the integrated model of Figure 11.2. This broad analytical framework includes internal and external learning and sees organisational learning as a process with two-way interactions between different levels. An *internalisation* process occurs when an internal learning process from individual to group and organisation is completed. We speak about an *institutionalisation* process when an external learning process is internalised. Further, following March and Olson (1975) and Huysman (1996), the model incorporates obstacles to organisational learning, central to our study (later) of CIMIC.

These processes of learning are often unbalanced and hindered by structural, cultural, and/or psychological obstacles. The obstacles provide an insight in how a learning process develops, and it reminds us that the assumed rationality in the process is limited by characteristics of humans and organisations. Table 11.3 defines and provides an overview of those obstacles.

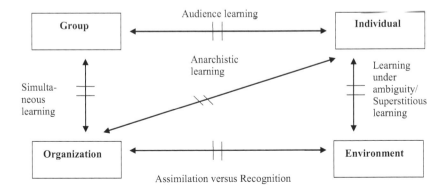

Figure 11.2 Integrated organisational learning model including obstacles

Table 11.3 Obstacles to learning

Learning Obstacle	Explanation
Audience learning	Obstruction in communicating personal knowledge to other members of the organisation.
Simultaneous learning	Different units in the organisation face confusing experiences.
Anarchistic learning	Individual action is not based on internalised organisational knowledge.
Superstitious learning	Incorrect conclusions are drawn about the impact of organisational actions on the environment.
Learning under ambiguity	Obstruction of knowledge transfer from environment to the individual. This occurs when changes in the environment cannot be clearly identified. Learning takes place, the individual affects organisational action, and the action affects the environment, but there is no insight about the meaning of these changes.
Assimilation	The inefficient capacity of the organisation to absorb external knowledge and to incorporate it in organisational processes.
Recognition	The imitation cycle from organisational knowledge to external knowledge and vice versa might lead to unconscious imitation of new knowledge. This can lead to the mismatch of information.

Source: Based on March and Olson (1975) and Huysman (1996).

The internal learning process might be obstructed by audience learning, simultaneous learning, or anarchistic learning. Audience learning obstructs the process by which personal knowledge is communicated to other organisational members. Simultaneous learning obstructs internal learning when different units in the organisation face confusing experiences. This can result in different and even conflicting learning outcomes. It is a barrier between the group and the organisation, as conflicting learning experiences between different units hamper the transfer of unambiguous knowledge. The obstacle of anarchistic learning occurs when individual action is not based on internalised organisational knowledge. In other words, the link between organisational knowledge and individual beliefs is disconnected (March and Olson 1975: 154–160).

The two forms of external learning – feedback learning and learning from other organisations – are both affected by two different obstacles. Feedback learning is the transfer of (coded) experiences, and this process might be hindered in two ways: superstitious learning and learning under ambiguity. The former occurs when incorrect conclusions are made about the impact of organisational actions on the environment (March and Olson 1975: 159). The latter entails the obstruction of knowledge transfer from environment to the individual. It occurs when changes in the environment cannot be clearly identified. Learning takes place, the individual affects organisational action, and the action affects the environment, but there is no insight about the meaning of these changes (March and Olson 1975: 159–160).

The traps and obstacles of learning from others are also twofold. The first relates to assimilation, that is, the inefficient capacity of an organisation to absorb external knowledge and to incorporate it in organisational processes. The second obstacle is one of recognition, which occurs when an organisation links the construction of organisational knowledge to the gathering of new external knowledge without recognising that this new information is coming from the external environment. This can lead to a mismatch of information or unconscious imitation of external knowledge (Huysman 1996: 98–105).

Organisational learning theory applied to NATO

Given the exploratory nature of this study and the complexity and richness of the context, a case-study approach is an appropriate research strategy (George and Bennett 2005). To that end, and following Yin (2009), a theoretical framework was first constructed (see previous section) and then applied to three different case studies: Bosnia, Kosovo, and Afghanistan. In each of these cases we have considered what obstacles NATO has faced while going through the organisational learning cycle. In doing so, we have specifically focused on the CIMIC concept.

Data were collected in several ways. First, thorough desk research was carried out. Literature on CIMIC was studied and relevant documents were collected from the CIMIC Centre of Excellence and from several NATO databases. These documents included *Allied Joint Publication (AJP)-9* on NATO CIMIC doctrine (NATO 2003); several Operational Plans; NATO military policy for CIMIC; and other strategic policy papers, guidelines, manuals, and evaluation reports on the translation and implementation of the doctrine of CIMIC.[3] As a next step, the authors and two research assistants held semi-structured interviews with key players at strategic and operational levels. The key players included CIMIC staff and planners working at Supreme Headquarters Allied Powers Europe (SHAPE); commanders; and military and civilian staff deployed under IFOR/SFOR (Bosnia), KFOR (Kosovo), and ISAF (Afghanistan). Also, the second author made three field visits to different areas in Afghanistan in 2005 (northern provinces), 2009 (Kabul and Kandahar areas), and 2010 (Uruzgan province in southern Afghanistan). During these visits, participant observations took place at staff meetings and briefings in the compound; mission teams were joined on several (multiday) patrols; and meetings were held with a variety of civilian NGOs, local leaders, and constructors.

The development of CIMIC

Across the missions in Bosnia, Kosovo, and Afghanistan, the concept of CIMIC and its implementation has changed significantly. In Bosnia, NATO decided its military forces were in need of a specialised capacity for civil–military cooperation. As a result, a dedicated CIMIC capacity was deployed from the commencement of the NATO operation in the mid-1990s. In accordance with the doctrinal and procedural documents, most troop-contributing countries had on CIMIC at that time, CIMIC staff mostly led in the civil–military liaison role at the tactical level. They were primarily occupied with initiating, executing, and outsourcing small-scale reconstruction projects. The enhancement of 'force protection' by 'winning the hearts and minds' of the local population was presented as the primary rationale behind these projects. In Bosnia, the purpose of CIMIC was to support the commander in reaching his military objectives. Particularly in the initial phase of the massive NATO operation, the 60,000 troops were given a military objective that focused on the cessation of hostilities and the establishment of lasting security. The American generals commanding the force rigidly stuck to this line. CIMIC activities were clearly not meant to amount to large-scale reconstruction, and the re-integration of war-torn Bosnia was not to become a military task. Civilian responsibilities rested with a hodgepodge of understaffed, underfunded, and poorly coordinated international civilian organisations (nominally overseen by the UN). NATO leaders frequently emphasised that support to the military operation, not 'nation building', was the goal of CIMIC (Brocades-Zaalberg 2006). In the course of 1996–1997 military forces gradually stepped up their support of the civilian component of the international effort, and so support of civil implementation gradually became the key to any level of progress. SFOR's CIMIC capacity, however, did not play a substantial role in this and the work was instead largely undertaken by SFOR brigades at the tactical level through liaison and small-scale projects.

The disconnect between the CIMIC concept and the requirements on the ground also came to the fore during NATO ground operations in Kosovo in 1999–2000. Here, CIMIC was planned in the same way as in Bosnia-Herzegovina (BiH): as a support function towards a military end. A UN-led civilian mission (UNMIK) was to become the interim government and oversee policing in the province. Yet, in practice, battalions participating in NATO's Kosovo Force (KFOR) exercised de facto governance in their area of responsibility. One of these was Dutch, operating in the Orahovac region. It had only two dedicated CIMIC officers, neither of whom had received any specific CIMIC training. Nevertheless, the Dutch battalion took over key responsibilities in the field of civil administration, policing, and the provision of basic public services such as electricity and water. The Dutch were certainly not alone in their attempt to fill the power vacuum, but not all national contingents were equally forthcoming in assuming these civilian responsibilities. According to the Dutch battalion commander, Lieutenant-Colonel Ton van Loon, his primary motive in taking on these tasks was to prevent Kosovan–Albanian insurgents of the Kosovo Liberation Army (KLA) from filling the power vacuum. As a result, CIMIC moved centre stage and was performed by regular military personnel and staff officers (Brocades-Zaalberg 2006).

Problems between the doctrine and practice of CIMIC became apparent again during the ISAF operation in Afghanistan. In its early years, the aim of ISAF was to assist the central government in Kabul get a grip on the Afghan provinces while simultaneously monitoring the formal authorities and unofficial power brokers. This placed civil–military interaction at the very heart of the ISAF mission and more specifically of the Provincial Reconstruction Teams (PRTs). One would, therefore, have expected CIMIC staff to play a pivotal role. However, a closer look at the distribution of tasks and responsibilities within ISAF shows that the majority of key civil–military liaison roles were taken on by other personnel. PRT commanders, often without reference to a CIMIC element, and relying on close cooperation with their political advisors, dealt directly and primarily with the provincial governor (see for example Rietjens, Soeters and van Fenema 2013). Meanwhile, in many Afghan provinces, ISAF mission teams consisting of approximately twelve persons penetrated the area to liaise with civil administrators and police at the district level. At all levels, non-NATO civilian advisors (political, development, and tribal advisors) mostly led in dealing with the international governmental and non-governmental organisations and the local judiciary. NATO CIMIC staff were hardly involved in these activities and were given only a residual role liaising with government departments in the provincial capitals.

Obstacles to organisational learning

From Bosnia via Kosovo to Afghanistan, NATO's thinking about civil–military interaction slowly but surely developed. Whereas it was merely a military tactical tool in Bosnia, interaction between military and civilian actors moved centre stage in Afghanistan. Yet NATO's CIMIC concept as it was laid down in *Allied Joint Publication 9* (NATO 2003) still focused on supporting the military commander through liaison and small-scale projects and could not keep pace with these new developments. The empirical evidence points to several obstacles that have hindered the organisational learning process. These are discussed next utilising categories elaborated as part of the integrated model of OL (Figure 11.2).

Audience learning (individual to group)

In all three cases, audience learning (that is, poor communication between individual and group) severely hampered NATO's internal learning process. There are three possible routes (or preconditions) by which audience learning could have been mitigated, none of which operated effectively in the cases we explored. The first is transparency (Popper and Lipshitz 2000). In this connection, we observed in the field that learning primarily took place through briefings and presentations and during individual hand-over/take-over periods. There were, however, no formal procedures to codify experiences and/or lessons learned during these events. For example, whereas some individuals had a hand-over/take-over period of two weeks and meticulously recorded their experiences, others simply vanished out of the mission areas without even speaking to their successors. And in cases when personnel did codify their lessons, they often did so in self-developed formats and reports. This led to fragmentation and hampered structural comparison and analysis. This problem was aggravated further by the short rotation periods, varying from four to twelve months (some personnel remained in theatre for two years, but these were exceptions). With Afghanistan's ISAF mission, NATO made several attempts to change this state of affairs by implementing an official lessons-learned process. During field visits to Kabul and Kandahar in 2009, the second author was present during the then most recent iteration of this cycle. As can be seen from Figure 11.3, however, it was highly complex; it also worked poorly in practice.

The second precondition for mitigating audience learning is by encouraging a climate to learn (Friedman, Lipshitz, and Overmeer 2001). Theory underscores the necessity of a climate that fosters enquiry, openness, and trust, but there has been little evidence of these qualities within NATO operations. Within KFOR, communication between different brigades (which, in any case, held different philosophies about CIMIC) was poor. According to Mockaitis (2004) 'the mission suffered from a lack of cohesiveness and consistency that [drove] more than one NGO around the bend'. And as far as ISAF has been concerned, the situation is even more negative. PRTs assumed a significant role in bolstering the ISAF effort. In some cases trained CIMIC personnel were responsible for managing the civil–military interface; but in many instances (see earlier) there were hardly any CIMIC people embedded in the PRTs, and the regular military filled in the positions relevant to civilian engagement. Further, PRTs were led by different nations and lacked clear command-and-control relations with the ISAF higher command; coordination of the aggregate PRT effort, therefore, proved very difficult. Further, the many national caveats that were in place among ISAF contributing nations complicated the relationship, with civil actors drawn from

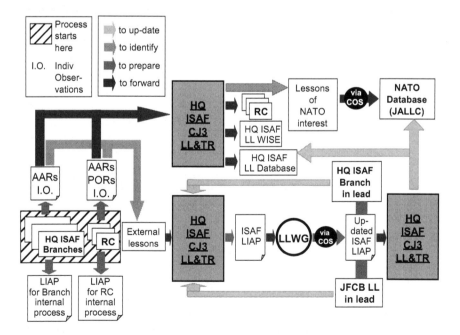

Figure 11.3 Lessons-learned process for ISAF

humanitarian organisations, the local population, and authorities. Often, ISAF personnel proved unwilling to engage with such actors if this entailed infringing operational restrictions such as patrolling by daylight only or working within clear geographic boundaries.

The third precondition for mitigating audience learning (Friedman, Lipshitz and Overmeer 2001) is organisational commitment. For various reasons, within NATO there was limited commitment to learning at all levels in both the Balkans and Afghanistan. At the political and strategic levels, lessons learned were not given much attention, as there was a concern these would reveal mismanagement and so fuel criticism towards the respective missions. At the operational and tactical levels, meanwhile, NATO preferred active military personnel to those dedicated to investigating lessons learned. This was understandable given often pressing military necessities. Additionally, commanders sometimes had limited interest in being open about what had gone wrong. Many of them were promoted after their deployment and thought that expressing criticism would be seen as indicative of operational failure (Rietjens 2008). The evaluations that many of the Dutch contingents made in Afghanistan illustrate this point. Most of them clearly stated that (significant) progress was being made, but rarely touched upon sensitive topics or negative experiences with which the contingent was being confronted.

Simultaneous learning (group to organisation)

A second important obstacle to NATO's learning ability relates to simultaneous learning. During the NATO mission in Bosnia as well as that in Kosovo, no clear and structured information (and lessons-learned) system existed. In Bosnia the relevant processes were oriented towards national military structures. In Kosovo many lessons were observed; these were often conflicting, however, due to various approaches being taken among the multi-national brigades. Such a state of affairs hindered the transfer of unambiguous knowledge to the strategic level. Moreover, the lines of communication between the operational and the strategic levels were poorly structured. NATO's Joint Analysis and Lessons Learned Centre (2006) has stated that many lessons-learned reports were produced, but that there was no systematic way of identifying conclusions of NATO-wide relevance. And despite this acknowledgement, the problem remained unsolved. One of the proposed solutions, the lessons learned process in ISAF (see Figure 11.3), was largely unable able to improve the situation.

Anarchistic learning (organisation to individual)

Anarchistic learning relates to interaction between organisation and individual. Organisational effectiveness is thus essential. Yet NATO as an organisation has struggled heavily with the role of CIMIC and with reconstruction in general. Although mainstream intervention literature points to the need to provide security first (Etzioni 2007), many counterinsurgency specialists (Kilcullen 2009;

Nagl 2002) emphasise the great impact reconstruction and development can have on winning the hearts and minds of the local populace. Many officers in the field were confronted with this dilemma (providing security or focusing on reconstruction). In their education and (pre-deployment) training they were, however, mainly instructed along classical military lines (Rietjens, van Fenema and Essens 2013). This made many military personnel unaware of the concepts of CIMIC and its embeddedness in the larger mission. It therefore remained unclear whether CIMIC should be used as a commander's tool to foster good relations with the local population or whether it was to be used to cover the total interface between the military and the great variety of civil actors. The individual military, and in particular its senior and flag officers, played a large role in this, leading to different approaches and preferences. Thus, in Kosovo, despite the strong recommendations of SHAPE planners, General Mike Jackson (the first KFOR commander) refused to incorporate a civil–military component into his force. It appeared that his previous experiences in Bosnia, as well as the influence of British military culture, contributed to that attitude (Brocades-Zaalberg 2006).

In addition to the influence of the individual military on anarchistic learning, doctrines and procedures have played an important role. During the operation in Bosnia (when NATO first seriously confronted CIMIC), it took a considerable period of time to develop relevant doctrine and guidelines. This was a result of the high number of actors involved actors, both military and civilian, and the disconnect between the tactical and operational levels (Brocades-Zaalberg 2006). Meanwhile, in Afghanistan there has been a great variety of units and branches focusing on the civil–military interface, including CIMIC, PRTs, civil-military cells, and development and influence teams. Both internally and externally, this has resulted in a lack of clarity on tasks, responsibilities and capabilities. From our field research it became abundantly clear that the military was either not aware of NATO doctrine and guidelines or simply did not bother reading them. Further, doctrine and guidelines were often slow to adapt to new and changing circumstances. In most cases, NATO forces were confronted with outdated documents that were not entirely suitable to their operational environment (Rietjens 2014).

Superstitious learning and assimilation versus recognition (environment to individual and to organisation)

In each of the obstacles described earlier, the cultures and practices of the different nations within NATO were crucial. When it comes to learning from the environment, the influence of the nations becomes obvious again. Information communicated from the tactical level to the different national organisations did not filter up to the strategic level (or did so only in small amounts) (see Joint Analysis and Lessons Learned Centre 2006).

Even more striking has been the lack of communication with civil organisations (Rietjens, Verlaan, Brocades-Zaalberg and de Boer 2009). This is clearly shown by the examples of SHAPE and the Allied Rapid Reaction Corps (ARRC) who completed their planning and preparation for deploying KFOR without reference to civilian stakeholders in the region.

Further, and contrary to the advice of many NGOs (Save the Children 2004), ISAF introduced the PRTs in many Afghan provinces as the main vehicles for facilitating reconstruction and development. Generally, civil organisations prefer not to be associated with the military lest they lose the confidence of the local population and their reputation for neutrality among parties to conflict (Rietjens 2008). Yet some interchange is nonetheless valuable, and non-governmental organisations (NGOs) with a stake in Afghanistan have been open to liaising with ISAF. NATO, however, in developing the CIMIC concept has been reluctant to learn from NGOs. The main reason for this lies in the structural organisational differences between military and civilian organisations (the former generally attach greater value to unity of command and control, top-down hierarchy, and discipline, whereas the latter are often horizontally organised and follow a consensus-based approach) (Rietjens, Soeters and van Fenema 2013).

In addition to learning from civil organisations, host nation actors within the local population have provided a wealth of learning opportunities for NATO. More and more, the Alliance has used polls to measure the attitude of the local population toward a large number of issues, including perceptions of the security situation or attitudes towards NATO troops. That said, many host nation actors have been wary of being associated with NATO troops for fear of hostile actions by insurgents. In addition, exchanging information has been hampered by other issues – a mistrust of foreign troops, the limited education of many local people, the short deployments of NATO personnel, and the conflicting motives of local power brokers (Rietjens, Verlaan, Brocades-Zaalberg and de Boer 2009).

Conclusion: exploring NATO

NATO-led CIMIC has developed considerably over the past twenty years. However, as this chapter has shown, it has done so in the face of many obstacles. Only few concrete relations between CIMIC capacities and their environment were found. The role of strategic command SHAPE was rather weak and many of its documents seldom met the eye of the military in theatre. National procedures and a mutual reluctance of NGOs and the military to engage complicated the institutionalisation of CIMIC within NATO still further. Organisational learning theory helps to shed light on those relations by allowing for valid inference when analysing the process of CIMIC's development.

NATO, to be sure, has all the ingredients for being a successful organisation. The most sophisticated weapons at its (nations') disposal, the best trained and technically equipped soldiers at hand. Yet, as our study has shown, when it comes to the institutionalisation of a new concept like CIMIC, the organisation appears to be a rather slow learner. Such cumbersome adaptation is perhaps not surprising. NATO was founded and designed during the Cold War for slow-onset disasters. Preventing a Warsaw Pact invasion for forty years along the Iron Curtain demanded long-term planning with a time horizon of five and sometimes more years. By contrast, contemporary operations are highly dynamic and often unforeseen. Notwithstanding the organisational changes NATO has undertaken over the past two decades, it still does not fully meet the demand of flexibility. Organisational learning theory provides a good insight as to why this is so.

For a start – and to address the questions of 'what is NATO (for)?' – the Alliance appears in our study to be less an institution and more a loose organisation of twenty-eight nations and many more individuals. Consequently, it has struggled both to institutionalise CIMIC and to fashion agreement among its members on a common and workable approach to civil–military coordination. Preferences within NATO are more often than not expressed and aggregated by the different member states and individual soldiers, whether in theatre or within international staffs. Conditioned by national demands, national military culture, and individual beliefs and habits, the aggregation of preferences in this context has been obstructed by national CIMIC strategies that have developed in parallel with, or even later than, NATO's own CIMIC concept.

Bearing in mind that the empirical findings in this study concentrate on CIMIC, we do not see developments in this regard as exemplifying NATO *pars pro toto*. However, given our own experiences in military organisations, including operational and strategic commands and operational deployment, we do consider CIMIC as an example for hypothesising about the development and implementation of other new concepts within NATO. If CIMIC has proven difficult to coordinate, how much more so will other emerging collaborative projects be, such as cyber and drone operations, which touch upon national political sensitivities among NATO's nations.

We could not give an answer to the question 'whither NATO?' in our chapter. What we could show is that a lot of work needs be done for the future – work that focuses less on high politics and regular summits (involving changing every two years organisational objectives and strategies), and more on organisational effectiveness as such. What is necessary is the will of politicians and the military alike to turn the organisation into a true institution. Otherwise, we remain pessimistic about a quick acceptance and implementation of the concepts necessary to ensure a healthy future for the Alliance.

Notes

1   We owe a debt of gratitude to two former researchers under our supervision, Willemijn Arends and Marieke Battink. Without their great analytical and theoretical skills we would not have been able to engage effectively with theories of organisational learning. We would also like to thank our colleagues at the Lisbon ECPR Joint Sessions 2009 and the follow-up meeting in Breda in 2010 for their comments. Over the years, many of our colleagues in Breda and elsewhere have commented on previous versions of this paper. Thank you very much to them also.

2   CIMIC is defined as '[t]he co-ordination and co-operation, in support of the mission, between the NATO commander and civil actors, including national population and local authorities, as well as international, national and non-governmental organisations and agencies' (NATO 2003: 1–1).

3   A full list of documents consulted is provided in the References section of this chapter.

References

Antonacopoulou, E. (1999). 'Developing Learning Managers within Learning Organisa- tions: The Case of Three Major Retail Banks', in Easterby-Smith, M., Araujo, L. and Burgoyne, J. G. (eds). *Organisational Learning and the Learning Organisation: Devel- opment in Theory and Practice*. London: Sage Publications.

Amersfoort, H., Moelker, R., Soeters, S. and Verweij, D. (eds). (2013). *Moral Responsibil- ity and Military Effectiveness*. The Hague: Asser Press.

Argyris, C. (1999). *On Organisational Learning*, second edition, Oxford: Blackwell Business.

Avant, D. D. and Lebovic, J. L. (2002). 'U.S. Military Responses to Post-Cold War Mis- sions', in Farrell, T. and Terriff, T. (eds). *The Sources of Military Change: Culture, Politics, Technology*, Boulder: Lynne Rienner Publishers.

Black, J. (2002). 'Military Change in Historical Perspective', in Farrell, T. and Terriff, T. (eds). *The Sources of Military Change: Culture, Politics, Technology*, Boulder: Lynne Rienner Publishers.

Boin, R. A. (2001). *Crafting Public Institutions: Leadership in Two Prison Systems*. Boul- der: Lynne Rienner Publishers.

Brocades-Zaalberg, T. (2006). *Soldiers and Civil Power: Supporting or Substituting Civil Authorities in Peace Operations during the 1990s*. Amsterdam: Amsterdam University Press.

Burnes, B. (2004). 'Kurt Lewin and the Planned Approach to Change: A Re-appraisal', *Journal of Management Studies*, 41(6): 977–1002.

Crossan, M. M., Lane, H. W. and White, R. E. (1999). 'An Organisational Learning Frame- work: from Intuition to Institution', *Academy of Management Review*, 24(3): 522–538.

Dekker, S. and Hansén, D. (2004). 'Learning under Pressure: the Effects of Politicization on Organizational Learning in Public Bureaucracies', *Journal of Public Administration Research and Theory*, 14(2): 211–230.

Easterby-Smith, M. and Lyle, M. A. (eds). (2003). *Handbook of Organisational Learning and Knowledge Management*. Malden: Blackwell Publishing.

Etzioni, A. (2007). *Security First: For a Muscular, Moral Foreign Policy*. New Haven: Yale University Press.

Farrell, T. (2008). 'The Dynamics of British Military Transformation', *International Affairs*, 84(4): 777–807.

Friedman, V. J. (2001). 'The Individual as Agent of Organisational Learning', in Dierkes, M., Berthoin Antal, A., Child, J. and Nonaka, I. (eds). *Handbook of Organisational Learning and Knowledge*. Oxford: Oxford University Press.

Friedman, V. J., Lipshitz, R. and Overmeer, W. (2001). 'Creating Conditions for Organi- sational Learning', in Dierkes, M., Berthoin Antal, A., Child, J. and Nonaka, I. (eds). *Handbook of Organisational Learning and Knowledge*. Oxford: Oxford University Press.

George, A. L. and Bennett, A. (2005). *Case Studies and Theory Development in the Social Sciences*. Cambridge: MIT Press.

Hayes, J. and Allinson, C. W. (1998). 'Cognitive Style and the Theory and Practice of Indi- vidual and Collective Learning in Organisations', *Human Relations*, 51(7): 847- 871.

Hedberg, B. (1981) 'How Organisations Learn and Unlearn', in Nystrom, P. C. and Strabuck, W. H. (eds), *Handbook of Organisational Design*, Oxford: Oxford University Press.

Huysman, M. (1996). *Dynamics of Organisational Learning*. Amsterdam: Thesis Publishers.

Huysman, M. (1999). 'Balancing Biases: A Critical Review of the Literature on Organisational Learning', in Easterby-Smith, M., Araujo, L. and Burgoyne, J. G. (eds). *Organisational Learning and the Learning Organisation: Development in Theory and Practice*. London: Sage Publications.

Huysman, M. (2000). 'An Organisational Learning Approach to the Learning Organisation', *European Journal of Work and Organizational Psychology*, 9(2): 133-145

Joint Analysis and Lessons Learned Centre. (2006). *NATO's Lessons Learned Process*. NATO Unclassified.

Kilcullen, D. (2009). *The Accidental Guerrilla: Fighting Small Wars in the Midst of a Big One*. Oxford: Oxford University Press.

Kim, D. H. (1993). 'The Link between Individual and Organisational Learning', *Sloan Management Review*, October: 37–50.

King, G., Keohane, R. O. and Verba, S. (1994). *Designing Social Inquiry: Scientific Inference in Qualitative Research*. Princeton: Princeton University Press.

Kolb, D. A. (1984). *Experimental Learning: Experiences as the Source of Learning and Development*, Englewood Cliffs: Prentice-Hall.

Krasner, S. (1984). 'Approaches to the State: Alternative Conceptions and Historical Dynamics'. *Comparative Politics* 16(2): 223–246.

Kuipers, S. L. (2004). *Cast in Concrete? The Institutional Dynamics of Belgian and Dutch Social Policy Reform*. Delft: Eburon.

March, J. G. and Olson, J. P. (1975). 'The Uncertainty of the Past: Organisational Learning under Ambiguity', *European Journal of Political Research*, 3(2): 147–171.

Mockaitis T. R. (2004). *Civil-Military Cooperation in Peace Operations: The Case of Kosovo*. Carlisle: Strategic Studies Institute of the US Army War College.

Morgan, G. (1997). *Images of Organisation*, London: Sage Publications.

Nagl, J. A. (2002). *Learning to Eat Soup with a Knife: Counterinsurgency Lessons from Malaya and Vietnam*. Westport: Praeger Publishers.

Nagl, J. A. (2010). 'Learning and Adapting to Win', *Joint Forces Quarterly*, 58(3): 123–124.

NATO (2003). *Allied Joint Publication-9, NATO Civil-Military Co-operation (CIMIC) Doctrine*, at: www.nato.int/ims/docu/ajp-9.pdf.

Noll, J. (2005). *Reforming Leadership: Dutch and Swedish Defence Organisations after the Cold War*. Göttingen: Cuvellier Verlag.

Pappalardo, J. (2004). 'Bosnia Commanders Point out Peacekeeping Lessons', *National Defence Magazine*, September, at: www.nationaldefensemagazine.org/archive/2004/September/Pages/Bosnia_Commanders3414.aspx.

Popper, M. and Lipshitz, R. (2000). 'Organizational Learning: Mechanisms, Culture and Feasibility', *Management Learning*, 31(2): 181–196.

Prange, C. (1999). 'Organisational Learning, Desperately Seeking Theory', in Easterby-Smith, M., Araujo, L. and Burgoyne, J. G. (eds). *Organisational Learning and the Learning Organisation: Development in Theory and Practice*. London: Sage Publications.

Reiter, D. (1994). 'Learning, Realism, and Alliances: The Weight of the Shadow of the Past'. *World Politics*, 46(4): 490–526.

Rietjens, S.J.H. (2008), *Civil-Military Cooperation in Response to a Complex Emergency: Just Another Drill?* The Hague: Brill Publishers.

Rietjens, S.J.H., Verlaan, K., Brocades-Zaalberg T. W. and de Boer, S. J. (2009). 'Inter-organisational Communication in Civil–Military Cooperation during Complex Emergencies: A Case Study of Afghanistan', *Disasters*, 33(3): 412–435.

Rietjens, S.J.H., Soeters J.M.M.L. and van Fenema, P. C. (2013). 'Learning from Afghanistan: Towards a Compass for Civil-Military Coordination', *Small Wars and Insurgencies*. 24(2): 257–277.

Rietjens, S.J.H., van Fenema, P. C. and Essens, P. R. (2013). "'Train as You Fight" Revisited: Preparing for a Comprehensive Approach', *PRISM*, 4(2): 17–30.

Rietjens, S.J.H. (2014). *The Comprehensive Approach: From 'Theory' to Practice to Theory*. Paper presented at NATO HFM-236 Symposium on 'Effective Inter-agency Interactions and Governance in Comprehensive Approaches to Operations', April, Stockholm.

Rosen, S. P. (1991). *Winning the Next War: Innovation and the Modern Military*. Ithaca: Cornell University Press.

Rynning, S. (2013). 'ISAF and NATO: Campaign Innovation and Organisational Adaptation', in Farrell, T., Osinga, F. and Russell, J. A. (eds). *Military Adaptation in Afghanistan*. Stanford: Stanford University Press. pp. 83–107.

Save the Children (2004). *Provincial Reconstruction Teams and Humanitarian – Military Relations in Afghanistan*, London: Save the Children.

Simon, H. (1991) 'Bounded Rationality and Organisational Learning', *Organisation Science*, 2(1): 125–134.

Terriff, T., Osinga, F. and Farrell, T. (eds). (2010). *A Transformation Gap? American Innovations and European Military Change*. Stanford: Stanford University Press.

Tettweiler, F. (2011). *Lernen in Interventionen? Evaluation am Beispiel der deutschen Afghanistan-Mission*. Berlin: SWP-Studie 22, September.

Vera, D. and Crossan, M. (2004). 'Strategic Leadership and Organisational Learning', *Academy of Management Review*, 29(2): 222–240.

Wiseman, E. (2007). 'The Institutionalization of Organisational Learning: A Neoliberal Perspective' in Proceedings of OLKC 2007 – 'Learning Fusion' at: www2.warwick.ac.uk/fac/soc/wbs/conf/olkc/archive/olkc2/papers/wiseman.pdf.

Yin, R. K. (2009). *Case Study Research: Design and Methods*, fourth edition, Thousand Oaks: Sage Publications.

NATO publications consulted

AAP-6, Glossary of Abbreviations used in NATO documents and publications, 1992.

ACE Directive 86–2 CIMIC 2000: Establishment of an ACE CIMIC capability, 13 January 1998.

AJP-01, Allied Joint Operation Doctrine, 1997.

Bi-SC Directive 86–3; Establishment of a Bi-SC CIMIC Operational Capability.

Bi-SC Guidelines for Operational Planning, 2001.

CINCSOUTH OPLAN 40104, Operation Determined Effort, the NATO Enforcement of the Peace Agreement in BiH, 20 October 1995.

Common Reference Document (CRD), SACEUR OPLANs 10407/10413, 24 July 2002.

Common Reference Document (CRD), SACEUR OPLANs 10407/10413, 8 October 2002.

MC 411/1, Military Policy on Civil-Military Co-operation, Euro-Atlantic Partnership Council, 6 July 2001.

NATO CIMIC Functional Planning Guide, March 2002.

SACEUR OPLAN 10405, Joint Endeavour, 16 December 1995.

SACEUR OPLAN 10407, Joint Forge, 27 April 1998.

SACEUR OPLAN 10407, Joint Forge, 17 June 1998.

SACEUR OPLAN 10407, Revise 1 Joint Forge, 16 September 1999.

SACEUR OPLAN 10407, Revise 1 Joint Forge, 25 October 1999.

SACEUR OPLAN 10407, Revise 2 Joint Forge, June 2002.

SACEUR OPLAN 31402, Final Draft, 28 October 1999.

SACEUR OPLAN 10413, Joint Guardian, 14 June 1999.

SACEUR OPLAN 10413, Final draft, Joint Guardian, 6 July 1999.
SACEUR OLPAN 10413 Final revise 1, Joint Guardian, 2 November 1999.
SACEUR OPLAN 10413, Revise 2, Joint Guardian, 19 December 2000.
SACEUR OPLAN 10413, Revise 3.

Index